Ghulam Murshid
48 Dovedale Avenue,
Ilford, Essex IG5 0QF UK

A POET APART

A POET APART

A Literary Biography of the Bengali Poet
Jibanananda Das (1899–1954)

Clinton B. Seely

Newark: University of Delaware Press
London and Toronto: Associated University Presses

© 1990 by Associated University Presses, Inc.

All rights reserved. Authorization to photocopy items for internal or personal use, or the internal or personal use of specific clients, is granted by the copyright owner, provided that a base fee of $10.00, plus eight cents per page, per copy is paid directly to the Copyright Clearance Center, 27 Congress Street, Salem, Massachusetts 01970. [0-87413-356-4/90 $10.00 + 8¢ pp, pc.]

Associated University Presses
440 Forsgate Drive
Cranbury, NJ 08512

Associated University Presses
25 Sicilian Avenue
London WC1A 2QH, England

Associated University Presses
P.O. Box 488, Port Credit
Mississauga, Ontario
Canada L5G 4M2

The paper used in this publication meets the requirements of the American National Standard for Permanence of Paper for Printed Library Materials Z39.48-1984.

Library of Congress Cataloging-in-Publication Data

Seely, Clinton B.
   A poet apart: a literary biography of the Bengali poet Jibanananda Das. (1899–1954) / Clinton B. Seely.
     p. cm.
   Includes bibliographical references (p.)
   ISBN 0-87413-356-4 (alk. paper)
   1. Das, Jibanananda, 1899–1954—Biography. 2. Poets, Bengali—20th century—Biography. 3. Poets, Bengali—Bangladesh—Biography. I. Title.
PK1718.D2613Z925   1990
891'.4416—dc20
[B]   88-40262
                                                                        CIP

PRINTED IN THE UNITED STATES OF AMERICA

To Gwendolyn Layne,

who, though she neither speaks nor reads Bengali,

understands Jibanananda's poetry

as well as anyone I have met,

Bengali or no.

Contents

Preface		9
1	Roots	15
2	The Kallol Era	40
3	Back to Barisal	81
4	The War Years: Prelude and Aftermath	146
5	Another Fling at Fiction	201
6	The Poetry of Politics	235
7	Posthumous Jibanananda	272
Notes		285
Select Bibliography		314
Index		329

Ghulam Murshid
48 Dovedale Avenue,
Ilford, Essex IG5 0QF UK

Preface

"You must meet Chunilal," insisted my acquaintance. "It was he who freed Jibanananda from where he lay, pinned beneath the tram car." I met Chunilal Dey in 1970, sixteen years after the death of Bengal's most cherished poet since Rabindranath Tagore. He sat at his usual place in the south Calcutta tea shop he operated on Rashbehari Avenue. Down this east-west thoroughfare in the middle-class Bengali neighborhood of Ballygunge run two sets of streetcar tracks. About ten strides or so from Chunilal's, one comes to the corner of Rashbehari and Lansdowne. Jibanananda and his family lived in their rented apartment on Lansdowne Road (since renamed Sarat Bose Road), just a half block north of the Rashbehari intersection. Some five blocks south lies Rabindra Lake, an extensive park where Jibanananda frequently went for solitary walks. On the evening of 14 October 1954, he was heading home from just such an outing. It was then, while crossing Rashbehari Avenue, that he stepped in front of an oncoming tram.

Chunilal heard the cries, he told me, and when he reached the scene of the accident seconds later he could see that someone lay trapped beneath the lead car. Chunilal, a stocky man, bent down, cupped his hands under one side of the tramcar and then, with that superhuman strength called forth when circumstances so demand, lifted it up off the track far enough for Jibanananda to be pulled free. Eight days later, due to complications from pneumonia, the acknowledged successor to Rabindranath as Bengal's poet laureate, Jibanananda Das, whose first name means "joy of life," died.

Chunilal did not know Jibanananda well. In fact, few if any people did, for he was a very private person who lived mainly through his poetry. Buddhadeva Bose, a well-wisher responsible for bringing Jibanananda's poetry to the attention of the Bengali world, wrote a fitting epitaph when early on he called Jibanananda "our most alone of poets." Perhaps that explains the presence of but one book-length biographical account in Bengali—none in any other language—of this giant of modern Bengali literature.

Though I had lived and worked for two years during the early 1960s as a Peace Corps Volunteer in Jibanananda's hometown of Barisal, I first came to know him only later, in Chicago, through his poetry. Jyotirmoy

Datta—himself a poet, former fellow at the Writers' Workshop in Iowa, and for a time visiting lecturer at the University of Chicago—introduced me to Jibanananda's wondrous world of words and images.

There were many others over the past two decades who have helped me to better understand Bengali literature that I might transform Jibanananda's life into a book. Invaluable were the many evenings in Calcutta spent with Buddhadeva, Jyoti's father-in-law, discussing everything from poetry to politics to the price of tea—especially and always poetry. Although I was not fortunate enough to know personally the subject of this biography, I did get the opportunity to meet with his widow, Labanya, and his two children—daughter Manjusri and son Samarananda—as well as his brother Asokananda and sister Sucarita, all of them most helpful in various ways.

Others who individually or collectively require mention are the staffs of the National Library and the Bangiya Sahitya Parishad in Calcutta, and Maureen L. P. Patterson and Alice Kniskern, James Nye, and William Alspaugh, all of the University of Chicago's Regenstein Library. To the Department of Comparative Literature at Calcutta's Jadavpur University I am deeply indebted, particularly to its former chairman, Naresh Guha, and faculty members Amiya Dev, Subir Raychaudhuri, Swapan Majumdar, and Shuddhashil Bose. For timely advice on the inevitable translation problems and more, I would like to convey my gratitude to Qazi Abdul Mannan, Pabitra Sarkar, and Soumya Chakraborty. And for those many, many intangibles, I thank Edward C. Dimock, Jr., Professor of Bengali and Bengali Studies at the University of Chicago, and George Steiner of Churchill College, Cambridge.

Though numerous persons assisted me in more ways than I can mention, there were various individuals who, by showing me materials in their possession or by calling my attention to some published piece, made my research that much more exciting and comprehensive. In this connection, I would like to thank the following: Arun Bhattacharya (particularly for his last and half-disintegrated copy of *Uttarsuri's* Jibanananda issue), Snehakar Bhattacharya, Gopal Bhaumik, Kalyan Kumar Bose, Nirendranath Chakravarty (particularly for his personal copy of the *Howrah Girls' College Magazine*), Amlan Datta, Satyaprasanna Datta, Shakti Dev (particularly for his personal copy of *Mayukh's* Jibanananda issue), Bishnu Dey, Amiya Kumar Ganguly, Sunil Ganguly (of Barisal), Haraprasad Mitra, Sunil Kumar Nandy (particularly for back issues of *Anukta*), Debabrata Ray, Saralananda Sen, Anandagopal Sengupta, and Kiran Sankar Sengupta. My special thanks go to the Foreign Area Fellowship Program, whose financial support made possible the study that resulted in this book.

I use a simplified transliteration scheme—no diacritics. This book is written for English speakers, who need not concern themselves with the Bengali alphabet; anyone who knows Bengali will be able to reproduce the original Bengali easily. Short and long vowels appear identical; retroflex and dental consonants are, likewise, indistinguishable. The inherent "a" vowel divides consonants that are not a ligature in the Bengali orthography. A number of my translations included in this book have appeared previously in journals, in certain cases in a somewhat different form. "Banalata Sen," "In Camp," "Naked Lonely Hand," "Beggar," "Blue Skies," and "In Fields Fertile and Fallow" appeared in *The Literary Review* (Madison, New Jersey); "What Sort of Sea Breeze Is This," "Hunt," "Night of Wind," and "Shadowy Figures" were published in *Practices of the Wind* (Kalamazoo, Michigan).

The reader may notice that I refer to Jibanananda Das as Jibanananda and Rabindranath Tagore as Rabindranath, a customary practice in Bengali, showing no disrespect. Also, those who might stumble over Jibanananda's name, take heart, for you are not alone. Over the years, his has surely been one of the most frequently misspelled names to appear in print, particularly when written in English. There are just too many *an*'s.

In one of his most quoted poems, Jibanananda wrote:

At day's end, like hush of dew
Comes evening. A hawk wipes the scent of sunlight from its wings.
When earth's colors fade and some pale design is sketched,
Then glimmering fireflies paint in the story.

Over three decades after the loss of this original and gentle man, it is surely time for those who cannot read Bengali to "see" the poetry he painted. Unless otherwise indicated, all translations in this book are mine, as are all misreadings—unintentional, I assure you.

A POET APART

1
Roots

My golden Bengal I love you.
Your sky, your breezes ever play through the flute of my heart.
O Mother, the fragrance of your spring mango groves drives me wild,
Ah me—
O Mother, what honeyed smiles I've seen upon your fields of late autumn.

—from Bangladesh's national anthem by Rabindranath Tagore

1

A whimsical figure appears to cavort on the map of the South Asian subcontinent—and it is a *sub* continent, having split off from Antarctica, drifting north until it made contact with Asia proper some fifty million years ago, then wedging itself under what we know now as the Himalayas.[1] The figure snuggles into the northeastern portion of modern India save where one outflung foot touches Burma and the other walks upon the Bay of Bengal. A little larger than Great Britain's Emerald Isle, verdant Bangladesh has four times the population (estimated at 100 million in 1986), making it the world's most densely peopled country. Ninety percent of that population (presently, about 90 percent Muslim, less than 10 percent Hindu, with Buddhists and Christians making up around 1 percent each) is nonurban, still living today in villages, in intimate contact with what Rabindranath sang lovingly of as his golden Bengal. A serenely beautiful land, Bangladesh nurtures the body and soul of a veritable nation of poets, though only one out of five Bangladeshis qualifies as literate.

More than a third of Bangladesh lies below the Tropic of Cancer. Fittingly, the summer or "hot season" (April to June) begins the annual cycle in this semitropical country. Bengal, for the most part, measures its years according to a solar calendar dating back to India's Scythian king Shalibahana (first century A.D.), as modified by the greatest of the Mogul emperors, Akbar (sixteenth century)—the year A.D. 1989 corresponding to three and a half months (January to mid-April) of the year B.S. 1395 (*bangla sal* or Bengali year) and eight and a half months of B.S. 1396. The Bengali year's twelve months—Baisakh (mid-April to mid-May), Jyaistha (May–June), Asarh (June–July), Sravan (July–August), Bhadra (August–September), Aswin (September–October), Kartik (October–November), Aghran (November–December), Paus (December–January), Magh (January–February), Falgun (February–March), and Caitra (March–April) —divide into six seasons, a system based on the ancient Indian lunar calendar: summer, monsoon or the rainy season, early autumn, late autumn, winter, and spring. Summer is the most uncomfortable, for the heat can be oppressive. Tempers grow short. But the summer brings something everyone enjoys—mangoes, unofficially Bengal's national fruit. With summer's end come clouds, harbingers of the monsoon as it moves up from the Indian Ocean, sweeping over India and the Bay of Bengal. Once the monsoon breaks, the beastly heat subsides, rice fields once again fill with rainwater, and tensions ease.

The rainy season has traditionally been a favorite with poets, for it is a time when husbands and wives, and lovers of all sorts, should be together. In fifth-century Sanskrit poet Kalidasa's *The Cloud Messenger* (*meghaduta*), an exquisite apostrophe of some hundred-plus quatrains, a semidivine *yaksa,* exiled far from home, implores an approaching cloud to convey his impassioned message to a distant lover. Bengal's own Rabindranath luxuriated through poetry in this season so dear to most of his countrymen's hearts.

When the monsoon ends, the skies clear, turning exceedingly blue. The autumns, both "early" as well as "late"—distinct seasons in Bengal, though the English rendering of *sarat* ("early autumn") and *hemanta* ("late autumn," also known as the "dewy season") would suggest otherwise—are delightful times. One rice crop is harvested, another planted. And Hindus celebrate then their main public festival, the Durga puja, a time to worship the goddess Durga and exchange gifts among family members. (Since the Muslim or Hejra calendar is lunar, about two weeks shorter than a solar cycle, Islamic holidays have become associated with no particular season of the year.)

Both autumn and spring, however, have their drawbacks, for during these periods, cyclones may build up in the Bay of Bengal, all too frequently ripping into the east coast of India or Bangladesh. One such devastating storm, the worst in recorded history, struck East Pakistan during November 1970. The West Pakistan government's perceived lack of concern for the disaster victims in the east wing (an estimated 500,000 died) contributed to heightened tensions between East and West Pakistan, with the consequent outbreak of civil war four months later, leading to Bangladesh's independence.[2] Since then other storms have hit this country, but, as with the Gulf Coast of the United States after being raked by a hurricane, life gradually returns to normal, although the loss in lives can never be forgotten.

Winters are mild and dry. In the gentle breezes wave coconut, palmyra, and the more spindly areca palms, the nut of which one chews with betel leaves. Here and there stand low lath houses wherein are cultivated the betel-leaf vines. Bamboo grows everywhere, as do a thousand and one other trees and creepers. Travel becomes much easier at this time of year: what in the rainy season lay under water has now turned to solid ground, capable of sustaining wayfarers on foot, by bicycle, or in bullock carts. Rice stalk stubble adorns empty fields. There is time for visiting, once the late harvest has been stored away.

Come spring, which starts in February, the days turn warmer. Little pots hang from the trunks of date palms just below the fronds, collecting the rising sap that will later be boiled down into molasses and brown sugar—or, by some, fermented to make toddy. Wherever one looks, flowers burst forth, and everywhere there are birds. Ubiquitous banana trees crowd around mud- and split-bamboo–walled, thatched-roofed village dwellings as well as the houses with tin and corrugated iron siding and the "pukka" brick edifices of the more affluent. Each cluster of homes or neighborhood has its "tank," a word of Portuguese origin which designates a man-made pond, sometimes bearing the name of the munificent man who had it dug. As the Bengali year draws to a close with water levels in these tanks now low, brief but furious storms, at times of cyclonic force, dampen the dry earth before the heat of summer returns and the annual cycle begins anew.

More than just a land refulgent with natural beauty, Bangladesh contains urban centers with intriguing histories. Near the towns of Bogra to the north and Comilla in the east stand remains called Mahasthan and Lalmai-Mainamati, respectively, the former probably containing the as yet unexcavated city of Pundaravardhana, which dates back to the time of the Mauryan kings (from the fourth century B.C.) and may have been visited by the Buddha; Lalmai-Mainamati was a thriving complex of Buddhist monasteries active from the sixth through the tenth centuries A.D.[3] Located just below Dhaka, Bikrampur (also spelled Vikrampur), first a Buddhist and then a Hindu political and religious center up to and through the Muslim period, still shows remnants of a later royal palace and grounds.[4] At the mouth of the Karnaphuli in the southeast corner of the country is the port city of Chittagong, base of operations from the sixteenth through the eighteenth century for Portuguese pirates who, along with the Arakanese, plied lower Bengal's waterways, raiding as far north as Dhaka itself and taking booty, and Bengalis to be sold into slavery.[5] To the northeast, in the low hills surrounding the town of Sylhet, one may still see the sprawling tea plantations, a legacy of Britain's East India Company.[6]

In the very center of the country lies Dhaka (the British spelled it Dacca), the capital city, with its Lalbagh Fort attesting to the sometime presence of the heirs of Genghis Khan and Tamerlane in this the eastern reaches of the Moguls' vast northern Indian empire. Persian-derived names of its streets and neighborhoods—Topkhana (arsenal), Peelkhana (elephant stables), Mahuttuli (mahouts' quarters)—recall the days when the Muslim dynasty or its surrogates ruled there. Hailed as the city of mosques, Dhaka seems to provide an Islamic house of worship on every other corner of its bustling streets and narrow lanes in the city's older section, which spreads out from one bank of the Buri Ganga or "Old Lady Ganges," a branch of the more famous river whose name it appropriates.

Dhaka boasts modern sections as well, including a new parliament building designed by American architect Louis Kahn. (Reciprocally, the United States herself owes a debt to Bangladesh's architectural genius, the late Fazlur Rahman Khan, and his revolutionary structural concepts, an example of which is one of the world's tallest buildings, Chicago's Sears Tower.) The old race track in the center of town has been converted into a park, complete with rides and amusements for children. Across the street stands the "Dacca Club," now just a social club, but in its day a bastion of British colonialism. Past Rokeya Hall, the women's residence named for the lady Begum Rokeya (1880–1932) who so tirelessly and effectively urged Bengali Muslim women to seek an education,[7] is the University of Dhaka, earliest and most esteemed of Bangladesh's postgraduate institutions. There taught Satyendranath Bose—for whom is named the boson, an elementary particle conforming to Bose-Einstein statistics. And from that same university on 21 February 1952, students and professors marched in support of their mother tongue.

Pakistan, then composed of West Pakistan and East Pakistan (present-day Bangladesh), had two "state languages"—Bengali and Urdu, the latter most current in West Pakistan, though even there very few people spoke Urdu as a mother tongue. English served as the link or "official language" of that physically as well as linguistically bifurcated nation. Toward the end of January 1952, Pakistan's prime minister reiterated in Dhaka the government's decision to make Urdu the state language for both wings of the country. Bengali-speaking Pakistanis protested. The February 21st march, conducted in defiance of government orders, ended in violence, with a number of Bengali students killed by the authorities. Instantly, those slain became martyrs, and 21 February one of Bangladesh's most important days of annual commemoration.[8]

Barisal, headquarters town for Bakhargunge District, sits upon one bank of the Kirtonkhola river on the northeastern fringe of Bangladesh's Sundarban jungle, named for its *sundari* trees and home to the majestic Royal Bengal tiger. It is the only district headquarters in Bengal not serviced by rail, for the British engineers (and the Pakistanis and Bangladeshis after them) found insufficient solid ground in this alluvial land crisscrossed by rivers and canals. North of Barisal, some fifty miles as the crow flies, lies Dhaka. To the west a hundred fifty miles or so is Calcutta, capital of the Indian state of West Bengal. Seventy-five miles straight south begins the Bay of Bengal. Barisal's surrounding countryside forms part of the low-lying, lush, semitropical Gangetic delta. The Ganges—her name changes to Padma when she enters Bangladesh from West Bengal—joins the Brahmaputra-Yamuna coming south out of Assam, then below Dhaka becomes one with the Meghna to form a massive river, so broad in places that its far bank disappears below the horizon. Further south the Meghna empties into the Bay of Bengal. Off from that mighty river meanders the Kirtonkhola. In this Bengal delta town of Barisal, Jibanananda Das was born on the sixth day of the month of Falgun in the Bengali year 1305 (18 February 1899) to Satyananda Das, schoolmaster and Brahmo preacher, and his wife, Kusum Kumari Das, occasional poet and full-time homemaker.

2

Jibanananda's immediate ancestors had migrated south from a village near Bikrampur, situated alongside the Kirtinasa, a branch of the great Padma and renowned for its destructive power. "In Bikrampur, the Munshi family is certainly not unknown," wrote Jibanananda's father, as part of a eulogy for his own father (Munshi being a title bestowed upon those lettered in Persian, the official language of the Moguls and of the East India Company's courtrooms until English replaced Persian for all official proceedings). "They were at one time wealthy and had a zemindary," continued Satyananda, "but through the negligence of the elders, that zemindary was lost and then ultimately destroyed by thieves and the Kirtinasa." Once relatively wealthy landowners (zemin is a Persian word for land; zemindar, an owner of lands; zemindary, the estate so owned), Jibanananda's ancestors became government servants of one sort or another in their adopted district of Bakhargunge: one was a records keeper, another a tax collector, another a government surveyor, and yet another a clerk in the courts.[9]

From his paternal grandmother, Prasanna Kumari Das, Jibanananda had heard tell of the powerful Kirtinasa, whose name means "glory-destroying." "Before we would go to sleep at night or when we were sick," wrote Jibanananda's brother, Asokananda, "our paternal grandmother used to sit beside the bed and tell us stories. We heard tales of the Kirtinasa from her. Grandmother was a Bikrampur girl. We were fascinated by her accounts of the rainy days there, of the Padma, and by stories about our ancestors. ..."[10] That lore included Rajballabh, an eighteenth-century rajah and patron of the arts whose twenty-one-spired palace was called "the Twenty-one Jewels," a reference that eventually made its way into Jibanananda's poetry. A sonnet composed shortly after his grandmother's death in 1930 begins:

> Carelessly, the Kirtinasa crumbled Rajballabh's glory;
> Yet the Padma's beauty outshines the Twenty-one Jewels—[11]

The Das ancestral village met a similar fate. "Sarbananda Dasgupta['s] ... home had been on the bank of the Padma in the village of Gaupara in Dhaka District's Bikrampur. Today that village no longer exists; it has gone to a watery grave beneath the 'glory-destroying' Padma," wrote Sucarita, Jibanananda's sister. Well before his home in Bikrampur was washed away by the Kirtinasa, Jibanananda's paternal grandfather, Sarbananda Das, had moved south.

> Sarbananda, for reasons of employment, left his parental home and came to Barisal. Later he was initiated into the Brahmo religion. And after accepting this religion, he considered unnecessary the "gupta," a distinguishing mark of the Vaidya caste;[12] from then on, our family was known as the "Das family." Relations with the ancestral home just faded away, and permanent residence in Barisal commenced.[13]

The Brahmo Samaj (an adjectival neologism from the name of the god Brahma, plus the word for community or society) is a reform Hindu sect created in Calcutta during the later 1820s as a reaction to European missionaries' criticism of Hindu practices.[14] Although all Brahmo beliefs and most practices can be supported by reference to Hindu scripture, many resemble those of Christianity. Brahmos theoretically do not acknowledge caste distinctions, which explains Sarbananda's switch from Dasgupta to Das. And Brahmos believe in the one, formless god of the Upanishads, instead of the multiple deities found in contemporary Hinduism. Idol worship is anathema to the Brahmo faithful—something which indirectly may have cost Jibanananda his first job, as we shall see.

The Brahmo movement was both religious and social, if those two attributes can ever be meaningfully separated in Bengal. During the nineteenth century, a great many socially progressive, liberal-minded Bengalis joined the Brahmo Samaj, and Brahmos in turn were generally considered progressive and liberal. (For example, the Samaj encouraged education of women.) In the twentieth century, however, Brahmos came to be thought of as rather puritanical. Indeed, the derogatory form of the name Brahmo—*bemmo*—implies a prude. But in the midnineteenth century, when the Samaj was firmly established in Calcutta and had branched out to the *mofussil* (i.e., everywhere outside of the cosmopolitan centers, Calcutta in particular), to be a Brahmo suggested that one sympathized with social and religious reform. It was then that Sarbananda Das joined the Samaj.

Initiation into the Brahmo Samaj resulted in less of an estrangement from Hindu society than conversion to Christianity. A number of educated and prominent Bengalis in Calcutta did convert, including the acclaimed "father of modern Bengali poetry." Madhusudan Dutt became Michael Madhusudan Dutt after his christening in 1843—against his father's vehement and violent opposition. Unlike Christian converts, Brahmos, from one perspective, were still Hindus, just as Protestants and Catholics are all Christians. But within the Hindu community not everyone looked upon initiation into the Brahmo Samaj with equanimity. Satyananda spoke of his father's acceptance of the Brahmo faith:

> Father had two sons, our elder brother and me, when he took up the Brahmo religion; later five more sons and four daughters were born. In order to appease the Hindu relatives, Father kept our elder brother within the Hindu community. And what shall I say about our Hindu relatives—none was wealthy then, but the love and affection I received from them during my childhood is a thing hard to come by these days. They used to take me home during the autumn puja holidays. In this way I acquired some knowledge about the Hindu community. Father had become a Brahmo when I was very young, and there are many things about the Hindu community which I have not had an opportunity to learn. Our elder brother remained for a long time within the Hindu community, and it was apparent throughout his lifetime that he had an affinity for our Hindu relatives. Several of his characteristics can be attributed to the fact that he lived for so long as a part of that Hindu society.[15]

Sarbananda helped found the Barisal branch of the Brahmo Samaj in 1861.[16] Except for that token gesture of keeping his eldest son in the Hindu community, he brought up his children to be good Brahmos. Even the eldest son, Haricaran, eventually accepted the faith. The second son, Satyananda, became a stalwart of the Samaj and remained so throughout his life.

Hand in hand with the progressive stance of the Brahmo Samaj went a general concern for education. Sarbananda enrolled Haricaran initially in what was then the only school in Barisal, the local district Zilla ("zilla" means district) School, then sent him to Calcutta to study at the newly opened Brahmo institution, City School. Later, both Haricaran and Satyananda also attended City College, the Brahmo Samaj's college in Calcutta. While studying there, the two brothers received word of their father's death from cholera (December 1885). They returned home for the *sraddha* (ceremonies in honor of the deceased), then journeyed back to Calcutta.

> When we returned to Calcutta, there was little time before the university exam. Unfortunately we two brothers failed to pass that time. In this

manner, along with the demise of our father, the hopes and expectations at the university vanished for both of us—just at the beginning of our youth. My father had been a worthy civil servant, and there is a general rule that if such a civil servant has surviving children or relatives, the government assists in maintaining the family by providing them some sort of employment. However, neither of us was ever afforded such assistance. Hence, the beginning of our youth marked the commencement of our struggle in life. Our elder brother got a job with the Post Office. I went to teach school in Habigunge. Subsequently, at the special request of our benevolent family friend, Durga Mohan Das, I secured a job in the Accountant General's office of the General Post Office. I was told then that if I persisted in that office, I would eventually draw a salary of Rs.300/- to Rs.400/-. However, we two brothers were not motivated by wealth: never was that the intention of the Lord. And so, after some time, I left to take my exams. In the meantime, I had joined the Braja Mohan School. Our elder brother, too, relinquished his position at the Post Office and joined the school.[17]

The Braja Mohan Institution, the official name of the school, had been founded in 1884 by one of Barisal's leading citizens, Aswini Kumar Datta. Satyananda would spend the rest of his life teaching school, while at the same time working actively and devotedly for the Barisal Brahmo Samaj.

In 1894 Kusum Kumari Das, aged nineteen, was married to Satyananda. Her family came from nearby Gaila, a village rather famous as the birthplace of a number of prominent members of the Vaidya caste. Both her father, Chandranath Das, and his elder brother, Kali Mohan Das, joined the Barisal Brahmo Samaj, Kali Mohan eventually becoming its minister. And, as his daughter would be, Chandranath was somewhat of a poet.[18]

Jibananda's mother studied up to the fourth grade in Barisal,[19] then, when the institution where she was a student closed, attended a Calcutta school, something in keeping with Brahmo attitudes but nonetheless quite progressive for a *mofussil* girl in those days. "My mother, Kusum Kumari Das, was born in the town of Barisal proper. She studied in Calcutta at Bethune School. Quite possibly she had studied up to the first class [highest grade]," her son noted. "Just after that, her marriage took place. She could very easily have passed the university's final examination. In this area, I believe, she was more competent than her children."[20]

In 1895, primarily through the efforts of Ramananda Chatterjee—one of the leading Brahmos of that day and Kusum Kumari's guardian during the period of her Calcutta schooling—a children's monthly magazine entitled *Mukul* ("Flower Buds") began publication in Calcutta. Sivanath Sastri, another renowned Brahmo and also friend of the Das family, lent his name to the journal as nominal editor. *Mukul* was associated with the Brahmo

Samaj's Sunday school. Its list of contributors included many of the leading figures in Bengali society, including Rabindranath Tagore and Upendrakishor Raychaudhuri, film director Satyajit Ray's grandfather.[21] Two other contributors were Kusum Kumari and Satyananda Das, the latter of whom wrote a short historical piece on Napoleon.[22]

Mukul published several poems by Kusum Kumari during its first year. One of these, "The Exemplary Boy" (*adarsa chele*) became a staple of poetry anthologies for Bengali children.

THE EXEMPLARY BOY

When within our country will that boy be born
Who not by words but by deeds grows big and strong!
Smiling face, expansive chest, a mind that's full of fire;
"I must indeed become a man"—this, his firm desire.

When danger draws near, advance ever forward.
Do not you have inside you, life—flesh and blood?
All only have two arms, two legs, for naught do you fear;
He who fully comprehends this, does he just cower there?

Who wants a lad whose eyes well up with tears, tell me,
Whose head begins to spin, when spoken to, merely?
With open heart, a smile that's broad, make this vow solemn,
"I must indeed become a man, for I am human."

The peasant's child and the son of a king
In our great world, each has his work.
So offer up your might, toil with heart and mind;
If you be truly "men," you'll bring honor to this land.[23]

In 1900, Satyananda and his brother-in-law, Manomohan Chakravarty, began publishing a monthly magazine, *Brahmabadi* ("The Brahmo"), mouthpiece for Barisal's Brahmo Samaj. It carried "discussions on the subjects of education, society, religion, and morals, but not politics."[24] In the initial years, Satyananda himself edited the journal, the duty later falling to Jibanananda's uncle, Manomohan. Besides articles on education and such, *Brahmabadi* regularly featured a poem on the first page of each issue and a "local news" section. The sheer volume of news published about Satyananda and his relatives identifies the Das family as a central and active component of the Barisal Brahmo Samaj. Manomohan composed many of the poems presented as the leading entry in the magazine, but a number were penned by Jibanananda's mother. (From the appearance of the first journal in their mother tongue, *Bamla Gajeti* ["Bengal Gazette"] in 1818, educated Bengalis have demonstrated a passion for publishing both periodicals and books, often featuring their own and their friends' writings in little—frequently irregular and sometimes short-lived—magazines.)[25]

Then Ramananda Chatterjee, in 1901 while posted away from Bengal in Allahabad, started yet another journal, a most respected Bengali publication by the name of *Prabasi* ("The Exile"). There, too, a few poems by Kusum Kumari appeared. Her greatest number of contributions, though, about a hundred poems in all, went to *Brahmabadi*. At some point she even published a volume of her children's poetry entitled *Poetry-Buds* (*kabita-mukul*), and later, *Puranic Tales* (*pauranik akhyayika*), featuring stories drawn from the ancient Sanskrit Puranas.[26]

Jibanananda had observed his mother composing poetry in between household chores or even in the midst of some of those tasks.

> Twenty-five, thirty, forty years ago there were a great many family members living in our Barisal house. I saw my aunt [Haricaran Das's wife] and my mother busy the whole day with housework. In those days our family's financial situation was not particularly good. But one is astonished today to think of how my aunt and mother, working tirelessly, and my grandmother, managing all, used to run a household so very successfully and energetically in the face of such adverse conditions....
>
> Mother didn't get much of a chance to write. She had married into a very large family where, however, there were educated persons and an atmosphere of learning. Nevertheless, it eventually became virtually impossible for such a woman of a not very well-to-do family of that day to do even a little of her own work now and then in between those unrelenting chores which continued throughout the day and night. Perhaps she did best to immerse herself in that consuming work and unselfish service rather than in poetry.... But had she written more, I believe now she could have contributed something unique to Bengali literature.
>
> There was a wonderful clarity in Mother's verse. I would often see her composing her fine poetry and prose. She might be extremely busy with various domestic chores—and at such a time *Brahmabadi* editor, Acarya [a term for teacher and also preacher within the Brahmo Samaj] Manomohan Chakravarty, would come in and say: "I need one of your poems for *Brahmabadi* right away. Someone is waiting to take it to the press." And Mother would take pen and notebook into the kitchen. There she could be seen wielding a cooking spoon in one hand and a pen in the other, as if she were writing a letter, with hardly a hesitation or pause. Almost right then and there she would give the poem to Acarya Chakravarty.[27]

Jibanananda's mother is also credited with saving her son's life. It was when Jibanananda was very young, before his brother Asokananda and sister Sucarita were born, that he fell very ill with an unspecified liver ailment.[28] As Asokananda pointed out, doctors in those days often prescribed a change of climate as a remedy for illness. Wrote Sucarita:

> Our elder brother was stricken once in childhood by a severe disease—he wasn't even expected to live. Mother and our maternal grandfather traveled with him to many healthy spots, to various new climes—Lucknow, Agra, Delhi. At that particular time our financial situation was not good at all. From old letters we come to know that our family and the relatives felt Mother's perseverance was self-destructive. Still, Mother remained uncompromising in her efforts. After spending a long time away from home, she returned with her child completely cured.[29]

Asokananda mentioned that his brother had a slight temper which would flare up at times and suggested that it might have had something to do with that childhood liver illness.[30]

Jibanananda was nearly nine years old before he started school formally, but his education had begun at home long before that. "Father was opposed to enrolling us in school at a young age. We learned reading and writing from our mother when we were small," wrote Asokananda of his brother and himself.[31] Then in 1908 Satyananda saw fit to place his eldest son in B.M. Institution, where he himself taught.[32]

B.M. Institution was destined to go through some rough times. In 1921, friction between the founder of the school, Aswini Kumar Datta, and the government gravely affected the institution and apparently caused Satyananda to resign his post of assistant headmaster. Earlier, in the spring of 1919 in the Punjab province of western India, General Dyer had ordered his troops to fire upon a crowd of some ten to twenty thousand people gathered together in an enclosure known as Jallianwala Bagh in the city of Amritsar, killing several hundred and wounding over a thousand. In protest against such barbarism, Rabindranath, knighted in 1915 by George V on the occasion of the king's birthday, resigned his knighthood, declaring in a letter to the viceroy, Lord Chelmsford, that "I for my part wish to stand, shorn of all special distinctions, by the side of those of my countrymen who for their so-called insignificance are liable to suffer a degradation not fit for human beings."[33] Mahatma Gandhi, disheartened by new legislation that allowed political defendants to be tried without jury and interned without trial, shocked by both the Amritsar massacre and the mild reprimand that Dyer received, and sensing a nascent national unity between Hindus and Muslims (the latter group disillusioned over harsh terms imposed on Muslim Turkey by the Treaty of Sèvres—1920), no longer advocated cooperation with the British.³⁴ A call in 1920 by Gandhi and Chitta Ranjan Das—the latter, Bengal's popular political leader whom Jibanananda would eulogize in one of his earliest poems—for withdrawal from government schools and colleges brought with it renewed efforts to implement "national," noncolonial education, more suited to the country's needs.³⁵

A decade and a half earlier, Aswini Kumar had stated publicly his views on national education.³⁶ The year following Bengal's 1905 partition (denounced by all Bengali Hindus and many Muslims as an attempt to weaken the political strength of the Bengalis), Aswini Kumar, in his capacity as head of the welcoming committee, addressed the Provincial Conference (chaired by Abdul Rasul, a Muslim barrister), an adjunct to the Indian National Congress and the only pan-Indian political force. Such notable figures as Surendranath Banerjee, Bipin Chandra Pal, Aurobindo Ghose, as well as Rabindranath who, in his capacity as chairman for a simultaneous literary conference, attended this 1906 session held in Barisal. The Swadeshi movement ("swa" is a Sanskrit prefix meaning "one's own"; "desh," a word for "land, homeland, country"; "i," an adjectival suffix) had commenced a couple of years previously, designed to encourage Indians to be self-reliant and buy Indian products instead of British imports. Aswini Kumar's welcoming address had to be delivered by someone else, for he was preoccupied with the chief government official, the Bakhargunge District Magistrate. On their way to the meeting that first morning, a number of the participants chose to march to the magistrate's quarters, singing what served as subjugated India's nationalist anthem, "Bande Mataram" ("Praise the Mother")—in defiance of prior assurances extracted from Aswini Kumar by the district magistrate. *Lathi-* (stave-) wielding police charged the marchers, spilling some blood.³⁷

In this opening address, in English, Aswini Kumar denounced the "dark day of partition" when the British sword "mercilessly smote their [Bengal's] sons and daughters] Mother."³⁸ On education, he declared:

> Our ideal and standard of life are not the same as those of western nations; the laws and habits that govern the oriental character are different from those that govern the occidental; the constitution of the oriental mind is different from that of the occidental. The system of education that is prevalent at present does not seem to take this into account. Are our boys trained in Indian thoughts, Indian histories and Indian traditions? It is next to impossible for those who have taken charge of our education to dive down into the depths of our national heart in which lie imbedded, maybe, beneath the slime of ages, precious truths that were propounded by the Hindu Rishis and Mahomedan Saints of old.³⁹

Invoking "National Education," he urged

> thousands and thousands to take up the Swadeshi vow, to demolish the citadels of conservatism and apathy which still stand as stupendous obstacles in the way of our industrial advancement, to secure the foundation of a number of Industrial and Technical schools on a humble scale with a model Technical Institute at their head, ... [40]

That was 1906—before Jibanananda, a lad of seven, had enrolled in any formal school at all.

The January 1921 issue of *Brahmabadi* took note of a local student movement and reported that a "national school" had been established in the old hostel at B.M. Institution. About 250 students assembled there, and various other persons volunteered both time and effort.[41] The February-March 1921 issue told of a number of students boycotting or quitting schools other than B.M. Institution, but then returning again. Four students were reported to have demonstrated their "noncooperation" by leaving the hall during the matriculation examination.[42] And then the April 1921 issue carried the news that Aswini Kumar had transformed the B.M. Institution itself into a national school.[43] In response to newly articulated demands for national education, its curriculum would include vocational training—specifically, technical classes and medicine. The school suffered the consequences of such a defiant, antigovernment act: part of the teaching staff resigned, and enrollment dropped off dramatically.

In 1921, as the national school underwent reorganization, Satyananda departed B.M. Institution to assume the position of headmaster at the Model School, an English high school that he himself founded.[44] Unlike a national school, Barisal's Model School gained accreditation by the authorities at Calcutta University.[45] There is no proof that Satyananda left B.M. Institution for reasons of political ideology. He might have been interested in the post of headmaster, a step up from being assistant headmaster at B.M. Institution. However, a statement by Jibanananda suggests political ideology may indeed have been the impetus behind Satyananda's resignation from where he had taught so long:

> Though he was concerned first and foremost not with another's but with his own country's dire economic and political situation, yet he perceived a distinction between the then current "nationalism" and true love of one's country. And though he viewed that so-called nationalism with suspicion, a feeling of identity with his country was for him a thing of which to be proud. Concerning the political movement, he did not favor petitions or assuming a begging posture. He realized that no country would experience lasting good fortune—no matter what political

change—if the separation which exists between the common man and the educated community is not at least partially eradicated. And though he was profoundly aware that during the more recent period there have been enthusiastic efforts to effect fundamental changes in society and the system of government—by near complete transformation of the ancient and even the nineteenth-century modes of thought—yet he firmly believed that the world does not really benefit by merely ever newer ideas or even by soundly rational acts unless and until men's inner defects are expunged. He placed emphasis on character and purity of consciousness— for all countries and for all men. He was of the belief that if these were not flawlessly maintained, the establishment of any apparently well-ordered political state or society would be but transitory; such a state would contain the seeds of its own destruction which would in turn cause its disintegration. And though his own feelings and thoughts on all these topics seem quite reasonable, he respected the ideologies of others who responded to the surging vital force of change.[46]

Satyananda, who "viewed that so-called nationalism with suspicion," was not alone in leaving B.M. Institution, for that same year headmaster Jagadish Mukherjee also relinquished his position.[47] The Barisal situation appears not to have differed markedly from a general Indian response to the national education experiment. Though "[n]ot many officials resigned or returned their titles," writes a prominent historian, "schools and colleges were disrupted for a time but substitute 'national' institutions soon wilted."[48] B.M. Institution may have continued to be a national school somewhat longer than most, simply because of Aswini Kumar Datta's forceful guidance. But then in late 1923, that patriot and educator died in Calcutta. One more year elapsed before B.M. Institution felt compelled, in its own self-interest, to forgo the national education scheme. According to *Jubilee,* a publication commemorating B.M. Institution's fiftieth anniversary (1884-1934):

> The new experiment lasted for four years. The number of students in the general classes fell down gradually to 67 in December, 1924. Jagadish Babu and the present proprietors, after careful deliberation and consultation with the leading men of the town, had the Institution reorganized on old lines under the University. The technical department had to be closed down for financial reasons. But the medical department continued to flourish. . . . [49]

Satyananda never rejoined the B.M. Institution staff, continuing on as Model School's headmaster until several years later when that school merged with another.[50] In 1927, he took a post as teacher of English at the local High English Girls' School.[51] Even when not formally teaching in front of a class, Satyananda instructed, preached, and wrote—and theorized about education, as we see in his article in *Brahmabadi* on Maria Montessori's approach to pedagogy.[52]

Jibanananda completed his studies at B.M. Institution well before it became a national school. He would have taken his matriculation examination in 1914 but for a rule that required a candidate to be sixteen years of age by 1 March of the year in which he planned to sit for the exam. And so he had to wait another year before he could take and pass his "matric," as it was called. During the years Jibanananda attended B.M Institution, headmaster Jagadish Mukherjee made a profound impression on this young student. Years later Jibanananda would write:

> ... it has been quite a while now since we graduated from the university. But from whom did we get our education? Or, at least, from whom did I? It was from three individuals. One was my father, one my mother, and one the headmaster of Braja Mohan Institution, Acarya' Jagadish Chandra Mukherjee. After graduating from that Barisal school, I have studied at many big colleges; I've attended the university. Yet today, upon arriving at the midpoint in life, I am ever aware of the fact that the very foundation of my life's education was molded in their hands.[53]

After passing the matric, Jibanananda for two years attended B.M. College, sister institution to the school with the same initials. At the I.A. or intermediate arts level, the student takes a combination of three fields. Jibanananda's was English, Bengali, and, of all things, chemistry.[54] He earned his I.A. degree in 1917, then went off to Calcutta where he enrolled at, not the Brahmos' City College, but Presidency College, then as now Bengal's oldest and most prestigious institution. While studying there for his B.A. degree in English, Jibanananda resided at the Oxford Mission hostel. This Church of England mission had a branch in Barisal, which accounted for the great number of boys from Barisal staying in that particular dormitory when attending college in Calcutta.[55] Moreover, Satyananda had translated into Bengali certain religious tracts, such as lives of the saints, for Mission publication, and, ever the teacher, had instructed the Barisal missionaries in Bengali.[56]

In 1919, Jibanananda received a B.A. honours degree in English from Presidency College, passing his examination in the second class, not the coveted first class for which all students strive. A special Brahmo "meditation service" was held at the Das residence, Sarbananda Bhavan, by the sons, daughters, grandsons, and granddaughters of the late Sarbananda Das to express their thanks and joy for the success they had had on various exams—M.A., B.Sc., and B.A.[57]

Jibanananda continued his studies in English jointly at Calcutta University and Presidency College, within Calcutta University's modified British higher-education system.[58] Simultaneously, he enrolled in the University's law college where his name appeared on the register for three years, 1919–22,[59] though he never sat for the final law examination. By 1922 he had passed, again in the second class, his M.A. examination in

English.[60] Sucarita attributed her brother's poor showing to a temporary illness he suffered just prior to taking the exam. Jibanananda wanted to wait a year before attempting the exam, so that he could be assured of a first-class score. Their father advised him not to waste a year's time, so he took it and, to his disappointment, ended up once again in the second class.[61] That second-class M.A. would return to haunt Jibanananda much later when, in his forties, he sought a teaching position in Calcutta.

One might wonder why Jibanananda, like so many of his fellow Bengali poets of that day, specialized in English literature. Why not Bengali? For him there was really no choice. It became possible to earn an M.A. degree in the "vernaculars" only from the year 1920 on,[62] and by that time Jibanananda had already committed himself to the formal study of the English language and its literature.

During 1919, Jibanananda, then a Calcutta college student, published rather shyly in the hometown, family-run *Brahmabadi* what may very well be his first public poem. Some four years previously, while still in Barisal, he had sent samples of his unpublished poetical endeavors to the ultimate arbiter of Bengali verse, Rabindranath Tagore. We do not know what poetry he submitted for appraisal; however, the senior poet's reply has been preserved and reads in part:

> There is no doubt but that you have literary talent, yet I fail to understand why you employ such imperious language etc. Such poetic affectation belittles real skill. Quality literature possesses a tranquillity which, when we see it disturbed, we begin to doubt the lasting nature of that particular writing. A show of force does not give proof of strength—rather, the opposite is the case.[63]

Four years later when Jibanananda's poetry first appeared in public, the poet's shyness manifested itself in the poem's signature line—instead of a full name, the poem bore the quasi-signature of "sri," a title comparable to that of "Mr." in English. (The annual table of contents for *Brahmabadi* that year, however, identified the poet more specifically as Jibanananda Das, B.A.) He would later contrast his poetry with his mother's. "The sweet jingle of words splashing through white water rivulets and the astounding unity of meaning," he wrote of her verse, "constantly tempted me; but from the very beginning, I traveled by another path."[64] His first composition proves an exception to that claim. Not only do the lilting meter and insistent rhymes mimic his mother's handiwork, but the very subject of the poem—an invocation to the new year—figured prominently in her poetic repertoire. Jibanananda's "Invocation for the New Year" (*barsa abahan*) was printed on the first page of *Brahmabadi* for the Baisakh number (the Bengali year begins with Baisakh—mid-April) of the year B.S. 1326 (A.D. 1919).

Initial poems for the previous three years had been contributions by his mother: Baisakh 1323, "Hope for the Year" (*barsa-asa*); Baisakh 1324, "New Year" (*naba barsa*); Baisakh 1325, "New Year" (*naba barsa*). Deferring to her son for the subsequent year, Kusum Kumari returned in Baisakh 1327 with "Wishes for the Year" (*barsa-kamana*). Jibanananda's contribution is short and quite sweet.

INVOCATION FOR THE NEW YEAR

There before the eastern portal
In brilliant blue, in shining passion
The morning sun awoke, arose
To a heavenly touch.

Upon the sky no cloudy shadows,
As if it were translucent heaven!
All the world without illusion
Is seen through charmed heart.

Gone is night, ah, gone away,
Calling out its last farewell.
Beneath some darkness deep and solemn
Those memories are kept.

Come, come hither, you the new one.
Gone is he the aged, pallid.
You today are deathless, you,
Now freed of all constraint.[65]

This first of Jibanananda's published poems shows considerable motherly influence, though he would not for long proceed in that direction.

Both his parents were well-read in English and Indian literature, as Jibanananda himself states in his reminiscences.[66] Literature, the reading and writing of it, had been an integral part of the Das family life. So too was teaching—that performed by his father in the various Barisal schools, as well as the religious and moral instruction both parents did in a less structured fashion at home and through the Brahmo Samaj. Like his father the teacher and his mother the poet, Jibanananda would spend the rest of his life both teaching—or trying to find a job teaching—and writing, both poetry and prose.

3

Jibanananda was born into a culture extremely proud, and justifiably so, of its literary heritage. The history of Bengali poetry (poetry and literature being synonymous until the nineteenth century when prose for literary purposes makes an appearance) dates back probably to the eleventh century A.D., possibly as early as the eighth century. An untitled collection of some fifty lyric poems, the so-called "Caryapadas," represents what many believe to be the earliest specimens we have of Bengali, albeit a very cryptic Bengali. (Hindi scholars claim the language is proto-Maithili, a dialect of Hindi, while the Assamese insist it is early Assamese, and the Orissans think of it as Oriya.)[67] The verses instruct the initiated, those who can decrypt the code words, in the proper beliefs and practices of Tantric Buddhism. The language may be eleventh-century. The manuscript itself, found by the eminent Bengali scholar Hara Prasad Sastri early this century in Kathmandu, in Nepal's royal Durbar Library, probably dates back no further than the sixteenth century.

Such is the case with nearly all texts in the Indian subcontinent: few, if any, predate the sixteenth or fifteenth centuries. The weather, hot and often humid from monsoon rains, coupled with white ants, and other natural calamities take their toll on the palm-leaf strips, the most common writing material, as well as any other "paper" on which manuscripts may have been written. Although Indian civilization produced some of the most ancient texts known to man today, the words themselves had to be passed on from the memory of one person to that of the next, or, if the text were committed to writing, copied and recopied onto fresh palm leaves as the older manuscripts began to deteriorate.

Virtually all of premodern Bengali literature is religious in one way or another, particularly that composed by Hindu poets. Baru Chandidasa's "Srikrishna Kirtan," one of the older (estimated dates extend from the fourteenth to the beginning of the seventeenth century)[68] and most important works in the literary canon, recounts via a collection of somewhat separable lyrics the pranks and exploits of Lord Krishna, cowherdsman-and-lover incarnation of the god Vishnu. In the late fifteenth century, there was born in Bengal a man by the name of Chaitanya, ardent devotee of Krishna and one whom followers considered to be an incarnation of both Krishna and Radha—the latter being Krishna's favorite milkmaid and paramour. Centered around Chaitanya, Bengali Vaishnavism flourishes today. Moreover, it can be found outside of India, in the United States, for instance, where one hears in public places the chant "Hare

Krishna" ("Hare" being the vocative form of Hari, one of the many Sanskrit epithets for Vishnu/Krishna).

Be the American converts what they may, Bengali Vaishnava poets of the fourteenth through the nineteenth centuries composed some of the finest devotional lyrics the world has known. In a sonnet full of love for his Bengal homeland, Jibanananda made passing reference to one of the most famous of these devotee-lyricists, Chandidasa[69] (as distinct from Baru Chandidasa), who had sung of his love for Krishna/Kanu—thank god, a requited love.

> On this dark night, thick with clouds,
> how can he possibly have come?
> But my friend is there, in the courtyard,
> drenched with rain
> and seeing him my heart bursts.
> O friend, what more can I say to you?
> I must have gained much merit in former births
> that he has come to me.
> But I do not control myself. In fear of my elders,
> I hesitate to go outside.
> Ah, as much pain and trouble as I have given him,
> when I see his sadness and deep love
> so much is my own heart pained.
> I would take the stain of infamy upon my head
> and burn my house with fire.
> His own sorrow he thinks joy, and sorrows at my sorrow—
> Chandidasa says, hearing of such love of Kanu
> the world is gladdened.
>
> (Trans. by Edward C. Dimock, Jr.)[70]

Hindus in Bengal pay homage to the entire Hindu pantheon but are either devotees primarily of Krishna (the Vaishnavas) or of the mother goddess in all her many manifestations. The latter are known as Shaktas, worshipers of Shakti, a name for the goddess representing the primal and feminine energy of the universe. Bengali Shaktas added their voice late to lyric poetry, but when they did so in the eighteenth century, first and foremost in the person of Ramprasad Sen, that voice proved new and startling. It was the cry of a petulant and neglected child cajoling his mother, the mother goddess—called Kali or Shyama/Syama ("the dark-colored goddess") or simply the Devi ("goddess"), among a thousand and eight different names—to turn her attention, her saving grace to the worshiper. Sang Ramprasad:

> I'm not calling you Mother anymore,
> All You give me is trouble.

I had a home and a family, now
I'm a beggar—what will You think of
Next, my wild-haired Devi?

I'll beg before I come to You,
Crying "Mother." I've tried that
And got the silent treatment.
If the mother lives should the son suffer,
And if she's dead, hasn't he got to live somehow?

Ramprasad says: What's a mother
Anyway, the son's worst enemy?
I keep wondering what worse You can do
Than make me live over and over
The pain, life after life.

(Trans. by Leonard Nathan and myself)[71]

Jibanananda acknowledges "Ramprasad's wild-haired Syama" in his own poetry.[72]

Throughout the medieval period of Bengali literary history, Shakta poets contributed amply to another genre that, along with the devotional lyric, epitomizes medieval Bengali literature: *mangal kavya* or, loosely translated, "auspicious story-poetry." Mukundaram Chakravarty's *Chandi Mangal,* a sixteenth-century narrative eulogizing goddess Chandi, is one of the most respected texts of the medieval period, both as sacred work and literature. *Mangal kavyas* demonstrate through their stories the benefits of worshiping the deity whose "mangal" it is and the suffering incurred by those who refuse to honor that deity. For example, Manasa, the goddess of snakes, has a number of *mangal kavyas* composed in her honor, the most popular of which being Ksetakadasa's *Manasa Mangal*. The central tale features the merchant Chand Sadagar from the town of Champa with his boat named Honeybee, his daughter-in-law Behula, and son Lakhindar. All manner of calamities befall Chand because he refuses to worship Manasa, the principal disaster occurring on the wedding night of Chand's seventh son, Lakhindar—the first six sons had been killed earlier by the goddess. Manasa sends one of her snakes to bite the bridegroom. Behula refuses to give her husband up for dead; instead, she places him upon a raft and floats downstream with the body. There she chances upon Manasa's assistant, Neto, who takes her to Amara, the abode of the gods where Behula dances flawlessly before Indra and the other deities, with Lakhindar's revival as her reward.[73]

Jibanananda weaves allusions to this medieval narrative into another of his sonnets. According to him, when Behula danced, all Bengal cried out in sympathy, sounding like the ankle bells she wore.

I have looked upon the face of Bengal—the world's beauty
I need no longer seek: in the darkness I awake and glimpse
In a fig tree, sitting beneath umbrella-like foliage,
The early morning magpie—I see all around piles of leaves
Of *jam,* banyan, jackfruit, cashew, *aswattha,* lying still;
Shade falls upon the cactus clump, upon the *sati* grove.
I know not when Chand from Champa, from his boat the Honeybee,
Had seen Bengal's exquisite beauty, the same blue shadows

Of cashew, banyan, *tamal.* Behula once on a raft upon the river—
When the moon's sliver died away behind some sandy shoal—
Had seen many an *aswattha* and banyan beside the golden paddy,
Had heard Syama's soft song, once had gone to Amara and when
She danced like a clip-winged wagtail bird at Indra's court, Bengal's
Rivers, fields, *bhant* blossoms wept like ankle bells upon her feet.[74]

Medieval Bengali literature was not the exclusive purview of Hindu poets and Hindu themes. Indeed, Bangladeshi scholars are quick to point out that not only are there fine Bengali narratives on Islamic topics, but Muslim poets in the medieval period were the first—and virtually the only—Bengali poets to compose secular tales. At the turn of the fifteenth century, Shah Mahammad Sagir wrote *Iusuf-Jalikha,* a romance based on the Joseph of the book of Genesis, and Zuleika, Potiphar's wife. Two centuries later in what is now Burma but was then the independent kingdom of Arakan, lying just south and east of present-day Chittagong, two premier Muslim Bengali poets, Daulat Kazi and Alaol, flourished under the patronage of the Arakan court. Alaol's *Padmabati* weaves a tale of intrigue and of beautiful, virtuous—and very Indian—women.[75]

In the nineteenth century, Bengali literature began to evolve gradually but fundamentally, two educational institutions in the burgeoning, new city of Calcutta indirectly contributing to that change. In 1800 the British founded a college at Fort William in order to instruct the East India Company's civil servants in the vernacular languages of British India. For this, the college required textbooks containing samples of Bengali. Poetry was readily available. Prose was not. William Carey, the Baptist missionary hired to teach Bengali, collected examples of conversational Bengali and wrote them up in a textbook of sorts entitled *Conversations* (*kathopakathan*). Carey also commissioned a work in Bengali prose, something new to Bengali literature. The result, Ramram Bose's *The Life of Rajah Pratapaditya* (*pratapaditya carit*). Serious Bengali prose literature would wait until the middle of the century to make its appearance, but with the work done under the egis of Fort William College, Bengali literary prose made its debut.[76] (A. T. M. Anisuzzaman, however, has argued persuasively that the early Bengali prose style itself appears far in advance of Fort William College, set by those Bengalis who worked for the East India Company, in business-related communications exchanged between factories.)[77]

Calcutta, headquarters during the nineteenth century for British governors-general administering their East India possessions, had become quite cosmopolitan. It would be known as "the City of Palaces" and "the Second City of the British Empire," as well as "the Paris of the East."[78] Among its leading citizens were numbered "Prince" Dwarkanath Tagore, entrepreneurial partner of Carr-Tagore & Co. and grandfather of Rabindranath Tagore, and Ram Mohan Ray, founder of the Brahmo Samaj. In 1816 a group of educated Hindu gentlemen, feeling the need for a college where their sons could receive a proper modern education, established Hindoo College, intended "to instruct the sons of the Hindoos in the European and Asiatic languages and sciences." An English-medium institution, its syllabus for the year 1828, for instance, reads like what one might expect to find in any liberal arts college in England or the United States: Oliver Goldsmith's histories of Rome and England, John Gay's fables, Alexander Pope's translations of the *Iliad* and *Odyssey,* Dryden's *Works of Virgil,* Milton's *Paradise Lost,* and a Shakespeare tragedy.[79]

As mentioned earlier, Persian had been the lingua franca of the Moguls, the rulers from whom much of the Company's possessions were acquired. In a foreign tongue, the British administrators meted out justice throughout the territory they governed. Then in 1835, English replaced Persian as the official language of the courts in British India. It was that same year in which Thomas Babington Macaulay, respected essayist and member of parliament who had come out from London to Calcutta to serve on the recently created Supreme Council of India, issued his famous or, to some minds, infamous Minute on Education, recommending English as the medium of instruction for schools under British control.

The British took seriously "the white man's burden." The issue before Macaulay was whether it would be better to educate the natives through the medium of one or another of India's vernacular or classical languages, or through English. Macaulay came down solidly on the side of English. And his reasons were not predicated solely upon the language, the ease or difficulty with which it could be mastered and used effectively, but on the richness of its literature. Macaulay wrote: "I have never found one among them [those Englishmen who advocated an Indian language, instead of English, as the medium of instruction] who could deny that a single shelf of a good European library was worth the whole native literature of India and Arabia."[80]

Such an attitude prevailed, even for a time among Indians. English carried with it prestige. Little wonder, therefore, that when Michael Madhusudan Dutt (1824–73), star pupil of Hindoo College, embarked on his illustrious literary career, he wrote in English. To a fellow student he sent a letter in the early 1840s, in English (all but a couple of his letters were in English, sparkling and vivacious):

> Good Heavens—what a thing have I forgotten to inform you of—I sent my poems to the Editor of the Blackwood's [Edinburgh Magazine] Tuesday last: I haven't dedicated them to you as I intended, but to William Wordsworth, the Poet. My dedication runs thus: "These Poems are most respectfully dedicated to William Wordsworth Esq, the Poet, by a foreign admirer of his genius—the author." Oh! to what a painful state have I committed myself. Now, I think the Editor will receive them graciously, now I think he will reject them.[81]

And reject them the editor in Edinburgh apparently did, for Madhusudan never mentioned them again.

After nearly a decade of writing English and of publishing with qualified success, Madhusudan had a change of heart: he would seek to make his literary mark in Bengali, his mother tongue, not English. With typical Madhusudan exuberance, he wrote again to that same college friend, telling of a daily regimen of language study which began at 6:00 A.M. with Hebrew, ended at 10:00 P.M. with English, and included Latin, Greek, and Sanskrit. Self-assuredly and rhetorically he asked, "Am I not preparing for the great object of embellishing the tongue of my fathers?"[82] As Madhusudan's own words indicate, his return to Bengali carried with it no hint of xenophobia. Quite the contrary. Referring to his magnum opus, *The Slaying of Meghanada* (*meghanadavadha kavya*), an epic based on an episode from the *Ramayana* and published in 1861 (the year of Rabindranath Tagore's birth), Madhusudan boasted Miltonic prosody:

> You want me to explain my system of versification for the conversion of your sceptical friend. I am sure there is very little in the system to explain; our language, as regards the doctrine of accent and quantity, is an "apostate", that is to say, it cares as much for them as I do for the blessing of our Family-Priest! If your friends know English, let them read the Paradise Lost, and they will find how the verse, in which the Bengali poetaster writes, is constructed.[83]

Madhusudan, well-read and a linguistic magician, drew upon his Indian literary heritage as well as elements of Occidental literature to produce something original and at the same time of his own tradition. Lesser poets and some of the emerging fiction writers, seduced by what they read in English, tended to imitate more than innovate. During the twentieth century, the anxiety of influence, as Harold Bloom called the phenomenon in a different context, plagued Bengali writers, as one or another of them would be accused of aping their Western counterparts. In the nineteenth century, however, the nature of that anxiety was somewhat different. Bankim Chandra Chatterjee (1838–94), the first Bengali novelist of significance (dubbed "the Walter Scott of Bengal") began his literary journal, *Bangadarsan* ("Mirror of Bengal") in 1872, lamenting in his introductory editorial the lot of those who wrote and published literature in Bengali. "Those elites, partial to English, are almost certain," he charged,

> that nothing worth reading could possibly be written in Bengali. They have determined that Bengali writers one and all are either devoid of taste, lacking writing style, or translators of English works. They are convinced that whatever is now composed in Bengali is either unreadable or a mere shadow of some English work, and why demean oneself by reading again in Bengali what is already available in English.[84]

By the end of the century, Bengali had proven itself to be a legitimate vehicle for literature, but the anxiety remained.

Politically, the East India Company's authority weathered the storm of the 1857 Sepoy Mutiny. Then in 1874, the British parliament voted to dissolve the Company, whose charter Queen Elizabeth granted in 1600, and Queen Victoria assumed the title Empress of India, thereby placing that jewel of jewels in her empire's crown.

In 1905, ostensibly to govern better a cumbersome administrative unit, the Bengal Presidency (consisting of the provinces of Bengal, Assam, Bihar, and Orissa) was divided in two, splitting Bengal itself down the middle, separating the western part with Calcutta from Dhaka and the eastern region. Incensed, Bengalis viewed this act as an attempt to weaken Bengal's political power. Besides verbal protests, such as those delivered at the Barisal conference, terrorist acts increased against the British Raj. It was during this period that Rabindranath Tagore composed two songs, "My Golden Bengal" (*amar sonar bamla*) and "Heart of the People" (*janaganamana*), which later became the national anthems of Bangladesh and India, respectively.[85] Partition of Bengal (in Bengali known as "banga bhanga" or "Bengal broken") lasted until 1912 when the British Crown, realizing its error, reunited the province but at the same time shifted the capital of British India from Calcutta to Delhi, traditionally the seat of power for rulers of northern India.

By 1912 Rabindranath, then in his fifties, dominated Bengali literature as no one before or after him has done. That year he had planned to visit the West for a third time. The night before he was due to sail, he fell ill. His doctors ordered him to postpone the trip. To recuperate, Rabindranath retired to the family's zemindary at Silaidaha, now in Bangladesh, near the banks of the Padma. During his convalescence, he translated into English a number of his Bengali lyric poems. After little more than a month, Rabindranath felt strong enough to travel and in May set sail.

Once in London he made contact with the painter William Rothenstein, whom he had met two years earlier in Calcutta.[86] Rabindranath let Rothenstein see the translated poetry. Impressed, Rothenstein showed the poems to W. B. Yeats, and Yeats in turn to Ezra Pound, who, as contributing editor in Europe for Harriet Monroe's fledgling Chicago poetry magazine, published six of them in the December issue of *Poetry,* marking the first time Rabindranath's verse had been printed in the United States. A month earlier, in London, the India Society at Rothenstein's urging had brought out a limited edition of *Gitanjali,* 103 of Rabindranath's translations with an introduction by Yeats. In the fall of 1913, with Rabindranath back at his school in Santiniketan (the name means "abode of peace"), word arrived of his winning the Nobel Prize for literature—the first of three Calcutta residents so honored, the others being Calcutta University professor C. V. Raman in 1930 for physics, and Mother Teresa in 1979 for peace. Though Pound would later completely reverse himself, at this moment he, like many in a Europe on the brink of war, stood in awe of this peaceful man from the East.[87] "When I leave Mr. Tagore," wrote Pound, "I feel exactly as if I were a barbarian clothed in skins, and carrying a stone war-club, the kind, that is, where the stone is bound into a crotched stick with thongs."[88]

At home in Bengal, Rabindranath, though never without his critics, would become known as Gurudeb, the respected guru or preceptor. As the third decade of this century opened, he held sway as the guru of Bengali letters. And it was during this same decade that a new wave of young Bengali poets and writers began to make their voices heard, among them a painfully bashful and retiring young English professor, Jibanananda Das.

2
The Kallol Era

> One cannot decide immediately whether his diction and syntax, his similes, etc. are good or bad—but one can freely call them unusual.
>
> —Buddhadeva Bose, from a 1928 editorial in *Pragati*

1

A third generation Brahmo, Jibanananda grew up in the *mofussil* town of Barisal, surrounded by Brahmo theology and Samaj activities. Yet neither he nor his siblings ever took a very active part in the Brahmo Samaj. None of them officially joined the Samaj.[1] "Firm in his own religious beliefs," wrote Jibanananda of his father, "he was sympathetic to other individual or congregational forms of religious practice—especially the practice of independence by fully aware persons. Of course, once in a while he would be saddened to think that his own children and native sons were not particularly inclined toward his beloved religion."[2] But their father instilled his love of learning and teaching in all three of his children. Sucarita, the youngest, became headmistress of Tamluk Girls' School. Asokananda took up government service as a meteorologist. And Jibanananda entered the college teaching profession, starting his checkered career in 1922 at his father's alma mater, the Brahmos' City College in Calcutta.

The City College faculty and staff provided in one sense an extension of the Barisal Brahmo Samaj environment. Many of the faculty members were Brahmos, of course. Moreover, a number of them hailed from Barisal itself. Some, including the principal, Heramba Chandra Maitra, had rather close ties with the Barisal Samaj, so at City College Jibanananda worked more or less among friends.

While teaching at this Calcutta college he began writing in earnest, the elegy first capturing his fancy. (Death, in one way or another, figures prominently, as we shall see, in much of Jibanananda's poetry.) His first published piece (excluding the New Year's poem in his hometown, family-run *Brahmabadi*) eulogized Chitta Ranjan Das, who died in 1925.

Deshabandhu— "Friend of the Country," the proprietary epithet of C. R. Das—led one wing of the Indian independence movement and was without a doubt Bengal's most beloved and influential political leader. Half a million mourners, Gandhi among them, followed the litter through Calcutta's streets to the Hooghly river ghat and the cremation ceremony. As is often the case in Bengal, honorable public figures are honored with poetry, a revered medium for Bengalis. Jibanananda titled his elegiac offering "On the Death of Deshabandhu" (*desabandhu prayane*), then later just "Deshabandhu," for inclusion in his first book.

> In Bengal's courtyard you plucked a song on Shiva's vina,
> O restless child, the revolutionary Padma was your river-mother.
> A cradle of fierce spring storms rocked your blood incessantly
> To the rhythm of surging waves. In your heart a million serpents celebrated,
> Hoods raised, weaving finer than the flailing snakes round Shiva's neck,
> Before your Shiva-trident vast opposing armies ever cowered.
> By your touch, O priest, new life appeared at once in what had been decayed.
> You, Vishnu's rending disc-weapon, had come, the vanquisher of cowardice.
> You shattered the Bengalis' disastrous, somnolent trance,
> You shattered the fetters of that dusty chain of fear,
> You shattered the goblet of wantonness with fierce pride, ascetic fervor
> When you stood a mendicant on the Orient's stage—before the entire world.
> Dressed as young Buddha, scorning all desires with a look askance,
> You flowed forth, the Gangetic source-spring of Indian thought
> For the wretched untouchable, for the good of all on earth
> Like thunder's rumble you chanted your mantra, O ascetic.[3]

And so on. Hindu gods Shiva and Vishnu and their iconography become metaphors for C. R. Das and his deeds. Deshabandhu compares with the young Indian prince, Gautama, who upon attaining enlightenment came to be known as the Buddha, the "enlightened one." And later in the poem, Savyasaci ("the one who draws the bow with the left hand, the ambidexter," an epithet for Arjuna), greatest Pandava warrior in the epic *Mahabharata,* does poetic service as Jibanananda tries to convey admiration for Bengal's recently deceased political figure:

> With a twang of the bow named Gandiva you said repeatedly, "Here, here I am!
> At epoch's end to India's Kuruksetra battlefield I have come, a new Savyasaci."

Jibanananda's paean to C. R. Das hints at the hyperbole found in coeval Kazi Nazrul Islam's (1899–1976) "The Rebel" (*bidrohi*), though Nazrul's egocentrism knows no bounds.

> Speak out, oh heroic one—
> Speak out—my head is held high,
> And seeing mine, the Himalayan peaks bow theirs!
> ....
> I am Dhurjati [Shiva], I'm the wild-haired sudden storms of April,
> I am a rebel, I'm the rebel son of the universal Mother!
> Speak out, oh heroic one—
> My head ever high.[4]

Known as "the rebel poet," both for this poem and his persona, Nazrul, while yet a teenager, quit school to join the Allied army, attaining the rank of havildar, a three-striped noncom native officer in the British infantry—but got no closer to the actual fighting than Karachi, Pakistan's port city on the Arabian Sea. Back home in Calcutta, he composed poetry to stir the blood. His *Fire's Vina* (*agni-bina*), a volume of impassioned poetry including "The Rebel," came out in 1922 and was forthwith proscribed because of its inflammatory nature. Twice the British government jailed him on sedition charges stemming from poetry he wrote and journals he edited. While imprisoned, Nazrul once undertook a fast that reportedly prompted Rabindranath to send him a telegram: "Give up hunger strike. Our literature claims you."[5] On the occasion of C. R. Das's funeral, Nazrul, the most prolific of Bengali songwriters, composed lyrics and music in praise of this fallen leader—a votive gesture similar in intent to Jibanananda's elegy.[6] Contemporaries, Nazrul and Jibanananda could hardly have been more dissimilar. Kazi Nazrul Islam—a Muslim, as the name indicates, and one of the very few Muslim poets in a field that Hindu (and Brahmo) writers dominated—was gregarious, boisterous, a self-assured rebel. Jibanananda demonstrated none of that flamboyance. But Nazrul's poetry proved infectious, and it momentarily infected the novice Jibanananda.

No literary masterpiece, "On the Death of Deshabandhu" did receive some words of praise, Asokananda recalled. One critic

> commented that he had thought when he read the piece that an older, established poet had composed it under a pseudonym. Later he [Jibanananda] placed no particular value on all that poetry. I cite the event for this reason: from the very beginning he entered the field of poetry well prepared, never giving evidence of what is called an immature hand.[7]

Contrary to his brother's opinion, this amateurish poem displays little indication of the Jibanananda to come.

Their mother turned out to be more critical, though more of this particular lyric's topic than of her son's poetic maturity or lack thereof. "After Chitta Ranjan's death," reminisced Jibanananda, "I composed a poem on him. Mother was herself a poet. In order to get her opinion, I sent her a copy of almost every poem of mine to appear on the pages of periodicals. By return mail she wrote: 'You have done well to write about Chitta Ranjan. But I asked you to write on Ram Mohan, or the Maharshi, too.'"[8] His mother had hoped her son would honor the religious leaders of their own Brahmo Samaj: its founder, Ram Mohan Ray, and the Maharshi or "Great Rishi," the epithet for Debendranath Tagore, Rabindranath's father and inspirational leader of the Samaj. If by chance Kusum Kumari had been worried that her son might actively join the independence movement, whose former leader he lauded in verse, she was mistaken. Jibanananda was then and continued to be apolitical.

Jibanananda's apolitical stance—reflected in much of his poetry—would be the cause of some hostile comments later on by Marxist-oriented critics, but for the time being his mother proved his stiffest critic. And possibly somewhat influenced by her criticism, Jibanananda published a panegyric poem in praise of the Hindu religious figure Ramdas, spiritual preceptor for Shivaji, that seventeenth-century Maratha general whose armies challenged Mogul hegemony in the central part of India known as the Deccan. Another of Jibanananda's lyrics lauded Bengal's own Vivekananda, missionary for the saintly mystic Ramakrishna. In the course of a visit to the United States during which he addressed the First World Parliament of Religions convened in Chicago (1893), Vivekananda, whose society remains active in the United States, probably initiated the oft-heard cultural cliché of the spiritual East and the materialistic West. Speaking in New York on the subject of his revered preceptor, Ramakrishna, Vivekananda suggested that

> ... when the Oriental wants to learn about machine-making, he should sit at the feet of the Occidental and learn from him. When the Occident wants to learn about the spirit, about God, about the soul, about the meaning and the mystery of this universe, he must sit at the feet of the Orient to learn.[9]

The South Asian subcontinent proudly possesses a rich endowment of religions. It also has had its share of religiously motivated mayhem, specifically bloodshed between Hindus and Muslims. Muslim armies invaded South Asia from the northwest through the Khyber Pass and at various times desecrated Hindu temples, demolishing "heathen" idols. Hindu armies retaliated. With the Moguls, most of the northern region came under the sway of Muslim rule. Much of the population, however, remained Hindu. It is argued that the British, seeing an advantage in disunity among the peoples they wished to rule, exacerbated the enmity between religious communities, adopting a "divide and rule" approach to maintaining power. Whether such accusations against the British are true, Hindu-Muslim animosity remains a fact of Indian life.

In the 1920s, events outside India adversely affected Hindu-Muslim relations in the country itself. During and just after World War I, Indians generally and the Muslims in particular fixed their attention on vanquished Turkey and the fate of the caliph—in some ways the titular head of the entire Muslim world. Nazrul Islam, for instance, composed in 1922 the poem "Kemal Pasha" (*kamal pasha*), boldly extolling the Turkish leader, presenting him as a war hero and leader of men. Indian Muslims took heart from Turkey's defeat of Greece that very year, viewing it as somehow a victory for Muslims and the caliphate, but when that same Kemal Ataturk abolished the caliphate in 1924, Muslim feelings of insecurity contributed to sporadic communal riots in India. C. R. Das, a Hindu, had gained the confidence of the Muslims and did much to mitigate ill will between Hindus and Muslims.[10] In 1926, the year following Deshabandhu's death, communal violence in Calcutta once again erupted. Jibanananda, as did Nazrul Islam, spoke out for communal harmony through many of his poems. In a work entitled "Hindu-Muslim" (*hindu-musalman*) published in June 1926, Brahmo Jibanananda referred to "us Hindus" and extended a friendly welcome to his Muslim brothers.

> In this sacred spot of greatest friendship—in this auspicious land of India,
> Hindu puja bells mix joyously with melodies from Muslim *namaz*!
> Hindu morning worship here begins amidst the Muslim call to prayer,
> The muezzins' call sounds throughout the very heavens.
> Fakirs say their beads at Eed; Hindu priests recite their mantras:
> At dawn and dusk, Vedic chants blend with the Koran's voice.
> Sannyasi and pir
> Here intertwine—as do the temple and the mosque.[11]

During the period beginning with "Deshabandhu" in 1925, Jibanananda published in several different journals. Both "Deshabandhu" and "Hindu-Muslim" came out in *Bangabani* ("Message of Bengal"), the journal that in the period 1923–26 serialized *The Path's Demand* (*pather dabi*) by Bengal's then most popular fiction writer, Sarat Chandra Chatterjee (1876–1938)—a novel (proscribed on charges of sedition) set in Burma and not unlike George Orwell's *Burmese Days* (1934), with its harsh indictment of British imperialism. A couple of Jibanananda's poems appeared in *Prabasi,* which had carried some of Kusum Kumari's poetry and much by Rabindranath. But these journals were not the vehicles of the avant-garde literary movement that began in Bengal in the 1920s.

One magazine's name, however, became synonymous with the new trend—that of *Kallol.* In 1923 *Kallol* ("Roaring Waves") began publication from Calcutta. Its two editors, Dinesh Ranjan Das and Gokul Chandra Nag, had been for the previous couple of years the nucleus around which a number of writers and artists gathered to form what they called the Four Arts Club.[12] These two men, from 1923 on, attracted the young and most avant-garde Bengali writers of the day. Gokul Chandra Nag died in 1925, but Dinesh Ranjan Das continued to edit the monthly journal until the early 1930s when it ceased publication for financial reasons—the fate of many a little magazine, both then and now.

Kallol was completing its third year of publication when "Blue Skies" (*nilima*) appeared, the first of Jibanananda's poems to come out in that magazine.

BLUE SKIES

Sunshine-glistening
Dawn sky, blue of midnight,
You show yourself time and again in endless splendor
Above this helpless city's prison walls.
Here thick coils of smoke overflow,
Harsh cooking fires ever glow here,
Blood-red pebbles smeared with hot desert breath,
Mirage-covered.
Hearts of countless travelers
Forever search desperately, not finding their way;
Their feet shackled by authority's firm chains.
O blue skies unblinking, you, O magician, have cracked
With your magic wand the very foundations of this prison of a
　　thousand injunctions!
Amidst humanity's uproar I sit in solitude and wonder
From what far mysterious place you wove your enchanted net
Then came alone to reality's bloody shores,
Spreading your blue wrapper over crystal lights,
A mute dream-peacock's wing!
Wiped from my eyes are the bloodstains of hunter-pierced earth,
Up flare fair lamp flames through limitless skies!
Sun-broiled beaches pallid with earth's tears,

> Tattered clothes, shaven-headed mendicants, pitiless this highway,
> This prison for the millions about to die,
> This dust—vast darkness encased in smoke
> Sinks within blue skies—into dream-widened, overwhelmed eyes,
> Into conch-white clouds in sparkling skies on a starshine night.
> Split is the withered cocoon of insectlike earth
> By your hesitant touch, O sleepless, far, fanciful realm![13]

"Blue Skies" displays Jibanananda's forte: a mix of sensuous and imaginative perceptions. Here he sees and "feels" a sky and a city at dawn. Later on, he will smell, taste, and hear natural phenomena such as the rising sun. His imagination-augmented eye will see more such things as an insectlike earth enclosed in its cocoon of darkness, bursting forth when the stars come out.

Of note in the poem is the manifest hostility felt toward the city by Jibanananda, a man of the *mofussil,* of the small town with its surrounding paddy fields and palm trees. As a professor of English in Calcutta, he resided within "this helpless city's prison walls!" Calcutta, Bengal's metropolis and the empire's second city, lured the madding crowd for various reasons, among them the employment a big city affords. There,

> Hearts of countless travelers
> Forever search desperately, not finding their way;
> Their feet shackled by authority's firm chains.
> ....
> ... pitiless this highway,
> This prison for the millions about to die

Jibanananda depicts the city itself as unprepossessing, shrouded in smoke. Anyone who has lived in Calcutta knows the haze of home cooking fires—small charcoal and coal burners, often lit with the aid of dried cow dung chips. Twice a day, once in the morning and then again at eventide, these stoves the size of water buckets are fueled, lit, and set outside to spare the kitchen the inevitable smoke. "Here thick coils of smoke overflow,/ Harsh cooking fires ever glow here," at dawn, and again at night "vast darkness encased in smoke" disappears within the sky.

It is the sky, that gift of nature not withheld even from urban dwellers, that provides escape for the city's prisoner.

> O blue skies unblinking, you, O magician, have cracked
> With your magic wand the very foundations of this prison of a thousand injunctions!

The lines that follow capture Jibanananda's essence.

> Amidst humanity's uproar I sit in solitude and wonder
> From what far mysterious place you wove your enchanted net
> Then came alone to reality's bloody shores,
> Spreading your blue wrapper over crystal lights,
> A mute dream-peacock's wing!

For most of his life he did sit alone, emotionally if not physically, and wonder—in most wonderful ways.

In February 1926 when "Blue Skies" appeared in *Kallol,* the right poem evidently found the right forum, for it caught the eye of a number of the younger writers. Acintya Kumar Sengupta in his memoirs *The Kallol Era* (*kallol yug*) remarks that he had been so struck by the poem that he immediately went to make the acquaintance of this unknown poet. Jibanananda resided at the time in Presidency Boarding, a rooming house just off Harrison Road (now renamed Mahatma Gandhi Road), within easy walking distance of both Calcutta University and City College where he taught. "You used to come often to Presidency Boarding," wrote Jibanananda to Acintya Kumar in response to publication of *The Kallol Era,* in 1949, "—then we would go out—often toward Chowringhee [a main street in central Calcutta]. Many things come to mind—of many irretrievable months, days, and moments."[14]

A couple of young writers, Premendra Mitra and Buddhadeva Bose, recalled that "Blue Skies" was the first poem by Jibanananda to come to their attention.[15] Both these men, as editors of two separate journals, were to do much to support their fellow poet. In that very same year, Premendra Mitra, with two others, brought out from Calcutta the second major outlet for the new literature, *Kali-Kalam* ("Pen and Ink"), a magazine that carried a number of Jibanananda's poems. And then a year later Buddhadeva Bose and Ajit Datta started publishing from Dhaka the third major voice of the young writers, *Pragati* ("Progress"). Though these three journals were by no means the only ones to showcase the avant-garde literature of the 1920s, they were its prime vehicles and set the tone for what came to be termed the Kallol era.

When Jibanananda's "Blue Skies" appeared, Buddhadeva, then only seventeen years old, was in his first year of college in Dhaka. But it was Buddhadeva as literary critic who in fact discovered and promoted the relatively unknown Jibanananda, ten years his senior. *Kallol* published Jibanananda's poems, although, according to Ajit Datta, the *Kallol* staff was not genuinely enamored of Jibanananda's work. "In particular, the editorial board of *Kallol* objected, perhaps, to giving up so much space to print his long poems. However, we," wrote Ajit Datta with pride, "happily and fondly printed those lengthy lyrics of his in *Pragati*."[16] *Pragati* not only printed Jibanananda's poems, Buddhadeva took it upon himself to argue Jibanananda's case in two editorials, the first pieces of criticism ever written on him.

2

Pragati began publication in June 1927. In August of that year, an obstreperous literary magazine reappeared on the scene. *Sanibarer Cithi* ("The Saturday Post") and its moving force, Sajani Kanta Das, played the role of aesthetic devil's advocate.[17] *Sanibarer Cithi* lampooned the litterateurs of the 1920s and 1930s, sparing few in its attempts to discredit satirically the avant-garde tendency of the day. One literary historian wrote:

> Sajani Kanta made his literary debut attacking Nazrul. Eventually nearly every renowned writer was savaged in his critical writings to the extent that being the object of his or *Sanibarer Cithi*'s barbs became a mark of success in the field of literature.[18]

Predictably, Jibanananda became the target of many of Sajani Kanta's barbed missiles.

Jibanananda's first book, *Fallen Feathers* (*jhara palak*), was published in the autumn of 1927.[19] It contained thirty-five poems, several of which had first come out in *Kallol* and *Kali-Kalam* and one from *Pragati*. He later denigrated the poetry in this book. "I am thinking about whether I should send you my first book of poetry," he wrote in a letter dated 2 July 1946, to someone who was about to produce a history of modern Bengali poetry. "I do not feel that this volume is of any significance."[20] Nevertheless, he allowed three of these thirty-five, but only three, to be included in a volume entitled *Jibanananda Das's Best Poems* (*jibanananda daser srestha kabita*) assembled and published in 1954 near the very end of his life. The selections were "Blue Skies," "Pyramid" (*piramid*), and "Back Then This Earth's" (*sedin e dharanir*), three poems that anticipate Jibanananda's future poetic concerns and motifs.

Possibly because India's attention had turned toward Turkey and, by association, to all the Middle East, Jibanananda's poetic gaze often fell upon lands west of India. But unlike Nazrul Islam's focus on the contemporary scene, Jibanananda's interest lay in the ancient civilizations of Babylon and Egypt. Egypt's pharaohs and queens, her pyramids and mummies held a special fascination for him throughout his life and especially during the earlier part of his poetic career. One of the poems in

Fallen Feathers is even entitled "Egypt" (*misar*), its first four lines alone liberally sprinkled with the words *mummy, sphinx,* and *pyramid*.[21] The pyramids gave an exotic flavor to any poem in which they appeared. More than that, these timeless structures allowed the poet to traverse eons with one stroke of the pen. And Jibanananda thought in terms of eons rather than years or a mere lifetime.

In "Pyramid"—whose title, of course, immediately situates the poem in the Middle East—time, death, and immortality are contemplated.

> The day wears on!
> At twilight's cloud-edge
> In the smoky silent evening
> The death bell of a new day tolls daily!
> Fires of the burning-ground blaze in the corpse of the century!

The narrator speaks to this symbol of death and antiquity:

> For whom, O sepulchre, do you sit alone today
> Like the body of some aggrieved spirit

And even when Jibanananda dwells upon the foreseen present, his imagery still exploits the past as he summons Memnon, the gigantic Theban statue of old, to herald the dawn:

> At the end of eternal night blazes forth
> The new sun!
> Up rises Memnon's voice unimpaired
> Along with the newly arisen dawn
> At the fleeting, threatening fingers of some hope beyond hope![22]

Such expansion of time and space remained a hallmark of much of Jibanananda's poetry. He lived in a fanciful world peculiarly his own, one which he experienced through senses heightened by a fertile, somewhat overwrought imagination and one which knew few of the limitations experienced by men who rely exclusively upon their physical senses. Much later in life Jibanananda tried bringing his vision back to actual and contemporary reality, but with uneven success. He shines when physical space and time are stimulants, not cinctures.

Though death pervades much of his poetry, Jibanananda's poetic world vibrantly lives. In "Back Then This Earth's," he anthropomorphizes nature so that dawn, the stars, wind, grass, even mother earth herself assume the trappings of life.

> Earth's umbilical cord was instantly torn asunder.
> I heard a mother's feeble weeping,

Mother earth—yours—calling to me from behind!
The damp grass called, and a cold month of late autumn, a swarm of fireflies!
The gaseous glow of red fields called me, as did a ferryboat landing by the cremation grounds![23]

Of course, personification of nature is not something new, any more than casting the earth or India or Bengal in the role of a mother. Bankim Chandra Chatterjee's novel *The Abbey of Bliss* (*anandamath*) (1882) depicts revolutionaries chanting the battle cry "bande mataram," Sanskrit for "hail Mother" and meaning hail to the motherland or mother India. (That cry, subsequently appropriated by real Bengali revolutionaries, can still be heard today as something of a second national anthem.) Bangladesh's national anthem, "My Golden Bengal," addresses Bengal as mother. Noteworthy is the intensity with which Jibanananda will animate Bengal, attempting to live or relive life through this nonhuman environment.

Fallen Feathers was not a roaring success, by any means. *Kallol* acknowledged the book's publication and added a few perfunctory comments on Jibanananda's poetry in general.

Fallen Feathers
—a book of poetry by Sri Jibanananda Dasgupta.

> Within a few short years Sri Jibanananda Dasgupta has firmly established himself in the field of poetry. The ecstasy of youth resonates in each and every poem by this young poet. There is much emotion in his meter, diction, and mood. His only fault: sometimes this emotion becomes unjustifiably extreme. It is obvious he was unable to avoid being influenced by Nazrul [Islam] and Mohitlal [Majumdar]; however, it seems that he has been able to incorporate those influences into his own personal style.[24]

Jibanananda had begun publishing under the name Dasgupta, that Vaidya caste surname that his grandfather shortened to Das upon joining the Brahmo Samaj. Like his grandfather and father, he too eventually dropped the "gupta." The book's title page and preface both give the author's name as Jibanananda Das. *Kallol* still knew him as Dasgupta, however.

Another review was written but never printed. Sarojendranath Ray, fellow Brahmo and English professor at City College, had been presented with a copy of Jibanananda's book. He regularly submitted both English and Bengali articles to Ramananda Chatterjee, who published them in either *Modern Review* or *Prabasi*. On this occasion, his review of *Fallen Feathers* failed to appear in print. As Ramananda later explained to Sarojendranath, while he himself had been willing to publish it, one of the assistant editors objected.[25] Sajani Kanta held the post of assistant editor for *Prabasi* at that time.[26] And, though his comments were never made public, Rabindranath responded to a copy of *Fallen Feathers* Jibanananda sent him. "You wrote me a letter, upon receiving the book; that letter is among my cherished possessions," stated Jibanananda in a note to the august senior poet years later.[27]

3

Sajani Kanta Das and his *Sanibarer Cithi* are important to an understanding of not only Jibanananda but all the avant-garde writers of the 1920s, this eccentric fellow providing a perfect foil for seeing the new literature more clearly. Moreover, although that journal, which has been referred to as a "literary goon squad,"[28] thrived on assaulting contemporary Bengali writers, nevertheless, one writer associated with the magazine, Mohitlal Majumdar, did provide some constructive criticism. Writing under the pseudonym of Satya Sundar Das—"Servant of Truth and Beauty"—Mohitlal acted as *Sanibarer Cithi*'s major theoretician.[29] In an article entitled "The Literary Ideal" (*sahityer adarsa*), Mohitlal defined the war the journal saw itself waging.

> In modern Bengali literature, there is an effort underway to create a new standard by reclaiming the besmirching mud from one's animal life, on the pretext of depicting the essence, the realistic picture of man. All these writers seem to have become mad—their anger directed against whatever is beautiful, not to mention the scriptures and rules of society. Whatever man by simple intuition knows to be despicable, which always was and always will be so—they call that the only truth; whatever solace and beauty there is in life they are bent on destroying. Is that a reverence for truth or the height of valor? Is true humanity based on smearing one's face with this mud! And so with the weapons of paper, pen, and ink, this circle of stalwarts [*Sanibarer Cithi*] is warring against that "false beauty."[30]

As the *Kallol* writers in the late 1920s became a recognizable literary force, they faced opposition of the above sort. The vulgarity—in the finest sense of that word—of their writing offended those who felt literature should be kept on a pedestal in humanity's museum for future generations to gaze at as they strolled by. The immortal works of art were not to be made of local mud but of purest marble quarried at a respectable distance from the ordinary folk. The noblest aspect of man—his mind, not his body—ought to be celebrated in these museum pieces. The immortal beings must speak an elevated tongue, befitting their position on the pedestal, not the riffraff's common gabble.

Sajani Kanta and company took such offense at the degradation of poetic diction into something which looked to them like prose that they created a portmanteau word to ridicule this new hybrid: *gabita,* made up of the *ga* from *gadya* (prose) and the *bita* from *kabita* (poetry)—a rough translation in English being "proetry." Sajani Kanta's term, in fact, anticipated what was to happen in the 1930s, for it was then Rabindranath and many others—Jibanananda included—composed what they respectfully called *gadya-kabita* or "prose-poetry." With the coinage *gabita,* however, Sajani Kanta attempted to disparage the poetry of the *Kallol* writers.

The *Sanibarer Cithi* issue following Mohitlal's manifesto ran a lengthy article entitled "The Crisis of Literature" (*sahitya-bibhrata*) signed by Sri Bararuci—"Mr. Eminent Taste."[31] The spoof presents an interchange in court between an elderly prosecutor (Rabindranath) and a young defendant (the young writers) during which the prosecution states the major issue in the case:

> There are many charges leveled against the young [writers], but the main regret is that they have taken literature from the elevated world of the mind down to the world of carnal desires.

The "great potentate," obviously Rabindranath, lectures the young offenders.

> The great potentate of literature spoke sadly—Woe is me, you kids are really immature. You don't even understand the essence of literature. There is a difference between realism and poesy.... The stuff of literature is not that of the body. Hold in check your mundane urges and "culture" your literary ones.[32]

In his reminiscences, Sajani Kanta included a more serious indictment of the *Kallol* writers, that of imitating the West and the concomitant loss of literary virility.[33] Bengali poets and writers have faced this charge of Western influence for over a century. In the nineteenth century, Bankim Chandra Chatterjee lamented the fact that his own countrymen assumed any good modern work in Bengali must be perforce a translation of some English book. In this century, no reputable critic would presume to accuse a serious Bengali author of out-and-out plagiarism from Western titles, but the accusation of "Western influence" leveled at a writer or his work always carries negative connotations.

On the basis of Sajani Kanta's criticism alone, he and Rabindranath should have been allies in 1927, for Rabindranath had long been apprehensive of the tendency to look abroad for inspiration.[34] In 1912, reflecting on the contemporary literary scene, Rabindranath spoke of "the excitement of the pursuit of English literature" and admitted that he had been moved no less than others. As a caveat he added:

However, our situation is very different from that of Europe's. The European mind's restlessness, European rebellion against constraining rules and regulations evolved out of her history and came to be reflected in her literature. There was a consistency between what was felt within and what got expressed outwardly. Because a storm had in fact arisen there, the thunder's rumble could be heard [in European literature]. The slight breezes which wafted from that European storm did not rise above a murmur in our society—but our hearts were not satisfied with that mere murmur. Consequently, in an effort to mimic the clap of thunder we tended to overstate our case, with a vengeance. It does not seem to me that we have been able to free ourselves from that tendency as yet.[35]

"Some persons here," declared Rabindranath in 1927 as he continued to warn his fellow writers against borrowing from other cultures (read, European), "consider the indignities presently imported into our literature from abroad as something of eternal worth. They forget that that which is eternal does not totally reject the past."[36]

Though of like mind with Rabindranath on this issue, Sajani Kanta did not seek a wider circle of friends and confederates, preferring to assault freely one and all. So, in August 1927, the same month in which *Sanibarer Cithi* resumed publication, he published in another journal an attack on Rabindranath and on one of his latest works, *Lord of the Dance* (*nataraja*).[37] Rabindranath took offense at the criticism. Sajani Kanta had assumed a pen name, Arasik Ray—"King of Bad Taste," an apt epithet, indeed. In December 1927, about to be found out, Sajani Kanta—afraid to face Rabindranath in person—wrote him a long letter of apology. Furious, Rabindranath dashed off a hurried reply.[38]

Along with regional dialects, Bengali has, theoretically, two standard forms of language, the "standard" itself varying slightly with time and place: colloquial or *calit,* and literary or *sadhu.* The *sadhu* language became relatively standardized during the nineteenth century, as Bengali prose literature itself matured. At the turn of this century *sadhu* was considered the only proper vehicle for literature. *Calit* or even dialect might serve as dialogue to lend color to a particular character, but the rest of a literary work would be *sadhu.* All journalistic writing was *sadhu,* as were public speeches. Though educated Bengalis might converse in *calit* Bengali, they wrote in *sadhu.*

By the second decade of the twentieth century a movement was underway to usher *calit* into the literary salon. The journal *Sabuj Patra* ("Green Leaf") began publication in 1914, with its editor, Pramatha Chaudhuri, and Rabindranath as chief contributors. It was through the pages of *Sabuj Patra* that *calit* made its debut in polite literary society. Today almost no one uses *sadhu,* save for an occasional newspaper editorial writer. But in the late 1920s quite the opposite was true; *sadhu* continued to be the preferred medium for serious writing. However, no matter which form of the language one chose to employ, the mixing of *sadhu* and *calit* was considered tantamount to committing a grammatical error.

Rabindranath's spontaneous reply to Sajani Kanta's belated confession takes on significance more for how it was worded than for what it said. "Even in Rabindranath's short notes," as Sajani Kanta put it, "I had never seen *sadhu* and *calit* forms of the language mixed together. But that day he had become so enraged that he committed the 'guru-*candali* error.'"[39] Guru-*candali* refers to the mixing of high style with low: gurus are usually Brahmins, of the highest caste, whereas *candalis* are female "untouchables," the lowest of the low in the caste system's hierarchy.

Sajani Kanta criticized Rabindranath more as a diversion than anything else, for *Sanibarer Cithi*'s concept of good literature corresponded rather closely to Rabindranath's ideas on, and practice of, the art. But the work of *Kallol* writers was another matter altogether. In order to facilitate its campaign against these authors, *Sanibarer Cithi,* from October 1927, ran a feature called "The Pearls" (*mani-mukta*) carrying the meaningful by-line: "Gathered by Mr. Diver" (*sriduburi karttrik ahrita*).[40] The editor explained: "*Sanibarer Cithi*'s diver dove into the sea of modern literature and gathered up many a pearl." This section quoted from other journals excerpts which *Sanibarer Cithi* found objectionable. There were those, friends as well as foes, who pointed out to Sajani Kanta that he gave offensive literature a wider audience at the same time as he annoyed some of his own readers—namely, those who concurred with him in his assessment that such literature should not be published, at all. Sajani Kanta responded, prefacing "The Pearls" with the following:

> We feel that today there is still a need to publish "The Pearls." For the convenience of those who, because of the obscenity, cannot take *Sanibarer Cithi* home without tearing out this section, we have perforated "The Pearls."[41]

Perforated the pages of "The Pearls" section were, in subsequent issues of *Sanibarer Cithi.*

Besides "The Pearls" *Sanibarer Cithi* ran another regular feature designated "News-Literature" (*sambad-sahitya*), an editorial section where the editor and friends could expound upon writers and their writings. What he lacked in "The Pearls," Sajani Kanta made up for in "News-Literature," not citing offensive passages from the moderns but simply passing comment upon the foibles of the writers or their works in general. Though Sajani Kanta obviously saw himself as employing acerbic wit to make his point, the humor in *Sanibarer Cithi* was often rather silly, the satire anything but subtle:

> There is a "red leaf" (*lal patra*) by the name of *Pragati*. Most probably it turned from green [an obvious reference to Pramatha Chaudhuri's journal *Sabuj Patra* ("Green Leaf")] to red—considering its tender age—out of embarrassment.[42]

On the last page of *Sanibarer Cithi*'s December 1927 issue, there appeared a full-page mock advertisement which read:

> WANTED—FOR RENOWNED BENGALI MONTHLY
> EDITOR
> ASSISTANT EDITOR
> CRITIC
> SHORT STORY WRITER
> NOVELIST
> KNOWLEDGE OF THE BENGALI LANGUAGE NOT NECESSARY
> APPLY _____, PATUYATOLA STREET

Kallol had its office at 10, Patuyatola Street, Calcutta.

Obscenity, nonliterary diction, and nonindigenous influences (that notorious Western influence) were the three big windmills with which *Sanibarer Cithi* jousted. Only, Sajani Kanta and his knights behaved sometimes less than chivalrously in their tilts—for instance, they did not hesitate to quote out of context. Sajani Kanta, in retrospect, held an image of himself and *Sanibarer Cithi* quite different from that perceived by others. His opponents, from his perspective, tried to depict his goals as something other than what they were:

> The young [writers] of that day and some among them who had advanced into middle age tried then and are still trying today to prove that *Sanibarer Cithi*'s crusade was against obscenity. That is not correct. Our holy war was proclaimed against pretentiousness, affectation, and the sensuous lip licking which goes hand in glove with weak and ineffectual writing.[43]

But despite these later protestations, Sajani Kanta had made obscenity one of his prime targets, whether or not he himself was fully conscious of what he was doing.

4

In its February 1928 issue, *Pragati* published Jibanananda's "Song of

Thirst" (*pipasar gan*), which drew the attention of crusader Sajani Kanta, the scourge of all things dishonorable in literature.

SONG OF THIRST

When I shall go away
Into some darkness, shall I again descend
With great thirst to this shore
Amid all of you!
Who gave me pain? Who loved me?
Forgetting all this, in search only of my body,
My nerves, veins, blood only
Upon this soil
Shall I descend!
Here and there—stopping—stopping—stopping
Shall I look for him
Who made his home
In the half light and shadows of this place!
That thirst which was in his frame of clay,
That pain—those lips, that hair,
Those eyes, hands, fingers
Stirred by joy through touch of flesh and blood—
That very body once inhaled the earth's scents,
Drank of her rice wine,
Heard her songs of water and of growing fields,
And saw the picture of that blue sky,
A woman's face—the figure of a man, a wife
Whose hand touched and still today feels warm—
Shall he return to all of them!
Loving like a true lover
Shall he come searching
A body only!
Lost who knows when to bits of bone
Upon this earth!

In darkness the ocean
Massaged my body. My eyes turned cold,
My lips, nose, and fingers
At his touch. My hair got soaked
In white flowers of foam.
Time and again on distant shores
Beneath starry skies
I, like a child, washed
In seas

And came to know and relish this body. Chest, face touched
By crimson sunshine—this womanish
Physique seemed kissed by him
In paddy fields!
He was my first lover who, traveling far off that October dawn,
Stopped for me!
My eyes again grew heavy
From his kisses!
This body—a listless girl
Gone limp at a man's caress,
Kissed by the juices of sunlight
Splashed upon the courtyard's flapping wings of flying sails
Some late autumn afternoon.
Ears pricked—
Listen, the song of falling dew
On a midnight in November.
Cold winds like blanched skeleton hands
Seize this body
And give it pain! This body, like some plentiful harvest,
Is ripped out
By the *jhumko* vinelike body-noose of woman,
Her lips, hair, eyes, her jasmine breath.
The pain returns!
Yet in this harvest field, the language of thirst
Will not be silenced. Who is that peasant,
Sickle in hand—severe—lustful?
He alone shall come and put an end to
All our painful joy!
Who is he! I do not know. Still today
We have not met.
Today in the body only, and its torments,
Are my wants. In my eyes, on my lips, in my hair
Only pain—only pain! In bud after bud
Only worms—wounds—stinging—
Today my heart craves!
While heading toward the stars
I lose the way and am reborn again and
Again a green plant in the earth's fields!
Through darkness, dew
Has sung in my ear,
Has poured its cooling fragrances.
The languid, drowsy virgin fingers
Of fog massaged my body.
Arousing an urge to touch
And smell. The listing sickle moon
Poured out its light—
Like the keen-edged kiss
Of a lover's lips!
He left me wounded,

In the greenish blood of vegetation!
Like the harvest this body of mine is rent
And wounded time and again—
Red sunlight of midday
Like fire!
Still I give pain,
And in return am pained!
Yet I want this joy of pain
In my green body!
Rosy light, a sip of sunlight,
Darkness, fog's knife
Seem to cut me. Particles of dust seem
Slowly to absorb me!
In field after field, in inert December
The scent of crops appears to
Ooze out from my chest!

Shall I regain
This body! Shall I descend
To pour the heat of blood
Upon this soil's lifeless dew!
Like the late autumn sun
Shall I squeeze between my fingers
The breasts of harvest?
Leaving one field
Shall I float to another and another
In this green land
Yet again! Shall I hear the song
Of rippling water? Shall I carry in my heart
That water's scent?
Shall I lose my way?
And come this way again!
Like insects
In these dusty beds
Shall I be crushed
By blows of grass blades!
Along with sorrow
Shall I gain joy!
My hair, like vines,
My fingers,
Petals—
Will they be bruised
By your fingers, hair!
Will flower
Injure flower! Once again
The keenness of this thirst of mine
Shall whet a thirst in all of you!
Shall the language of hunger
Blossom forth

Within your chests! Shall I fall
Upon the cultivated fields of earth
Again—
While heading for the stars.[44]

In the March 1928 issue of *Sanibarer Cithi*, Sajani Kanta wrote:

> Professor Jibanananda Dasgupta has in the poem "Song of Thirst" in the February issue of *Pragati:*
> 1) drowsy virgin fingers
> 2) Shall I squeeze between my fingers/The breasts of harvest?
> 3) My fingers, /Petals—/Will they be bruised/By your fingers, hair!
> 4) ... fingers/Stirred by joy through touch of flesh and blood—
> 5) —fingers/At his touch. ...
> OH THAT FINGER![45]

Jibanananda's fingers seemed shockingly frank, scandalizing Sajani Kanta, so his feigned indignation suggests.

The poem struggles with a theme dear to Jibanananda's heart: reincarnation. We see this concern of his in other poems, for example, "Tangerine" (*kamalalebu*):

TANGERINE

> When once I leave this body
> Shall I come back to the world?
> If only I might return
> On a winter's evening
> Taking on the compassionate flesh of a cold tangerine
> At the bedside of some dying acquaintance.[46]

In "Song of Thirst" the narrator contemplates a rather nebulous terrestrial return. If these two words—nebulous and terrestrial—seem to be logically at odds with one another, that is as it should be. Life, death, and possible rebirth cannot always be comprehended logically. Jibanananda skews the very concept of reincarnation to conform to his own views and quandaries about life and death. Reincarnation, as the word itself suggests, normally implies a reappearance within carnal matter. In one of the untitled sonnets posthumously published, we find a straightforward carnal embodiment:

> When again I return to the banks of the Dhansiri, in this Bengal,
> Not as a man, perhaps, but as a *salik* bird or a white hawk,
> Perhaps as a crow of dawn in this land of autumn's new rice harvest,
> I'll float upon the breast of fog one day in the shade of a jackfruit tree.[47]

But the narrator of "Song of Thirst" fantasizes several earthly reinhabitings, enjoying a multitude of sensuous experiences, including the herbaceous, a theme which occurs in the poem "Grass" (*ghas*), for instance, with its concluding lines, "Let me be born grass in grass, descended from the savory dark/Of some rich grass-mother's body."[48]

For all the terrestrial imagery in "Song of Thirst," the nebulous quality remains, heightened by fluidity in gender as Jibanananda switches from masculine to feminine and back to masculine. Bengali, with no pronominal gender, allows for more lexical sexual ambiguity than does an English translation. The third-person pronoun may translate as either "he" or "she" or even "it." Nouns, such as "woman" are, of course, not sexually ambiguous, but such words occur infrequently in this poem. Ambiguity is fostered not only with respect to sex but also in regard to the form of reinhabiting the narrator envisages—is it carnal or vegetable, or a nebulous terrestrial combination of both?

The tension set up between pleasure and pain mirrors this ambiguity, a tension that persists in much of Jibanananda's poetry. To live in human society means to suffer emotionally. But to live as a nonhuman brings with it suffering as well, only of another ilk: the blows of grass crush insects, and the earth has pangs of thirst. Even so, for Jibanananda, sensuous experience is a good unto itself, a verification of the value of life, however difficult, whatever the form. Life, he tells us, inexorably seduces, over and over tempting him back from his journey to the stars, to know again "this joy of pain."

5

That March (1928) proved momentous in the history of Bengali literature. The *Kallol* coterie and its detractors had been exchanging insults. Both sides were wary of the seductive style of that senior man of Bengali letters, Rabindranath, who had to be consciously resisted if one were to achieve an independent identity, so the younger writers felt. But Rabindranath was not easily denied. He would not sit idly by while others inveighed against him or subverted what he considered to be the proper direction for Bengali literature.

The previous year Rabindranath had gone to visit Java and Bali. Just before sailing, he contributed to the new journal *Bicitra* ("Variegated") the article "The Essence of Literature" (*sahityer dharma*).[49] Unbeknownst to him, "The Essence of Literature" caused a furor among his junior colleagues who sensed that their literary efforts were being impugned. While on board ship, without any inkling of the hostile reaction with which his previous essay had met, he wrote a companion piece entitled "Literary Innovation" (*sahitye nabatwa*) which he submitted to *Prabasi* upon his return to Bengal in October.[50] In those articles Rabindranath argued—as Mohitlal Majumdar had done earlier in *Sanibarer Cithi*—that literature should not be a reflection of man's gross animal nature but of a more refined universe, and that it should not partake of Western liberal morality and sociopolitical views.[51] That it could be imitated by writers of lesser ability was one of the weaknesses of a brazenly new literature flavored with what he viewed as an artificial concoction. Rabindranath wrote:

> The unskilled [poets] try ever so hard to make up for their own inadequacies by means of imitation. Harshness they see as prowess and impudence as manliness. Since without the help of stock phrases they have no power to proceed, they garner and maintain a number of these stock expressions of newness specific to this contemporary era. When Indian curry is imitated in English kitchens, the curry powder is prepared according to a fixed recipe and then kept in bottles.... These sorts of prebottled stock phrases are now available for modern literature—they have become "reality curry powder" in the kitchens of unskilled writers. One ingredient in this [powder] is ranting and raving about poverty, another is pandering to the libido.[52]

Rabindranath's remarks aroused some suspicion, totally unfounded, that he sided with *Sanibarer Cithi* against *Kallol*. As acrimony between factions as well as toward Rabindranath himself increased, some people felt that all concerned needed to discuss the matter rationally, in a structured setting. Asked to mediate, Rabindranath reluctantly agreed to do so and that March convened a two-day conference at Bicitra Bhavan (no connection with the journal *Bicitra*), a part of the Tagore ancestral home in the Jorasankho neighborhood of north Calcutta. During that conference, for which he acted as master of ceremonies, keynote speaker, and moderator, Rabindranath, then in his late sixties, lectured his younger guests on how both to behave and to compose literature, repeating in the main the ideas put forth in his two essays. "The conference was called to arbitrate the disagreement," wrote Acintya Kumar Sengupta, "which had arisen over the direction and standards of modern literature. Actually it was not to arbitrate but simply to listen to whatever Rabindranath had to say."[53] In a question-and-answer session at the end of the second day, asked point-blank whether he approved of *Sanibarer Cithi*'s form of literary criticism, he called it an improper, "fundamentally cruel" literary method which he did not condone.[54]

The conference had little noticeable effect on those in attendance. Sajani Kanta continued to churn out his inane criticism. The more vociferous *Kallol* writers cried foul at Rabindranath's censure of them and then returned to their business as usual. Jibanananda, who had not participated in the meetings, went on publishing his poetry throughout this literary maelstrom.

Though the opposing parties had not come to terms, something positive and quite unanticipated resulted from the Bicitra Bhavan confabulation. Rabindranath, whether subconsciously influenced by the progressive youngsters or not, would write a lyrical novel, *The Last Poem* (*seser kabita*),[55] which demonstrated once again his genius and eternal modernity. Buddhadeva and the *Kallol* set were profoundly impressed:

> All that which we had attempted yet had not quite been able to accomplish, Rabindranath had just done—so easily! so completely! with such grace! It seemed as if the novel were ours, that is, a work for the young writers specifically, an oblique reprimand by Gurudeb intended to instruct us. We were stunned to see Rabindranath's "modern" image.[56]

Now the *Kallol* coterie would have not only to contend with *Sanibarer Cithi* but to struggle anew to break that stupor of admiration for Rabindranath—as Amit Ray, the main character in *The Last Poem*, declared—a stupor that many of them considered their worst enemy.

6

In sharp contrast to what appeared in *Sanibarer Cithi,* Buddhadeva Bose published a serious critical statement on Jibanananda's poetry in *Pragati*'s September issue, the first attempt by any critic to understand this uniquely modern poet. As Buddhadeva pointed out, Jibanananda, though modern, did not epitomize literary modernity as it came to be defined in the 1920s. The atypical Jibanananda traveled "a previously unexplored river in Bengali poetry. To date," wrote Buddhadeva,

> he enjoys no popularity. Rather, many seem indifferent or even hostile toward his writings. Unlike Acintya Kumar Sengupta, he has not immediately attracted countless imitators. The reason for this is perhaps that it takes some time to appreciate fully the rasa of Jibanananda's poetry, ... his poetry must be read deliberately, calmly and must be comprehended gradually.[57]

Buddhadeva chose an appropriate term in *rasa*, a word rich with meaning in Indian aesthetics. Rasa's first gloss is "juice," as in the juice of an orange, for instance. By extension, it means "essence" or "the essential element." Early on, Sanskrit aestheticians designated rasa, or a focus on a central emotion, as the sine qua non of good literature. Eight individual rasas (for some critics, as many as ten) came to be identified: *sringara* (love), *vira* (heroism), *bibhatsa* (disgust), *raudra* (anger), *hasya* (mirth), *bhayanaka* (terror), *karuna* (pity), and *adbhuta* (wonder). Later theoreticians refined the concept of rasa to mean not any one of various emotions but the essence of those emotions—feeling itself, rarified and divorced from anything specific.[58]

Sanskrit literature, like the Sanskrit language itself ("sanskrit" means "perfected, refined"), was aimed not at the common man but at a very cultured, learned audience. A member of such an audience was called a *rasika*, one who had become educated in aesthetics and therefore could apprehend and appreciate rasa. In Bengali, these terms do not always carry the same range of meanings they have in Sanskrit. *Rasika,* as an adjective, has as one of its common meanings in Bengali "witty" or "fun-loving" and does not necessarily or even primarily refer to one versed in literature. Rasa, besides its basic definition of juice, still connotes the stuff of good literature, though it has lost the specialized denotation given it in Sanskrit poetics. In Bengali, one speaks of a fine work of modern literature—or even film—as having rasa, that "something" which makes the work artistically succeed. Buddhadeva draws upon the various connotations of rasa, Sanskritic and Bengali, when he suggests that one must take time and train oneself—as a classical *rasika* would be trained—to appreciate the rasa of Jibanananda's poetry.

Despite his mention of rasa, Buddhadeva does not laud Jibanananda's poetry as a contemporary Sanskritic incarnation. Far from it. Other critics also, but Buddhadeva in particular, argued strongly that Bengali, though spawned of Sanskrit (as Portuguese, for example, carries the genes of Latin), should be treated by its poets as an autonomous and respectable tongue. Just as English can be written with a highly Latinate vocabulary, so too Bengali possesses a rich storehouse of accessible Sanskritic words. (India's national anthem is written in such heavily Sanskritized Bengali that some Indians will swear the language is in fact Sanskrit, not Bengali.) In the 1920s, diction had become a topic of debate in literary circles and a target for *Sanibarer Cithi*. Of Jibanananda's poetic diction Buddhadeva observed, "His main characteristic we notice is that he attempts to compose poetry avoiding as far as possible Sanskrit lexical items, using instead only indigenous words. Consequently, his diction has become totally his own—I do not believe it would be easy to copy."[59]

Jibanananda had fashioned for himself not only a unique diction but an entire poetic and very personal world in which he was content to live. His poetry does not jar the reader as much of the so-called modern, realistic literature of that day did. His poetry, as Buddhadeva put it, enchants. "For certain, he is a total romantic," wrote Buddhadeva,

> from his toenails to the hair on his head. In one sense, he may be called the antithesis of Premendra Mitra. Premendra stands fully alert to all the ugliness and harshness of the real world. The cruelty of real life causes him constant distress. . . . Jibanananda completely denies the existence of

this worldly life. He takes us by the hand to a wonderful secret world—perhaps we might some day gaze upon that enchanting world in a dream.[60]

The August 1929 issue of *Pragati* carried one of Jibanananda's more puzzling and at the same time intriguing poems—"Sensation" (*bodh*).

SENSATION

Into the half light and shadow I go. Within my head
Not a dream, but some sensation is at work.
Not a dream, not peace, not love,
Inside my heart a sensation is born.
I cannot escape it
For it places its hand in mine,
And all else pales to insignificance—futile so it seems.
All thought, an eternity of prayer,
Seems empty.
Empty.

Who can go on like the simple folk?
Who can pause in this half light and darkness
Like the simple people? Who can speak
Like them, anymore? Who can know
For certain anymore?—Who seeks to understand
The carnal savors anymore?—Who knows the joys
Of life again, like everyman?
And sows seeds like everyman anymore?
Where is that relish? And who, hungry for harvest,
Has smeared himself with the scent of earth,
Has anointed himself with the scent of water,
Has gazed toward light with rapt attention,
Has gained a peasant heart,
Who would any longer remain awake upon his earth?
Not a dream—not peace—but some sensation is at work
Within my head.

When I walk along the beach, or cross from shore to shore
I try to ignore it.
I seize it as I would a dead man's skull
And wish to smash it on the ground. Yet it spins like a living head
All around my head,
All about my eyes,
All about my chest.
I move, it too comes along with me.

I stop—
It too comes to a halt.

As I take my place among other beings
Am I becoming estranged and alone
Because of my mannerisms?
Is there just an optical illusion?
Are there only obstacles in my path?

Those who were born to this world
As children,
Those who spent their time
Giving birth to children,
Or those who must give birth to children
Today, or those who come to the sown fields of this world,
For to give birth—to give birth—
Is not my heart
Like theirs, their heart and head? Is not their mind
Like my mind?
Then why am I so alone?
Yet I am all alone.
Did I not raise my hand to see it hold a peasant's plough?
Have I not drawn water in a pail?
Have I not often gone with sickle to the fields?
How many wharfs and rivers have I been to
Like those who fish?
Algae from a pond, the smell of fish
Engulfed my body.
—All these tastes,
—All these I've had. My life has flowed
Like unchecked winds.
My mind slept as I lay beneath the stars
One day.
All these desires
I knew once—unchecked—unbounded.
Then I left them all behind.
I have looked upon woman with love.
I have looked upon woman with apathy.
I have looked upon woman with hate.

She has loved me,
And come near.
She has paid no heed to me.
She has despised me and gone away when I called her time and again,
Loving her.

Yet it was actually practiced one day—this love.
I paid no attention to her words of contempt,
No attention to the wrath of her hate,
And went my own way. I have forgotten
That star—the sinister influence of which
Blocked my path of love over and over again.
Still, this love—this dust and mud.

Within my head
Not a dream, not love, but some sensation is at work.
I leave all gods behind
And come close to my heart—
I speak to this heart.
Why does it mumble to itself alone like churning waters?
Is it never weary? Does it never have a moment's peace?
Will it never ever sleep? Will it not enjoy just
Resting calmly? or not know the joy
Of gazing at the face of man?
Of gazing at the face of woman?
Of gazing at children's faces?

This sensation—only this desire
What does it gain, immense—profound?
Does it not wish to leave the beaten paths
And seek the starry span of the sky? Has it vowed
To look upon that man's face?
To look upon that woman's face?
To look upon those children's faces?
Those sickly shadows under eyes,
The ears that cannot hear,
The hunchback—a goitre that arose upon the flesh,
A spoiled cucumber—chancred pumpkin,
All that is within man's heart
—All that.[61]

What is this sensation? The Bengali title, "*bodh*," which shares a common root word with the "buddha" or "enlightened one," could be translated as awareness, consciousness, or even inspiration. The feeling is not one of love, peace, or a dream. It cannot be ignored or escaped. And once it works its will in one's heart and mind, that person is no longer like his fellow man. He cannot behave as ordinary people do. He is alone, even when physically among others.

This particular poem has spawned numerous interpretations marked by a variety of rather insecure grapplings with that ambiguous term "sensation" or *"bodh."* One analyst equates it with the "agony of creation," calling it an overpowering urge that eventually exhausts the poet, prompting him to seek repose in death.[62] Another critic sees *"bodh"* as a necessary adjunct to poetic inspiration, as intense and unintelligible disquiet which helps the poet transcend life's familiar realities to produce something new.[63] Yet another reader of the poem dismisses *"bodh"* as nothing more than a kind of neurological disorder peculiar to intellectuals of modern, urban, industrial cultures.[64]

Along with his readers, Jibanananda himself struggles to understand the unsettling feeling which impels him to be an explicator of the world around him, and which sets him apart from "the simple folk." Once, in other lives, the narrator was as other men—his life simple, and flowing "like unchecked winds," his mind asleep while he "lay beneath the stars." But that was "one day." Now, a feeling shadows him, overwhelmingly insisting that he "remain awake upon this earth," and chronicle that awareness, however painful or lonely the task. Separate, aware, inspired, he has become a poet: an observer of the "starry span of the sky" as well as of the "chancred pumpkin"—all that which is within man's heart.

Like an unwilling Bodhisattwa, this "apprentice Buddha" wears the mantle of awareness, which for him mutates into implacable creativity. He cannot know the joy of merely gazing upon the faces of fellow human beings. Just as Gautama was driven to abandon desire in order to attain enlightenment, so too does Jibanananda's *"bodh"* compel him to leave behind all desires and "come close to [his] heart."

Although "Sensation" appears at a relatively early moment in his career, it is a remarkably astute statement of the manner and consequences of poetic inspiration. A decade later, Jibanananda will write an essay entitled "On Poetry" (*kabitar katha*) in which he alludes to the making of a poet and the forces of creative inspiration. But here, using the metaphor of "enlightenment" or "awareness," he sets out, for all the world to see, the loneliness and desperate biddings which characterize his life and, by extension, that of other men who are prompted to gain the "immense—profound."

In the same issue of *Pragati* which carried "Sensation," Buddhadeva wrote a second critique of Jibanananda and his poetry, once again focusing on diction. In that article an aficionado of Jibanananda's poetry speaks to someone who had never heard of him:

Look here, by this time we should have realized that Bengali's umbilical link with Sanskrit was severed long ago. Bengali is now a completely independent, adult language—her grammar, her rules and regulations, her spirit is different from Sanskrit's. . . . yet, amazingly, Bengali poetry even now demonstrates favoritism for Sanskritic words and is still unable to free herself from Sanskrit conventions. Beautiful damsels yet stand beside fenestrae with locks of hair falling loose. They gaze upon their countenances in looking-glasses, redden the edges of their feet with lac dye, and recline upon cool and pure white couchettes. In the heroines' hands are lotuses and wristlets of jasmine etc., though these fashions went out of style in this country long ago. How much longer are we going to grovel before the door of Sanskrit and belittle our own mother tongue? It seems that Jibanananda Das has understood our error. One sees in his work an effort to elevate diction as far as possible to pure Bengali. ... Why shouldn't we call a window a window [instead of a fenestra], a bed a bed [instead of a couchette]? ... Of all the words that have found their way into our spoken language ... are we going to deprive our poetry of that vast fund of vocabulary which, for some reason, we keep quarantined away from the poetic world? Why should we not make poetry natural and straightforward by using the idioms of our spoken language? ... the language of Jibanananda's poetry is the purest Bengali, for it is nothing but Bengali.[65]

What is "pure Bengali"? The question lends itself to no easy answer, for that period or today. Linguistic purity, like racial purity, falls into the realm of chimerical fancy. But Buddhadeva implies there can be degrees of purity within a language. He reminds his readers of the obvious—the difference between a highly Sanskritized, self-consciously elevated style of Bengali (*sadhu*) and a Bengali that reflects more of the spoken idiom (*calit*)—then suggests that *calit* represents a purer Bengali than *sadhu* and that Bengali poetry ought to be written in this more genuine form of the vernacular. As T. S. Eliot pointed out, "Every revolution in poetry is apt to be, and sometimes to announce itself to be, a return to common speech."[66] The *Kallol*-fomented revolution proved no exception, but Jibanānanda, as was his way, did not conform to the typical revolutionary.

Buddhadeva does not say that Jibanananda wrote in *calit* Bengali; he says he wrote in "pure Bengali," an important distinction. This so-called "pure Bengali" corresponds to no common speech, nor any regional dialect, nor Jibanananda's own argot. As Buddhadeva stated in his earlier article, Jibanananda created a diction "totally his own," avoiding in the main the highly Sanskritized vocabulary of *sadhu* Bengali while at the same time employing both *sadhu* and *calit* verb and pronominal forms. The grammatical indiscretion that had shocked Sajani Kanta in Rabindranath's riposte Jibanananda committed unabashedly in his poetry of this period. From the poem "Sensation" come these lines:

> Those who were born to this world
> As children,
> Those who spent their time
> Giving birth to children

The Bengali reads:

> *janmiyache yara ei prithibite*
> *santaner mata haye,—*
> *santaner janma dite-dite*
> *yahader kete geche anek samay*

The first word, *janmiyache,* is a *sadhu* verbal form; *yara,* the second word, a *calit* pronoun. *Haye, dite,* and *geche* are all *calit* verbs; *yahader* is a modified *sadhu* pronoun. This mixing of forms came and went with Jibanananda. Today there is hardly a Bengali poet worth his salt who writes in anything but *calit*. Then, however, this flaunting of convention seemed a bold move.

Earlier that year, Jibanananda's last poem to appear in *Kallol* (the journal ceased publication that very year) had contained what might be labeled unpoetic diction.

> Out there sea sounds can be heard,
> A skylight overhead,
> Birds on wing talk to one another.

And further on, in this poem entitled "Birds" (*pakhira*):

> Beyond the sea on an even farther shore
> Upon some polar peak
> Had lived all these birds.
> Buffeted by blizzards, they flocked
> To the sea,
> As does man, oblivious to his own death.
> In brown—golden—white—bright wings,
> In little rubber-ball-like breasts
> Were tucked their lives—
> Just as death extends a thousand miles before the sea
> So, too, it reaches deep and true.[67]

Buddhadeva recalled his first reading of this poem and the excitement he felt upon encountering "skylight," "little rubber-ball-like breasts," and death present for "a thousand miles before the sea." Words such as *skylight, rubber ball,* and *mile* (Jibanananda used the English words in Bengali script), acceptable enough in common Bengali parlance, had not appeared in respectable poetic diction of that day. Buddhadeva thrilled at the ease with which these "prosaic" foreigners came effortlessly alive in Jibanananda's poem. Looking back on what his fellow poet meant to the *Kallol*-era poets, Buddhadeva credited Jibanananda with giving them courage to be innovative. Sunil Ganguly, one of today's most gifted fiction writers and himself a poet, summed up Jibanananda's achievement in one sentence: "And to this very day the greatest revolutionary in the world of Bengali poetry is Jibanananda Das, for he demonstrated the courage to break down the customary worship of words."[68] Sunil might have said that he broke down the caste hierarchy of words, for with the entree of Jibanananda into poetic society, lexical untouchability began to disappear. The whole range of vocabulary used by a Bengali—whether rustic or sophisticated, indigenous or foreign—became acceptable for use in poetry.

Bengali, no less eclectic than English, borrows when need be.[69] Though much of its vocabulary—even its *calit* vocabulary—derives from Sanskrit, modern Bengali is flush with words from Persian, Arabic, Portuguese, English, and those for which no satisfactory etymology has yet been proposed—the "local" words, of unknown origin. Jibanananda infused life into poetic diction in general and his poetry in particular with the unpretentious use of living expressions. The language in which he composed may not have been the language he spoke, but he had demonstrated that any and all language was poetic language. Neither Jibanananda's diction nor Buddhadeva's articles went unnoticed by *Sanibarer Cithi,* but the self-styled literary censor ranted and raved, without observable effect.

7

Beginning with August 1928, Sajani Kanta published serially in *Sanibarer Cithi* a work entitled *Nakur Thakur's Ashram* (*nakur thakurer asram*), a satire on what he considered to be the swelling ranks of quack gurus preying upon gullible Bengalis. Nakur, the greedy holy man, he conceived of as an insectivorous plant, suggesting that such persons lure their unsuspecting clients, then consume them and their money. The September installment's vivid description of how this botanic guru sucks the life out of his victim transgressed standards of decorum and earned Sajani Kanta, for all his quixotic crusading and Comstockery, the charge of violating Section 292 of the Indian Penal Code, an offense against public decency and morals. Found guilty, he was fined Rs.50/-.[70] Literary magazines of that day sold for around eight annas (half a rupee) a copy, so a fine of fifty rupees could be considered nominal.

As though that were not retribution enough, Sajani Kanta was arrested on another charge in the very same month in which his obscenity trial began. This ironic turn of events may have delighted the *Kallol* folks, but in fact it was no laughing matter. The previous December he had had the proud fortune, as he put it, to publish the Indian edition of the American author Jabez T. Sunderland's book *India in Bondage*. In May 1929, Calcutta police confiscated copies of the Sunderland book from the office of Prabasi Press and from the home of *Prabasi*'s editor, Ramananda

Chatterjee, then arrested the book's publisher and printer, Sajani Kanta, on a sedition charge. A cursory glance at this polemic reveals the reason for the British government's actions, as does the foreword to the first edition: "In this Twentieth Century after Christ, ought any nation in the world to be held in forced subjection by another? Then why great India?"[71]

The sedition trial began that June and, including appeals, extended into 1930 when both men were found guilty and fined more punitively: Rs. 1,000/- each.[72] Besides these two trials, Sajani Kanta had been threatened with legal action by Naresh Chandra Sengupta—lawyer as well as writer—over a satirical article on the latter that had appeared in *Sanibarer Cithi*. And then in August of 1929, as the obscenity trial drew to a close, the editor of *Sanibarer Cithi* came under threat of being sued as a result of yet another article's unauthorized republication.[73] But Sajani Kanta felt not only the legal scepter's punishing clout. He had in 1929 been hit by the "thunderbolt" of a new but short-lived magazine and, early the next year, bludgeoned with the "cudgel" of another such publication.

The thunderbolt struck in April 1929, just as legal proceedings for the first trial got underway. In that month, several of the *Kallol* group, Acintya Kumar Sengupta, Buddhadeva Bose, and Bishnu Dey foremost among them, brought out a magazine entitled *Mahakala* ("The Great Death," a common epithet for Shiva, lord of destruction). As Sajani Kanta described the journal, it had a black cover upon which, written in letters of fiery red ink, a subtitle of three words blazed forth: *sanibarer cithir asani* ("*Sanibarer Cithi*'s Thunderbolt").[74] *Mahakala* editors were punning on the words *sani* (meaning Saturn), *sanibar* (Saturn's day or Saturday), and *asani* (thunderbolt). The latter at first glance appears to be a negative ("a" is a negative prefix) of *sani,* but in fact is a non-negative word in its own right. The negative connotation, however, was certainly intended, as were the multifarious connotations of this word ranging from thunderbolt (the god Indra's punishing weapon) to Shiva, the great destroyer himself.

Acintya Kumar wrote of the appearance—and disappearance—of *Mahakala*:

> At this time, in the company of recently assembled friends, a new magazine by the name of *Mahakala* made its debut—in reply to *Sanibarer Cithi.* Just as *Sanibarer Cithi* rudely insulted Bengali literary persons of stature—such as Rabindranath, Sarat Chandra [Chatterjee], Pramatha Chaudhuri, Dinesh Chandra [Sen] and Naresh Chandra [Sengupta]— [this magazine] disparaged several other respectable persons—those whom *Sanibarer Cithi* favored. . . .
> Be that as it may, *Mahakala* didn't last. The reason was simple: we lacked the shrewdness needed to run this sort of publication—the right mix of contempt and affability, of the light with the serious, of ribald abuse with detachment and Vedantic theology. In these areas, *Sanibarer Cithi* was a master.[75]

According to Sajani Kanta, *Mahakala* survived only three months.[76] However, the institutionalized counterattack on him and *Sanibarer Cithi* did not end with *Mahakala*'s demise. The first three months of 1930 saw the publication of a magazine named *Rabibarer Lathi,* literally "The Sunday Staff," a weapon meant to stave off "The Saturday Post" (i.e., *Sanibarer Cithi*). The latter magazine, wrote Sajani Kanta, outdid *Mahakala* in vituperation.[77]

Prior to the appearance of *Rabibarer Lathi,* however, *Sanibarer Cithi* went out of business. In fact, the last months of 1929 proved fatal to a number of magazines. *Pragati* published its final issue in October 1929, which included a poem by Jibanananda titled somewhat prophetically "Song of Leisure" (*abasarer gan*). *Kallol* ceased publication in December of that year. *Kali-Kalam,* after coming out irregularly during the latter half of 1929, printed its last issue in January 1930. With these magazines gone, Jibanananda lost his publishing opportunities; between October 1929 and September 1935 only one of his poems saw print. The *Kallol* era over, he would wait six leisurely years for Buddhadeva Bose and Premendra Mitra to launch *Kavita,* wherein his poetry again would find a regular publisher and an appreciative audience.

8

In 1928, before *Kallol* folded, Jibanananda's first teaching position came to an end. Some writers have seen a direct connection between the loss of his job and the poetry Jibanananda composed. Other persons argue that his poetic avocation had nothing to do with the termination of his employment at City College.

The year began under a cloud of political tensions of two kinds: nationalist (between Indian nationalists and the colonial powers) and communal (between Hindus and Muslims). During this period of heated emotions, the distinction between nationalist and communal tended to blur. Infringement upon absolute freedom of religious expression elicited defiance staunch as that from any Swadeshi freedom fighter. Some Hindus, for instance, were incensed equally by prohibitions against chanting the politically inflammatory "Bande Mataram" as by restrictions against making music and beating drums in front of a mosque. So, despite the solidifying catalyst of nationalistic feelings, parochial loyalties kept Bengal fragmented. As political tension increased, communal disturbances became more prevalent. Educational institutions provided focal points for releasing some of that tension.

Attached to the Brahmo Samaj's City College stood a students' residence hall, the Ram Mohan Ray hostel, open to boys of any religious faith. However, except for the Sunday morning lecture delivered by Principal

Heramba Chandra Maitra, no congregational religious observances were allowed within the hostel compound. The Brahmo Samaj especially opposed idol worship, forbidding any such activity on the premises. But in January, as the unpopular British parliamentary commission headed by Sir John Simon steamed toward Bombay, certain newspapers and leaders called on Indians to stand up for their rights. It was time for an uncompromising challenge to existing authority, and City College—its Brahmo staff, along with the college rules and regulations—represented an authority.

Saraswati, goddess of learning, is understandably a favorite among students. During the latter half of the 1920s, the popularity of the Saraswati puja—the annual ritual worship of the goddess's image which takes place in late January or early February—had been increasing. Simultaneously, hostilities intensified among religious communities in Bengal. Barisal's own *Brahmabadi* had carried an editorial comment on the matter the previous year:

> The past few years have witnessed throughout Bengal a strong interest in this particular puja [Saraswati]. Its religious significance vis-à-vis the society, however, is no longer interpreted in the manner in which it once was. This year the puja and accompanying activities were performed in many urban schools and "religious preservation" societies. It is with profound regret and sorrow we find that in the foul winds of enmity Calcutta's vile hostility of old between Hindus and Muslims is causing again today all these lamentable and objectionable incidents in connection with this joyous festivity.[78]

Hindu students of City College celebrated the puja in previous years. But according to one account, performances of it in a City College hostel itself had been disallowed from 1917 on, by order of Principal Maitra. Students were free, however, to worship outside the hostel compound.[79] Then, very early on the morning of 27 January 1928, in the spirit of defiance, Hindu students of Ram Mohan Ray hostel conducted a Saraswati puja within the compound walls. "The students had secretly made all the arrangements," wrote Binod Bihari Banerjee, a colleague of Jibanananda at City College. "They had brought in the image in the dead of night and just before dawn called for the priest. The puja was begun in the courtyard of the hostel."[80]

Binod Bihari recalled that Brajasundar Ray, another City College professor and a Brahmo with Barisal connections, showed up at his door to say that a Saraswati puja was in progress. The two of them hurriedly went to Principal Maitra's quarters and upon his advice paid a visit to the university vice-chancellor, Jadunath Sarkar, who forbade the use of physical coercion.[81] Two days later, the following item appeared in an English-language newspaper:

SARASWATI PUJA IN CALCUTTA—INCIDENT IN CITY COLLEGE
STUDENTS' BOLD STAND

> The S.P. passed off peacefully in Calcutta this year but for a sad incident which took place at the Rammohon Ray Hostel attached to the City College.
>
> It is reported that the students of the Rammohon Ray Hostel arranged this year to perform the puja to the Goddess Saraswati in the adjoining hostel compound. But as it was against the usual custom of the hostel authorities the Superintendent, Babu Brojo Mohon [sic] Ray was reported to have asked the students not to perform the puja in the hostel compound and to remove the deity from there.
>
> The students, it is said, to assert their rights paid no heed to the order of the Superintendent. Thereupon the Superintendent, it is reported, in an angry mood attempted to enter the enclosure where the deity was installed but the students did not allow him to do so.
>
> This created a good deal of resentment between the Superintendent and the students and the Superintendent left the place finding no other alternative. The puja was performed without any further trouble.[82]

The problem at City College, however, did not melt away with the ceremony's completion upon immersion of the idol. The offenders, ordered to apologize, refused to do so.[83] Instead, the students took their own version of the story to the press, concluding with a plea:

> We appeal to the Hindu public to keep their eyes on the progress of these events and on the subsequent actions that the college authority is determined to take upon the students for no other offence than that they could not abandon their religion on their admission into the Hostel and observed their religious festivals according to their faith.[84]

City College did try to punish the boarders by fining the accused miscreants.[85] In a matter of months, things deteriorated to such a degree that the administration closed the college for a premature summer vacation.[86]

The affair did not end there. Battle lines were well drawn. On one side stood those who felt that Hinduism had been affronted and the rights of Hindus infringed by City College's Brahmos. The opposing side, comprised mainly though not entirely of Brahmos, felt that the college authorities had every right to establish rules of behavior for students within the confines of property under the college's auspices. The fight drew many respected and influential combatants. Subhas Chandra Bose, protégé of the late C. R. Das and probably the most influential Bengali political figure of the day, took up the Hindu boarders' cause, while Rabindranath was one of City College's distinguished advocates. Ramananda Chatterjee, a Brahmo, carried many of the pro–City College statements in his *Modern Review* and *Prabasi,* statements by Rabindranath and such notables as Dinabandhu

(C. F.) Andrews and Annie Besant. Even Sajani Kanta and *Sanibarer Cithi* joined the fray, poking fun at the sanctimonious stance assumed by fellow Hindus who claimed their religion had been defiled by the Brahmo touch.[87]

The situation, however, proved no laughing matter for City College. Enrollment fell off, financially hurting the institution. From the Sadharan Brahmo Samaj's annual report for 1928, one gets an inkling of just how dire the crisis had become:

> The number of students in the current session is fifty per cent of what it was last year. At the end of the last session, the services of eleven members of the staff were dispensed with. And yet a very heavy deficit had to be provided for.[88]

Among those eleven professors was Jibanananda Das, after six years still the junior-most member of the English faculty, and the only one of that department to be dismissed.[89]

It seems reasonable to assume that Jibanananda, though a fellow Brahmo, lost his position due to a retrenchment policy following the Saraswati incident. Indeed, a number of persons argue very strongly that simple economics alone forced out Jibanananda. But there are others who believe his poetry had something to do with it.[90] At the time, few people other than immediate family, colleagues, and some of the *Kallol* writers took notice of this bashful Brahmo's dismissal. Those proved to be busy times, and there were other issues, political and literary, to think and shout about. The convention held at Bicitra Bhavan and presided over by Rabindranath had taken place in March that year, and the feud between Brahmo college and the Hindu community continued throughout the summer months. The firing of Jibanananda became a significant issue for debate only much later, after he had achieved fame.

In 1949 Acintya Kumar Sengupta's *The Kallol Era* came out, serially at first and then in book form the following year. Of Jibanananda and City College he wrote:

> Jibanananda used to be a lecturer at City College. I have heard that the authorities were indignant because he had conceived of the dark face of a breast in his poem entitled "Harvest" [*sasya*]. They snatched away his job on the malicious charge of obscenity. As far as I am aware, Jibanananda was the first sacrifice offered on the chopping block of obscenity.[91]

Jibanananda read what Acintya Kumar had written about him as the book appeared serially. Moreover, he took the trouble to respond to his friend, correcting one point in another passage of those reminiscences which, in his opinion, qualified as a misstatement. "I did not go just three or four but a hundred or more times to that office of *Kallol*'s," wrote Jibanananda in a letter. "You used to go in the afternoons—I would go toward morning."[92] That was all he amended of Acintya Kumar's statement regarding him. The point made about obscenity costing him his job went unchallenged.

The next public pronouncement on the subject came in 1968, well after Jibanananda's death. Buddhadeva contributed a small drama to a special issue of the weekly *Desh* ("Country") devoted to "obscenity and literature," which read in part:

> Elderly writer: I was just thinking of another matter. You do know the story of Jibanananda losing his job, don't you?
> Professor (chuckling softly): That "doe in heat" [*ghai harini*]!
> Elderly writer: The poem "In Camp" had just come out in *Paricay* ["Acquaintances"]. Then one day as he arrived at the college, Jibanananda was summoned to the principal's office. That was the very same college where Jibanananda had studied; the principal had been his teacher. As Jibanananda entered the room the elderly gentleman got to his feet and shaking a copy of *Paricay* said, "You wrote 'doe in heat'? 'Doe in heat,' you wrote that? Out, get out this instant!" And Jibanananda, with his awkward stance, his bashful sidelong glance, suppressing a nervous burst of laughter, slowly went out.[93]

Acintya Kumar, when asked about the source of his information, replied that Jibanananda himself told him he lost the City College appointment because of poetry he had written. Buddhadeva, replying to the same question, said that in literary circles it had been just something everybody knew, that Jibanananda had lost his job due to alleged obscenity in his poetry.[94]

Buddhadeva's article drew a retort from Sarojendranath Ray, Jibanananda's colleague in the English department at City College. He advanced the argument of retrenchment, stemming from the Saraswati puja incident, then added:

> Mr. Maitra was known to be a man of high moral principles and most eloquent. There are many stories about his high morality. A few of these even he had heard and was amused by. It is not surprising that a tale should be composed connecting his morality and the loss of Jibanananda Babu's job. Buddhadeva Bose is not the only one; others have done this too.[95]

In general, Brahmos—the great reformers of the nineteenth century—had earned a reputation for being morally rigid. As mentioned earlier, the word *bemmo,* the derogatory form of Brahmo, today means prude.[96] Prudish or no, moral development had always been a central concern of this religious community. The Students' Weekly Service, for instance, a Brahmo young people's organization founded in Calcutta in 1879, dedicated itself to "building character." In the 1920s this phrase meant not only abstaining from smoking and drinking but also from frequenting the professional theatre, in which women of ill-repute supposedly performed.[97] As late as 1932, Barisal's own *Brahmabadi* carried an editorial note voicing Brahmo displeasure as well with the cinema, or bioscope, as it was then called.

> Falling Standards—In education, morality, religion, the society, etc., in all fields Barisal is falling from that high standard of old. It is impossible to discuss fully all these matters in this journal; today we shall cite but one perversion of the ideal in only one such field. Even after so much discussion, so much deliberation, once again a bioscope has found a place in Town Hall. No matter how many reasons there are supporting this, in these difficult times—and measured against Aswini Kumar's pure, high standards [Aswini Kumar was responsible for having Town Hall built]—it is thoroughly indecent.[98]

As Sarojendranath stated, there were many stories, possibly apocryphal, concerning Principal Maitra's personal high moral standards, or puritanism, depending on one's point of view. A commonly heard tale, related by Nirad C. Chaudhuri in his *Autobiography of an Unknown Indian,* goes as follows:

> The spirit of Brahmo morality is perhaps best illustrated by an anecdote about Principal Heramba Chandra Maitra, a very notable Brahmo in his day. He, it is said, was one day walking down Cornwallis Street in Calcutta when a man asked him where the Star Theatre was. Annoyed by this query of unsavoury associations, Principal Maitra, it is reported, at first replied, "I don't know," then, realizing that he had told a lie, ran back to the man and this time said to him: "I know but I won't tell." The anecdote is certainly apocryphal, but it is true in its spirit.

Zealous Brahmos, Nirad tells us, "vowed as sternly to eschew ... the theatre because the actresses were *demi-mondaines,* as they vowed to shun debauchery, falsehood, or drunkenness."[99] It is little wonder, then, that Buddhadeva and others might have assumed that Jibananda's poetry—which so scandalized a magazine editor such as Sajani Kanta Das—contributed to Jibananda's dismissal from the Brahmos' City College.

The advocates of both positions, particularly Buddhadeva, commit factual errors that undermine the validity of their statements. Jibananda had never been a student at City College, and Heramba Maitra was not his former teacher. The poem "In Camp" appeared in *Paricay*; but *Paricay* did not begin publication until 1931, whereas Jibananda left City College in 1928. The assertion that poetry played a role in the loss of his job stems from supposition. Yet evidence for the opposing view is only circumstantial. Sarojendranath Ray insists that Heramba Maitra never read current Bengali magazines or books of contemporary literature.[100] Nevertheless, it seems unlikely that he would not have at least heard of *Sanibarer Cithi* and Sajani Kanta's criticism of one of his own English faculty. There was a Saraswati incident, one consequence of which was City College's retrenchment policy. However, that this retrenchment alone cost Jibanananda his position cannot be indisputably proven.

For whatever reason, Jibanananda found himself out of a job in mid-1928. Not until the end of 1929 did he obtain employment again, this time at the recently established Prafulla Chandra College in Bagerhat, a very small town in Bangladesh situated about halfway between Calcutta and Barisal. He stayed there for only a few months before accepting a position at Ramjas College in Delhi where the vice-principal was Sukumar Datta, himself a prominent Barisal figure and nephew of Barisal's most illustrious citizen, Aswini Kumar Datta. Again, Jibanananda remained only a short while at this post, from December 1929 to March 1930.[101]

Prabhash Chandra Ghosh, a colleague and friend of his at Ramjas College, maintained that Jibanananda felt lonely and unhappy in Delhi. But he did have at least one other friend there, Sudhir Kumar Datta, another Brahmo from Barisal. Sudhir Kumar lived at a hotel by the name of Raisine, located in New Delhi. Jibanananda's college stood on what he referred to as "the barren, waterless hilly tract of land then called 'Kala Pahar' [renamed Anand Parvat] on the outskirts of Delhi...."[102] The two men would meet regularly in the evenings, with Jibanananda sometimes taking Sudhir Kumar to his college club. "Our college was on a hill, quite far from Old Delhi, farther still from the New Delhi of the Raisine," wrote Jibanananda years later, remembering Sudhir Kumar. "It was December and extremely cold then in Delhi—even colder on the hill.... but ignoring all this inconvenience, he came and began to stay with me on that 'marooned' mountain."[103]

No matter how dissatisfied he might have been in Delhi, Jibanananda did want to retain his teaching position there, according to Prabhash Chandra. He planned to get married and then return to Ramjas College. In pursuit of that end, he requested Prabhash Chandra and others on the staff to approach the principal on his behalf, asking that he, Jibanananda, be granted tenure and a short leave in order to go home to wed. The principal turned down these requests, and Jibanananda's job in Delhi came to an end some four months after it started.[104]

Despite what occurred at Ramjas College, Jibanananda was set on marriage. According to his wife, his parents summoned him from Delhi so that arrangements could be made. Labanya Das's guardian had actually proposed the union. Labanya Das (née Gupta), her two sisters, and a brother were born in the town of Senhati. They lost their father and mother within four months of each other when Labanya was only seven. Though her father, Rohini Kumar Gupta, remained a Hindu, his two older brothers, Amritalal and Biharilal, had joined the Brahmo Samaj. Amritalal, a preacher at the East Bengal Brahmo Samaj in Dhaka, became Labanya's guardian. It was he who approached his coreligionists (and Vaidya co-caste members, though caste should not matter to a Brahmo), Satyananda and Kusum Kumari Das, with the offer of marriage between his niece and their son.[105]

Amritalal had become concerned that his niece might get involved in anti-British political activities. "While I was studying for the I.A. degree at Eden College, Dhaka, I grew a little too interested in politics," explained Labanya. "My uncle (the late Amritalal Gupta) realized immediately what was happening, perhaps. And so, without any notice—that is, without giving me time to understand what was going on—he went ahead and arranged my marriage. Not only that, he didn't even let me know that a professor from Ramjas College, Delhi, was about to come to have a look at me."[106]

Then one day Amritalal summoned Labanya home from the student hostel. There was a muddy field to cross on the way from the hostel to her uncle's house, she recalled, and at the time she wore a rather plain cotton sari with a decorated border. As she entered the house, her uncle informed her that a guest had arrived and that she should prepare tea and sweets. When she brought the refreshments into the sitting room, she still had on that mud-splattered sari. A single guest sat there, a dark-complected twenty-eight- or twenty-nine-year-old man wearing a simple dhoti (the skirtlike lower garment worn by Bengali Hindu gentlemen) and *panjabi* (the loose, collarless slip-on shirt worn by both Hindus and Muslims), staring at the floor.[107]

Custom has it that a young man look over the bride-to-be his parents have chosen and give his assent. After that gentleman had seen and registered his approval of her, Labanya's uncle immediately solicited her consent to the marriage. Following much cajoling—for Labanya showed more interest in the potentially exciting experience of college and clandestine politics than in the prospect of marriage—she eventually agreed to wed. Buddhadeva Bose, Ajit Datta, and one or two other writers attended the ceremony, which was performed according to Brahmo rites by Manomohan Chakravarty, Jibanananda's uncle, at Dhaka's Brahmo temple on 9 May 1930. Several days later, the newlyweds arrived by inland steamer at Barisal. In keeping with the practice followed in most of Bengali society of having married couples live in the husband's parents' household, Jibanananda and Labanya took up residence with his family at Sarbananda Bhavan, the Das's simple dwelling at the corner of Bogura and Gorosthan

Roads in Barisal proper. There, on May fourteenth, young Labanya performed the "bride-rice" (*bau bhat*) ceremony where the newly arrived wife cooks and feeds rice to her in-laws, thus establishing herself as part of the husband's household.[108]

Labanya's marriage interrupted her studies for the time being, and her budding political career was nipped before it blossomed. The couple's first of two children, daughter Manjusri, arrived in 1931. Later, Labanya returned to educational pursuits, completing her bachelor's degree in 1935 at the local Barisal college. Notice of her accomplishment appeared in *Brahmabadi*.

> Achievement of Women—Daughter-in-law of the Brahmo Samaj's Satyananda Das B.A. and wife of professor Jibanananda Das, Labanya Bala, mother of a five-year-old daughter, received her I.A. and now has passed the B.A. examination from B.M. College.[109]

A son, Samarananda, was born in 1938, completing their family.

It probably never can be determined for certain whether Jibanananda really did want to return to Delhi after his marriage or whether he was content to remain in his native Bengal. I would guess that he indeed knew contentment at being home again, for he loved his homeland with a passion and would soon write sonnets which speak of that affection. True, others before and after Jibanananda have expressed their love for Bengal. Erudite Madhusudan, punning on the first element in his name (one meaning of *madhu* being something sweet, specifically "honey"), began his poem "To Bengal" (*bangabhumir prati*) as follows:

> "My native Land, Good night!"—Byron
> Remember, Mother, this slave of yours,
> I beg thus at your feet.
> Were my mind's desire
> In fact not to transpire,
> Still, please don't make your lotus heart
> Devoid of what is sweet.[110]

Rabindranath's song begins forthrightly: "My golden Bengal I love you." Jibanananda's professions of love are equally sincere, but at the same time uniquely Jibanandian, as we shall see.

3
Back to Barisal

... As the helmsman,
His rudder broken, far out upon the sea adrift,
Sees the grass-green land of a cinnamon isle, just so
Through the darkness I saw her. Said she, "Where have you been so long?"
And raised her bird's-nest-like eyes—Banalata Sen from Natore.

—Jibanananda Das, "Banalata Sen"

1

The first half of the 1930s found Jibanananda newly wed, back in Barisal, and unemployed. Not until 1935 did he formally resume college teaching in the English department of Barisal's Braja Mohan College, then the largest *mofussil* college in all of Bengal.[1] *Fallen Feathers* had come out in 1927. His second book, *Gray Manuscripts* (*dhusar pandulipi*), would not be published until 1936, even though nearly all the poems in that volume had already appeared in print by 1930.

Between these first two books, Jibanananda composed, but did not publish, a considerable amount of both poetry and fiction, even an unfinished, untitled novel dated 1933.[2] The fiction published thus far reveals new facets of Jibanananda: his handling of a down-to-earth, idiomatic, conversational Bengali and his ability to invent a make-believe world that is true to life, peopled with, in some cases, characters bearing a decidedly autobiographical aura.

The beginnings of this 1930s prose phase, dominated by the short story, coincided (as did a later one when he was to produce several novels) with a time of great change in Jibanananda's life. In his early thirties, he had to adjust to living with another human being, one quite unlike himself—the young, very beautiful, and spirited woman whom he had only recently met and wed. After more than a decade of living alone but of being busy (first as a student in Calcutta and then as a professor in Calcutta, Bagerhat, and Delhi), he now had a new domestic life, back home in Barisal, to which to attend, as well as the full-time pursuit of writing. Having resumed college teaching in 1935, he would again in 1946 decide to abandon that vocation (permanently, so he thought, though it did not turn out that way) and, moreover, to leave his ancestral home for the vagaries of journalism and life once again in Calcutta. But at this juncture in his life, Jibanananda's real and figurative worlds seem to have coalesced, for his fiction has an immediacy and clarity much of his poetry would never attain.

All but one of the five short stories and three novels thus far published are written in a standard, very colloquial (*calit*) idiom (the one exception being composed in an equally standard form of the elevated, or *sadhu,* language). None of the uniquely personal, idiosyncratic hybrid Bengali found in Jibanananda's poetry appears in his prose. The latter, though fiction, is reflective of the real world, stated in real-world terms. Dialogues have the feel of authenticity, conversations flowing naturally, unself-consciously. The vocabulary is extensive, rich, and apt. In short, Jibanananda takes full command of the language of fiction in order to depict vividly a very matter-of-fact human environment—this in contrast to both the domain and the language of his poetry which, for the most part up to now, have fallen outside the mundane, quotidian universe.

What transpires in his fiction is conveyed primarily through interactions among real, generally middle-class, educated Bengalis in Calcutta or some *mofussil* town setting comparable to Barisal. The issues that concern them often revolve around love, unrequited or in some cases, due to the marriage of one protagonist to someone else, unrequitable. In his poetry, Jibanananda frequently casts the narrator in the role of the wounded party:

Your body—
You brought it near once—then, the crowd
Day and night
Called you away, I don't know where—these eyes
Saddened—and I, torn apart—torn asunder—and so many days,
So many nights passed walking the paths of the world.[3]

This is my song
And though you've come, you'll never hear it.
Tonight my call
Will float away upon the winds of the path, but
Still a song comes to my heart.
. . . .
Only you one day—one night's
Gathering of men and women
Called you away—how far?[4]

She has loved me,
And come near.
She has paid no heed to me.
She has despised me and gone away when I called her time and again,
Loving her.[5]

In the fiction, likewise, it is usually a man who, sometimes cuckolded and sometimes just spurned, plays the aggrieved role, often pathetically so:

The doctor arrived. A young upstart Westernized fellow.

He turned his head this way and that, letting his eyes take in the room around him. During a span of five minutes he brushed something from his "suit" a good seventeen times. Upon gazing for a moment at my loose shirt made of country cloth, he himself felt embarrassed. Somehow or other—as he wiped the perspiration from the back of his neck, from his eyes, nose, and mouth—he had to sort out this patchwork of ragged lives.

Still he came, nightly.

Precisely as the day vanished and shadows thickened in the sky.

Suddenly, like the shadows.

He said, "Let me see your glasses."

I took them off slowly and handed them to him.

"My god—what thick lenses! These'll ruin your eyes!"

"What am I to do?" I said, with a burst of nervous laughter.

He spun my glasses around, danced them up and down, swung them side to side, all the while talking volumes, lecturing.

I didn't understand a thing.

Hadn't listened.

I only realized that he was going on talking.

Just that and nothing more. . . .

He returned my glasses to me.

I responded, "That's it?"

"How did your eyes give out? I suppose it was at a young age."

"What's done for is done for."

He stared at me, as though he sought to maintain his feeling of disgust, thinking, "It is I who keep going that rotting body you call a person."

To him, such a grievous insult to humanity seems utterly unbearable.

Before I could say anything, Reba brought in the tea.

There was a crack in the cup, in the saucer too.

Reba felt more chagrined by this than did the doctor. She didn't quite know what to say to extricate herself.

She was jabbering away, Reba was.

Through the vacuity of my lenses, my craving soul dissolved, I cast a glance at the two of them.

They took no note of me.

I was enjoying myself, leaning back against our flaking wall, eyes closed.

For no particular reason.

The doctor wasn't budging—Reba, too, seemed ensconced.

She finally had what she wanted.

They talked on and on.

With eyes closed I thought to myself, "I could tell you all that—what you two are saying—all that, and with more flair and gesticulating. I could say that. I could say that. I could say all that. No matter what I may be, it is I who am able to exclude myself, not you people—you are incapable."

The more worked up they got, the more disheveled they became and—it seemed to me—the more ridiculous they were.
What are they to me!
So this is their love!
If she had only let me love her!
Reba said, "He's asleep."
For a few minutes, complete silence.
Then sounds of kissing.
The both of them, fidgeting, eagerly, furtively.
Again, total silence.
Alone in the darkness, as the room turned cold.
Repulsive or pleasant!
I cannot know for sure.
I call Reba and am staring into her face.
I've got it, I've got it, I've found that faith, that confidence.
Her countenance was no less fine that day she filled the cupped *sal* leaves with day-old rice and gave that to the beggar. No—no—repulsive it cannot be! It is beautiful—beauty's finest hour!
Reba says, "Why did you call?"
It was as though a caged bird gained its freedom—her voice was such. Even I have gained the sky again.
Regained the light that lights the sky—all of it. Light is indeed far greater than darkness.
Far greater.
There is no higher truth than that expansive sky.
"You were calling!"
It wafted over my entire body. Reluctance, shyness, fear, and loathing—all these seemed to a great extent to lift away.
That confidence—upon this rotting corpse.
"You called!" A bit longer and two pairs of petals round the eyes would have had to close.
Before such happened, Reba went away, just like that.[6]

So ends one of Jibanananda's earlier short stories, with the main character feigning sleep while wife and visitor to the house—a young doctor—compromise the marriage.

Mostly set in Calcutta, Jibanananda's fiction conveys a tension between life in the city and that in a rural environment. The *mofussil* town contains denizens every bit as venal as those found in Calcutta, but the surroundings of such a place and of Bengal's myriad villages have their abiding lure. Another of the short stories from the early 1930s ends with a married woman, Saci, propositioning an unmarried man, Somen, to escape together to the romantic life far from the city's throng. As the story concludes, Somen, unemployed and a bit of a vagabond, visits Saci in the middle of the day, when her husband is away at the office. Until this point, the reader has had no cause to assume that Saci is unhappy with her role as wife of a successful business man.

Back to Barisal

From the next room Saci brought out a box of Havana cigars and placed it on a teapoy in front of Somen.

As he picked one out, he commented, "I haven't had a Havana for I don't know how long—"

Saci had returned to where she'd been sitting.

Somen lit his cigar—

For a brief moment Saci saw herself as a prostitute of sorts—one so raised from childhood, adept at serving—only that, nothing more. At the same time, Saci seemed to Somen as though she were feeling slightly meretricious—like some very expensive harlot who, for an instant, had flashed through Somen's heart—prohibitively expensive, yet someone who yearned to become close to him—but of course, for that one fleeting instant only.

Saci ruminated on whether she had been remiss as a hostess.

Her sari—quite clean—still then, had she done everything right?

Her hair put up in a bun—would it be proper to let it flow loose—or, maybe she should have braided it? What if she had gone barefoot, lining her feet with the traditional red dye, instead of wearing showy Bijapuri sandals.

Had she put kohl around her eyes? an iridescent dot upon her forehead?

Such a toilette was part of her life once—Somen had even witnessed that. And today Saci seemed overcome by a desire to show him that once more.

"I remember," said Somen, "that day along the bank of the Bakmohana river when I let you enter that jungle of *bhantasyaora, juili, mayanakanta,* and *alok* vines. About a mile from your house. Your head tilted confidently as you proclaimed, 'Of course I know my way—I've done it many times!' But you hadn't, not even once. And you got lost in amongst the mango and jackfruit and bamboo groves. Then I, like some young *rui* fish, came swimming down the river, nibbling at your slender *sarapunti*-like gills. Ah, that river—the fragrance of those reeds—night—darkness—the stars—damp sands—how many, many days your cool body ruled my heart—"

He smiled slightly, then went on, "But today there's no question of reliving all those experiences—retelling them is by itself somehow wrong."

"Why?"

"You're never going to regain that village life—at least not with such intensity. No, Saci, it's impossible. That's why I too cannot return to the village. I don't even want to think about it, about what the village is like—the *telakuco* vines, clumps of cactus, the wild *dhundul* roots have faded far into some darkness, some moonlight. We are no longer there—we're not part of all that any longer—what would we do with it all now! When from the window of my Calcutta rooms I gaze out and see off in the distance red blossoms bursting forth upon a leafless *simul* tree, I think of the sorrow, the intense longing for the village which, in truth, might have consumed me, and I conclude, in light of the demands of this new life, all that other becomes ludicrous—I've thought so for a long time now. And even though I yearn to impose fresh demands on this new life—nevertheless, when they impose themselves, they'll find me up to the task, for sure—"

He looked at the continuous stream of smoke rising from his cigar and added, "When the honey's gone, it's gone—for whom it's meant, it's for them alone. Yet, from Calcutta's heart it's not just foul humors that ooze, it might be any fluid—collected as required."

Saci, after a long period of silence, said, "Let's go to the village—"

"Which village?"

"Where we were—"

"On the banks of the Bakmohana? In that *bhantasyaora, mayanakanta* jungle?"

Saci nodded her head, "Yes—there too—"

Somen responded, "Impossible."

"I've been thinking for some time now that I would go—"

Shaking his head Somen asked, "How are you going to go?"

Saci thought for a moment, head bowed.

After a bit, she raised her head and asked, "Why?"

"Because," replied Somen, "you'll want to return again—"

"And why shouldn't I return?"

His cigar had been held loosely between his fingers. He now tightened his grip, adding, "Why would you return?"

"Why wouldn't I?"

Somen said, "If I were to go with you out there among the wild flowers, *dhundul, kalami* vines, and bamboo groves, I could not return. But mark it well, we are not what we were—neither I nor you. You now feel the urge to wander—the same sort of urge that tempts a man to go see the Taj Mahal causes you momentarily to be inclined toward embarking on some excursion. Maybe you'll shed a tear, embrace me, let me kiss you—rest your head on my shoulder and cry, maybe—maybe even wish not to return—maybe even let me have you—but all that's for a single afternoon, Saci, an afternoon, swathed in village field and jungle and deadly seductive—or for an evening—a single night. At dawn you'll swim that river to where you were a girl of twelve or thirteen. And who's to stop you? A woman transformed is beyond reach. I am capable of change—lasting change. You, though, just for the fun of the trip."

Somen absentmindedly tossed his cigar butt onto the cement floor, then said, "That's the difference between men and women."

He got up.

At least for this one afternoon Saci had become that Saci of old.

Today, right now, he could take advantage of Saci for whatever he himself required—she was ready for that, even eager. But on this sofa? As it had happened that day by the Bakmohana river, in the shadows of the jungle, beneath a starry sky, with the smells of the water nearby.

It hurt just to think of it—it hurt to think.

He couldn't bear to remain in the room a moment longer. Another Havana in hand, Somen was out on the street before he knew it.[7]

Back to Barisal 87

In the late 1940s, writing from Calcutta, Jibanananda concluded his novel *Sutirtha* with a permutation of just such a scene.

One of Jibanananda's short stories from this early period is quite unlike the rest of his fiction. Even its language is unique, for "Company, Alone" (*sanga, nihsanga,* the title given by the publishers) was written in *sadhu,* Jibanananda's only publication to date, including essays, to exhibit that elevated form of Bengali and, thus, to experiment with linguistic conservatism. The subject matter of this story likewise contrasts with that of his other fiction, for it has only one character, the narrator, who is writing a letter to his wife of three years. Absent are the interactions between characters which dominate his other fiction. Absent, too, is the city. Though unidentified by name, Barisal, undoubtedly, serves as the setting, as anyone familiar with that town will recognize from the few permanent landmarks mentioned. The anonymous main character assumes once again the role of the injured lovelorn, a not uncommon persona in both Jibanananda's poetry and prose. Unseen elsewhere in his prose is the incredible richness of the physical world that surrounds this monologist, an extraordinarily sensitive narrator who sees more, feels more in his casual and uneventful stroll about town than most people would. This epistolary story, with its luxuriant description of a part of Bengal, foreshadows (or maybe simply reflects, for its dates are uncertain) a sizable series of sonnets which Jibanananda may have been working on at the time. Be that as it may, in its descriptive flights this work itself exudes poetry:

This time, it seems, you plan to remain at your father's for quite a spell. I haven't written you for some time—our marriage is three years old—three years, of course, is not long—many marriages remain new and vital ten-fifteen, twenty-twenty-five, even fifty years. Each and every day, at least three to four days a week, they feel they have to exchange letters.

But both you and I know, had our lives been arranged like theirs, no path of escape would have been found in this world.

For a long time now you have not sought word of me, and I, for my part, have written you nothing—this void, though, is deeply gratifying. I seek to keep this life of mine brimful of just such emptiness and silence. Do you know what I crave? There is a certain charming village path, white with dust, that meanders by *baici, mayanakanta,* and *babala* trees, cactuses and wild *aparajita* creepers—beside it stands the unabated exhalation of a certain field—green grass there, filled with *syama* and *dewali* and grasshoppers and *kac* bugs, *sudarsan* insects fly about, yellow-, orange-, tobacco-brown-, blue-colored butterflies flutter to and fro throughout the afternoon among the wild flowers—here and there a few *palas, arjun,* and *hijal* trees, dense *ulukhar* weeds, the kingfisher's dazzling wings, in one particular spot, nearby the soft scents of grass, there at one far corner of the field where the forest's lord, the *aswattha* tree, for ages has composed its shade and yielded sanctuary night and day to *salik, bulabuli, kokil,* and the crow, there let me build my one-room hut of straw, and let me write and smoke cigars and pass my days.

Were I to have arranged my life just so, I know you would have not objected. An urge would stir in you to render your companionship to me, thinking me lonely.

And a bit later on, in more specific terms, he tells her of the time they were together:

I don't know whether you remember or not, but even while you were here, I used to keep a jug of water in my own room at all times. If thirsty, I myself would get the water. I never asked you to pour me a glass. But I appreciated that. Even now when I reflect on it I realize your company spared me from deep loneliness. It still does; it always will. Is there any grander attainment to be had in this world? Of course, I held a quite different opinion eight years ago. I wasn't yet married then. I used to think I would have my wife massage my feet, she would brush back the hair from my brow, and would fan me—

And much, much more!

But when you came into my life I saw that you did none of that. Nor did I even want it. Gradually within my heart some sort of snake-charmer's flute began to play. I couldn't tell from whom this melody came. Throughout day and night, from the side of a village path, from thickets of *ulukhar,* from the sky, from the breast of a still and exquisite afternoon, I used to be overwhelmed just pondering who it was that produced such a melody. Yet I very much enjoyed it, so deep and unknown. I had once loved someone whom I have lost—was this her joy personified? No, not that. Neither was it you—nor I. It was just a constant, deep and pleasing sound—as one walks on unimpeded, it is in coconut palm fronds, in the light brown wings and white throat of the hawk, in the colored sails of boats at dawn, in the fierce sunshine, in the Meghna and Dhaleswari rivers' swelling breasts of flood waters, in sweet *madhukupi,* a sea of *kas* grasses, in clusters lush with *dron* blossoms, in vermilion on the forehead of some lifeless, gorgeous woman, in twilight clouds, in fog upon a winter's eve, upon the lonely loom of dreams woven with sad, shy eyes—it is the tune they play—it is the sound of that.

Whether this melody is in your life I don't know. If it's not—procure it. It provides life with profound support.[8]

The manuscript for the preceding is dated, in Jibanananda's own hand, May 1933. He and Labanya were married in that same month three years earlier. Both theirs and the fictional letter writer's marriage would have been three years old in 1933.

2

The lush, highly poetic language of the preceding prose story, in which Barisal's milieu becomes translated into words, is analogous to the language of an entire volume of lyrics, composed at this very same time or, at most, a year later. His poetry notebooks, more than forty in number, span the years from 1931 right up to his death in 1954. One of these, bearing the date March 1934, contains sixty-odd sonnets and a few pieces not in sonnet form. This collection, edited somewhat by the poet's brother, was published posthumously and, based on an expression that appears in one of the poems, entitled *Bengal the Beautiful* (*rupasi bamla*). In his introduction, dated 31 July 1957, Asokananda wrote, "Twenty-five years ago, in a short expanse of time, these poems were written while the poet had been seized by a particular emotion. All these poems are a product of the late *Gray Manuscripts* period."[9]

The sonnet has been a productive poetic form in Bengali since the middle of the nineteenth century, when Michael Madhusudan Dutt adopted medieval Bengali *payar,* fourteen-syllable lines arranged in rhymed couplets, and adapted it to the sonnet. With typical Madhusudan flair, he mailed from Versailles in 1865 a Bengali sonnet entitled "Poet Dante" (*kabi dante*), together with accompanying French translation, to Italy's king, Victor Emmanuel II, on the occasion of Dante's six-hundredth birth anniversary—an offering described by Madhusudan as "une petite fleur orientale." In reply, the king's minister wrote that his sovereign was pleased "the Italian genius finds an echo on the shores of the Ganges" and felt Italy would be "the ring which will unite the orient with the occident."[10] Politically, the king's aspirations came to naught. The sonnet, however, "is the only poetic form borrowed from another language which still grows in Bengali and promises a very long life," writes Sisir Kumar Das. "Other European poetic forms have been introduced into Bengali by other poets, but the Italian exotic which Michael Madhusudan Datta planted on the shore of the Ganges has flourished and blossomed abundantly, and Bengal has made it her home."[11]

Jibanananda, just one in a long line of Bengali practitioners of this verse form,[12] published his first Bengali sonnet in *Gray Manuscripts* (1936). But much earlier, he had written other poems of this genre. Like Madhusudan, Jibanananda foreshadowed his Bengali sonnets with some in English. For example:

> I have felt the breath of autumn wind,
> With the fragrance of spring still in my heart;
> I have touched, shiveringly, the skirt
> Of Autumn—her treasures nervously gleaned;
> She laughed not like summer, nor grinned
> Like the wind-weary phantom-girt;
> Nights that out of winter dart
> To her own winning sadness she is pinned.
>
> With a flower, or two—a vanishing scent,
> A flash of smile on her demure face,

> She walks with a light half-spent
> By life and half in death's embrace;
> She looks like a lady that is gracefully bent
> To track the lost lover's fading trace.[13]

The editors of *Mayukh* ("Luster"), wherein the lyric appeared in a special Jibanananda issue following the poet's death, cautioned readers not to take this English poetry for anything but private Jibanananda juvenilia, composed around 1919 when he began his public career as a Bengali poet with "Invocation for the New Year," published in the family-run *Brahmabadi*.[14] The rhymes may leave something to be desired, but the poem is noteworthy for a number of reasons. Jibanananda used that same Petrarchan sonnet structure, or octave and sestet—the form also preferred by Madhusudan—in most of the poems in the 1934 notebook. And autumn, evocative of impending death here, was to be the season he concentrated upon in subsequent poetry. Death, a prominent feature of this poem, will be a recurring theme in Jibanananda's later work, as will be the personification of nature as beautiful woman. In the title *Bengal the Beautiful,* the word *beautiful,* as an adjective, is feminine; it may also be a feminine noun glossing as "beautiful woman." And so, the two words of the title could be thought of as in apposition: Bengal, the beautiful woman.

In a letter written in the early 1930s to Bishnu Dey, Jibanananda mentions his English poetry, unfortunately without reference to a specific poem. Upon reflection some forty years later, Bishnu Dey himself could only surmise that it must have been poetry given to him to read and criticize.

> Sarbananda Bhavan
> Barisal
> 18.10.31
>
> [salutations]
>
> I received your letter and was titillated with chagrin to learn that my English poems are not worth submitting. Actually I gave up writing such poetry a long time ago. Of course, I don't know what I might do in the future. I hope to bring my Bengali verse along with me to Calcutta. I'll be going to Calcutta toward the end of November.
>
> It was good to learn about everybody. I hope I'll be able to see everyone when I'm in Calcutta. I haven't heard from Prabhash Babu; has he gone to Delhi? When did *Paricay* come out? What's in it? It piques my curiosity, terribly. Are you staying in Calcutta for the puja holidays? It's still better than a month before I can get to Calcutta.
>
> Hope you all are well.
>
> J.[15]

We may never know whether the English poetry to which Jibanananda alludes contained sonnets. We do know that in the early 1930s he composed in Bengali a number of poems of fourteen lines divided structurally—by rhyme scheme though not by contrast between proposition and resolution—into octaves and sestets. That Jibanananda, who seems to have revised his poetry extensively, could have quickly composed, as his brother suggests, nearly sixty well-constructed sonnets with few or no revisions seems highly improbable. The presence, toward the end of the notebook, of longer poems and possibly even fragments of poems, replete with emendations, implies the poet may have used this notebook, from March 1934 on, to copy or recopy his revised sonnets as well as poetry which had not been reworked. No matter the actual span of time in which these sonnets were written, one must agree with Asokananda that his brother was genuinely inspired. But all this having been said, the question still remains as to why Jibanananda never published this poetry during his lifetime.

To write some sixty sonnets eulogizing Bengal presupposes intense emotional involvement with one's environment. And Jibanananda's sonnets are not intellectual constructs, no matter what the outward form might suggest. Visceral, sensuous statements, they speak of a romantic's childlike heart reexperiencing love. If overheard as he talked to himself in such exuberant outbursts, the poet might have burned with embarrassment, for these comments are almost too personal. Through such private exercises, Jibanananda relives Bengal to the fullest, an animal-vegetable-mineral rural Bengal, not the human society of cosmopolitan Bengal.

> There is a place in this world—the most beautiful, compassionate.
> There the green delta is awash with honey-sweet grass;
> Trees have names like jackfruit, *aswattha,* banyan, *jamarul,* cashew.
> There in clouds at dawn awakes the *nata* fruitlike red round sun.
> There Varuni resides at the mouth of the Ganges—and there Varuna
> Yields abundant river waters to the Karnafuli, Dhaleswari, Padma, Jalangi.
> There a white hawk is as full of movement as betel leaves in the wind.
> There a spotted owl is as subtly young as the smell of paddy fields.
>
> There the citrus branches droop in darkness upon the grass,
> And the buzzard flies away home upon dark evening breezes.
> There a yellow sari clings fast to some beautiful woman's body—
> Sankhamala is her name. In no other river, on no other grass of
> This vast world will you find her—Bisalaksi had granted her a boon,
> And so she was born amidst the paddy and grass of blue Bengal.[16]

Bisalaksi—literally, the large (*bisala*) eyed (*aksi*) one—signifies one of the auspicious names for the Bengali mother-goddess, more commonly known as Durga. The poem makes a simple statement: There, by the grace of goddess Bisalaksi, go I. Fairy-tale princess Sankhamala represents

Jibanananda and everyone else fortunate enough to have been born in Bengal, the world's most beautiful and compassionate place, where rivers empty into the Bay of Bengal, in which dwell the Hindu god of waters, Varuna, and his wife Varuni. Jibanananda had seen little of the wider world, but he had been away from his Bengal for several months while in Delhi. That may have been enough to convince him of his *mofussil* homeland's merits. A recitation of Bengal's vegetation, birds, and rivers becomes an incantation, conjuring up Bengal before the mind's eye.

Lest anyone doubt his sincerity, Jibanananda cites other seemingly desirable places which in his opinion cannot compare with his beloved home:

> Who would leave this delta to seek beauty on the paths of the world?
> The dry banyan leaves seem to call forth a tale of the end of an age:
> They are strewn along the many paths through fields in lonely
>   November.
> Who would reject them and set out for a foreign land? I shall not
> Give up *basamati* paddy fields for Malabar or the hills of Ootecamund.
> I shall not watch the palm trees nod heads to an ocean's song in some
> Other land—which brings to heart that dream of cardamom flowers
>   somewhere, and
> Cinnamon as Varuni sits unbraiding her hair. I shall not set out upon
>
> The path of the world. Falling *aswattha* leaves in pale white dust,
> When in this midday no one is around—not even a bird—
> Only lush grass spread out upon the ground, over gravel,
> Or one or two doleful sparrows turning over some pieces of straw,
> And those *aswattha* leaves lying there in pale white dust:
> That is why this life left not this path to wander elsewhere.[17]

Malabar is the lush coastal region of southwestern India; Ootecamund, a hill station located in south India. Hill stations are vacation resorts, refuges from summer's heat. Even such a resort or the palm-treed beaches of the Malabar Coast, the exotic lands of cardamom and cinnamon, cannot compare with Bengal and her fields of fragrant *basamati* rice. A November day, the rains long since ended, the ground now dry, leaves strewn about, a common little sparrow or two, an empty field and no one to distract him—the poet recalls again why he has never forsaken Bengal for parts elsewhere.

One life span seems not sufficient—one physical form inadequate—to experience all of Bengal's wonders:

> When I return to the banks of the Dhansiri, to this Bengal,
> Not as a man, perhaps, but as a *salik* bird or white hawk,
> Perhaps as a dawn crow in this land of autumn's new rice harvest,

> I'll float upon the breast of fog one day in the shade of a jackfruit tree.
> Or I'll be some young girl's pet duck—ankle bells upon her reddened feet—
> And I'll spend the day floating on duckweed-scented waters,
> When again I come, smitten by Bengal's rivers and fields, to this
> Green and kindly land, Bengal, moistened by the Jalangi river's waves.
>
> Perhaps I'll watch the buzzards soar on sunset's breeze.
> Perhaps I'll listen to a spotted owl screeching from a *simul* tree branch.
> Perhaps a child scatters puffed rice upon the grass of some home's courtyard.
> On the Rupsa river's murky waters a youth perhaps steers his dinghy with
> Its torn white sail. Reddish clouds scud by, and in the darkness, coming
> To their nest, I shall see white herons. Among them all is where you'll find me.[18]

Would that he could come back to the Dhansiri (a metonym for Bengal but also a river which flows not far from his native Barisal) in the form of a bird upon the fog, or a duck floating on one of the numerous tanks green and fragrant with duckweed. Perhaps, in some unspecified form, the poet would simply observe Bengal: the birds, a child playing, a young boatman on the Rupsa. Jibanananda probably just so watched dinghies (another Indian gift to the English language) upon that river which lies between the town of Khulna and the small community of Bagerhat where he taught for a short time in 1929. He must have been ferried across that flood several times on his way to and from his college.

Though the flora and fauna and rivers are real, few actual people appear in this poetry, and seldom do any of them possess a human relationship with the poet. Those with whom he does interact stay anonymous, simply "you." And the reality of these beings, especially the women, remains very much in doubt. They are for the most part wispy figures, unlike the other cast of characters prominent in these sonnets: Bengal's fairy-tale, folk-tale, historical and mytho-historical figures.

Through the sonnet relating their tale, Chand from Champa and Behula establish a continuity of experience, for back then they had seen Bengal's beauty just as the poet sees it now. Chand enjoyed the sights of beautiful Bengal when he sailed her rivers out to the Bay of Bengal on his trading voyages. Behula, the epitome of virtue and fidelity, gazed upon Bengal's natural beauty, as she floated downstream with her dead husband.

Manasa Mangal allusions inform a second sonnet in the *Bengal the Beautiful* collection:

> Ah birds, were you not there at Kalidaha once? Through whirlpool winds

> Did you not squawk your high-pitched calls that midday in July,
> In this Bengal? All day today amongst this rumbling rain storm and
> Cloudy overcast, Chand Sadagar and Honeybee, his dinghy, come to mind.
> When was it that they sank at Kalidaha, under just such stormy skies?
> Did not then too countless birds glide and dive across such blackened winds?
> Today all day a flock of river gulls, out in these monsoon rains and
> Gathered on a sand bar in the Dhaleswari, appear as if afloat at Kalidaha.
>
> This flock of birds appears to be not of this day and age at all.
> And this river, the Dhaleswari—this sky, as though not of today at all.
> Does Manasa reside within the cobra-hooded cactus grove? She does indeed.
> Is not this river Kalidaha? Ah, there at that ghat did I not glimpse
> The face of Sanaka, bun undone, hair flowing loose? How sad and pale and
> Worn-out is all truth. This dream of yours is true, said Manasa herself.[19]

The mythical Kalidaha takes its place in Bengal's *mangal-kavya* tradition as a site on a river or in the ocean where the goddess either makes an appearance or causes destruction.[20] In the *Manasa Mangal,* merchant Chand's seven ships are sunk there.

Several other sonnets contain references to both the *Manasa Mangal* and the *Chandi Mangal.*

> ... in this sweet world of Behula and Lahana
> I gave my heart to the path that's covered with dust of their feet (p. 19)

> ... I saw the black crow
> Covered green jungle of betel-nut palms—Srimanta, too, had seen such (p. 37)

> ... there the grove of *jam,* lichee, jackfruit,
> Touched by the feet of Dhanapati, Srimanta, Behula, Lahana (p. 39)

> ... —torn bits of wet straw
> Seem to lie soft on fields, as Sanaka had held to her breast (p. 48)

Sanaka, the wife of Chand Sadagar; Lahana, the elder wife, and Srimanta, son of Dhanapati, are featured in the *Chandi Mangal.*

Jibanananda also refers to historical and mytho-historical figures: Ballal Sen, a king of ancient Bengal; Rajaballabh, whose glory was destroyed by the Kirtinasa river; Arjuna, from the *Mahabharata* epic; the Buddha and Confucius; the renowned medieval Bengali poets Mukundaram,

Chandidas, Ramprasad, and Rayagunakar (Bharat Chandra Ray); and the man in whose memory Jibanananda had written one of his first poems, "Deshabandhu" Chitta Ranjan Das. Absent, or nearly so, from this collection of poetry is an actual, living person, for Jibanananda's Bengal emphatically does not consist of real human society, only static human life. Humans—maidens with reddened feet, a child scattering puffed rice, the young boatman—form a *tableau vivant,* functioning as elements of the natural surroundings as do rivers and trees.

Throughout his life, Jibanananda shunned contact with all but a very few people. Death provides one way of insulating oneself from other humans, and death pervades his poetry. But the sonnets alone express more than an obsession with death. In one, the poet will return by transmigrating into Bengal's flora and fauna, avoiding humankind altogether. In another, he will leave the physical environment only if taken away by death. And therein lies the dilemma, setting up a tension between the exuberant, positive emotions toward Bengal and the allurements of death. The collection, consisting of more than mere nature poetry, is a clear statement of Jibanananda's version of the existential quandary.

> Your child will one day quit your bosom, turning from
> Bengal's breast to go away. At which time the stars will fall,
> Slipping from the sky's soft blue bosom, sinking into
> Cold. Everywhere gorgeous paddy one day will have fallen in the
> Fog. Perhaps the night owl will sing its song in darkness,
> Will snatch me up like a field mouse into death's house,
> The smell of chaff sticking to my desiring heart, yet in my eyes
> Blue death, sleepless, a bent moon, an empty field, the scent of dew.
>
> Who after all knows when death is coming—when that storm in
>   Kalidaha
> Will snap the lotus stalk, pluck the life out of the gull, a hornbill?
> I do not know. Yet may I die within these fields and ghats,
> Not by the black Yamuna. May the fragrance of these river waves
> Cling to my eyes, mouth. May my Bengal the beautiful stay awake
>   upon
> My breast. And may I remain lying beneath her like Ardhanariswara.[21]

Kalidaha here provides a folkloristic allusion to death. The "black Yamuna" whose waters appear much darker than the Ganges when those two mighty rivers converge at Allahabad, flows beside Delhi, that city where Jibanananda had taught for several months. To live in Delhi, away from Bengal, would be insufferable. But Jibanananda speaks not of living but of dying, preferring to die in Bengal than in Delhi. Physical Bengal will stay with him even after death, so he hopes, as he desires to become the half male (himself) and half female (Bengal) Ardhanariswara, a form of god

Shiva whose left "half" (*ardha*) is "woman" (*nari*) and right half is the "male god" (*iswara*). This same Shiva, in Hindu iconography, lies supine as a corpse, while upon his chest stands goddess Kali. Ramprasad, that poet who often sang of himself as the child of the neglectful goddess-mother, resonates throughout this sonnet. Here, too, Jibanananda assumes the role of the child. But whereas Ramprasad deemed the world an illusion to be transcended, an inhibition of his perception of truth, Jibanananda considers the physical world, in particular Bengal, as the only reality. To leave his home would be catastrophic: the world itself would end, the stars fall. But he must die, as must everyone. So he wishes to die in Bengal, to become physically a part of her—as the deity Ardhanariswara is one body comprised of two halves—and to have her rest upon his bosom, as Kali stands astride her recumbent mate.

In other poems, Jibanananda gives death more immediacy with mention of the funeral pyre and cremation ground:

> As long as I might live I yearn to see the sky, gone elsewhere
> Into skies as blue as *aparajita* vines—bluer still.
> I want to watch the dawn's own herons, kingfishers swooping high
> Wringing with their wings the sky, going somewhere during
> The month of September. I wish to sit upon the grass of Bengal,
> For I've roamed the world and borne in heart the age's sorrows.
> I'll drift with the Dhansiri's flow toward Bengal's burning ground
> Where Ramprasad's wild-haired Syama still comes today,
>
> Where some lovely lady's body, embroidery-bordered sari clad,
> Rides a funeral pyre of sandalwood—a parrot on a mango branch
> Forgets to speak; where resides the greatest beauty—melancholy;
> Where the lotus withers; where for long Bisalaksi has not spoken;
> Where one day Sankhamala's, Chandramala's, Manikmala's
> Bangles used to jingle—ah, will they ever jingle once again![22]

Ramprasad sang worshipfully to his mother Kali or Syama or Tara. As Kali she assumes her terrible or destructive aspect. As Bisalaksi or Durga, she presides over prosperity, victory, and mankind's fortune. Though Durga, she has failed: she has not brought back that good fortune of old symbolized by the jingling bangles on childhood's fairy-tale princesses. Although the poet takes consolation from physical Bengal, the fact of death persists, residing in the burning ground alongside life's greatest beauty—melancholy. The beautiful woman had been yet within the mainstream of life, for she wears a married woman's decorated sari instead of Hindu widow's weeds, a plain white dhoti. The grief-stricken parrot, normally a talkative bird, sits speechless. Since the parrot (*suka-sari*) symbolizes love in Indian mythology (the parrot serves as vehicle to Kama, the Hindu god of love), a parallel between a female parrot and the lovely lady can be inferred, as the lone male parrot upon the tree limb empathizes with the husband of this dead woman who rides the sandalwood pyre.

The funeral pyre appears in a number of these sonnets:

> ... she will watch and see who came when to build
> The pyre out of mango wood (p. 14)

> ... when was it her bones fell upon the funeral pyre?
> When was it (p. 21)

> ... when I awake again, I see my funeral pyre filled with
> The grass of Bengal (p. 23)

> When did the heart's day of love end—only its pyre lies
> There (p. 64)

In fact, cremation grounds comprised Bengal: "You came to the land of cremation grounds—" (p. 43).

His own death, toward which he will "drift with the Dhansiri," Jibanananda transforms into a pleasant, nonthreatening sleep:

> I shall fall fast asleep one day within your starlit night.
> Perhaps even then youth will linger in my heart—my young days
> Still will not have ended. Good. Sleep comes—grass of Bengal
> Underneath my breast, eyes closed. On the mango leaves of Bengal
> The green beetles asleep, and I too lie sleeping with them:
> I'll sleep on content in this field—this grass—speechless,
> The tales of my heart slowly wiped away. There'll be many fresh
> New celebrations of life's sweet wounds, against the current
>
> In all your busy minds. Yet, young man, when with your fingernails
> You'll rip this grass up and go along, when Manikmala at dawn
> Comes by this path to pick red banyan flowers and sour *kamranga* fruit,
> When the yellow leaflets of the *sephali* blossoms fall upon the grass
> In some soft autumn, just how far the *salik,* the wagtails fly today,
> How strong the sunshine, clouds—I'll sense all as I lie in death's darkness.[23]

The tension eases, for the narrator, though dead, will continue to experience Bengal, the physical senses living on while he "sleeps."

Bengal the Beautiful has met generally with approval, certain readers considering it Jibanananda's most successful book. In 1971, during the Bangladesh liberation war, poems from this collection became viewed as expressions of the quintessential Bangladesh for which the Mukti Bahini ("freedom army") fought. Twice during the war's nine months, new editions of *Bengal the Beautiful* were published. Not just the general reading public but academe, likewise, has esteemed these sonnets. The University of Chittagong's anthology of Bengali poetry (selections made by that institution's Bengali Literature Committee for the Bengali curriculum) includes five poems by Jibanananda Das, three of them sonnets from *Bengal the Beautiful*. Those who praise these poems usually do so for their depiction of deltaic Bengal's lush landscape.

The book has not received unanimous acclaim, however. A serious criticism comes from Alok Sarkar, himself a poet and a publisher of some of Jibanananda's poetry:

> When the *Bengal the Beautiful* poems are placed side by side with poems such as "A Day Eight Years Ago" or "Sensation," we can understand how great an enemy to poetry are impure emotions, diluted poesy, and artistic flaccidity.[24]

No one would argue with Alok Sarkar on the merits of the two poems to which he refers. Likewise, one might concede that from a certain perspective Jibanananda exudes an almost overweening passion for Bengal's physical beauty, a rapture that nearly smothers the reader with a surfeit of rich images and motifs. However, if these sonnets are seen as pieces of a montage combining powerful emotions trying to come to terms with overpowering beauty, then the lyrics taken collectively assume an added dimension, becoming a visual history of a poet's unresolved struggle to cope with the unendurable: mortality in the face of astonishingly seductive life.

Jibanananda himself characterizes the relationship of the individual lyrics to the whole body of poetry.

> These are not each separate, independent entities but rather of one body in an all-encompassing sensation. Though retaining their individuality like the scattered dwellings of rural Bengal, they depend upon one another complementarily.[25]

It also seems reasonable to conclude that Jibanananda was working out and working over some of what he would use in his later poetry. Writes Sanjay Bhattacharya, Jibanananda's friend, supporter, and, for one volume, his publisher:

> Perhaps at that time he wished to build for himself an idol of faith in that lonely abode of his and, in fact, had gained peace. When I read his posthumously published (and thus not by his own volition) *Bengal the Beautiful* poetry, it strikes me that the seeds of the "moment's peace" from "Banalata Sen" are precisely within *Bengal the Beautiful*, ... [26]

The "moment's peace" Sanjay makes reference to is from the title poem,

"Banalata Sen," of Jibanananda's third book. ("I am a weary heart surrounded by life's frothy ocean. /To me she gave a moment's peace—Banalata Sen from Natore.") Sanjay argues that Jibanananda had lost faith in the real world, then regained a faith of sorts—in a fantasy land of his own construing, embodied in the *Bengal the Beautiful* and *Banalata Sen* volumes. Whether one accepts Sanjay's thesis, his insightful observation about the relationship of *Bengal the Beautiful* to *Banalata Sen* can be understood on two levels. First, the seeds of what Sanjay interprets as a renewed faith, brought to fruition in *Banalata Sen,* are contained in *Bengal the Beautiful.* Those "seeds" of the moment's peace that the poet obtained from Banalata Sen not only exist in *Bengal the Beautiful* but are, to extend Sanjay's point a bit, Bengal herself. Bengal gave the poet peace, as did Banalata Sen. And therefore physical, folklore Bengal becomes Banalata Sen.

Secondly, on a more mechanical level, what Sanjay calls seeds—present in *Bengal the Beautiful,* germinating in *Banalata Sen*—can be thought of as images, motifs, and particular words. The "paths of the world," almost a leitmotiv in *Bengal the Beautiful,* resounds in "Banalata Sen." Grass, the title of two poems, one of which was published in *Banalata Sen,* seems a ubiquitous element of *Bengal the Beautiful.* The owl, an earlier favorite with Jibanananda, would continue to be in his repertoire, as would the mouse and owl together. Sankhamala, the Dhansiri, a golden hawk, orange sunlight, and a naked hand all appear in *Bengal the Beautiful* and subsequent poetry, much of it in *Banalata Sen.* Many other correspondences exist between *Bengal the Beautiful* and later poems. Correspondences within the sonnets of this collection itself, moreover, suggest that the poems, to rephrase Jibanananda's own words quoted in Asokananda's introduction, taken as a composite, form a single verbal painting of rural Bengal.

Jibanananda had an interesting relationship with the Petrarchan sonnet, that paragon of the love lyric. As noted above, early in his career he composed his own romantic sonnet, in English and to nature. From a notebook which antedates by a few years that of the *Bengal the Beautiful* manuscripts, we find several more Bengali Petrarchan sonnets, none of them published in his lifetime. A short lyric, also unpublished, in a notebook dated 1931 may shed light on why this verse of somewhat conventional form remained in manuscript:

No matter how new the poetry I invent
You will all come forth and say: that age is gone, that was the fashion
   once.
There has been plenty of all that.
Thank goodness our imaginations tore through enchantment's snare.
Like myna birds our pens, pointed toward illusion's peak,
Have pierced the sky of blue.[27]

Although Jibanananda does not say what "new poetry" he feared would be considered passé, he might have been referring to his Petrarchan sonnets of the same period, particularly those in which he reveals his overwhelming love for Bengal.

Bengal the Beautiful may represent something he had to write, yet which he chose, for any number of reasons, not to publish—one of those reasons being the absence of a sympathetic publisher who would champion his verse. *Kallol* and like journals had long since ceased publication. *Kavita* did not appear until September 1935. In the interim of more than five years, Jibanananda published but one poem and that in a magazine, *Paricay,* whose editorial board did not appreciate his sort of poetry.

3

Paricay, one of Bengal's most sophisticated literary and intellectual journals, began as a quarterly in July 1931. Sudhindranth Datta, its founder, edited the periodical for the first seven years and then jointly edited it with Hiran Kumar Sanyal. Following the issue of June 1943, Sudhindranath relinquished control of his magazine altogether. Subsequently, *Paricay* became the mouthpiece for Leftist writers and critics. Contributors during those initial years make up an impressive list of some of the leading Bengali intellectuals in all fields, from physical science (in the person of Satyendranath Bose) to political science (with Susobhan Sarkar writing on the Russian Revolution) to poetry discussed by editor Sudhindranath himself and Rabindranath Tagore, among others. Articles on religion, philosophy, music, and ancient history found their way into *Paricay,* as well as reviews of European, Russian, American, even Chinese literary works, some but not all of that literature being in English translation. The scope of this magazine was truly impressive. Bishnu Dey and Buddhadeva Bose, along with nearly all the prominent modern poets of the day, contributed.

The advent of *Paricay* caused considerable excitement among the literary set. Buddhadeva received his copy during the period of his M.A. examinations and could hardly wait to finish his exam that day so he might see what the first issue held in store.[28] Jibanananda expressed his excitement about *Paricay,* as seen in his letter to Bishnu Dey. Part of this enthusiasm, no doubt, was due to the dearth in Bengal of magazines progressive enough to be acceptable to former *Kallol* writers.

The initial number carried Sudhindranath's manifesto on the nature of poetry, "The Emancipation of Poetry" (*kabyer mukti*), by some accounts prologue for the drama of modern Bengali poetry to be played out during the coming decade.[29] In that essay, Sudhindranath spoke of the poet as verbalizing mankind's thoughts rather than expressing his own ideas. Of poetic language, a point of contention during the 1920s: "... the modern poet, at times and because of association of ideas, extends equal treatment to all words, refined or not, old or new, indigenous or foreign." And as for the grumblings over growing complexity, convolution, and obscurity in modern verse: "... there are two sides to this difficulty: the reader's and the poet's. It is unjust to blame the poet for incomprehensibility which has its origin in the reader's indolence."[30] Though some of Sudhindranath's statement may sound like an apologia for Jibanananda, such was not the case. These two men approached poetry quite differently.

Paricay's third issue, January 1932, carried Jibanananda's controversial poem, "In Camp." Bishnu Dey had personally solicited a contribution from Jibanananda, yet once the poem arrived, it proved somewhat of an enigma to the *Paricay* staff. The term *ghai,* as in *ghai harini* (the latter word meaning "doe"), was particularly bothersome.[31] From context, the term appears intelligible, but none knew what the word actually meant. Contextually, *ghai* seems to suggest estrous, such connotation of sexual excitement making the poem rather controversial. The word's denotation continues to be imperfectly understood to this day. An Assamese word, *ghai* glosses as "a bird used as a decoy to ensnare other birds" or "a full-grown male bird; a decoy bird." And, the verb *ghai pat-* is rendered as "to attract wild birds to a snare through a decoy bird." Jibanananda transferred the decoy definition from the male bird to a female deer. There seems to be no doubt that sexuality constitutes this decoy's lure. Like a doe in heat to stags, Jibanananda's poetry has proved irresistibly alluring to readers. But like the very expression *ghai harini* itself, that same poetry at times bemuses those readers.

The poem received a mixed reception at best from the *Paricay* personnel. Sudhindranath wanted not to print it at all.[32] The near total absence of Jibanananda's poetry from the first seven years of *Paricay* indicates Sudhindranath's opinion of his fellow poet's work. Hayat Mamud cites a statement by Asok Mitra that Jibanananda was never really accepted by the various aristocratic literary circles (i.e., Sudhindranath, among others). In a footnote Hayat Mamud writes: "Incidentally, we have heard that Sudhindranath did not acknowledge Jibanananda as a poet; even after Jibanananda's demise, Sudhindranath remained silent about him."[33] True, but little more than a week after Jibanananda's death, Sudhindranath explained that silence in a letter to Sanjay Bhattacharya:

> #6 Suite
> 6, Russel Street
> Cal. 16

[salutations]
I've been suffering from a fever and congestion the last two weeks.

That's why I was unable to attend Jibanananda's *sraddha* ceremony yesterday. For the very same reason I've been tardy in answering your letter.

My mind has gone utterly blank—for many a day now—I have absolutely no time, because of the pressures of trifling, yet income-earning tasks. If I were to sit down to write something on Jibanananda in this condition, it would be showing him disrespect. Therefore you must excuse me.

I trust you are well. Please come by one day. 1 November, 1954.

Yours,
Sudhindranath Datta[34]

Though Sudhindranath may not have attended the *sraddha,* he was anything but unmindful of Jibanananda, for he visited him in the hospital the two days before Jibanananda died.[35] Still, his critical views remained. Following Jibanananda's death, Buddhadeva Bose brought out a special Jibanananda memorial issue of *Kavita* in which was included a photograph of the manuscipt, replete with emendations, for a poem posthumously entitled "She" (*se*). Sudhindranath, noting the many revisons, said words to the effect of "why such effort for so little?"[36] His main criticism of Jibanananda's poetry seems to have been that it literally lacked integrity, that it was not an integrated whole. Some of Jibanananda's poems do appear to ramble desultorily, for Sudhindranath, an anathema.[37]

Not only in poetry but in life style, Jibanananda and Sudhindranath could hardly have been further apart. The latter epitomized the cosmopolitan gentleman. He wore slacks and a shirt, sometimes coat and tie. Alcoholic beverages were served in his home. His spoken language was English.[38] He had traveled widely, first in 1929 accompanying Rabindranath to Japan and America and later that year through Europe on his own. He even taught for a while at the University of Chicago. Sudhindranath's poetry is scholarly, cerebral, Sanskritic. He by no means spurned his mother tongue, which in fact he did much to refurbish, but his use of it is akin to that of a philologist's, uncovering buried meanings inside linguistic relics now encrusted with modern connotations. Jibanananda was almost antischolastic in his idiosyncratic use of Bengali.

As stated above, Sudhindranath would have rejected Jibanananda's "In Camp." Bishnu Dey argued, however, that he personally had requested a contribution from Jibanananda for publication in *Paricay* and therefore the magazine perforce must publish it, which *Paricay* did, January 1932.

IN CAMP

Here on the edge of the forest I pitched camp.
All night long in pleasant southern breezes

Back to Barisal

By the moon's light
I listen to the call of a doe in heat.
To whom is she calling?

Somewhere the deer are hunted tonight.
Hunters entered the forest today.
I too seem to catch their scent,
As I lie here upon my bed
Not drowsy at all
In this spring night.

Forest wonder everywhere,
An April breeze,
Like the taste of moonlight.
A doe in heat calls all night long.
Somewhere deep in the forest—beyond the reach of moonbeams—
All stags hear her sounds.
They sense her presence,
Come toward her.
Now, in this night of wonder
Their time for love arrives.
That sister of their hearts
In moonlight calls them from forest cover—
To quench their thirst—to smell—to savor!
As if this night's forest were free of tigers!
No clear fear fills those stags' breasts tonight,
Not even the shadow of uncertainty.
There is only thirst,
Excitement.
Perhaps wonder wakes in the cheetah's breast as well at the beauty of
    that doe's face.
Lust-longing-love-desire-dreams burst forth
In this springtide night.
Here is my nocturne.

One by one deer come from the wooded deep,
Leaving behind all water's sounds in search of another assurance.
Forgetting tooth and claw, they approach their sister there
Beneath the *sundari,* bathed in moonlight.
As man draws near his salty woman, lured by scent, so come those
    deer.
I sense them—
The sound of their many hooves.
In moonlight calls that doe in heat.
I can no longer sleep.
As I lie here
I hear gunshots.
Again I hear the sounding guns.
The doe in heat calls once more in the light of the moon.
As I lie fallen here alone
A weariness wells within my heart

While I listen to the sound of guns
And hear that doe's call.

Tomorrow she will return.
In the morning, by daylight, she can be seen.
Nearby lie her dead lovers.
Men have taught her all this.

I shall smell venison upon my dinner dish.
... Has not the eating of flesh ceased?
... But why should it?
Why must I be pained to think of these deer—
Am I not like them?
On some spring night
On one of life's wondrous nights
Did not someone come into the moonlight, call me too, in the pleasant southern breezes
Like that doe in heat?
My heart, a stag,
Forgetting the violence of this world,
All caution cast to the winds—all fear of the cheetah's eyes—
Had not it yearned to possess you?
When, like those dead deer, the love in my heart
Lay caked with blood and dust,
Did not you, like this doe, live on
Through life's wondrous night
One spring night?
You too had learned from someone!
And we lie here, our flesh like that of dead animals.
All come, then fall in the face of separation—separation and death—
Like those slain deer.
By living-loving-longing for love, we are hurt, we hate and die,
Do we not?

I hear the report of a double-barreled gun.
That doe in heat calls on.
No sleep comes to this heart of mine
As I lie here, alone.
Yet one must silently forget the thunder of those guns.
Night speaks of other things upon camp beds.
They by whose barrels deer perished tonight,
Who relished flesh and bone of deer upon their dinner plates,
They too are like you.
Their hearts too wither there in sleeping bags.
Thinking—just thinking.

This pain, this love resides everywhere,
In the locust, the worm, in the breast of man,

In the lives of us all.
Like those slain deer in spring's moonlight
Are we all.[39]

As far as anyone knows, Jibanananda never in his life went on a hunting trip. In one other poem about deer hunting ("The Hunt" [*sikar*]) does he express his disapprobation of the hunter. The specificity of the term *ghai*, if it is indeed an Assamese word meaning a live bird used as a decoy, implies that Jibanananda had some contact with persons who spoke Assamese or with hunters or both. According to his brother, at no time did Jibanananda travel to Assam. He did, however, make the acquaintance of a hunter by the name of Muniruddin, whose other occupation was that of local Barisal brick mason. Asokananda described the man:

> He had a tall, muscular body, chest of steel. When Muniruddin, wearing boots and a black coat, gun in hand, would set off with his brother for the Lakhutiya or Kasipur jungles with that heroic brazen air, at those times he cut a very different figure. At such moments we didn't have the courage to go up to him. We used to stand staring in his direction from afar—out of respect mixed with fear. When he was doing his masonry work, during a break when he was in a good mood, we would hear all sorts of hunting stories from him. My elder brother collected a lot of minutely detailed facts from him about hunting.[40]

And their grandmother, Prasanna Kumari Das, used to tell the boys stories of the hunting exploits of their uncle, a deputy conservator of forests. Their Barisal home even had the uncle's trophies of antlers, wild water buffalo horns, and a tiger's head hanging on the wall.[41]

Of course "In Camp" is not about deer hunting at all but about people, the narrator in particular, and human relationships. The poem suggests that there may have been a woman in Jibanananda's life, a lover who spurned him. (He will rarefy her to "Creation" or life itself, in his own note on the poem.) Corroborating biographical information does not exist: In the opinion of his close relatives and friends, he never had anything even remotely resembling an affair, before or after marriage. Nonetheless, many other poems seem to refer to a relationship with a woman, several addressing a woman by name.

The fact that the relationship may not have been real does not invalidate the emotions expressed. Jibanananda employs a somewhat complicated paradigm of lured, lure, and hunter to declare those feelings. A decoy doe in heat calls out to the forest stags, not to satisfy her own urges but to entice those deer within range of the hunters' guns. She solicits for a destructive force, so strong her appeal that the deer lose all fear of their natural predators. Then the guns sound, and the deer fall prey to the hunters.

The poem's narrator passively and fairly distantly audits this event, extrapolating from what he hears, filling in details from his general knowledge of the area and possible circumstances. Though he has, presumably, come with the hunting party, he lies on his camp cot when the actual hunting and killing happen. Unclear as to how closely he associates with the hunters, initially he states, "I pitched camp," and then, "I seemed to catch their [the hunters'] scent." But later he partakes of the venison dinner along with the hunters. Blame for both the actual killing and the art of deception falls squarely upon the men's shoulders. They have taught the doe to lure, to be insensitive to her fellow deer, although the smells and the state of being in heat are natural phenomena and thus not under her or their control.

The narrator then sets up a paradigm for those that destroy or aid in the destruction of their fellow beings: Hunters represent corruptive human society, which teaches others cruelty for society's gain; the doe, the natural object of love; and stags, those who are hurt by human society. The narrator then inserts himself into that paradigm. Am I also not like them—my heart, a stag, which died one night, while "you," the alluring doe, survived to entice again? Did someone teach you to do what you do?—for it cannot be natural. Then toward the end of the poem, he conflates the paradigm by equating "you" with the hunters. Now there are two equivalents for the "you"—she both solicits for others and kills on her own. And we—mankind—fall prey to her destructive powers and to the human society manipulating her. The reader never knows the identity of "you," or exactly what she did. From Jibanananda's perspective, she betrayed his love. Enticed by her, he should have been wary of the violence in her world. But love makes him vulnerable to life's cruelties. A sadder but wiser and less trusting man, the narrator observes in the last stanza that love means pain and that all who love, be they worm or man, become victims. This doe in heat—guileless and yet guilty—continued to be one of Jibanananda's most powerful metaphors for existence: Bengal, life itself, lured, while men, society, human relationships in general remained deadly dangerous.

Sajani Kanta Das, through his *Sanibarer Cithi,* which had resumed publication in September of 1931, heaped ridicule and scorn on this latest of Jibanananda's poetic efforts.

> It is quite touching that the poet, through the medium of poetry, has uttered the personal feeling of a doe in heat separated from her lovers and also the innermost thoughts of her "heart"-brothers.
>
> The reader, perchance, does not understand what a "heart"-brother is. The poet has said that a "sister of their hearts" is calling to all the brother deer of the forest "to quench their thirst—to smell—to savor!" We know of paternal and maternal cousin-brothers and cousin-sisters. This is the first time we have met a "heart"-sister. . . .

Perhaps wonder wakes in the cheetah's breast as well at the beauty of that doe's face.
Lust-longing-love-desire-dreams burst forth
In this springtide night.
Here is my nocturne—.

And finally I realized why the poem is called "In Camp"! With that dash placed after the word "nocturne," the poet has suppressed the juicy account of his nocturnal secrets and has left us unsatisfied. ...

But let me digress for a moment. We realize many people blame *Sanibarer Cithi* for being obscene and say that by quoting obscene passages, we increase the respect for such writing and also its circulation. We request these people to keep the following in mind.

Paricay is a quarterly of "high-class" cultural entertainment. Rabindranath gave it his affectionate blessings, and Hirendranath Datta contributes to it. *Paricay* has acquainted us more than once with what sort of repugnant obscenity a publication, with which individuals of the stature of Rabindranath and Hirendranath are associated, can and does proffer. The poem "In Camp" is just an extreme example of this. And therefore—under whose tutelage does the circulation and respect for this class of writer increase? Let the common reader be the judge of that.[42]

In a rare moment of self-exegesis, Jibanananda defended "In Camp" against Sajani Kanta's accusations of obscenity. This rebuttal, which never appeared in print during his lifetime, gives us an inkling of not only what he is trying to say through this particular lyric but also both how his background in English literature informs at least one of his poems as well as how he saw himself in the world of contemporary Bengali poetry.

A couple of words, it seems to me, need be said about my poem "In Camp." After I had completed the piece, I felt I had written it in simple, straightforward language, no doubt, but still then, perhaps, some might fail to comprehend the poem. In actuality, the sense of this lyric has proved so utterly elusive to many that they in turn have, without fear of contradiction, labeled it obscene.

"In Camp" is not obscene, to be sure. If there is one constant, unwavering melody which pervades this composition, it is the melody of life's helplessness—for all life, that of man, of worm, of locust. In Creation's hand we all are absolutely helpless—it is this which "In Camp" hints at, and this alone. The poem's melody—that violence results, boundaries blur twixt hunter and hunted, slaughter and solicitation—the world is not so much bothered by such behavior as it is saddened—saddened and made to feel vulnerable. In the poem "In Camp," the narrator feels it is not just the vulgar deer hunters who glorify luring then killing, it is as though Creation herself were just such a hunter and the lives of us all were her prey. As though everywhere proceeds apace the never ending readying of love-life-dream's annihilation—just such a readying as in *King Lear*: "As flies to wanton boys are we to the gods; They kill us for their sport."

In Bengali literature, at least in poetry, the particular melody—that of unmitigated, merciless vulnerability ("Like those slain deer in spring's moonlight/Are we all.")—whether such a melody has been heard before, I cannot say. But it can be said without hesitation that present-day Bengali writers and the reading public are at most only slightly acquainted with this melody. Granted, people can be offended by that with which they are unacquainted, that which jars the familiar mode and manner of thinking. Be that as it may, the poem "In Camp" is least of all guilty of a charge of obscenity. One might surmise the sort of critical comments that would result were this lyric to be translated into English, German, or French and recited in foreign literary circles: there would ensue an analysis of that specific melody of "In Camp" about which I have just spoken. Except for those one or two of prurient minds—they possess the unlimited ability to tease out from within this poem what their appetite requires. This is their one and only ability, however. Measured against their standard of prurience, "In Camp" is indeed obscene—but, for them, the stars in the sky would be considered immodest when they come out at night. Shelley's "soul's sister" is, to the Western poet, critic, and general reader, an endearing expression. But "sister of the heart" (I am indebted to Shelley for my locution)—only they who are most prurient would read into these few words prurience and nothing more. About Muteykeh (a mare), Browning has said, "She was the child of his heart by day, the wife of his breast by night." Who knows what folks would say about Browning!

In Bengal there are many trees and plants besides the *sajne*. The lowly *sajne* may be unaware of the *sundari,* which covers the vast Sundarban jungle—likewise, prurience remains forever far removed from and completely unknown to the soul of the true literary critic.[43]

Not all of Bengal's poets in this year of 1932 remain mired in the naïveté of sophomoric literary battles. But alas, if such could only have been the case! How pleasant life would have been, luxuriating in the exquisite joy of mindlessness, afoot the easily accessed, easily traveled pathway—packing plain and simple notions.[44]

4

After "In Camp," Jibanananda did not publish another poem until Buddhadeva Bose and Premendra Mitra, along with Samar Sen, began to edit this century's preeminent Bengali poetry journal. *Kavita* concerned itself exclusively with Bengali poetry and criticism of poetry—or, as Buddhadeva himself put it, devoted itself to poets:

... *Kavita* had begun not as a poetry magazine but as a poets' magazine. In other words, it was not exactly our aim that in every issue some poetry—even some good poetry would be printed; we wanted to encompass all the contemporary streams of genuine poetry. A most fortuitous coincidence aided us. All the poets of the thirties who had introduced a new vision and a new melody, whose activities without a doubt constitute the first significant event in Bengali poetry since Rabindranath—the start of their journey and ours, as publisher, coincided.[45]

With the advent of the quarterly *Kavita* in September 1935, Jibanananda began to publish again, ten poems in the first year alone. Only associate editor Samar Sen had more poems (16) published during that first year. Buddhadeva Bose, with ten, matched Jibanananda's output. During the following year, the number of poems contributed by Jibanananda (13) exceeded that of all other contributors, and such was the case for the third year when his contributions numbered ten. He also published an essay that year entitled "On Poetry" (*kabitar katha*) and a review of one of Buddhadeva's books (*Kankabati* [*kankabati*]). Jibanananda had obviously found once again an appreciative editorial staff. The first issue of *Kavita* carried his "Before Death" (*mrityur age*):

BEFORE DEATH

We who have walked deserted stubble fields on a December evening,
Who have seen over the field's edge a soft river woman scattering
Her fog flowers—they all are like some village girls of old—
We who have seen in darkness the *akanda* tree, the *dhundul* plant
Filled with fireflies, the moon standing quietly at the head of
An already harvested field—she has no yearning for that harvest;

We who have lived in the darkness of a long winter's night, who have
Heard wings flutter on a thatched roof in captivating night—
The smell of an ancient owl, now lost again in the darkness!
Who have understood the beauty of a winter's night—wings buoyed up
 over
Fields brimming with deep joy, herons calling from *aswattha* tree
 limbs;
We who have understood all this secret magic of life;

We who have seen wild geese escape injury from a hunter's bullet
And fly away into the horizon's gentle blue moonlight;
We who have placed a loving hand upon the sheaves of paddy;
Like the evening crows, we who returned home full of desire;
Smell of a baby's breath, grass, sunlight, a kingfisher, stars, sky—
We who were aware of these as we came and went throughout the year;

Who have seen green leaves turn yellow in the November darkness,
Light and *bulabuli* birds frolicking in the windows of a cashew tree,
A mouse rubbing chaff over his silklike fur on a wintry night,
Waves forming in gray odors of rice and pouring down twice daily
Upon eyes of lonely fish, a duck in evening's darkness on the bank of
 a pond

Catching scent of sleep—the touch of a womanly hand carries him off,

A golden hawk calling from the window of a minaretlike cloud,
Beneath a wicker vine a sparrow's eggs appearing so hard,
A river ever smearing its banks with fragrance of soft water,
Roof thatching casting shadows in deep night upon a moonlit courtyard,
Smell of crickets in the green wind of April's outlying fields,
Thick juice oozing with heavy desire into bluish custard apples' breasts;

We who have seen the red fruit fallen beneath the thick banyan,
The crowds of deserted fields seeing their faces in the river,
However blue the skies, yet finding one that is even bluer;
Who upon the paths have seen soft eyes casting their glow on the earth;
We who have seen evening each day flow over rows of betel nut trees,
The dawn appear every day simple and green like a sheaf of paddy;

We who have understood after many a day, month, season gone by
That daughter of the earth who came near and in the darkness spoke of
Rivers; we who have understood there is another light within
The fields, ghats, paths: its afternoon grayness is in our bodies—
As we let go our seeing hands, that light remains constant:
Kankabati of the earth floats there and attains a body of pale incense.

Before death what more do we wish to understand? Do I not know that
The face of gray death awakes like a wall at the head of all prostrate
Reddened desires. Once there was a dream in this world—there was gold
That attained silent peace, as though by some magician's need.
What more do we wish to understand? Haven't we heard the call of wings
As the sun faded? Haven't we seen the crow fly off into fields of fog![46]

Except for the final two stanzas, this poem is a fairly straightforward evocation of life's natural beauty. It represents a poet's vision, to be sure, for only a poet has that "autonomous substance of imagination"—a phrase from Jibanananda's essay "On Poetry"—which allows him to see "over the field's edge a soft river woman scattering/Her flowers of fog; ..." For "All are not poets," he wrote, "some are. And they who are, are so because in their hearts there is the autonomous substance of imagination, ... "[47] The "we" who have loved, seen, and understood are poets. Only a poet sees "A golden hawk calling from the window of a minaretlike cloud." Only a poet understands "all this secret magic of life."

Kavita's April 1938 issue was a special number devoted to criticism and the theory of poetry. Buddhadeva solicited a contribution from Jibanananda, who obliged him with "On Poetry," wherein Jibanananda defines what makes certain people poets instead of poetasters:

All are not poets, some are. And they who are, are so because in their hearts there is the autonomous substance of imagination, and within imagination, thought and experience, and because behind them are the past centuries to help them, and with them the new poetic radiation of the modern world. But this help is available not to all, but only to those who have imagination and the essence of experience and thought within imagination. It is these persons who fall into the mood of creating poetry by encountering the complexities of this world. ... I for one cannot understand those who maintain that poetry has to be created consciously, by someone who has been fully initiated into the entire poetic tradition of his own country and the rest of the world.[48] ... in the rough and tumble of this disjointed world of man there comes a time when even the most humble conscious supplications seem to cease. Then it is as if in the silence and darkness of a little world the heart begins to glow like a candle and slowly the genius and faith of poetic creation becomes [sic] manifest. The moment this wonderful experience abandons our hearts, poetry ceases to be born—written, instead, is verse. Verse—which contains moral and social teaching, various mental gymnastics, and an abundance of doctrines to prick the reader's mind before anything else and most of all. Yet the influence of such verse is ephemeral; the reader gets no delight from it, but only feels a satisfaction of a lower order, seeking in vain for the glow of the body of poetry.[49]

Jibanananda obviously believed deeply in the "autonomous substance of imagination." Later that same year a young poet from Dhaka, Kiran Sankar Sengupta, wrote requesting an introduction to *Dream-Desire* (*swapna-kamana*), his first book of poetry. In Jibanananda's only book introduction (the book came out in December 1938), he speaks once again of imagination as being an essential element in the creation of true poetry:

We often receive polished poetry from the young writers. But this particular poem [one of the poems in this book] should give us confidence in Kiran Sankar because it is one of his comparatively modern compositions and not merely a clever piece. Many people can sense sincere emotion. However, it seems to me that others besides me will perceive the near-complete realization in this poem of the transformation of it [the sincere emotion] by the autonomous substance of experience and thought within imagination which is itself from within the heart.[50]

Life's natural beauty, as the narrator sees in "Before Death," comes primarily from the late autumn or winter months when days are dark longer than they are light, when the fields have been harvested. This season in no way symbolizes morbidity for him—quite the contrary. He seems to relish the darkness, the fog, and the solitude of such times. Here again from his essay:

Poetry and life are two different outpourings of the same thing; life as we usually conceive it contains what we normally accept as reality, but the spectacle of this incoherent and disorderly life can satisfy neither the poet's talent nor the reader's imagination. It is the creation of poetry that appeases the poet's conscience, brings tranquillity to his intellect, and satisfies the reader's imagination. And yet poetry does not contain a complete reconstruction of what we call reality; we have entered a new world. If we should imagine a new water in place of all the waters of the earth, a new lamp in place of all its lamps, then it may be possible to discard all days and nights and human beings and desires, all the dust and stars and skeletons of creation, and conjure a new usable order that would be poetry, existing by virtue of a secret relationship with life, a new and gray-hued relationship maintained through subterranean tunnels.[51]

The "grayness" in poets' bodies (see "Before Death"), then, represents that "new and gray-hued relationship," a relationship between poetry and life—neither white nor black but something in between, not shiny bright and new, but new nevertheless, both old and new at the same time. This is certainly a poet's perception of something more than the mere physical, analyzable components of reality. He sees a larger whole, a "new usable order that would be poetry," bearing that constant gray hue in all things: fields, ghats, paths. That afternoon glow does not depend solely on human sensory perception, for the sensorially perceived world of "incoherent and disorderly life" satisfies no one. We all, presumably, can perceive that which "we normally accept as reality." But the poet sees more. At a point in this perception, he can let go with his "seeing hands," his sensuous intuition, and proceed to that realm away from "all the waters of the earth," away from "all the lamps." There the experiences of the moment become timeless, transcending the physical earth. Folk-tale character Kankabati, if not his Muse—which I think she is—certainly symbolizes the genuine poetic insight that though a "daughter of the earth" and "bound to dwelling in time and earth" is yet transcendent and eternal.[52]

If before death we, the poets, have perceived this secret, subterranean relationship between life and poetry, if we have truly perceived, then what more is there to understand? That perception is an end in itself. That relationship needs no "human beings and desires." It needs no mundane world. And so death becomes acceptable. In the seventh stanza of "Before Death," the narrator speaks of poetic perception. In the eighth, he is prepared for death, for he has seen the world through a poet's eyes. Here, as in so much of his early writings, we see beautiful nature juxtaposed with Jibanananda's struggle to come to terms with death.

Editors frequently sent copies of their magazines to Rabindranath Tagore. Individual poets, too, often submitted their work to him for favor of comment. (Jibanananda himself had done just that, once before he had become a published poet and again after *Fallen Feathers* appeared in print.)[53] Any statement from Rabindranath was highly prized by even the more rebellious poets, for he continued to be acknowledged as the guru of Bengali letters right up to his death in 1941. And so, according to the practice of the day, a copy of *Kavita* went to Rabindranath, who obliged Buddhadeva Bose with a reply in which apropos of "Before Death" he wrote, "Jibanananda Das's poem, full of pictorial beauty, delighted me."[54] Pictorial this poem certainly is, especially the first six stanzas.

5

The second year of *Kavita* began with a full-page ad announcing an October 1936 publication date (the book appeared in December) for Jibanananda's second work, *Gray Manuscripts,* and subsequent issues continued to herald the new book:

> All that poetry of Jibanananda's which was published during the initial stage of the modern literary movement in *Kallol* and other magazines and which aroused much praise and scorn is collected together in this book. Moreover, the comparatively recent poems, "In Camp," "Vultures" and from the first issue of *Kavita,* "Before Death," are also included. Altogether, one complete phase of development of this most alive and mature poet is to be found in *Gray Manuscripts.*[55]

Jibanananda was preoccupied in Barisal. Responsibility for guiding his work into print fell to Buddhadeva, who had left Dhaka and settled in Calcutta several years earlier. The name of D.M. Library, publishers and booksellers in Calcutta, appears on the title page of *Gray Manuscripts,* but in fact Jibanananda was officially the publisher, as he had been for his first book and would be for the succeeding one. Being publisher meant simply that he supplied the money. Manuscripts had to be readied for the printer, proof sheets corrected, cover designed (done by Anil Krishna Bhattacharya, who had designed covers for both *Pragati* and *Kavita*)—Buddhadeva took care of all these arrangements. And Jibanananda dedicated *Gray Manuscripts* to Buddhadeva, who had done and would continue to do so much to introduce him to the Bengali reading public.

Most of the seventeen poems in this volume, as the ad indicated, had appeared in print prior to 1930—eleven in *Pragati,* two in a journal called *Dhupchaya* ("Chiaroscuro"), and one in *Kallol*. Jibanananda in his introduction notes that he wrote all seventeen poems between 1925 and 1930:

> Nine years later, my second book of poetry is being published. Its name, *Gray Manuscripts,* gives its own introduction. All the poems in this book were composed between 1332 [1925/26] and 1336 [1929/30].... Today those magazines are no more—*Pragati, Dhupchaya, Kallol*—nearly all

the poems in this book were published once in those magazines. I have many unpublished poems of that same period with me—and though their rights [to publication] are no less than many of the *Gray Manuscripts* poems—still then they remain with me today, becoming even grayer. Aswin, 1343[56]

From among those unpublished poems he chose one, "Vultures" (*sakun*), for the first edition of *Gray Manuscripts*. Not Petrarchan, this sonnet consists of four stanzas in Dantean terza rima with concluding couplet for a rhyme scheme of *aba bcb cdc ded ee,* something novel for Bengali poetry—though Pramatha Chaudhuri had written three-line rhyme-linked stanzas earlier, but not sonnets.[57] Shelley's "Ode to the West Wind," composed of five terza rima sonnetlike stanzas, was no doubt well known to Jibanananda, the English professor. One draft of "Vultures" can be found in a notebook dated Paus–Magh 1338 (1931–32) in which there are also Petrarchan sonnets, never published in his lifetime.

VULTURES

Vultures sail the whole afternoon from field to field through
Asia's skies. They've watched man—his markets, haunts, and hovels.
The still, outlying lands belong to them. There, where the field's harsh

Silence stands beside the sky, like another sky, the vultures
Alight together from hard clouds, as though, smoky-gray, the weary mythic
Elephants that guard the skies had fallen, leaving distant lights. All these

Forsaken birds descend to earth upon Asia's fields for a few moments only—
Then mount again their huge swart wings and fly to palm trees, horns of hills,
An ocean's shore. Gazing on the earth's beauty, they watch seafaring

Ships crowd the dark of Bombay's harbor, then glide away to soothing
Malabar, circle the sad corners of some minaret, those many vultures,
Oblivious to birds of this world, then drift as if to some far shore of death.

The Vaitarani river or some morose lagoon, divorced from life,
Weeps, stares to see when into deep blue fades that horde of Huns.[58]

The Vaitarani, like Greek mythology's river Styx, is that body of water in Hindu mythic lore that dead souls must cross. The primary connotation of Huns here is not that of ravishing hordes, although vultures do ravish carrion. These Huns—strangers to society, preferring the "still, outlying lands"—are travelers, traversing all of Asia. The Vaitarani or some lagoon, around which these birds of morbidity gather, separates life in this world from the realm of the dead. Vultures travel in both worlds, this one and that "far shore of death," whereas the "birds of the world," as well as men, cannot. In the initial stanza of a poem from this period, entitled "Vaitarani," we find:

> It was as if at sometime I'd come back from the grave,
> The Vaitarani gave me leave to go.
> And spreading vulture wings, black, I flew on toward this world.
> Seven days and seven nights I flew. If only there were light—
> Light of this earth, of love.
> The Vaitarani river gave me leave.[59]

Elsewhere in this lyric Jibanananda converses with vultures, sees his home again, thinks of being incarnated, and finally returns, a weary vulture, to the Vaitarani and the other side of reality. In "Vultures," he observes from this side only, that of the living.

In the second (1956) and all later editions of *Gray Manuscripts,* the poet's brother included fifteen additional poems, among them "Vaitarani." Asokananda explains:

> ... As I searched for all those "even grayer" poems, I found that many of them no longer exist; they are beyond reclaiming, due to insect damage. Only two notebooks could be collected. From these two notebooks a total of fifteen poems have been added in this edition. Those poems in which the resonance and times of *Gray Manuscripts* are fairly strong were given priority. In certain poems, of course, one may notice that hint of independence characteristic of the post–*Gray Manuscripts* period. Perhaps these poems mark an interim period in his evolving stream of poetry. The poems are arranged basically in order of their composition without relying on their transitional nature.[60]

Of the fifteen additional poems, nine are terza rima sonnets, among them "Rivers" (*nadi/nadira*), published in the same issue of *Kavita* (September 1936) announcing publication of *Gray Manuscripts.*

RIVERS

Only a bramble berry copse, mimosa clumps, a forest of *jam*
And cashew, elsewhere an *arjun* tree, with all its shade. What is
That river saying day long as she draws them near? Who is this river?

Her life sends a flash of awe through my heart: where no people are—
Only the river—I go there and hear the sounds. I listen. The midday
Jalapipi birds have long heard such sounds. As I walked the deep banyan-

Leaved paths I too heard, was pained: my heart stunned that one
Noontide by the water's scent: it seemed a child had died—my heart
That child. As much as rivers hope from light and sky, had I not hoped

As much once? only once? Who were they who came and said:
"There are no trees—sunshine—clouds—no stars. The sky is not for you!"
Yet why for a thousand years has the river received all this? Why does

The river live in a child's heart? This river with its sounds no longer
Brings wonder to my heart. To the hearts of men, rivers are lost—
ended.[61]

A child's imagination, that tenuous link we establish between ourselves and nature, fades as we grow up and away from the natural world. At some point, adults inform us that the sky is just the sky, not something personal for us only. Luxuriating in nature, so much a part of *Bengal the Beautiful,* resonates in "Rivers," but here the narrator assumes an adult's perspective as he bemoans his loss of contact with nature. In *Bengal the Beautiful* the grown-up child attempts to reestablish and relive that innocent contact. It was this poem, expressing that most modern of attitudes, alienation, which Jibanananda chose to publish back in 1936. *Bengal the Beautiful*'s effusive, childlike emotions he kept out of print during his lifetime.

Jibanananda, in the late 1920s and early 1930s, experimented with formal poetic structures: sonnets, and Spenserian stanzas in a couple of poems included in *Gray Manuscripts.* Satyendranath Datta, the Bengali metrical genius, had made a great impression on Jibanananda, as is evident from the latter's first book, *Fallen Feathers.* Later, he would indicate his disdain for Satyendranath's poetry, for the "triviality of the content of his verses" and a "form, more resonant than subtle, more clever than really critical or important, ..."[62] In *Gray Manuscripts* and during the early 1930s, Jibanananda concentrated on poetic form and methods of poetic expression. In his review of *Gray Manuscripts,* however, Buddhadeva Bose makes no mention of the larger formal structures as such but dwells at some length on meter, which Jibanananda, he writes, has "bent, twisted, wound and woven ... according to his will." His meter is "unhurried, as if intentionally made to pause, uneven and unpolished."[63] There is a good reason why, in a review written during the latter half of the 1930s, attention would be paid to meter: it had become what diction, sex, and foreign influence were in the mid- to late 1920s. Meter now divided the moderns from the more traditional poets.

Buddhadeva, furthermore, declares that Jibanananda in *Gray Manuscripts* shows himself to be a nature poet.

> In one sense all poets are nature poets, as I've said previously. Yet, not all poets are given this designation since nature is not the single or dominant subject matter for them. For many poets, nature is a backdrop for the various experiences of human life. For many, it is an indulgence of the senses, and for some, it is merely a reflection of the condition of our hearts. There is no poet who has not deeply felt nature, but the number of poets who have realized and expressed all of life through nature herself is small. These in particular are "nature poets."[64]

To Buddhadeva's ways of thinking, only one modern Bengali poet could be termed a true nature poet: Jibanananda Das. Even those of his poems which seem to be concerned with love were still basically nature poems, Buddhadeva argued, for "the natural environment looms much larger and more alive in the poet's imagination than does the woman of his love."[65] As for influences, there were Keats, the Pre-Raphaelites, and something reminiscent of the young Yeats, too. But, having said all this, Buddhadeva reiterates that, in the final analysis, Jibanananda's creative power and his vision remain uniquely his.

Distance and solitude pervade this poetry, notes Buddhadeva. There are fairy tales drawn from worlds other than our own and wonderful, sensuous pictures:

> The abundance of pictures and their distinctiveness are noteworthy in Jibanananda's poetry, one observes. Whatever imagination he has expressed through the many similes and allusions is all of the nature of appearance, not of thought; it is born out of feeling, not cogitation. Jibanananda is the least metaphysical, the most physical among our poets; his writing is the least intellectual, the most reliant upon the physical senses.[66]

Jibanananda possesses extraordinary skill as a word painter, Buddhadeva declares. "Moreover, the pictures are not just visual but tactile and olfactory, primarily tactile and olfactory." And, he concludes, Jibanananda ranks as "one of the major poets of the modern period and I consider *Gray Manuscripts* to be his first mature book."[67]

Buddhadeva remarks that to date (March 1937) there had not been adequate mention of Jibanananda in any criticism dealing with modern Bengali poetry. He himself had discussed Jibanananda's poetry in two articles in *Pragati* (September 1928 and August 1929). Sajani Kanta Das, of course, mocked several of Jibanananda's poems in *Sanibarer Cithi*. Then, in April 1937, a review of *Gray Manuscripts* was printed in *Paricay,* the same magazine that had reluctantly published "In Camp." Not as enthusiastic as Buddhadeva, this reviewer was nevertheless favorably disposed toward Jibanananda's poetry. Though *Gray Manuscripts* "as a whole sometimes appears fuzzy and lackluster," certain individual poems, "In Camp" among them, qualified Jibanananda to be placed "within the highest echelons of modern poets." The reviewer assayed the degree of poetic distance from Rabindranath: Mohitlal Mazumdar being completely under the senior poet's spell; Bishnu Dey's poetry showing near-total freedom from that influence; and Jibanananda falling somewhere in midspectrum.[68] (Like it or not, in the 1920s and 1930s poets and critics alike had to live with the omnipresent Rabindric standard.)

By the latter half of the 1930s, things were looking up for Jibanananda. He had a job. There was a very sympathetic magazine editor in the person of Buddhadeva once again in a position to print his poetry, this time in *Kavita*. His second book of verse had come out. And a few people, though only a few, were beginning to view his work with a modicum of respect.

6

Upon receiving his personal copy of *Kavita*'s second issue, Jibanananda had written to Buddhadeva:

>Sarbananda Bhavan
>Barisal
>23.12.35

[salutations]

I was delighted to get the December issue of *Kavita*. I've been terribly busy grading the "Test Examination" papers, and so this reply has been somewhat tardy.

I very much enjoyed Rabindranath's poem, your "Kokil, O Kokil" [*kokil, ogo kokil*] and Samar Sen's poetry in this *Kavita*. You have written a marvelous poem, focusing upon that *kokil* [the Indian cuckoo]. Among all the compositions on the subject written either in Bengal or elsewhere, this particular poem of yours is as unique as it is excellent—I've read it over time and again—and each time it seems new and "refreshing," and my heart laments. "The Compassionate One" [*dayamayi*] reminds one of Browning's "Dramatic Lyrics"—just as forceful and savory—but the style and flavor are completely your own.

In many ways writing done late in life tends toward "dotage," but I'm fascinated and quite impressed to see how Rabindranath's youthful imagination forever flows in an unfathomable stream. The opening lines of his "Holidays" [*chuti*] poem in particular left me enchanted—the entire poem excels from beginning to end.

Samar Sen's "achievement" in these two issues of *Kavita* is nothing short of remarkable; he possesses a "continuously poetical quality of mind." This talent of his, I trust, will take him far.

I read "Obsession with Modernity" [*adhunikatar moha*] and your other comments. Do we have here both "propaganda" and "snobbery"? One need only glance at the various magazines and journals of this land to gain a profound sense of just how valuable and necessary all such impartially level-headed, introspective, luminous criticism really is.

And how well has *Kavita* been received? How many copies are printed per issue? Will you be staying in Calcutta for the Christmas vacation?

I shall be sending several poems for the next issue of *Kavita*.

Hope you are well.

Sri Jibanananda Das[69]

One of his four poems in that December 1935 issue—namely "Banalata Sen"—was to become his most famous composition. It has been artistically rendered into English by a number of persons. In fact, Jibanananda made his own translation; my own version follows his, for comparison. (Though these translations differ markedly, they are made from the same original—Jibanananda has exercised poetic license, as it were.)

BANALATA SEN

Long I have been a wanderer of this world,
Many a night,
My route lay across the sea of Ceylon somewhat winding to
The seas of Malaya.
I was in the dim world of Bimbisar and Asok, and further off
In the mistiness of Vidarbha.
At moments when life was too much a sea of sounds,
I had Banalata Sen of Natore and her wisdom.

I remember her hair dark as night at Vidisha,
Her face an image of Sravasti as the pilot,
Undone in the blue milieu of the sea,
Never twice saw the earth of grass before him,
I have seen her, Banalata Sen of Natore.

When day is done, no fall somewhere but of dews
Dips into the dusk; the smell of the sun is gone
Off the Kestrel's wings. Light is your wit now,
Fanning fireflies that pitch the wide things around.
For Banalata Sen of Natore.

(Trans. by the poet)[70]

BANALATA SEN

For thousands of years I roamed the paths of this earth,

From waters round Ceylon in dead of night to Malayan seas.
Much have I wandered. I was there in the gray world of Asoka
And Bimbisara, pressed on through darkness to the city of Vidarbha.
I am a weary heart surrounded by life's frothy ocean.
To me she gave a moment's peace—Banalata Sen from Natore.

Her hair was like an ancient darkling night in Vidisa,
Her face, the craftsmanship of Sravasti. As the helmsman,
His rudder broken, far out upon the sea adrift,
Sees the grass-green land of a cinnamon isle, just so
Through darkness I saw her. Said she, "Where have you been so long?"
And raised her bird's-nest-like eyes—Banalata Sen from Natore.

At day's end, like hush of dew
Comes evening. A hawk wipes the scent of sunlight from its wings.
When earth's colors fade and some pale design is sketched,
Then glimmering fireflies paint in the story.
All birds come home, all rivers, all of this life's tasks finished.
Only darkness remains, as I sit there face to face with Banalata Sen.[71]

Ceylon (present-day Sri Lanka) and Malaya need no explanation. Bimbisara/Bimbisar and Asoka/Asok once ruled ancient India. Vidarbha, later known as Berar, and Vidisa/Vidisha, also known as Malwa, are cities, as is Sravasti, whose artisans gained fame with their excellent craftsmanship. In contrast, Natore is a small, ordinary, *mofussil* town in Bangladesh, and Banalata Sen is just a woman's name. Her true identity has been a favorite topic for idle speculation among all manner of literary buffs. However, as far as anyone knows, the name Banalata Sen corresponds to no real person. Its significance lies partly in its commonality. Sen indicates one of the Vaidya caste, Jibanananda's own caste—if that mattered to an apostate Brahmo. Banalata has, like all Bengali names, a literal meaning: *bana* glosses as forest and *lata,* a vine or creeper. Together, the name means "a sylvan vine," something Jibanananda with his proclivities for the natural environment of Bengal, the beautiful, might covet.

But there is fashion in names, as in most of man's creations. "Lata," as the second element in a woman's name, proved popular in Jibanananda's parents' generation—one of his aunts had the name Snehalata, as did the title of a novel by possibly the first woman novelist in Bengali, Kusum Kumari Raychaudhuri. The first edition of *Snehalata* came out in 1296 (1889–90). That same author published books entitled *Premalata* and *Santilata,* named for their eponymous heroines. The novel *Swarnalata* (1873), by Taraknath Ganguly, enjoyed considerable popularity during the latter part of the nineteenth century. Rabindranath's short story set in the Calcutta of the 1880s, *The Broken Nest (nasta nir)*, has as one of the main characters a sister-in-law by the name of Charulata. So, though the name Banalata may be significant for being ordinary, it also carries with it the sense of a past generation, a generation that represented security and nurturing parents.

Jibanananda produced one of his most tightly constructed lyrics in "Banalata Sen." Throughout he relies upon *payar,* that oldest and most common of the Bengali meters. The three sestet stanzas rhyme *ababcc,* the first stanza exclusively of twenty-two unit lines (8-8-6), a pattern found frequently in the *Bengal the Beautiful* sonnets. The latter two stanzas display varied line lengths. Each stanza funnels the reader's attention from the massive to the minute. All three taken together likewise exhibit comparable movement from large to small. From the world, an ocean, kingdoms, a city, we move, in the first stanza, to the focal point, an individual woman. From a kingdom, a bustling commercial city, an island, we again move, in the second stanza, to that individual woman. From an entire day, to the onset of evening, to the very end of that day and its activities, in the third stanza we once more come to rest in front of that individual woman. The first stanza spans worlds of ancient kingdoms. The second stanza begins to focus upon that woman but always connecting her with the vast worlds—her hair with Vidisa, face with Sravasti: the massive and the minute approach synthesis. The third stanza concentrates on the minute: a hawk, fireflies, and finally the individual once more. Not only in space but also through time, these stanzas, as well as the whole poem, move from presenting reigns of kings as mere moments, to a moment's peace as an eternity.

This peculiar and characteristically Jibanananandian manipulation of historical time and place has not gone unnoticed by literary critics. Of "Banalata Sen," Dipti Tripathi writes:

> Among the poetry reflecting this historical sense, "Banalata Sen" must be mentioned first and foremost. Such a synthesis of the "timeless" and the "temporal" had not occurred previously in Bengali literature. The poet was pained by the ungratifying nature of love, hurt by the absence of beauty in the present age. And so he sought the real essence of love and beauty in the larger area of geography and history. Behind Natore's Banalata Sen, confined in time and place, lies the expanse of geography and the depths of history. By combining these two dimensions, this little lyric poem takes on the stature of an epic.[72]

The "you" of *Gray manuscripts* and some of the *Bengal the Beautiful* poems has now received a proper name: Banalata Sen, a comforting individual who differs from the rest of human society. She understands the poet, in this poem at least. Conversely, he does not shun her as he does the rest of human society, which has always wearied him, from the time of

Bimbisara to the present. The historical dimension intensifies emotions he has in this brief human life. Jibanananda uses historical as well as geographical imagery to extend the stage upon which his subjects play and, by so expanding the venue, he increases the force of his statements. Contacts with the human world have hurt him—the "I" of the poem—a lot. Since that human world spans the length and breadth of South Asia and ranges from historical time to the present, the hurt he feels seems all the greater.

The poet states directly that Banalata Sen gave him "a moment's peace" from the surrounding "frothy waters" of life. The last two lines of the poem leave unresolved the ambiguity as to whether Banalata Sen symbolizes death—both comfort and a rest from tiring life. Certainly, Banalata Sen represents solace, and Jibanananda conveys this quality of hers by the famous image in the second stanza's last line: bird's-nest-like eyes. Not an idiom or trite simile in Bengali, "bird's-nest-like" challenged the reader then—and still now—to synthesize given cause (the nest) and imagined effect (protection and rest).

Jibanananda employed the same image elsewhere. As mentioned earlier, he did not much enjoy the time in 1929–30 when he taught at Delhi's Ramjas College. Sudhir Kumar Datta, fellow Brahmo from Barisal and a year or so his junior provided some companionship. They saw each other frequently. When Jibanananda first arrived in Delhi, Sudhir Kumar met him at the railway station. Of Sudhir Kumar on that occasion, Jibanananda wrote, more than five years later: ". . . across his face, [that smile] of bird's-nest-like assurance and shelter."[73] Banalata Sen provides that same sheltering comfort and reassurance by raising her bird's-nest-like eyes to the poem's weary, wayfaring speaker. It cannot be known for certain which came first, the statement about Sudhir Kumar (d. June 1935) or the poem "Banalata Sen" (published December 1935), nor whether Jibanananda conceived of the image when he saw his friend in 1929 or much later after Sudhir Kumar's untimely death, as Jibanananda recalled that meeting at the Delhi station.

Banalata Sen shows up in another poem nine months later, also published in *Kavita*. "Thousands of Years Merely Play" (*hajar bachar sudhu khela kare*) has six *payar* lines with rhyme scheme *ababcc,* a stanzaic structure identical to "Banalata Sen." Initial references in both lyrics to a time span of thousands of years loom large; penultimate lines speak of life's business being finished; and, notably, Banalata Sen figures in both poems.

"Thousands of Years Merely Play" exists in two published versions. The one which came out in *Kavita* became an entry in the first edition of Jibanananda's fourth book, *The World at Large* (*mahaprithibi*) (1944) and again in his seventh book, the last to be published in his lifetime, *Jibanananda Das's Best Poems* (*jibanananda daser srestha kabita*) (1954).

The Signet Press *Banalata Sen* (1952), his sixth book (a greatly expanded edition of a 1942 volume by the same title), contains the other version. Only in their setting do the two differ.

THOUSANDS OF YEARS MERELY PLAY

Thousands of years merely play like fireflies in darkness.
Pyramids all about. The smell of coffins.
Moonlight upon sand. Here and there shadows of date palms
Like disintegrated columns. Assyria stands dead—humbled.
Stench of mummy on our bodies: all of life's business is finished.
"Remember?" she asked. I queried merely, "Banalata Sen?"[74]

THOUSANDS OF YEARS MERELY PLAY

Thousands of years merely play like fireflies in darkness.
All about the abode of eternal night.
Moonlight upon sand. Here and there shadows of *devadaru* trees
Like disintegrated columns. Dwaraka stands dead—humbled.
Sleep's scent on our bodies: all of life's business is finished.
"Remember?" she asked. I queried merely, "Banalata Sen?"[75]

The one poem employs Middle Eastern imagery, the other Indian. Middle Eastern imagery predominated in Jibanananda's first book, *Fallen Feathers*. But there it functioned almost literally, to situate the context of the action. Later, his Middle Eastern imagery does not so much denote the literal as connote distance of time and place, analogous to the function history and geography play in a poem such as "Banalata Sen." Middle Eastern imagery adds an element of the non-Indian exotic, thus serving to distance further what is already distanced by historical and geographic imagery.

Given the similarity in function between historical-geographic imagery in general and Middle Eastern imagery in particular, Jibanananda apparently felt that he could substitute Indian for Middle Eastern imagery with no detriment to the poem. Indeed, "Thousands of Years Merely Play" works as well with Dwaraka (capital city of lord Krishna's ancient kingdom) in place of Assyria, and with Indian *devadaru* trees instead of date palms (which grow in India, though those in the poem are surely desert palms of Egypt or Assyria). Neither pyramids nor mummies are literally crucial to the poem, but they intensify the sense of vast yet unified time, specified in the first line by "Thousands of years." The mention of Assyria and Dwaraka serves the same purpose.

This six-line poem reprises the three-stanza composition "Banalata Sen." To understand "Thousands of Years Merely Play" one must already be familiar with Banalata Sen and what she represents. Unfortunately, the shorter poem tries to do much of what is done in the longer composition, but does so less effectively. The six lines move from the vast impersonal to the intimate relationship with Banalata Sen. The intervening lines, however, get in the way. There is no real movement. The first and last lines show little nexus. The environment in which the narrator and Banalata Sen find themselves expands, takes on an exotic flavor owing to the historical allusions, but in "Banalata Sen" there is genuine movement—a progression from ancient to immediate present. The references to antiquity add specificity to the places through which the character in the poem has been wandering. "Thousands of Years Merely Play" presents a relatively static scene.

The statement in "Banalata Sen" that life's business is ceasing ("All birds come home, all rivers, all of this life's tasks finished") has been prefaced by activity. The entire poem, up to that point, has focused on the actions of life ("For thousands of years I roamed the paths of the earth"). When a similar statement is encountered in "Thousands of Years Merely Play" ("All of life's business is finished"), it comes as *non sequitur,* for hardly anything of life and life's business has been depicted. One could read some meaning of solace into the brief exchange between the narrator and Banalata Sen—and in fact the poem "Banalata Sen" suggests this is the correct interpretation—but the preceding lines do not provide much help in leading the reader to draw this conclusion. The failure of this poem, except as chorus to the longer one, underscores an aspect of "Banalata Sen" crucial to its success: proper magnitude. One can only wonder if "Thousands of Years Merely Play" might not have been a wisely rejected stanza from an early draft of "Banalata Sen."

Middle Eastern imagery comes to be just a part of the more general category of historical-geographic imagery. A *Bengal the Beautiful* sonnet queries: "Didn't they see the dream, Rome, Assyria, Ujjaini, Gaur-Bengal, Delhi, Babylon?"[76] And in a poem published in the third number of *Kavita,* the poet strings Assyria, Egypt, and Vidisa together in one line:

WINDY NIGHT
(*haoyar rat*)

Last night was thick with wind, a time of countless stars.
All night long, a vast wind played within my mosquito net.
At times that net swelled like a monsoon sea's belly.
Tearing loose from the bed every once in a while
It would try to fly to the stars.

Back to Barisal

Now and then it seemed to me—perhaps while half asleep—that there was no mosquito net over my head at all,
As it soared like a white heron upon a sea of blue wind, skirting the hip of the star Swati!
Last night was such a marvelous night.

All the dead stars awoke last night—there wasn't the least little space in the sky.
I saw the gray faces of all the world's beloved dead in those stars.
In the dark of night, in *aswattha* treetops, those stars glittered like a lusty hawk's dewy eyes.
The huge sky gleamed in the moonlit night like a shining cheetah stole upon the shoulders of Babylon's queen.
Last night was such an amazing night.

Those stars in the bosom of the sky that died thousands of years ago,
They, too, brought with them through the window last night countless dead skies.
Those stunning women I saw die in Assyria, Egypt, Vidisa,
Seemed last night to stand shoulder to shoulder, javelin in hand, in far-off mist and fog at the sky's horizon:
To trample death under foot?
To proclaim full victory for life?
To excite the sullen, frightful stupor of love?
I was overwhelmed—overcome,
As though torn by last night's compelling blue tyranny.
On the sky's endless, expansive wings
The earth, like some insect, was swept away last night.
From the sky's bosom came the lofty winds
Sighing through my window,
Like so very many zebras of a verdant land, startled by the lion's roar.

My heart filled with the scent of a vast green grassy veldt,
With horizon-flooding blazing sunlight scent,
With the restless, massive, vibrant, woolly outburst of darkness,
Like growls of an aroused tigress,
With life's untamable blue intoxication!

My heart tore free from the earth and flew,
Flew up like a drunken balloon into an ocean of blue wind,
To the mast of some distant constellation, scattering stars as it flapped away like some mischievous vulture.[77]

7

The preceding poetic flight of fancy, as significant for its form as it is delightful, is one of Jibanananda's several prose poems. Prose poetry in Bengali became and then ceased to be an issue all within the span of a decade, the 1930s. It was Rabindranath who had rendered some of his Bengali lyrics into English prose, publishing them as poetry in 1912 under the title *Gitanjali*. Prompted by the acceptance as poetry of his English prose renditions, Rabindranath asked himself, as he tells us in the introduction to his first volume of prose poetry in Bengali, *Postscripts* (*punasca*) (1932): "Can the poetic essence be instilled in Bengali prose, as it is in English, without maintaining the obvious jingle of verse meter?" And he answers, predictably in the affirmative: "It is my belief that poetry's authority can be greatly increased through the frank medium of prose."[78]

By the mid-1930s, prose poetry had become all the rage in Bengali literary circles. Jibanananda's and a few others' excepted, most of the poems in *Kavita*'s first issue were composed in "prose meter" (*gadya-chanda*). *Kavita*'s third issue, in which "Windy Night" appeared, carried an editorial devoted to prose meter. There is no connection, the editorial declared, between English free verse and Bengali prose meter. Free verse is verse; Bengali prose meter is prose, not verse. With prose meter, the editorial asserted, one says what one wants to say and no more. Pound and the Imagists' Manifesto were then cited. Among specific guidelines for writing prose poetry, the editorial urged poets to avoid as far as possible Sanskrit synonyms for common words. Jibanananda's poetry in particular was lauded as exemplary in that regard—reminiscent of Buddhadeva's earlier editorials in *Pragati* praising Jibanananda's unique poetic diction.

Meanwhile, Rabindranath himself became wary of the enterprise. In an essay contributed to the December 1936 number of *Kavita,* entitled "Prose Poetry" (*gadyakabya*), he offered tempering admonitions: yes, prose poetry is fine, but—beware of this and what about that and pay heed to the other thing.[79] During the next year, "vexed by prose poetry," as Sanjay Bhattacharya put it, Rabindranath undertook to compile an anthology of Bengali poetry.[80] The following year, 1938, *An Introduction to Bengali Verse* (*bamla kabya paricay*) came out. By fiat of Rabindranath, no prose poetry was there anthologized.[81] Buddhadeva criticized severely this conservative collection and, in reaction to it, commissioned his own anthology, *Modern Bengali Poetry* (*adhunik bamla kabita*), published two years later. By that time, however, prose poetry no longer held paramount significance in the world of modern Bengali verse. But while it was a hot issue, during the mid-1930s, Jibanananda had composed a few such prose poems, "Windy Night" among them, as was the following pictorial fantasy:

NAKED LONELY HAND
(*nagna nirjan hat*)

Darkness once again thickens throughout the sky:
This darkness, like light's mysterious sister.

She who has loved me always,
Whose face I have yet to see,
Like that woman
Is this darkness, deepening, closing in upon a February sky.

A certain vanished city comes to mind,
In my heart wake outlines of some gray palace in that city.

On shores of the Indian Ocean
Or the Mediterranean
Or the banks of the Sea of Tyre,
Not today, but once there was a city,
And a palace—
A palace lavishly furnished:
Persian carpets, Kashmiri shawls, flawless pearls and coral from waters round Bahrain.
My lost heart, dead eyes, faded dream desires
And you, woman—
All these once filled that world.

There was orange sunlight,
Cockatoos and pigeons,
Dense, shady mahogany foliage.
There was orange sunlight,
Much orange-colored sunlight,
And you were there.
For how many hundreds of centuries I have not seen the beauty of your face,
Have not searched.
The February darkness brings with it this tale of a seashore,
Sorrowful lines of fantasy domes and arches,
Fragrance of invisible pears,
Countless deer and lion parchments, graying,
Stained glass rainbows rippling over drapes—
A fleeting glow from
Room through anteroom to further inner room.
Momentary awe and wonder.

Sweat of ruddy sun, smeared on curtains, carpets,
Watermelon wine in red glasses!
Your naked lonely hand

Your naked lonely hand.[82]

Here, too, as in "Banalata Sen" and so many other of his poems, sits a woman, only her hand (or arm—the Bengali word means both hand and arm) in view. Here, too, time is measured in centuries, and locale extends from India to the Mediterranean. Here, a poet's passionately imaginative view of sunset. He "recalls" a fantasy palace. And then, with help from the setting orange sun, turning red as it sinks, he splashes before the reader's eyes a profusion of sensuous images—cockatoos, lush foliage, a castle's outlines, uncommon fruit (pears), parchmentized lion and deer hides. Color and more color, hot and sweaty, smeared on already vivid carpets and curtains, watermelon wine made redder by red glasses. And suddenly, amid all this color, there lies an unadorned hand, ostensibly of that mysterious woman whom Jibanananda has named in some poems and left unnamed here.

He had developed a somewhat similar evening scene in *Bengal the Beautiful:*

> One day I grew upon the paths of the world: my body
> Walked the soft grassy paths; I sat upon the grass
> And saw stars play like fireflies in curiosity's infinite
> Sky; glossy wet river banks fill with water's scent
> In darkness; I hear the swish of whose soft saris,
> See unoiled hair; who come with words to console—
> Gray cowrie-shell hands—naked hands in an evening breeze
> Visible; near yellow grass lie the gorgeous sad wings
>
> Of a cold dead butterfly. I look; I stop and stand quietly:
> Orange color spreads over the evening sky—crows appear blue.
> I sink into a crowd of people—I talk—hold hand in hand.
> Some profound wonderment of somewhere seems hidden within that
> Compassionate, doleful hair—I sleep alone beneath the stars.
> An owl's gray wings speak with fireflies the whole night long.[83]

Here the poet begins with the physical world: grass, stars, the smell of a river. With senses attuned to his environment, he catches the sound of unstarched saris as some women pass by. Their hair, like their saris, indicates that they are not dressed up to go out socially but are probably engaged in some domestic chore. The narrator notes their bare hands (no bangles), ruminating on what thoughts lie hidden inside a person with whom he holds hands. At this point he restrains the fantasy about being with a woman, returning to sensuous perception of this natural world. In short, the poet never really "gets off the ground" in this sonnet. Although elements that stimulate his fantasy in "Naked Lonely Hand" are present here—an orange sunset, bare hands—the sonnet remains grounded in Bengal, whereas "Naked Lonely Hand" runs free in his imagination.

That Jibanananda can perceptively observe nature is demonstrated in much of his poetry. That he can likewise empathize with the natural, nonhuman world comes through clearly, particularly in the poetry of the 1930s:

THE HUNT
(*sikar*)

Dawn:
Sky, the soft blue of grasshopper's belly.
Guava and custard apple trees all around, green as parrot feathers.
A single star lingers in the sky
Like the most twilight-intoxicated girl in some village bridal chamber,
Or that pearl from her bosom the Egyptian dipped into my glass of Nile-blue wine
One night some thousands of years ago—
Just so, in the sky shines a single star.

To warm their bodies through the cold night, up-country menials kept a fire going
In the field—red fire like a cockscomb blossom,
Still burning, contorting dry *aswattha* leaves.

Its color in the light of the sun is no longer like vermilion
But has become like wan desires of a sickly *salik* bird's heart.
In the morning's light both sky and surrounding dewy forest sparkle like iridescent peacock wings.

Dawn:
All night long a sleek brown buck, bounding from *sundari* through *arjun* forests
In starless, mahogany darkness, avoids the cheetah's grasp.
He had been waiting for this dawn.
Down he came in its glow,
Ripping, munching fragrant grass, green as green grapefruit.
Down he came to the river's stinging, tingling ripples,
To instill his sleepless, weary, bewildered body with the current's drive,
To feel a thrill like that of dawn bursting through the cold and wizened womb of darkness,
To wake like gold sun-spears beneath this blue and
Dazzle doe after doe with beauty, boldness, desire.
A strange sound.

The river's water red like *macaka* flower petals.
Again the fire crackled—red venison served warm.
Many an old dew-dampened yarn, while seated on a bed of grass beneath the stars.
Cigarette smoke.
Several human heads, hair neatly parted.
Guns here and there. Icy, calm, guiltless sleep.[84]

Sundari trees situate this poem in the Sundarban jungles south of Barisal, whence the narrator sees Venus in the morning sky. Sensuous as ever, Jibanananda verbally paints dawn, employing humans at first only as elements in a simile modifying the natural surroundings. The twilight-intoxicated girl warrants explanation. In many Hindu Bengali weddings, the ceremony takes place at the bride's home. Friends and relatives of the bride traditionally keep the newly married couple awake most of that first night, teasing the bride-groom and chatting with the bride, a variation of shivaree. One maiden, undoubtedly excited by the whole affair, managed to stay awake the entire night. Juxtaposed to this thoroughly Bengali miss are the exotic Egyptian lady and her pearl pendant, drawn from Jibanananda's stock of Middle Eastern imagery.

The hunters, presumably Bengali, are accompanied by some non-Bengali servants who stay up most of the night, guarding the camp and trying to keep warm. These real humans, undistinguished, contrast sharply with the distinctive women of the similes. As the sun rises, the color of their fire fades, contrasting with the forest's natural morning luminescence. Men are not the only ones who must get through the cold night. A deer spends his night on the move, struggling to preserve his life from the clutches of the predaceous she-cheetah. A new life, a new day awaits him as his body draws sustenance from the light and the water and the grass around him.

These tableaux, which capture scenes lasting a few minutes' duration, are followed by the murderous shot. The deer who had successfully, with great effort, avoided the cheetah falls prey to man. The beauty that the poet dwelled upon so long, those few moments that he detailed, drawing them out to several stanzas, have been destroyed. The rest of the poem consists of curt, clipped sentence fragments: ugliness, to be passed over as quickly as possible. With obvious contempt, the narrator points out the significant attributes of these men: their vapid tales, cigarettes, groomed hair, and guiltless sleep.

In a posthumously published poem, Jibanananda paints a different picture of a very different hunt:

A TALE OF THE SUNDARBAN JUNGLES
(*sundar baner galpa*)

A deer waded into river waters of dawn.
All last night a cheetah stalked him—
For the whole moonlit night, that sleek she-cheetah chased deer shadows.

Wind-footed shade she followed,
Like desire.

Flush desire born of jarring beauty,
Not from envy.
Last night, a cheetah salivated at the sight of such a handsome face.
In March moonlight last night
Through a land of purple shade, silver dew,
Through a realm of latticed windows,
Through the warmth of green and saffron breezes,
Through orange-colored wine of moonlight cast on grassy clearings
The two of them made up a forest dream last night,
This deer, this cheetah.
Moonlight's soft sinews shaped a picture with their bodies,
Painted an exquisite portrait of a woman with a cheetah's body
Running like the wind behind her longed-for young man—
The interwoven branches weaving checkered carpets on their bodies—
At breakneck speed,
A thousand walls of leaves,
Opened up like windows
By March winds,
Turning indigo again like darkened tunnels
And in amongst those rich deep shadows of mahogany
He becomes a mahogany deer,
She, a bluish wooden cheetah,
Enveloped by darkest night
Like a placid sea
Passionately swelling, flooding, inundating cave after mountain cave.

In a fountain of silver moonlight,
In a fountain of wind
Their bodies burst forth again like so many golden flowers.
Off they ran like a crystalline cascade,
Now lost behind a veil of azure shadows,
Then from within those shadows mining diamond moonlight,
Plucking strings of a tambura darkness,
Splitting open watermelon winds.
Now they find the moon, these two,
Now they lose it.[85]

Such living vicariously through nature formed the stuff of much of his poetry during this period:

GRASS
(*ghas*)

With light, soft green, like tender lemon leaves,
The world was filled this morning.
Grass green, like unripe grapefruit—and just as fragrant—
Deer tear with their teeth!
I too would drink, like green wine,

> The fragrance of this grass, glass after glass,
> Would knead the body of this grass—rub my eyes upon it,
> My feathers on the grass's wings,
> Would come forth from the delicious darkness of some lush grass-mother
> To be born as grass in grass.[86]

Instead of focusing upon the deer, Jibanananda directs his attention to the grass. Grass figures prominently in many of the *Bengal the Beautiful* sonnets, so too the concept of transmigrating not into a man but into nature.

8

Jibanananda truly enjoyed names for names' sake. The "you" of the *Gray Manuscripts* poetry often assumes a proper name in his subsequent works, the *femme* of "Banalata Sen" a case in point. The 1952 expanded version of *Banalata Sen* contains a variety of names, with seven of the thirty lyrics named for his fantasy women: Banalata Sen, Sankhamala, Sudarsana, Syamali, Suranjana, Sabita, and Sucetana. One Sephalika Bose appears suddenly (and momentarily) in the poem "Deer" (*harinera*). In "She Who Merged into the Skies" (*akasalina*), the narrator again addresses a Suranjana, and he recalls a girl by the name of Arunima Sanyal in a poem of the same period entitled "The Wild Ducks" (*buno hans*). (Arunima's name was Asrukana Sanyal in the original poem published in *Kavita*. Arunima appeared as such in *The World at Large* [1944] and all subsequent collections.) Sankhamala shows up several times, in different poems—one wherein she is featured:

SANKHAMALA
(*sankhamala*)

> Who was that woman who, leaving the deep forest path
> In the dark of evening, came and called to me?
> She said, I want you:
> I have searched the stars—on wings of fog
> For your pained eyes, bluish like the fruit of cane reeds.
> I have searched for you there—where light descends
> Into river waters of evening to become the body of fireflies,
> Spreading its gray owllike wings through November darkness
> Along the Dhansiri river
> From rice paddy to paddy like a golden stairway.
> I searched for you in my lonely owllike heart.

I saw her body, filled with melancholy bird hues.
The bird that clasps the damp *siris* tree limb in evening's darkness—
Upon its head, the crescent moon,
The hornlike crescent blue moon that listens to its warble.

Her face was white as cowrie shells,
Her two hands, cold.
In her eyes burned the red pyre
Of cashew wood: Sankhamala appeared within that fire,
Her head to the south.

The blue darkness of a hundred centuries
Seemed within her eyes
Her breasts
Like comforting conch shells—moist with milk—of an ancient
  Sankhinimala.
This world once possessed her, but no more.[87]

A fantasy, fairy-tale woman of old searches for the narrator in the first stanza, she herself being described in the rest of the poem. Similarity between the names Sankhinimala (Sankhini, one of the four categories of women as defined by the Sanskrit texts) and Sankhamala (literally, "garland of conch shells") may have been uppermost in Jibananda's mind as a way of adding richness to his female character.[88] In sonnets cited earlier, Bisalaksi granted this same Sankhamala the boon to be "born amidst the paddy and grass of blue Bengal." And Bengal is "Where one day Sankhamala's, Chandramala's, Manikmala's/Bangles used to jingle—ah, will they ever jingle once again!" In one sonnet in *Bengal the Beautiful,* Jibananda describes some of what transpired in his mind as he wrote about such women as Sankhamala:

As I sat down to write all these poems, alone in my heart,
Dew dripped from *calata* leaves in the moonlight,
Banks of the pale Dhansiri river rested calm, fogbound:
Bats, dark wings spread, sketched lines of desire across cold
Moonlight. Cupping a flickering lamp flame, Manorama appeared,
With her, a swarm of ancient honeybees—maidens who offered
Mango buds in winter's night, brought cold milky meat of
Custard apples. I saw them in the dim light: this poem was

Written with their dark hair in mind, the shape of their
Cowrie-shell-like gray hands in mind, and for their hearts.
How many centuries ago did their compassionate conch-shell-like
Breasts—their yellow saris—milky bodies—wonderful hearts
Go away into this world's most peaceful cold house of solace:
In my sad dream which lingers on, they wake from sleep.[89]

Not only this poem but much of Jibanananda's poetry of the 1930s, early 1930s in particular, was written with the dark, unoiled hair of these imaginary women in mind, and written for them, "for their hearts."

Even a lyric unquestionably based on a Western model displays the Jibananandian flavor, and that woman:

O HAWK
(*hay cil*)

O hawk, golden winged hawk, in this afternoon of damp clouds
Cry no more, soaring beside the Dhansiri river!
Her languid eyes, like cane reed fruit, come to mind through your lamenting melody!
She, who with her beauty has gone far away, was like fair princesses of the earth;
Why do you call her back again? O, who so loves to dig at my heart
And reawaken the pain!
O hawk, golden winged hawk, in this afternoon of damp clouds
Cry no more, soaring beside the Dhansiri river.[90]

"O Hawk," like so many of Jibanananda's poems published during *Kavita*'s early years, shows correspondences with other poems published around the same time as well as with the sonnets of *Bengal the Beautiful*.[91] From the latter come these examples: "... I don't understand why *bhanta* and *amsa* moss forests talk in the wind—why the hawk cries"; "... the warm wind from field's edge/Sighs like a hungry hawk in this March darkness"; and "... you sang many a day/Flying like a golden hawk through skies of sunshine and clouds—."[92] Furthermore:

The afternoon grows damp with clouds. Beside the river a lone hawk
Perches on a *jarul* tree branch staring toward the opposite shore.
Pigeons fly off into the little niches in the courtyard. Honeybees
Abandon cucumber vines. Black clouds gather in the January skies.
Ants steal away with their dead butterfly, sprinkling soft dust
From its wings onto the grass. For a few moments *salik* birds scuffle
Noisily on a mango branch. A "speak-to-your-wife" bird calls his spouse
No longer—his yellow wings seem to be lost among the jackfruit and

Palas trees. Nor is the mistress of the house in the courtyard—
The husking pedal lies idle: who will husk the paddy?—she had not
For a long time now, nor does she come to dry her hair in the sun.
She does not bathe this noon. Seed rice is sprouting in the storeroom,
Still she does not come. Who will fry the puffed rice this afternoon?
O hawk, golden hawk, will that fair princess ever live again?[93]

The sestet's absent woman constitutes yet another element in Jibanananda's Bengal. But the hawk and the maiden are not nearly as integrated as they are in "O Hawk," which connects the cry to the memory of the woman to the pain that memory causes, whereas this sonnet presents a series of pictures and merely hints at emotion for the vanished girl.

One of the finest poems Jibanananda ever wrote came out in *Kavita* in March 1938.

A DAY EIGHT YEARS AGO
(*at bachar ager ekadin*)

It was heard
They took him to the morgue.
Last night in the February dark
When the crescent moon, five days toward full, had set
He'd had the urge to die.

A wife had lain beside him—a child, too.
There had been love, hope, in the moonlight.
Then what ghost did he see? why was his sleep disturbed?
Or maybe he hadn't slept for days. Now, lying in the morgue, he sleeps.
He had sought this sleep perhaps.
Like a plague rat, maw smeared with frothy blood, neck slack
In the bosom of some dingy cranny, now he sleeps.
Never again will he wake.

"Never again will you wake
Never again will you know
The unremitting, unrelenting grievous
Pain of waking."
As though some stillness stretched its camel's neck
Through his window
And said these words to him
When the moon had sunk into strange darkness.

But the owl is awake,
And the decrepit, putrefying frog begs a few moments more
Among anticipated warm affections—beckoned by another dawn.
I sense all around me the unforgiving opposition
Of my mosquito net, invisible in the swarming dark.
The mosquito stays awake in his blackened monastery, in love with life's flow.

Flies alight on blood and filth, then fly again to sunlight.

How many times have I watched the play of winged insects on waves
   of golden sunshine.

An intimate sky it would seem—some pervasive life force
Controls their hearts.
The grasshopper's constant twitching, caught in the mischievous
   child's grasp,
Fights death.
Yet in that foremost darkness after moonset, you, a coil of rope in
   hand,
Had gone alone to the *aswattha* tree,
Knowing that the grasshopper's life, or the *doyel* bird's, never meets
   with
That of man.

The *aswattha* limb,
Did it not protest? Did not fireflies in cordial throngs
Appear before you?
Did not the blind and palsied owl come and
Say to you: "Old lady moon has sunk in the flood, has she?
Marvelous!
Let's now catch a mouse or two!"
Did not the owl screech out that raucous news?

This taste of life—the scent of ripe grain in an autumn afternoon—
You could not tolerate.
In the morgue, is your heart at ease
In the morgue, in that suffocating stillness
Like a flattened rat with blood-smeared lips.

Listen,
However, to this dead man's tale. He lacked
Not love of woman,
Nor did married life's expectations
Go unfulfilled.
From time's churnings emerged a wife
And honey, the mind's honey
She let him know.
Never in this life did he shiver
In the cold of hunger's draining pain.
And so,
In that morgue,
Flat out he lies upon a table.
I know, yet I know,
A woman's heart—love—a child—a home—these are not everything,
Not wealth nor fame nor creature comforts—
There is some other perilous wonder
That frolics
In our very blood.

It exhausts us—
Exhausts, exhausts us.
That exhaustion is not present
In the morgue.
And so
In that morgue
Flat out he lies upon a table.
But every night I look and see, yes,
A blind and palsied owl come sit upon the *aswattha* branch,
Blink her eyes and say: "Old lady moon has sunk in the flood, has she?
Marvelous!
Let's now catch a mouse or two!"

Oh profound grandmother, is today still so marvelous?
I too, like you, shall grow old—shall cast old lady moon across the
 flood, into the whirlpool.
Then we two together shall empty life's full store.[94]

The event is simple enough: a man commits suicide. Why he does so, we never know. The narrator, thinking aloud, seems to insinuate a case for suicide, though he counters that idea in the final stanza, his ambivalence contributing to the poem's spellbinding tension.

So far, a dated manuscript copy of this poem has not surfaced, and thus there is no way of knowing for certain when Jibanananda composed it. The title itself implies that, whenever written, the poem's stimulus existed at least eight years earlier, 1930 or before. And indeed, a morgue or "corpse-cutting room"[95] did exist in Barisal well before 1930. Asokananda Das wrote, following his brother's death:

Right from childhood we two [brothers] walked past the cremation grounds on the outskirts of Barisal; sometimes we gazed in awe toward the "corpse-cutting room."[96]

The man in the poem had been taken to a morgue. His urge to die had come upon him the night before, when the waxing moon, in its fifth phase, had sunk into darkness on that Falgun (February/March) night. A moon in its fifth phase, not quite half full, would set just before midnight. The day of the sixth phase (*sasthi*) of the moon is the goddess Sasthi's day. Even though not a caste Hindu, Jibanananda was by no means ignorant of Hindu lore. Sasthi, the goddess of children, both nurtures the newly born and provides new life. The man may have hanged himself in order to be born anew.[97] He may have wished to live not as man but in some other form. "Knowing that the grasshopper's life, or the *doyel* bird's, never meets with/That of man," while he is still a man, he may have chosen to end this human existence so that he might become part of the natural, nonhuman universe. In a sonnet from *Bengal the Beautiful,* Jibanananda wrote:

When I return to the banks of the Dhansiri, to this Bengal,
Not as a man, perhaps, but as a *salik* bird or white hawk,
Perhaps as a crow of dawn in this land of autumn's new rice harvest[98]

In "Grass" he had said as much: "[I] Would come forth from the delicious darkness of some lush grass-mother/To be born as grass in grass."

The man hangs himself from an *aswattha* tree (also referred to as *pipal/pippal*), another name for *Ficus religiosa,* or "holy fig tree." It is closely connected with the Buddha, for under just such a tree did he gain enlightenment. "A Day Eight Years Ago," on one level, recounts Jibanananda's vicarious reliving of the Buddha's tale. The Buddha-like character in the poem had suffered. Perhaps sleepless for days, he had borne "the unremitting, unrelenting grievous/Pain of waking." There was an intangible, perilous exhaustion, the riddle of which required solving. The man had a wife and child, love and hope. He had not lacked food or shelter. He had tasted life, smelled the ripening wheat in autumn. But he had not been swayed from his purpose. Finally, beneath the Bodhi Tree—the tree of wisdom—he understood what man must do to overcome the sufferings of the world. He was fully enlightened: he was dead.

The *aswattha,* besides its Buddhist association, has other religious significance. One definition of *aswattha* is that tree which lives a long time without opposition: *a* (unopposed) + *swa* (eternity) + *stha* (to stand). Another offers a somewhat different etymology but arrives at basically the same meaning: *a* (not) + *swattha* (temporarily standing)—and adds that the *aswattha* is the tree of *samsara* or the tree of this world. Such a meaning is found in both the *Upanishads* and the *Bhagavad Gita.* One of the many, many exegetes of that latter text comments:

> The word *aswattha* means that which is not today as it was yesterday. This word refers to *samsara* or phenomenal existence. It is imperishable but not constant and steady.[99]

The character in "A Day Eight Years Ago" hanged himself on the tree of *samsara,* the tree which, though imperishable, ever changes. Neither reader nor narrator may know for sure whether that man's life, like the tree, was imperishable, simply changing into some other form such as that of a *salik* bird, or white hawk, or crow of dawn, or grass.

Almost a year and a half earlier, Jibanananda had published a poem in which an *aswattha* tree spoke its mind:

SAID THAT *ASWATTHA* TREE
(*balila aswattha sei*)

Said the *aswattha* tree slowly: "Which way are you headed,
Where do you want to go?

We've all been neighbors so long, so very, very close.
Your sun-stained straw huts, they're standing yet.
And here you go forsaking home and lands,
Heading where, what path—I have no idea.
You've wrapped up your belongings, even the broken bowls, that leaky pot.
Now where are you set on going?

"Not fifty years have passed, why, it seems just yesterday
Your grandfathers, fathers, uncles
—yes, I remember them well.
Here on the edge of these very fields they bought land, built their straw huts.
And on this land, on these paths with all this grass and paddy, trees and *nim* and *jamarul,*
They paid off their debt of sorrow with life's hope, hunger, and exhaustion.
Standing here I watched it all—it seems like just the other day.

"You won't stay any longer? Which way are you headed?
I suppose there's greater peace somewhere else—more hope?
A deeper sense of life, I suppose?
And that's why you'll go there to build your huts of hope.
But, no matter where you go, life itself does not change.
No matter where you build your hope-filled huts, a tale of hunger, dreams,
A tale of pain and separation shall show itself in graying hair."
So said that *aswattha* tree, trembling in the darkness overhead.[100]

The *aswattha* tree, that imperishable tree of life, had watched life change. Generations lived and died within its purview. Then some inhabitants of the area were about to leave, in search of a greater peace. Jibanananda had returned to Barisal in the 1930s, back to the land of his ancestors. And so, as if empathizing with the *aswattha,* he spoke as poet for it, admonishing those about to leave their homeland for the anticipated better life elsewhere. That same tree of life would protest another exodus, when a man with his hanging rope approached one of its limbs.

Death always fascinated Jibanananda. The sonnets of *Bengal the Beautiful* teem with tension between life and death. There the poet had been trying to answer the unanswerable: Does death deprive one of Bengal? "A Day Eight Years Ago" wrestles anew with the problem, with the emphasis shifting to the nature of the suicidal urge—why man chooses death.

In an elegy for his friend Sudhir Kumar Datta, whose eyes he likened unto bird's nests, Jibanananda stated that "death is like a second returning of life itself." Later on in that same essay he wrote:

It seems to me that as long as we are alive and continue to come in contact with death, we shall see various sorts of images, shall see dreams, we shall ask questions, shall fantasize. But, concerning this matter, we can prepare no maps, no "timetable." It is not possible to travel blissfully to that far shore and then jovially return to this side, like just so many "American tourists."[101]

Even after the moon had drowned and all was utter blackness, the owl remained awake, alive, searching for food. Even the old, half-dead frog begged for yet a few more minutes or another dawn sun. The mosquitoes, in the darkness of their Buddhist "monasteries" (*samgharam*), did not resign themselves to that suspended state of animation known as religious meditation but instead fought furiously to sink their proboscises into life's bloody stream. Flies would even feed on carrion and filth just so that they too could live and dart about in sunlight; other insects, some of the smallest and lowest forms of life, lived life fully, sporting in the sun's life-sustaining light. Every being seemed possessed by an irrepressible, boundless sense of life. Even the helpless grasshopper in the hands of some mischievous child struggled single-mindedly against death.

Nature intensifies the poignancy of this human's behavior. If life is so precious to other living beings, why did he value his own so little? If he could see what price others would pay for life, why did he give his up freely? Had not other living creatures protested his unnatural act? Had not the *aswattha* branch protested? Had not the fireflies—flashing symbols of life in the darkness—shown him light, life, golden flowers? Had not the screech owl screamed that life goes on even in the dark, that darkness in fact presents a fine opportunity to catch a few life-sustaining mice?

About a third of the way through the poem, Jibanananda switches from the impersonal third person to the personal second person pronoun of direct address. This change of voice deepens our sense of horror as the suicide confronts his hanging tree. We have made contact with him now, speaking to him directly. That emotional quickening then subsides as the narrator views the corpse in the morgue, well after the dramatic meeting of man and tree. He muses, in a somewhat detached manner, on why the suicide took place. He understands—or thinks he does—that there is something intangible in man's blood, something that exhausts the life force.

Even so, every night the she-owl, now old and blind but with hope in her heart still, remains as enthusiastic as ever about living. Out of habit, instinct maybe, she screeches out her excitement. The moon has set again. Again she will hunt a mouse or two, despite her blindness. Is exhausting, blinding life still so wonderful? Presumably she would answer yes. She has lived to a blind old age and now sits upon the hanging tree, the tree of enlightenment, or of *samsara*. And yet she reaffirms life. With that observation, the narrator rejects suicide and affirms (for the time being anyway) a life like the owl's. He will not commit suicide, but instead will feast on life, continuing to struggle, to fight against death. Unless one struggles, he dies like a rat. All creatures must actively feast on life, as the owl does. A rich, lush environment alone does not suffice to sustain life. The suicide had all a man could physically want. Even so, he did not seize the day and feast on life.

The last stanza of the poem notwithstanding, Jibanananda is much more interested in the death and its causes than in the owl and her life-sustaining mice. In fact, the whole poem, but for the last stanza, investigates why the man brought about his own demise. Had he seen a ghost? Had dark silence, craning its camel-like neck through the window, whispered to him to commit suicide? Both possibilities are impossible to confirm.

But a third factor that may have caused the suicide is present in everyone: Jibanananda, at least, senses that this suicidal something dwells in him, in his very blood.

> There is some other perilous wonder
> Which frolics
> In our very blood.
> It exhausts us—

This something results in a weariness the sleep of death may alleviate, but "it" remains a mystery. What I translate as "perilous wonder" (*bipanna bismay*) causes weariness which results in that suicidal urge. The poem hinges on this phrase, though the English translation may not be forceful enough to convey its importance. The man confronts the *aswattha* tree at the poem's emotional peak, but the overriding question is *why* did he commit suicide. Just what is this "perilous wonder"?

Dipti Tripathi concludes that "perilous wonder" represents the mental agony of creativity:

> This perilous wonder is creativity's agony. In the poem "Sensation" [*bodh*], too, the poet spoke of this oppression of creativity—
> > Not a dream—not peace—not love,
> > Inside my heart a sensation is born!
> > I cannot escape it
> Against this super force the poet is helpless. Unlike for worldly people, love, children, affluence, fame cannot bring out one's true identity for the poet. Moreover, he is weary from that perpetual struggle with the unrelenting emotions of creativity.[102]

Another critic, Rabindranath Samanta, understands the term to be an expression of the awe Jibanananda felt when looking upon death and being drawn by its strange magnetism. He, too, sees a connection between "perilous wonder" and "sensation":

The poet looked upon death itself with a sensation of wonder. Jibanananda was primarily a poet of the wonder-sensation. With this feeling of wonder—like that of the romantic poets, toward grass, flowers, stars, rivers, and women—he gazed in utter wonder at death, too, and the irresistible magnetism of death. That man had everything and now has made death is very own; that man was alive yesterday and today is dead. As the poet seeks the reason for the astonishing act, he is stunned, wonderstruck.[103]

The word *bismay* shows up a number of times in Jibananada's poetry. It glosses as "wonder" and "surprise," but one can feel wonder and surprise at any number of things. A poem from the expanded edition of *Gray Manuscripts* displays affinities to "A Day Eight Years Ago":

BIRD
(*pakhi*)

Exhausted, you are fast asleep, and so
To whom can I, in tonight's moonlight, tell of
My feeling of wonder—and the source of this wonder
Which came from the stars—for you are not awake.

Upon my breast weighs this bird.
Bird or moth? Bird or firefly?
Brown gold blue down, hidden in more down.
He came alone on such a winter's night

From some still grass,
From sheaves of paddy sometime, somewhere
From an egg of silk he came and caught
The shivers, this shivering thrill.

In moonlight, in winter's cold
Whom had he sought? How far did he wish to fly?
Had deserted fields of stubble pained
Him? Where in the world is there no sorrow?

No, no, the look on his face was of dreamy courage.
He had not known pain—but put his faith in
Splendiferous life.
Down, beak, feathers—these were his pride.

In moonlight, in winter's cold,
Though he had to come into these hard hands of mine—
With death abundant all around, why do I balk at granting that
To you? Am I too not a bird, nestled in hard, unseen hands. And none

Saddened will hesitate to cast me away. I know I won't by some mistake
Be spared. Yet, as I place a gentle finger on this colored cotton ball
Wet with the night's dew, I see, quietly examining,
A fear, it seems, surrounds those golden,

Glistening eyes. This bird, so small—yet he had learned all. What wonder—
That fear and pain are present in the hearts even of creation's smallest creatures.
Not hope, not longing, neither love nor dreams,
But all about in this world hangs the scent

Of separation. Such sorrow is in their hearts too,
Theirs too. It weighs upon that richly colored plumage.
But why? Why had these golden eyes searched for an ocean of moonlight
And then again sought some far universe? Why?[104]

A bird lies dying, though our narrator "balk[s] at granting that," preferring euphemistically to speak of him as sleeping. He speaks to the creature directly in the second person and about it in the third person, a shift of voice used more dramatically in "A Day Eight Years Ago," where occurs this same paradigm of the poet speaking to and about a dead subject. There the subject was a man who had taken his own life; here the subject is on the verge of death. Here again, however, the poet asks, why death. Or, rather, he asks why it came to live if it is only going to suffer and die. "This sorrow is in their hearts too," he declares. And he, the poet, will die some day; he too is held in the hard, unseen hand of death. The world reeks of the stench of separation—the separation of life from the living world. At first the poet thinks this bird, a dumb animal, dies happily. But then, on closer scrutiny, he sees that the bird, too, suffers as does man. Sorrow, fear, and pain exist within that heart, behind the colorful exterior plumage. That realization causes our narrator to feel *bismay*.

The final poem in *Bengal the Beautiful,* one of the few nonsonnets, contains the phrase *ascarya bismaye* ("in astonished wonder"). This poem and one of the sonnets provide two other contextual environments for Jibanananda's feeling of "wonder."

Some day no one will find me any more in this foggy field, that I know.
My heart will cease to travel then—will enter the cold and peaceful
Room, or comfort may come somewhat slowly. To forget these fields
Of the earth may take time. And toward a few *salik* birds of the fields

I shall gaze in astonished wonder for a time from in my bed of darkness.

Or do the golden hawk's wings still today from afar come floating
On fog of fields? And still today head toward that bald *aswattha* tree
   as evening turns to gold?
And do field mice eyes among soft rice stalks still gaze toward stars

As evening falls? Have bees not built a hive even today from a densely
Foliated *jam* branch? With honey eaten do they still today fly through
Evening breeze and fog—how far—or someone burns fallen *calata*
   leaves
Beneath the honey hive—bees fly out—fall—lie dead on the grass—

It hurts to think of it. If I would but live on the earthly paths—
But enough of that, I have never ever seen well the spotted owl's face—
Such a bashful bird—do the gray wings dance upon those waves of
   fog?
When seven stars shine forth does she descend into the dense breast

Of some *gab* tree? Does the light of fireflies not fall through dark holes
In *jiuli* and *babala* trees? Little children oblivious to guardians' fears
Search for a *jhimjhim* bug's green flesh in darkness, lost among
   akanda trees
Beneath a *makal* vine in the blue water of dew, but no one will find it.

And do the golden hawk's wings—his wings still today come floating
On fog of fields? And still today head toward that bald *aswattha* tree
   as evening turns gold?
And do field mice eyes among soft rice stalks still gaze toward stars?
I shall gaze in astonished wonder for a time from in my bed of
   darkness.[105]

And:

> Here life's current ebbs and flows—and they sleep silently
> This evening on mud floors—the smell of dark and dust clinging
> To their eyes and mouths. An owl sings upon a *kadam* branch.
> It seems one day perhaps only this moonlight will remain on earth,
> Only this cold. All night long this spotted owl will talk—
> From jackfruit limb then branches of the *hijal* she will call
> To a *sapamasi* bug—that day paddy will wave in darkness before
> Lips and eyes of mice—bats' black wings on *karamaca* leaves
>
> Will wring out fog and fly away into a farther blue fog,
> And no one will see that. On that day I shall no longer see
> The wonder of the village path—all will sleep on: as dead men
> Sleep tonight, as the leaves of *aswattha* and *jhau* trees
> Are withering, rotting most quietly in sleep tonight,
> As dead women sleep—as upon their breasts sleep their saris.[106]

Jibanananda used *bismay* in various contexts, at times to indicate his own restless, continuing awe at life's glories, especially as found in his beloved Bengal, at times to convey a fascination bordering on horror engendered by the very idea of death. Particularly telling, given his avocation as poet—and therefore as sensitive chronicler—is his characterization of that wonder as "perilous," for its coursing in the blood can in and of itself exhaust its possessor to death. Unlike the suicide, however, Jibanananda is much more the grasshopper in a child's grasp, or the blind old owl—struggling to participate in life's wonders rather than merely gazing upon them from a "bed of darkness." Our poet does not understand the suicide who turns away from "life's full store," search as he might for an answer to the why of the fateful journey in which self-death was wrested from the tree of life. Jibanananda will accept death only if he is snatched up "like a field mouse into the house of death," despite the exhaustion, the "grievous/Pain of waking," the knowledge that his life, too, rests in "unseen hands" that will not hesitate, someday, to cast him away. Sheer poetic skill and force of vision enabled Jibanananda to wonder so wonderfully aloud in "A Day Eight Years Ago." He plumbs the depths of the ambiguities and tensions that create the life-death dichotomy[107] and scrutinizes the play of exhaustion and seduction that forms the mosaic of "this foggy field."

4
The War Years: Prelude and Aftermath

> During the forties with all the hullabaloo from poets partial to revolution, Jibanananda, that votary of solitude, trod a saner path toward the society to be, lighting the way with a different sort of poetry.
>
> —Sanjay Bhattacharya, *Poet Jibanananda Das*

1

Politics, during the late 1930s and the two following decades, profoundly affected Bengali literature. In 1937, *Paricay*'s reviewer of Jibanananda's *Gray Manuscripts* had spoken of two classes of modern poets, differentiated according to their degree of independence from Rabindranath. That reviewer also commented upon such literary qualities of Jibanananda's poetry as meter and diction. By the late 1940s and 1950s, it was neither Rabindranath nor formal literary features but political criteria against which many critics measured the literary arts.

A Bengali literary history of the 1940s must consider the Communist Party of India and the Bengali writers who embraced Marxism. During previous decades, the literati deemed themselves divided along modern-traditional lines. Rabindranath proved to be both modern and traditional, and influential in both camps. But Rabindranath aside, modernity and tradition were the two general rubrics under which writers fell—until the 1940s when Marxism became a compelling influence. Some writers became Communists outright; others were sympathetic; still others were not. Some writers banded together in opposing literary-cum-political groups; others remained independent of any political affiliation. Jibanananda participated only peripherally in such groups, but his poetry came to reflect a greater political awareness than it had previously displayed.

In 1928 the sixth World Congress of the Comintern established a strict sectarian posture for Communist Parties everywhere. Members were true Communists, all others shunned as the enemy. The Party indulged none of the socialist, Left-leaning organizations. At the seventh World Congress of the Comintern in August 1935, that sectarian stance gave way to a *front populaire* philosophy, with the adoption of the Dutt-Bradley Thesis—"The

Anti-Imperialist People's Front in India."[1] One result of this policy of cooperation and alliance was the formation of an All-India Progressive Writers' Association (AIPWA),[2] the first conference of which took place in Lucknow, April 1936. In his presidential address the respected Urdu and Hindi writer Munshi Prem Chand declared that literature must contain "an impulse toward social reconstruction, the power to reflect the hard realities of life—in short we want a literature which may produce in us movement, change and restlessness."[3] Though organized by the Communists, the AIPWA supported and received support from non-Communist writers, too. A second AIPWA conference, presided over by Rabindranath, convened in Calcutta, December 1938. Shortly thereafter, the organization collapsed.

Though the AIPWA disintegrated, integration of literature and politics progressed unabated. Pranabendu Dasgupta writes about this decade:

> I have spoken of the significant poets of the forties as a major group in a very particular sense; however, that group was not undivided. And it must be kept in mind that the primary impetus for the divisions was politics or the poets' attitudes toward politics.[4]

Abu Sayeed Ayyub called this shift in literary focus the Communism and near-Communism phase, characterizing it, with but few exceptions, as rather sterile. He labeled "leftism" the literary fashion of the day ". . . and, the less competent a writer is, the more anxious he is to be à la mode."[5]

Two men in particular, Sanjay Bhattacharya and Satyaprasanna Datta who edited and published *Purvasa* ("The East"), reacted vehemently against the intrusion of Communist ideology into poetry.[6] Leftist ideological presence was real enough. However, Sanjay's perception of the Bengali literary situation around 1940 proved singular, for he held even Buddhadeva and his magazine, *Kavita,* to be Communist camp followers.[7]

In 1944, Jibanananda's fourth book, *The World at Large,* was published by Purvasa Ltd., Sanjay and Satyaprasanna's publishing concern. According to Satyaprasanna, who did the printing himself, that volume formed part of the effort to check Communist infiltration of literature, by reviving "romanticism" (he spoke the English word) in poetry. Jibanananda's book, in Sanjay's estimation, would go a long way toward reestablishing romanticism's credentials and thus exert a positive, anti-Communist influence on the course of Bengali poetry.[8]

Like Buddhadeva Bose, Sanjay Bhattacharya had been active throughout most of the 1930s, advancing the cause of modern literature—as he understood it. He himself wrote as well as published other writers in *Purvasa*. But unlike Buddhadeva, Sanjay became emotionally involved with politics and tended to mix literature with matters political in a rather idiosyncratic blend. In 1939, after an anti-Hitler, anti-British issue (which appealed to no Bengali constituency at that precise juncture in history), *Purvasa* of financial necessity folded—regular publication resuming only after a hiatus of several years, in 1943. During the interlude, however, editor Sanjay did not sit idle. Premendra Mitra and Acintya Kumar Sengupta, according to Satyaprasanna, approached Sanjay about bringing out another magazine. Both Sanjay and Satyaprasanna felt reluctant to embark on a new publishing enterprise, for they planned to resume *Purvasa* again at some future time. Nevertheless, in September 1940, one year after *Purvasa* fell silent, a poetry quarterly entitled *Nirukta* raised its voice with Premendra Mitra and Sanjay Bhattacharya as joint editors.

Reluctantly or not, Sanjay agreed to undertake *Nirukta* for specific purposes, one of which was to stem Communist literary incursions while advancing the cause of that romanticism he so cherished.[9] The journal's title—not without significance—suggests a further aim: *nirukta* means "categorically or explicitly or clearly stated." Modern Bengali poetry, some felt, had become an unintelligible, sickly babble. *Nirukta* was there to heal the sick. Part of Premendra Mitra's editorial in *Nirukta's* initial issue spoke to that point:

> Briefly stated, it is our feeling that there are sufficient symptoms manifest in contemporary Bengali poetry to suggest the existence of an unhealthy perversion. And this is not just our feeling; from Rabindranath's letter, quoted in the current issue, it is quite evident that the perverse direction Bengali poetry is heading worries and pains him. This sick poetry could easily have been silently ignored were it not for the present danger of contagion it carries with it. But censure and criticism alone are not sufficient antidotes against infection. The best means of warding off infection is to maintain a healthy and sound standard of poetry; toward this end we have brought out *Nirukta*.[10]

The letter by Rabindranath mentioned above bears the date 22 August 1940, and begins:

> I was happy to learn that several of you are about to publish *Nirukta*. For some time now there has been an unabated increase in the number of persons seeking poetic fame via the non-poet's path of obscure discontinuity of thought and of stuttering, perverted meters.[11]

As already noted, Rabindranath had soured on the metrical experiments of the 1930s. And by the 1940s, the intelligibility of poetic thought—or lack thereof—loomed large as an issue in Bengali literary circles. *Nirukta* had been founded ostensibly on the principle that "obscure discontinuity of thought" was unpoetic.

There appears to have been another and more personal reason for publishing *Nirukta*: resentment toward Buddhadeva and *Kavita*. Sanjay gives us some inkling of this emotional dimension:

Because *Kavita* had become a Stalinist camp, he [Premendra Mitra] relinquished his editorship of *Kavita* and came into *Purvasa*'s so-called Trotsky camp, to battle dictator Buddhadeva Bose in a verbal war. Even though I was attacked by Buddhadeva from the second issue of *Kavita* onward, yet I, as the secondary editor of *Nirukta,* did not raise the least little protest against Buddhadeva. Rather, by reviewing Buddhadeva Bose's poetic accomplishments, I fulfilled the duty of one of his enthusiastic readers. It was Buddhadeva who had assailed me, after deleting my poem from the second issue of *Kavita;* twelve years later, fearing the demise of *Kavita,* it was Buddhadeva who invited me again to contribute poetry to *Kavita.*[12]

The rift between Premendra Mitra and Buddhadeva may have been based on politics, may have stemmed partially from their differing opinion regarding poetry, but probably derived from a combination of causes. The dissension between Buddhadeva and Sanjay, however, seems to have sprung from an incident that occurred just after *Kavita* began publication. Purvasa Press actually printed the first two issues of that quarterly. For the second issue, Satyaprasanna Datta typeset one of Sanjay's own poems, without the editors' permission. Incensed, Buddhadeva excised that poem from the issue, and, by the third issue, *Kavita* had a new printer.

For whatever purposes, Premendra Mitra and Sanjay Bhattacharya began publishing their excellent poetry quarterly in September 1940. Sanjay considered Jibanananda Das the featured poet in this new publication:

> At the very beginning of the forties, the second year of World War II, it was not only the ailing Rabindranath but several post-Rabindric poets, too—Premendra Mitra in the forefront—who felt uncomfortable about the type of social consciousness which bellowed forth in Bengali verse and which at the same time rejected [true] poetry. At that point, the *Purvasa* group took refuge in the poetic genius of Jibanananda Das for the purpose of preserving Bengali poetry's own best interests.[13]

Nirukta, the journal devoted to healthy, romantic, intelligible, non-Communist poetry carried in its first issue Jibanananda's poems "Movement" (*gatibidhi*) and "Ascertainment" (*nirdes*).

MOVEMENT

The way in stands ever open,
And once inside the way out too is there:
A path of light into open field from forest's darkness
And from the field's light again into darkest night,
Or, leaving homey pleasures, for the company of a woman—jester—
  fly.

All this represents the wanderings of the body.
It may go, asleep.
(But the path of full consciousness stretches even further.
Light and darkness mean nothing to it.)
The ostrich roaming all day in the sunlight
Blinds himself perhaps by burying his head in sand—
Maybe out of modesty.

I've learned beloved truth from reading books,
Gained strength from some plague-ridden land,
Loved a woman,
Or, overwhelmed, I went to share with everyone another truth,
On a clear autumn night, most decorative and bright—
Or, to offer sincerest consolation to the farthest stars,
But anxiety, like a wet dog on a rainy night
From door to door, shakes off malice.

It stirs at the very roots of all the tall trees
By the river—far below trance.
It drinks the decoction of philosophers' teeth
Within the carcass of a rat—discarded sweet potatoes—dead meat.
Cognizant, we prepare ourselves,
For there remains a long prologue—
It will be understood (if there is some humility in our eyes)—
Why beautiful peacocks had created the ostrich
In a melody of the weaver's loom—in the sun's melodic scale.[14]

ASCERTAINMENT

Now again time by itself sports in the wind
With a thin and worn weaver's shuttle.
"To whom had they given the slip after playing
In the cascade's noose—that early morning,
The *hariyal* bird, the gray *cital* fish?"
Saying this, two "speak-to-your-wife" birds laughed.
That laugh sparkled upon the cascade,
Pouring over rounded pebbles.
Along with brilliant fish, the dawn's cascade
Tickled time's shuttle.
Irritated time thus went in search, in some other matter,
Of a partner for his own rule-bound heart.

If the light is blown out in a puff of time,
Whom does it harm—whom will it harm?
Maitreyi—Nagarjuna—Kautilya in silence[15]
Consider that question as they bend over black stones.
Two and two is still three, four, five.
Riddle and refutation remain alive like cascade's jingling.[16]

It is difficult to understand why Premendra Mitra and Sanjay published two such opaque poems in the maiden issue of the magazine whose name meant "categorically stated." The adjective *durbodhya* or "not easily intelligible" had often been applied to Jibanananda's poetry of this ilk. Neither of these lyrics found its way into any of the volumes published by Jibanananda during his lifetime. The only exegesis in print of either verse consists of a brief statement by Sanjay that "Movement" does not present a very hopeful picture. Citing the first four lines, he declares that the poet finds no spiritual purpose or intent in that light into the open field—a light that shines upon life—and concludes that Jibanananda had begun to prepare the twentieth-century mind (presumably for life in the twentieth century).[17]

B.M. College colleagues, some partial to Jibanananda's nemesis, Sajani Kanta Das, took special glee in mocking the bashful English professor and his seemingly befogged Bengali poetry. Heramba Chakravarty, professor of Bengali, reminisced following Jibanananda's death:

> I remember today how I had attacked him, publishing a satirical poem entitled "Spiky Catfish in Blue Waters" (*nil jale simimach*). At first his eyes got that embarrassed, doleful expression. Then in the following instant, his queer burst of laughter chased away those clouds of sarcasm. The high priest of sarcasm, however, was Professor Narendralal Ganguly, now Principal of Dum Dum Motijhil College. Jibanananda Babu was deeply hurt by such adverse criticism of his poetical talents.[18] He would restrain his critics with that pathetic, helpless expression of a little boy just beaten with a switch. I'm not sure whether he was angered by the insults in *Sanibarer Cithi,* but he used to be very curious. As soon as he heard an issue had arrived, he would come to me and read the (not Jibananda) section.[19] And then offering up that unique, erupting laugh, he would go off silently. It was as if his dream-veil of poetic imagination had not been disturbed in the least.[20]

Ramesh Chandra Sen—chemistry professor, ardent Rabindranath admirer, and personal friend of Sajani Kanta[21]—composed a number of satirical verses aimed pointedly at what he deemed to be the gibberish of Jibanananda's (and all the modern, post-Rabindranath poets') idiom.

IS THIS ALONE SOLACE(?)
(*ei sudhu santwana*[?])

There's a hornbill's nest atop imperishable banyan,
Lyada bugs are into *chatim* tree blossoms.
Parrot and insect, amid the dense sun's flowing hair,
Satisfied the world's urge to live.

Grandmother fries up some rancid breaded shrimp
Golden on the outside, cholera within—
An American girl seems like rice-straw smoke
Beneath the posturing smoke, carbon black.

Rows of smoky-eyed owls
Spreading their blue tongues beneath the window,
Not a side-glance, a golden necklace—
Give me some water chestnuts, some yellow baby bird eggs.

Half of a *jam* berry in a beautiful cave.
Is this alone solace for the slabbery poet?[22]

2

Perhaps Jibanananda's "not easily intelligible" quality can best be demonstrated by observing five serious students of modern poetry grapple with the same lyric. If "In Camp," with its doe in heat, troubled *Paricay*'s management back in 1932, "Dance of Twilight" (*godhulisandhir nritya*), published in that same journal—but with a somewhat different editorial board—in 1939 could have been dubbed a veritable conundrum.

DANCE OF TWILIGHT

Where crowded porticos—at the end of the world
Lie fallen—silent—broken—
There behind tall *haritaki* trees
The red—round sun of a winter's afternoon

Quietly sinks—into moonlight.
Only an owl alone sits in the *aswattha* tree
Staring out, watching a golden ball-like sun
And the renowned face of a silvered caselike moon.

Beneath those *haritaki* branches flash diamond sparks
And jubilant white crystalline waters:
The shadowy shape of a human head—stillness—
Brown leaf scents—*madhukupi* grass.

Several goddesslike women:
Their men: deeds, tender-aged ones;
Within their hair and hair buns: freshly born clouds of hell,
Beneath their posturing feet is the grass of Hong Kong.

There hidden waters turn pale, then again as diamonds,
Rustling leaves make no noise;
Yet they sense in the decrepit roar of cannons
That Shanghai is being destroyed.

There several gregarious women,
Gesturing with hair and eyes beneath an intimate moon,
Gifted women; men both local and foreign
Will not rise up again, maddened in blood of trade and war.

They draw them gradually with profound kisses
But human sleep yields no flavor as their heads
Lie on cotton pillows; with waves upon this lowly worldly field
By breezes of that pulverized earth—by Varuna

They take them along a crooked path into the *haritaki* grove—in moonlight.
The days of cut glass sunshine of trade and war
Have all ended; in their braids are unresponsive clouds of hell,
Beneath their posturing feet are Scorpio—Cancer—Libra—Pisces.[23]

Sunil Ganguly presented a short piece of criticism on "Dance of Twilight" in what was one of the better, albeit short-lived, critical journals in Bengal during the latter half of the 1960s, *Kavita-Paricay*. He began with a rather belittling paraphrase:

Several destructive women somewhere in a jungle forest have begun to dance in the early moonlight. Round about them are several young men. This is the subject matter of the poem—nothing more. Now one can research various philosophical points and tear one's hair. But that little bit *is* the poem.[24]

He goes on to point out what he feels to be metrical errors, and accuses Jibanananda of having overindulged in end-rhymes and alliteration and of having inserted meaningless or inappropriate words simply for sound effect. Furthermore, Sunil takes issue with the title: Jibanananda meant to imply the twilight of civilization, quaking with the tremors of war. But then the poem moves quickly from twilight in the first stanza to moonlight for the rest of the poem. The title should have been simply "Dance," he suggests. And since there is moonlight, the reader may conclude that after twilight and war, the world is not plunged into complete darkness but remains illuminated from the moon's glow. In something of a summation, Sunil restates the poem's "subject matter":

Waves of dance come wafting by, even where the world is being devastated by the throes of war. This is indeed true, for war can destroy nothing of the world; it is within man himself that the destruction has commenced. Such is the message of this poem—the rest is just ambience or, in other words, just words. When one excludes the message, that which remains is poetry.[25]

As might be expected, Sunil's article drew rebuttals. Two critics explained away Jibanananda's seeming metrical missteps as mixed meter or printing errors,[26] or as an expression of the poet's freedom and of the strength of *payar,* which can be scanned two different ways.[27] But by far the most enlightening aspect of the several rebuttals: no two persons could agree on what Jibanananda's poem communicated. Naresh Guha wrote:

> The main difficulty with Sunil Babu's explication is this: I cannot find in the poem itself where several destructive women somewhere in a forest jungle have begun to dance in the early moonlight. It is my feeling, moreover, that this poem is a profound jest.[28]

Arun Kumar Sarkar disagreed with both Sunil and Naresh Guha:

> The former saw within the poem a picture of a pleasing dance; to him, "the dance is paramount in this poem." It is the latter person's feeling that "this poem is a profound jest." The opinions of both these men seem to me most quizzical. For until now the meaning conveyed to my mind by the poem under discussion was not that of dance nor of jest—and please don't be startled to learn—but that of pervasive melancholy.[29]

Manabendra Banerjee sees the macabre in the goddesslike woman's dance of death. The women, not goddesses but goddesslike, are in fact whores, Manab tells us. Their profound kisses become kisses of death as men perish through both war and commerce in Britain's colony of Hong Kong:

> We can understand why clouds of hell are born from within
> their hair buns as we recall the Chinese and Japanese adage:
> women are the gates of hell.[30]

But Manab, though he renders interpretations of many other elements in this poem, has difficulty situating the action geographically. Are the crumbling porticos that of a zemindary mansion, in which case the poem, with its *haritaki* and *aswattha* trees, would be set in Bengal. Or, are these porticos a part of the colonial architecture of British Hong Kong, in which case the trees present somewhat of an enigma.[31]

A fifth commentator, Sanjay Bhattacharya, interprets the poem stanza by stanza.[32] He considers "Dance of Twilight" to be one of Jibanananda's finest compositions or "visions." To Sanjay, the title does not signify civilization's twilight due to war, for the war is over: "The days of cut glass sunshine of trade and war/Have all ended. ...." The "juncture" (*sandhi,* as in *godhulisandhi,* quite literally "the juncture of twilight") in the title implies not day's end but the close of the war:

> The war has ended, and young men and women are dancing together in celebration of the peace. The poet realizes that this momentary peace is a prelude to another war or revolution. ... That time when the past war and the future revolution come together is a moment of peace—Jibanananda wished to call such time "twilight." ... The "vision" of Rabindranath's *Balaka* is that of the eve of World War I, and the "vision" of Jibanananda's "Dance of Twilight" is that of the eve of the Chinese revolution.[33]

If the relatively apolitical Jibanananda of the 1930s could in 1939—based on what had been happening between Chiang Kai-shek and Mao Tse-tung during that decade—predict the outbreak of hostilities between Nationalist and Communist forces in the autumn of 1945 just months after the surrender of Japan, then one would have to agree with Sanjay's assertion that Jibanananda was a visionary poet. More likely, Sanjay simply forgot that "Dance of Twilight" had been published during the first half of 1939 and not around the end of World War II. (It was later included in the volume *Darkness of Seven Stars* [1948], which might have influenced Sanjay's perception of when the poem had been composed. A manuscript version of this lyric can be found in one of the notebooks dated December 1937 in the National Library's Jibanananda collection.)

These five divergent readings emphasize the fact that much of Jibanananda's poetry becomes something less than intelligible by the beginning of the 1940s. Perhaps Jibanananda is making a statement about the nature of civilization as he understood it, but his communication remains incomplete and ineffable. He has not provided prose exegeses of his poetry (the posthumously published note on "In Camp" is the sole exception), nor did he discuss specifics of it in letters to friends. And so five Bengali critics—two of them university professors of comparative literature, and four out of the five established poets—understand Jibanananda's poem in five very different and not at all complementary ways.

3

Dhurjati Prasad Mukherjee wrote to Sanjay in the early 1940s, apparently in response to an invitation to contribute an essay on Jibanananda to the forthcoming *Nirukta:*

These days Buddhadeva considers Jibananda [*sic*] Das a superior poet. I too have been attentively reading his work. I enjoyed the last several poems. However, I still cannot grasp what he is all about. When I do, I'll write something; no one need encourage me to do so. I had a conversation with him one day this past summer vacation but couldn't accept what he said about poetry. If I were to write something just now, I would probably not do him justice simply because our difference of opinion would pose a hindrance to my appreciation. I must have time to forget "his opinions." Do you understand?[34]

Abu Sayeed Ayyub spoke of Jibanananda Das as Bengal's most confused poet. The poems of the *Banalata Sen* volume Ayyub enjoyed—Jibanananda could feel, perhaps better than any of his fellow poets. But he could not formulate, failing miserably when he tried to set forth a philosophy of life. The *Banalata Sen* poems work wonderfully as poems, as personal, emotional statements of sensation. Ayyub conceded that even some of the post–*Banalata Sen* sociological observations succeed as poetry. Jibanananda possessed the ability to observe and to empathize with a peasant or beggar as well as to mourn the death of a deer. However, Ayyub reiterated, the philosophical poems fail, because the philosophy fails, if indeed it is actually intelligible.[35]

Sanjay wrote an article on Jibanananda for *Nirukta*'s very last issue (June 1943) in which he suggested a reason for the ever increasing complexity of his friend's verse. Complexity here becomes a somewhat more impersonal, less subjective word than unintelligibility. And in fact, Jibanananda used the word *jatil* (complex), not *durbodhya* (not easily intelligible), when referring to his own work. Wrote Sanjay:

> Perhaps, because he has been forced to enter into another world [a material world] after the first world [a world of feeling] had been shattered, he finds no assurances in his mind about the certainty of this second world. This anxiety causes his thinking, his language to become ever more complex. Let us conclude with the poet's own words concerning his present poetry: "Currently my poetry has become complex (*jatil*). There is little favor for my latter poetry. Be it a fault or a virtue—this element is not unnatural; it is merely one phase in the life of poetry. If I have the strength, the will, and maintain a true heart, I may perhaps advance poetry toward the future."[36]

Ambuj Bose offers a rather interesting explanation for the complexity of Jibanananda's poetry. And though Ambuj Bose's observations do not seem altogether valid, his suppositions beg serious consideration and may even suggest why the poetry of this World War II period became intelligible only with difficulty. He first points to the language in these poems, a particular language of an individual mind, a language of the feelings of an individual who has studied in English, thought in English. Often when one is reading this poetry it seems that a Bengali artist who was raised with English notions has done an amazingly tasteful translation of English poetry.[37]

He goes on to state that Jibanananda's expository prose—as employed in his essays—reveals likewise a strange variety of Bengali and one that would translate easily into English. From experience, I can assure Ambuj Bose that this is not the case. Jibanananda's essays are as difficult to render into English as they are to read in Bengali. And likewise, I question the assertion that this poetry reads like a translation from English, although the inference bears pondering: Jibanananda may have been trying to think in terms of an intellectual system quite foreign to him. Forcing his language to communicate ideas that he himself only partially understood, ideas on war and peace and the future of human civilization, he produced only partially intelligible poetry.

Nirukta's second issue (December 1940) contained two more of Jibanananda's poems, "Beggar" (*bhikhiri*) and "Night" (*ratri*), both of them far more readily comprehensible than those in the initial issue.

BEGGAR

I got one pice[38] at Ahiritola,
I got one pice at Badur Bagan.
If I could just get one more,
I'd walk away with dignity
—he said, stretching out his hand in the dark.
It was as if a blind man yearned with all his being to weave cloth,
But his efforts become as the conch shell craftsman's saw in crippled hands.

I got one pice while roaming through the parks,
I got one pice at Pathuria Ghata.
If I could just get one more,
I'd have some rice husked
—he said, extending his neck till the light from the gas lamp fell upon his face.
But in the crowd—on Harrison Road—was a deeper sadness.
A world's mistake: a beggar ignored. The world's failing.[39]

This poignant little poem shows Jibanananda, the humanist, at his best. He sees the beggar, hand outstretched, craning to gain recognition. Whereas he fantasized Banalata Sen, now he sees an actual human being.

He also sees the city. He had, of course, been to Calcutta many times before, having been a student there for four years, and teaching at City College for six more. On various other occasions he had visited Calcutta. Now he sees the city strongly and clearly—the fantasy world of "unreal domes and a palace" ("Naked Lonely Hand") temporarily superseded by the very real world of Calcutta, replete with her beggars.[40]

If indeed *Nirukta* stood in literary, political, and personal opposition to *Kavita,* as Sanjay seems to have believed, such differences of opinion did not prevent Jibanananda from contributing freely to both journals. In December 1940, the same month "Night" appeared in *Nirukta,* another poem by the same name was printed in *Kavita.* Both focus upon night in Calcutta.

NIGHT

There a while ago—in a huge palace—in one corner
An extension lecturer's lamp burned steadily.
Even now night has not yet really set in upon the walls;
Gas lights burn hot in the streets,
And still the sun is aglow as it fades.
A sales clerk stares quietly pondering still
Upon a ladder whether from that upper shelf
A book or pale insect—or dust—or spider will come out.
These lonely sentrylike rickshaws have not yet been lowered—
They remain lost in the crowd's squeeze.
A man stands in countless
Alleyways simultaneously,
Like a symbol of the heart of everyone of this world.
From this night into much deeper nights
In Kalutola, Pathuria Ghata, Mirzapur
On the sidewalks of Esplanade
In Malanga Lane, and Creek Row,
In Cockburne Lane—
If a pair of horns were to appear on that fellow's bald spot,
But the magician has stolen his wig and fled.
If I were to leave you here on night's edge
And go
I would go
Not from the world.
This night all night everything of life
Is here.
Dew noiselessly falls from
The *tittiraj* tree,
Striking the wings of a pair of crows.
More dew falls upon yellow straw
Like a fine mist of wind.

The War Years: Prelude and Aftermath 159

Where and when did you become lost?
All the stars overhead judicious as knives
Cutting the thread of time, cutting through the continuous thread
   of time.
The transparency of night poured over my eyes:
A grapefruit heats up somewhere, a spider top-spins around,
A court jester laughs, a queen's body turns cold.
Rivers like children—children, distant, like rivers.
The blue light of beggars and crowds fades as the ends of heaven
   are approached.
Hell's multifarious drumming beats from the foreheads of
   children.[41]

NIGHT

Lepers open the hydrant and lap some water.
Or maybe that hydrant was already broken.
Now at midnight they descend upon the city in droves.
A motor car passed by, coughing like a goat,

Scattering sloshing petrol. Though ever careful,
Someone seems to have taken a serious spill in the water.
Three rickshaws trot off, fading into the last gaslight,
As though by the power of some magician.

I turn off, leave Phear Lane, defiantly
Walk for miles, stop beside a wall
On Bentinck Street, at Territti Bazar,
There in the air dry as roasted peanuts.

The warmth of intoxicating light kisses my cheek.
Smell of kerosene, lumber, shellac, gunny, leather
Blending with the hum of dynamos
Draws taut the bowstring.

Draws taut the dead and conscious worlds,
Draws taut life's bowstring.
How long ago did Maitreyi chant her lines of verse,
Or immortal Attila conquer kingdoms?

Even now, from an upper window, half asleep, a Jew
Sings in her inimitable style.
Our forefathers smile to think of what we call song—
And what we call gold mines, oil wells, and paper mills.

Several Anglo lads stroll by, dressed smartly.
A grinning Negro leans casually against a post,
Cleaning the briar pipe he holds in his hand

> With the confidence of an old gorilla.
>
> To him the great night of the city seems
> Like the jungles of Libya.
> The animals, however, are orderly, overpaid,
> And indeed wear clothes, out of modesty.[42]

As in "Beggar," Jibanananda's "Night" poems observe Calcutta. Not coincidentally, both sets of observations take place at night, when one sees and yet remains unseen. Darkness shielded the reticent Jibanananda from too direct a contact with humanity while at the same time allowing him to peruse the urban environment's "flora and fauna." Kalutola, Pathuria Ghata, Mirzapur, Esplanade, Malanga Lane, Creek Row (he later worked in a newspaper office on Creek Row), Cockburne Lane, Phear Lane, Bentinck Street, Territti Bazar—all, as locales or streets, make up the Calcutta landscape.

In the month of August 1941, Rabindranath Tagore died at the age of eighty, his death marking the end of the twentieth century's dominant and sometimes domineering Bengali literary influence. "That there is no figure, and presumably none likely in the near future to be of Tagore's eminence in our literature goes without saying,"[43] wrote Jibanananda some eight years following Rabindranath's death. Of his influence, Jibanananda noted:

> Examine the literature of any country and one finds the age so masterfully mirrored in all its human richness through the poetry of that country's greatest poet that all other contemporary practitioners of the art, when they venture out on the diverse, dispersed paths of that era and seek to express themselves—be it through pure emotion or controlled language, through poetic suggestion or buried meaning—find it nearly impossible to avoid that master poet.[44]

There were then and are now excellent Bengali writers, well respected and literarily influential, but none attaining Rabindranath's prominence. He held sway till the end. As mentioned earlier, Rabindranath wrote *The Last Poem* in his sixties, showing the younger writers a piece of modern fiction that they themselves envied. In his seventies, Rabindranath had been instrumental in introducing prose meter into Bengali poetry.

Now the poet was dead. Many writers paid their respects, in print, to the great man. Sanjay and Satyaprasanna issued a special number of their temporarily defunct magazine *Purvasa,* which carried two poems, one of them by Jibanananda, entitled "Rabindranath" (*rabindranath*). *Paricay,* in November 1941, published a special issue in memory of Rabindranath for which Jibanananda composed another poem entitled "Rabindranath." A number of persons brought out special monographs, not necessarily connected with any established magazine. In July of the following year, there came from Pabna, a *mofussil* town now in Bangladesh, one such occasional publication, *The Twenty-fifth of Baisakh (pancise baisakh)*—Rabindranath's birthday—a collection of poems compiled by one Jyotirindra Maitra, to which Jibanananda contributed a third poem entitled "Rabindranath." Early on in his career, he had written—though he did not publish—yet another poem with the same title.[45] Then again, in the very last year of his life, Jibanananda published a fifth poem likewise entitled simply "Rabindranath."

RABINDRANATH

"There shines a light in the heart of man,
And that is why everyday honeyed sun and stars. . . ."
Some sort of words like this were heard a while ago.
Today that speaker seems

So far away.
Because our present history
Is held in winter's chill
They think Shiva's primal sounds of beauty, of creation

Have fused into that final dissolution.
Yet worth returns
To shores of newer times, like universal truth,
By effort, hope, and the consciousness of man.[46]

A more optimistic poem would be hard to find, a greater compliment, difficult to imagine. Rabindranath's poetry becomes a particularized instance of the original and universal sound, of Shiva's primal sounds of creation and beauty. When aligned with his two coequals, Brahma and Vishnu, Shiva assumes the role of destroyer. But all three Hindu gods serve independently as creator, preserver, and destroyer. One of Shiva's five-fold activities is that of creation (*sristi*). And it is Shiva who is associated with the arts, whose one of a thousand and eight epithets is "instigator of all arts."[47] Beauty, though presently in winter's clutches, will be born anew, in new poetry. Such a statement reflects Rabindranath's own view of art and artistic creation, as an individual and temporal manifestation of the universal and infinite. In his *Gitanjali* he had sung:

Thou hast made me endless, such is thy pleasure. . . .
   This little flute of a reed thou hast carried over hills and dales, and hast breathed through it melodies eternally new.[48]

During a 1916–17 lecture tour of the United States, he said, "Our individual minds are the strings which catch the rhythmic vibrations of this universal mind and respond in music of space and time. . . . Of course, our creations are mere variations upon God's great theme of the universe."[49] Once again, says an optimistic Jibanananda, resonances of Shiva's creativity will be particularized in individual works of art. The last line of Jibanananda's poem echoes his own assertion to Sanjay in the early 1940s that with "the strength, the will," and "a true heart," he might contribute to poetry's future development. This fifth "Rabindranath" poem came out in 1954. Jibanananda would go through a trying period, poetically, before he could say with confidence that something of real genius would indeed return to his, or to Bengali, poetry.

Following Rabindranath's death, Jibanananda wrote the essay, "Rabindranath and Modern Bengali Poetry," his first major statement regarding poetry since "On Poetry" appeared in *Kavita,* in 1938. In the earlier essay, Jibanananda contended that the poet should practice his own profession, not that of a philosopher or sociologist:

> Each thinking being has a special genius; he is an expert in his own domain. The poet, too, is a success in his world, that of poetic creativity. It may seem to us that since he has wisdom of a sort, the poet can make valid pronouncements concerning economics, sociology, political science, and various other realms of the intellect. We must realize it is not so. The pseudo-poet is of course an expert in all areas, as is the pseudo-philosopher. But the man of whom his native talent has made a poet or painter or musician makes his mark not as a wise thinker, but only in the realm of art. If we demand the best of a man of talent, not something second-rate, we can have it only within the confines of the realm where his talent is rooted in its own unquestionable method of development.[50]

This statement should not be construed as precluding the poet from actively partaking in practical, nonartistic life, Jibanananda warns. However, the poet can only make extraordinary contributions in the realm of art.

By 1941, Jibanananda had given ground to those forces that chose to war on society's evils with the weapon of poetry. He had by no means reversed his stance, but poetry and life appeared not so distinct for him in 1941 ("Rabindranath and Modern Bengali Poetry") as they had seemed in 1938 ("On Poetry"). Rabindranath himself integrated, Jibanananda concedes, observations on social justice with poetry.

> All those new poets in our country who look with derision upon the more exalted feelings compose their poetry in a voice now slick and scintillating, now coarse and crude—in verse or in prose meter—a poetry which exudes irony and is ever ready to unmask society's injustices throughout the world today. Rabindranath's goals are the same, yet he

usually expresses his aspirations through the passion of pure poetry. Their attitude differs from Rabindranath's in this respect: they are intellectuals who blithely disallow for that flash of inspiration and are staunchly opposed to the intrusion of any sort of rarefied essence of art [rasa] in literature.... But if one accepts literature as a mirror of the age (even a merciless mirror of a decaying age), still then journalistic and propagandistic writing differs from poetry in that the former lacks unity, purity, and freedom of inspiration rarefied through experience, the very qualities which inform poetry.[51]

Jibanananda does not actually concede that literature is or should be a reflection of the times, but he entertains this viewpoint as a possibility.

Though the master poet was no more, Bengali poetry would live on, to be sure, but Jibanananda feels less than sanguine about the times, an attitude which becomes ever more reflected in his poetry. "Glory" (*garima*) appeared on the first page of *Nirukta,* September 1941:

GLORY

On a blustery day a hawk, like this very heart of mine,
Suddenly swooping upward snatching on high
Perhaps desired the blue sky.
Yet lovers will be vanquished by demons;
And won't the irate universe scoff?

When was it that that old, golden bird
Fell at our feet.
He had fervently entertained life.
Yet today more huge than the sky—alone
Dead. Death—dear today, I am by its hand painted on a canvas.

The afternoon's whole red sun shines all around.
The river water's melody flows along, listening attentively.
Though they aren't firmly ordered within my heart
I am intent upon this sky, wind, river.
All these tokens will remain as so many objects of glory.
Or maybe glory—once people have breathed deeply the winds of this century and
The stock market has fallen—will appear in the clever and the shrewd.[52]

Jibanananda has fallen prey to cynicism as well as bemusement: that which he cherished—which the hawk, his heart, loved, "this sky, wind, river,"—will be vanquished by demons. He no longer controls the direction of his vision, for the world's natural beauties are not now "firmly ordered" in his heart—they have become "tokens," "so many objects of glory."

This poem represents the other end of the spectrum from "Sensation," where Jibanananda made us privy to his struggles with the proddings of poetic creation. Now, with a sad, almost bitter tone, he announces the death of the soaring hawk, the loss of nature as subject for his (and all romantics') inspiration, and the conquest of his world by "the clever and the shrewd." Painted on a canvas, he becomes just one more element on the *pat* (a storyteller's illustrated scroll), instead of the master painter of his beloved Bengal.

The fatigue expressed in "Banalata Sen" emanated from a very personal feeling. Death or rebirth in the nonhuman world seemed preferable to the exhaustion of life. But life wasn't evil, just personally tiring. Now Jibanananda perceives the world and its societies as something with which one must contend. Restful sleep or death no longer affords a solution. The poet, drawn out of himself, revises the intensely introverted statements of *Bengal the Beautiful* and *Banalata Sen* to comment on the plight of mankind as a whole.

In that same month, two of Jibanananda's poems came out in *Kavita*, one of them entitled "Grass" (*ghas*). The first poem by that name had appeared in *Kavita* nearly six years earlier, wherein Jibanananda luxuriated in grass. Sensuous—green, fragrant, juicy—it seduced him to become part of it, to be born or reborn as grass. In the later poem, grass has died.

GRASS

Death shriveled his body, discarding it upon the river's bank.
Frothy light licked him in midday.
Green winds came and smoothed out what was
Wizened on earth, taking him into their motion.
Encouragingly, talkative waters sleeked down his body—
But—the debt to time gradually
Called him away into ugly, stiff nakedness.
Then when hell went to open its natural, ancient gates
It saw his bones
Had suddenly hidden in *kanasona* grass, like grass.
From then the grass of this world amuses[53]
For six months a jackass, and an intellectual for a subtle six more.[54]

Grass dies, but life is reborn. Dead, wizened grass doesn't go to hell but hides itself in living grass. The phenomenon of life and the annual cycle of renewed life, epitomized by grass, occupies the minds of sensitive, intelligent men; that same grass serves as fodder for dumb animals. In its own way this second "Grass" poem is as sensuous as the first: licking light, smoothing green winds, and encouraging waters that wet the body, making it soft and sleek. But the grass is dying or dead throughout most of the lyric.

And the poet, the observer, speaks from a distance. Whereas in the first "Grass," the narrator wanted to drink its fragrance, to squeeze its flesh and to rub its plumage, and ultimately to be born as part of grass, he simply observes grass in the second poem. He personifies grass and feels, through personification, what the grass feels, but he is not lost in its world. The "subtle intellect" tells the reader that there is a world of men, too, which the poet recognizes. In the earlier "Grass" and other poetry of that period, this awareness of the world of men had been absent.

A poem entitled "Shadowy" (*abachaya*), also published September 1941, in the special Tagore issue of a magazine called *Jayasri* ("Goddess of Victory"), illustrates further Jibanananda's new awareness of the human world around him.

SHADOWY

Today at dawn acute exhaustion.
Today in the afternoon, too, acute
Melancholy weighs upon the earth's breast.
All day in the field a peasant adds two
And two and comes up with three.
He has nothing anywhere to harvest.
The whole night long he lies cowering
Beside chilled skeletons.
Not a thing does he disown.

2

A river flows in choppy waves.
It has nothing but its water.
Morning became afternoon at some point
And, too, the century we knew passed away.
It probes for swallow nests.
On the bank of that river
Upon its brown mud fall leaves.
All this is common simple certainty.
On my finger, too, a yellow leaf
For as long as it exists. Somewhere in a nearby tree
A *kokil* sings at cold emptiness,
And comparable to that bird's frightful single-mindedness
Is the surety of times changing in this civilized world.
Afternoons die again and again.
He knows not by what substance he is to be satisfied:
Old rough drafts—or revolution.[55]

Jibanananda acknowledges the existence of the common man, the peasant, toiling for little or no gain. From this depressing scene the poet shifts his attention to a river. Time, like water, flows by continuously and rather imperceptibly. Nature continues. Rivers flow on, but human civilization seems bent on terminating one age and starting anew—World War II giving proof of this urge. Man, dissatisfied, seems unwilling to continue on as he is. Does he really know how to become satisfied? The Communists advocate revolution. Will that appease humanity, or do older ideas contain the solution? Jibanananda remains uncertain as to how humanity will, or even should, proceed. Subtly didactic, this poem reveals a poet sensing pessimistically that utopia is not imminent. Man will be dissatisfied, no matter what happens, and there will be another end to yet another era sometime hence.

In December of 1941, Jibanananda published in *Nirukta* a poem of six stanzas, uniform of rhyme scheme and in a meter that had been introduced to Bengali by Rabindranath, a meter (called *matrabritta*) in which Jibanananda hardly ever wrote. The meter fairly mocks the subject matter, albeit playfully, for the poem tells of four beggars, a woman and three men, who, our narrator imputes, play at formalities—one beggar, a vizier or minister, another, a rajah or king, and the third man, an enforcer of regal law. The three and their female guest are domiciled upon the sidewalks of Calcutta. Even the title, "Lighter Moments" (*laghu muhurta*), contrasts ironically with both the formal poetic structure and the lightly portrayed but deadly serious statement on poverty and the plight of Calcutta's poor. A portion of this poem became part of the narrative of Allen Ginsberg's Indian journals:

> "Three beggars
> washing their hands in the grey wind,
> drinking the grey wind from their cupped palms
>   on the corner of Bentick [sic] Street
> Downtown Calcutta near the
>   Post office quiet wide street
> Three beggars over a pot
>   cooking in the gutter charcoal—
> An old woman comes near, wanting
>   the warmth of the Fire—
> And they gossip about who got the
>   Houses of Calcutta,
>   who won and lost all the money—
> Who remembered thighs on the
>   bed of down—"
>
> (Adaptation by Allen Ginsberg)[56]

From the first page of the last issue of *Nirukta*'s second year (June 1942), another poem of social statement:

IN FIELDS FERTILE AND FALLOW
(*ksete prantare*)

A simple creature had lived in many an emperor's realm
When finally one day he gazed four or five yards ahead
And saw no emperor anywhere, yet still no revolution,
Only the silence of a peasant and his bullock in the noonday field.
As afternoon in Bengal's fallow fields edged forward
Blending gradually with estuaries
While Babylon and London rose and fell—
Yet he kept his back turned.
The afternoon was such that laborer
Came with ladylove.
When man dies, his mummy's tomb sprawls out
In a mile of sunlight.

2

Once again afternoon fades into estuaries.
The whole day long a single peasant worked
The field with his bullock.
This century turns shrill.
Long shadows cast by trees
Stretch over Bengal's fallow fields.
Daylight hours for here, for this era, are gone.
And the peasant, unawares, caught in the lingering of March–April twilight
Yet stands steadfast, gazing upon afternoon.
Nineteen forty-two, it seems.
But is it really nineteen forty-two?

3

He holds no hope of peace or passion, anywhere.
He was born, he will die one day.
He had come to the field with the rising sun.
At sunset he left.
He slept soundly, for he knew the sun would rise again.
That night, dew played
With primeval memories.
A peasant's wan plough,
All those dark lumps overturned by plowshares,
A world about a quarter mile long
He worked all day now lies
Unturned. Real or false?

4

Blinded by the brilliance of a bloody flood, this simple creature

Finds no relief as yet.
Here the earth is uneven
With its cracks and fissures of an April field.
There are no other promises.
Mere stacks of straw extending for two or three miles,
And even then, not like gold.
Only the sound of scythes drowns out the world's cannons,
Pathetic, meek, without refuge.
There are no other promises.
As water birds scurry about, the afternoon river listens intently
To the melody of its own waters.
Has the cultivator, the human being of today, arisen from an amoeba
Through purposeless expansion
From a comedy of errors in the blue-covered ocean?
Buddhist shrines, the cross, ninety-three, and Soviet myths and promises
Are the histories of eras ending.
Life amid the shoreless sea
Perhaps understood all this, and Naciketa rather than Praceta
Instantly became the favored model
For the first and final man in common humanity's sunlight.[57]

A famine was fast descending upon Bengal as Jibanananda's thoughts turned outward toward human society. What he comprehended did not reassure him. Great civilizations have come and gone but the simple peasant lives on. Revolution, which the Communists had promised, had not materialized, nor would it. Even so, a cataclysm occurred: the ending of an age. The Bengali word for a devastating famine is *manwantar,* or, quite literally, the changing or termination (*antar*) of a period presided over by the mythical Manu, son of Brahma. The famine of 1943 would take a heavy toll of lives in Bengal.[58] Moreover, the world was at war. A farmer's sickle proves pathetically impotent against the destructive cannons, though it may drown out their roar. Much blood had been spilled, but to no one's benefit, the peasant certainly as bad off now as he had been. In fact, had man or organic life generally progressed at all, evolving from the sea, from the lowly amoeba utterly without purpose—a mere comedy of errors?

The Buddha, Christ, the French Revolution, and the Russian Revolution—through metonymy "Buddhist shrines, the cross, ninety-three, and Soviet myths and promises"—call attention to several cataclysmic events in the course of human history. These are not beginnings of new eras, to Jibanananda, but endings of old ones. The Buddhist *caitya* or shrine usually contains a relic of the deceased Buddha; the cross marks the end of the human life of Jesus. Louis XVI was beheaded in early 1793; the Reign of Terror raged during the autumn of ninety-three when Marie Antoinette went to the guillotine. Russia's Revolution is characterized as just so many myths and promises.

These four symbols signal the end of eras. Did they endow the world with hope? Had Buddha's teachings or Christianity made the world a better place? Did the Reign of Terror or Communism bring social and economic justice to "common humanity"? Unfortunately, man seems to make no moral or ethical progress. As with the present age, eras continue to come to an often violent end: "Somewhere in a nearby tree/A *kokil* sings at cold emptiness,/And comparable to that bird's frightful single-mindedness/Is the surety of times changing in this civilized world." Naciketa is the lord of fire; Praceta, the lord of the sea. Life seems to have somehow understood the principle of might, to have been drawn to the sheer destructive, all-consuming force of fire. And, in the eyes of Jibanananda, that life rejected Praceta as it evolved onto dry land; man turned from the nurturing sea to idolize Naciketa and fire.

His work continued to appear not only in *Nirukta* but also in *Kavita,* which from June 1941 was edited solely by Buddhadeva Bose. (Premendra Mitra had left *Kavita* and now co-edited *Nirukta* with Sanjay.) *Kavita*'s March 1942 issue offered no poetry by Jibanananda but did announce the "One for a Pice" (*ek payasay ekati*) series. His *Banalata Sen* booklet would be published later that same year as part of this series, which featured sixteen poems by a single poet at a price of four annas (four pice to the anna), or one pice per poem.[59]

A nostalgic reflection on his former poetic world, "One's Natural State" (*swabhab*) appeared in *Kavita,* June 1942:

ONE'S NATURAL STATE

Though once there were within these eyes of mine many a river
As dawn would dawn anew in this land of ours,
Still, there could be seen a solitary river—
A solitary woman, when the fog would lift,
Following the contours of that river's bank—
The statue of her comes and stands
Like tranquil dignity of the human body
Amid a perfect golden circle of the sun.
It was as if the sun's entire, all-encompassing perimeter
Were a part of her.
If after all this time I importune
Time to retrieve all that,
He would show those memories to me in sympathetic lights
As night took hold in one or two late autumn evenings.
Though people by the thousands on the earth today
Die like insensate flies—
Still, a woman once
Thinking frightful, natural thoughts like

"In sunshine shall forever water flow through waters of dawn's rivers."
With words like those and in the most mundane of ways she disappeared.[60]

A similar poem, entitled "Hard Times" (*durddin*) had been sent to Jagadish Bhattacharya—with a letter dated 23 May 1940—for publication in his journal *Vaijayanti* ("The Banner"). The magazine, which began publication six months earlier, closed down operations that very same month, and the manuscript for "Hard Times" and three other poems by Jibanananda remained with Jagadish Bhattacharya, unpublished.

HARD TIMES

Though once there were within these eyes of mine many a river
As dawn would dawn anew in this land of ours,
Still, there could be seen a solitary river—
A solitary woman, *with a rabbit in her arms,*
Following the contours of that river's bank—
The statue of her comes and stands
As though cut from white cloth by an artist's scissors
Amid a perfect golden circle of the sun.
It was as if the sun's entire, all-encompassing perimeter
Were a part of her.
If after all this time I importune
Time to retrieve all that,
He would show those memories to me in *candle* lights
In this pale walled room covered with yellowish paper.
A young woman seems long since
To have cut out her own silhouette—and entered
Into the sun—and then forgotten to come out,
She had her pure white rabbit.
That today there are no rivers on the earth—no sun—
Is all the fault of these crippled times.[61]

The natural and the fanciful were that day (1940) no more, due to the crippled, paralyzed—literally "kneeless"—times. By 1942, hundreds of thousands were dying and would continue to do so in a world war, and later in an "era-ending" famine. But a woman, maybe nature, once thought not of death but of rivers. She too is no more. Almost simultaneously Jibanananda's lyric voice faded as the times' stark reality forced its way into his poetry, smothering his very lyricism.

4

The Communist Party of India (CPI), declared illegal in 1934, had worked since the seventh Comintern (1935) to establish an anti-imperialist people's front, an antifascist *front populaire*. In March 1942, a twenty-one-year-old Leftist writer, Somen Chanda, "was assassinated while leading railway workers belonging to a union of which he was the organizer to attend an anti-Fascist meeting at Dacca."[62] Apparently realizing they had the basis for unity among writers, the Leftists revived the All-India Progressive Writers' Association, renaming it the Anti-Fascist Writers' and Artists' Association.

On March 28 [1942], Ramananda Chatterjee, the doyen of Indian journalism presided over a largely attended public meeting where the various diabolic aspects of fascism and the role of the writer and the artist in the fight against fascism were discussed by well-known literary fighters [*sic*]. A committee was set up to organise the Anti-Fascist Writers' and Artists' Association; it included such significant names as Jamini Roy, than whom there is none more creative among India's painters; Atul Gupta and Ayyub, leading critics; Satyen Mazumdar, Hiran Sanyal and Sajani Das, editors all of them; and finished prose writers, Naresh Sen Gupta, Manik Banerjee and Tarashankar Banerjee; masters of the fiction-form, Buddhadeva Bose; Amiya Chakravarti (of Santiniketan), Bishnu Dey, Subhas Mukherjee and other poets.[63]

Ramananda, the venerable old Brahmo still edited *Prabasi* and *Modern Review*. Under his chairmanship, writers and artists of all political persuasions could comfortably unite.

As protest against the Somen Chanda killing, a number of writers issued a manifesto,[64] and

a book of poems dedicated to the memory of their colleague resulted. Amiya Chakravarty, Buddhadeva Bose, Bishnu Dey, Samar Sen and Subhas Mukherjee are among the contributors. The book takes its name *Prachir* (*The Barricade*) from the spirited chorus of the opening poem by Amiya Chakravarty: ... [65]

Some Dhaka-based writers, reacting to Somen Chanda's death, brought out another publication, a fortnightly entitled *Pratirodh* ("Resistance"). One of the joint editors of this venture was Kiran Sankar Sengupta. (Some four years earlier, Jibanananda had written the introduction to Kiran Sankar's book of poetry, *Dream-Desire*.) *Pratirodh*, which began June 1942 and lasted only until the middle of January 1943, billed itself as "a biweekly

Marxist and anti-Fascist literary magazine," published on behalf of the "Dacca District Progressive Writers' Association." Not only Jibanananda but also such politically disparate poets as Buddhadeva Bose, Sanjay Bhattacharya, and Subhas Mukherjee contributed in the autumn of 1942 to *Pratirodh,* Jibanananda's poem "Feeling" (*anubhab*), solicited sometime during the summer of that year:

FEELING

Shall we not travel once again the amazing path?
Something well worth seeing yet remains somewhere.
From the Atreyi river to the vast ends of the Bay of Bengal;
Dawn proceeding from west to
A Bengal of evening's deltaic shores;
As salt seas well up in her—
All that the sun creates with sunshine—
And besides this, silence.

As a huge moon slowly comes to rest
Standing at the head of Bengal's fields—
Besides what nature gives of her own heart
There is no other moonlight anywhere.
Though not a widower, yet like his shadow
All this gains control here of men's hearts.
This land is sprinkled with light of the ocean, of the sun
All is bought and sold among men with copper.
The owl of a worthless storehouse unknowingly flies
Into moonlight, like some luminescence.
Today it is not peace—it is not happiness,
It is not pain, either;
As we sought to abolish discriminatory differences, endless divisions arose,
Are being exhausted—in this sort of classless, selfless feeling.[66]

The narrator's actual feeling (*anubhab*) remains diffuse. He allows fleeting thoughts about physical, natural Bengal to waft through his mind. The sensation which lingers is a product of the times. "Today it is not peace—it is not happiness,/It is not pain, either." Jibanananda, in fact, does not articulate a truly personal response. Instead, he draws upon current political, impersonal vocabulary. It is a "classless" feeling. But Jibanananda is no propagandist here. He points out the partial results of the struggle for classlessness: endless divisions. These divisions may fade away, or they may be eliminated by force, or they may linger on—he does not say (know) for sure.

And while various political machinations were taking place, Jibanananda's poetry continued to appear in a number of other journals, as well as in *Nirukta* and *Kavita*. Though Buddhadeva stated he had been unaware of Sanjay's feelings of hostility toward him, *Nirukta* and *Kavita* did give the impression of being in competiton with one another. Both welcomed Jibanananda, and Jibanananda obliged both with contributions, at least twice with poems of the same name: "Night," in 1940, and two years later, "Various Choruses" (*bibhinna koras*) (*Nirukta,* September 1942; *Kavita,* October 1942).

VARIOUS CHORUSES

one—

Several white geese still glide along
Slowly upon the river of our hearts.
We have lived in peace—for many a day
With our wedded women for many a day.

We have seen our children on the maidan in the light
Scattered about of their own accord—barely countable.
We have stared at the strange crowd and have seen the heads of the people,
Have seen the household deities, horns out of stone.

We have hung pictures of the city's grandfathers—
Pictures of the city fathers from the walls.
We circumambulate this big city of ours
Trying hard, it seems, to express

That meaning, that something[67] by which we shall be immortal.
We have taken what is our due;
And by the time we said what we had to say
The *natia* plants, it seems, had been nibbled away.

But again they turned green, replenished
According to the needs of our children—our children's children.
Time spinning in just such a cyclic pattern
Can suddenly turn obstinate as a mule

And follow some other geometric course,
Some other philosophic revolution of ideas.
But will our children, all our children's children, though aware of this,
Remain firm avoiding that frightful intercourse of beauty and the fool?

If they were to die, caught up in the turbulent current of time,
If, in the rubble of this darkened palace,
They were to gaze upon the jackal and the owl and cry—
Then the dream would be true; at such a time life's realities

Would be stripped away from material things.
Were the last family of man to disappear, who would return
The realities of life? I have become obsessed at times
With just such a strange dream.

two—

Time, like a worm, eats into our country.
Our children will one day become the elders.
They will take their stand in life upon self-evident truths.
And perhaps there remains in their hearts

Some anxiety over this. On the maidan, in parks
Today they orate, seeking to shed life's poison.
They spend many a shortened winter's day
In their fine flowing shirts like so many circling pigeons.

Radiance from the ocean's sunlight seems to descend
Upon our land like a bluish wave.
Our grandfathers and fathers, too, knew it as an adage;
And we too once had such an interchange
Of ideas—but in the dangers of these woeful times
We have lost that deep trust.
Though we have slept on the dark earth beside someone or other,
Though we have awakened in the morning beside someone—all year
  long

We must recall, must recognize him or her, too.
Is she time? is she life? a cousin? a whore? a wife?
The family of man has come to a halt upon the edge of time.
And because once they were known, we know them today

As we hoard dark superstitions, laughing softly.
Familiarity, tested time and again in place after holy place,
Lies piled in stacks of paper in a kingdom of pale knowledge.
Even our children are not of our own hearts.

We, halfway down the path, rest in the afternoon shade.
One world has been destroyed before us;
To resolutely demand another world
Requires

Youth like the morning sky.
That morning never appears without the dark counterpart night.

In the west the setting sun, the specks of dust, the microbes make
   known
Their restless grandeur and leave the earth to man in debt to
   mankind.

three—

All day long are heard the sounds of rice stalks or of sickles.
The peasants walk with deliberate steps.
The panting from their shadowy bodies
Cuts through the gloom of the century.

From time to time several planes pass over.
And as a covey of *hariyal* birds
Flies by one wonders how far man can go alone
Walking on his two feet.

All these thoughts, however, are mind's frivolity.
The sky reddened,
Not from cannons, for even today
Nature has sway here.

Night, on its dark path to sleep,
Once again draws together the children of one world
As the sunlit day of men and intellectuals
Becomes empty in its heartlessness.

That night has come; our children are embroiled
In debts owed family and strangers.
The sound of the dove belongs not to evening, not to morning.
But in between in only this Behula and death.

four—

Now the character of history has proceeded far.
Both enemy and friend have gazed toward the western sun.
Who was it that unwound his turban, waiting for the harvest,
For the sun from the east, and then left saying
He had wished to sink into the dark night?

We, in our own opinion, in the opinion of others, of all,
Are not like just so many dodos among flocks of dodos
On the lonely beaches of time—
But rather, we are controlled by our dispositions.
This is a transition either into life or into death, so it seems.

Is the sky's pale color that of dawn, or the dark of evening?
Is this expansive sea to be crossed?
And though we are many, we are now alone.

As we cause the extinction of the species, those last remaining dodo
   birds,
As we approach we hear the sound of the dove,
Or is it the unfathomable cacophony of dodoism.[68]

And, in *Kavita*'s October 1942 number:

VARIOUS CHORUSES

Our lifetime has passed many a day on this earth
And now the daylight hours hear death's sound.
Once I had thought
The ear might find pleasure in foul times
With a wink to the heart, lulling it asleep.
But that darkness has drawn much closer, denser today.
Through cracks and crevices in our walls
An even greater retribution works its will.
The minds of our children, slipping away from the house,
Assimilating the appeals of Vibhisana and Nrisimha,[69]
Proceed from dawn toward afternoon,
Then ignoring night return again at dawn.
Still they have no place to live,
Though we built in blind faith a home
One day a long time ago; still they have nothing to eat,
Though, with eyes to the soil, we sowed
The earth with rice one day. They have lost all else;
Their minds, having traveled the land of worries and yet
Extraordinarily holding to pleasant thought,
Have lost somewhere the path before them,
And behind—a restless silence fills our home.
We with eyes open have walked many a day now
The paths of the city; we have worked and enjoyed the fruits
Of wealth; we have with our votes become one with public opinion.
We have read books with implicit trust.
And though with our wedded women, on life's stage, we sin
With every letter of our signature, articulating sinful lies,
And though our faith be lost, still we have not lost that sexual
Single-mindedness of life; still there is no love anywhere, even after
   so long.
There are signs at every intersection of the city's main streets;
One dead body embraces the corpse of another
Though frozen in terror—perhaps by some second death.
Our experience, knowledge, women, yellow harvest of late autumn
Go here and there, each in search of its own heaven.
No one objects, however—for there is no way;
Slipping away from one's proper place, yet everyone remains in

His proper place. At the end of the century this
Sort of pervasive rule descends. From the afternoon veranda all the decrepit
Men and women gaze out to the edge of the fading sunlight, out toward the sun:
Like an unbroken circle of cut glass.

2

The continent is spread out all about like a desert:
As far as the eye can see—I feel.
But many persons at our window
Take it to be like the ocean's light, beckoning one to cross over;
They stare the day long toward this enigma.
To see their faces one feels
They hear the ocean's song perhaps;
Such absorbed wonderment blends well with
Their frightened faces. They have long
Wandered about our land like corporeal objects.
They witnessed the defeat of man in combat with material divinity.
Perhaps the strength of matter was victorious due to its superior intelligence,
Or perhaps due to divinity's unconquerable power—
For so long now it had heard us expound upon
The utter superiority of its own power.
But the speech is ended when applause becomes intense.
They know all this.
In this darkness of ours, crops in deserted fields
Grow strangely in clumps and patches yet
Give the illusion of a beautiful picture.
Far distant within the hub of the city today at dawn
They who have created nothing, their unaltered minds
Awake in regimentation and set to work—and sleep at night
Like some familiar memory.
From this is born tumult, snatching and seizing, premature death,
Family squabbles, blind superstition, flattery, fear, and despondence;
And that is why the smiley-eyed sailors came from the sea's far shore;
The half-Shiva-half-woman manifestation of the deity,
More tangible in times of sorrow than God,
Casts its soft shadow from the foot of the Himalayas to
The libido of Uncle Sun's sailors.

3

Green breezes float over grass.
Or perhaps the grass is green.
Or, as one recalls a river's name, the river itself appears all around
And remains visible till afternoon.
Rolling in joyous waves, under eyes of countless suns,

To the right and left
It gazes upon man's sorrow, fatigue, luster, half-fallen boundaries.
Upon reaching nineteen forty-two, once again it wishes to gain
New glory, flowing into canals of blind darkness, blood, smoke.
More girls than even blades of grass,
More dead men, nineteen forty-three, forty-four, than even rivers.
Above the cannons, through sunlight and blue sky, stainless swans
Leave the Indian Ocean and fly toward another sea—
Translucent like spotty clouds, rolling.
Yet they are birds of death passing through sweet air.
As they came suddenly into the path of sunlight, an endless trumpet flower,
A pointed face of steel blooms from their shoulders, beneath the blue.
Do the watchful masses proceed at least today?
Have lust, injustice, blood, bribery, scandalmongering, fear
Wanted to thieve from the house of emotions, devoid of love and wisdom?
Have the waters of the great ocean ever been still, like one well-known for truth—
Did they recognize their own white-capped
Nest of water beneath the rarefied atmospheric blue?
If not, then is the swelling ocean a lie?
Yet it is not a lie: the sands of the sea push up the darkness of the netherworld,
Become blind by time-honored qualities, and later become illuminated.[70]

The poems speak to the precarious present and, directly addressing the reader like Greek dramatic choruses (the word *chorus*, in both titles, is a Bengali transliteration of the English word), alert him to the nature of the times. Characters of the drama act and interact while the chorus interprets that action.

Once again the statement: An era ends, as does the familiar. "Our lifetime has spent many a day on this earth/And now the daylight hours hear death's sound." We thought we were building a world, building a home, growing food. Yet there is nothing for our children. They are restless. What we provided does not suffice. We have lived a lie and know it; not love but instinct kept society going. And now at the twilight of the era, "decrepit/Men and women gaze out to the edge of the fading sunlight, out toward the sun."

The narrator's surroundings seem a desolate desert, incapable of sustaining life. Yet others, those who would see a utopia on the other side, take the setting sun for the ocean's light. That light beckons man to cross the sea, sea being a common symbol for the mortal world in which man struggles and suffers. To cross the sea implies (metaphorically, in Shakta bhakti poetry, for instance) the attainment of release from *samsara*; in

1942, it might mean attainment of a utopian socialist or communist state, or independence from Britain. (Gandhi had launched his Quit India movement in August 1942, declaring that Indians would not fight Britain's war and that the British must get out of India. Subhas Chandra Bose, who had absconded to Germany and organized the India National Army from Indian prisoners of war, now commanded the INA in Burma which, in conjunction with the Japanese, was advancing on India's eastern borders. Via radio broadcasts, Subhas Chandra urged his fellow Indians in India to take up arms against the British and to welcome the Japanese as their liberators.) But, the chorus asserts, people are uncertain, fear written on their faces. The light, the sun (Japan's symbol), presents an enigma: Many are unsure of what if anything waits on the other side of the sea of night.

Our narrator-chorus reminds his audience of a time with green grass and rivers. In his mind's eye he sees a river, now witness to contemporary man's plight. And does that river, time's river, cut channels of blind darkness, blood, and smoke? Is that the new glory? The old glory had been nature herself: "sky, wind, river." As man closes this era and the cannons spew out death, the stainless swans (airplanes) fly away. The waters of life are now so agitated that these swans, bivalent symbols of nature and destruction, fly on, not even recognizing their own watery nests below. But, the chorus—*Kavita*'s "Various Choruses"—holds out some unspecified hope for the future.

Nirukta's "Various Choruses" ends on a more uncertain note. The chorus asks whether the present time represents the end or the beginning. "Is this expansive sea to be crossed" or not? Do we hear the sound of the now-extinct dodo bird? In October 1942, Jibanananda published another poem in which he used the dodo image to suggest possible imminent disaster for mankind:

SONG OF THE SEA OF LIGHT
(*alosagarer gan*)

In pallid sunlight, congested waves of mankind
Stretch out to the east, the south, the north.
Upon their farther shores the sun, in the year nineteen hundred
    forty-two,
Looking on as this afternoon light of today

Sinks quietly. It was sinking so
When Uttara's fetus aborted, and some time
After the death of the Buddha—when Lenin ceased to exist.
Several singing *hariyal* birds, chatting

> With the Bay of Bengal, search a path toward the west
> Amid clouds the color of oranges
> As agitation over man's present concerns
> Sinks into "all-clear"-like fuzzy emotions
>
> And darkness and night's cacophony.
> The *hariyals* of Bengal! Saffron clouds to the west!
> We human beings—even today—both alive and dead—in the light
> Of the sea, have forgotten those dodo birds' extinct conscience.[71]

Once again, Jibanananda portrays a sunset over a sea that may or may not be crossed. That sea, with its waves of mankind, surrounds us. He calls the reader's attention to endings of eras, to death, which coincided with just such a setting of the sun. He speaks of Uttara's child, Pariksit who, stillborn in the sixth month of pregnancy, was revived by Krishna.[72] Then when Yudhisthira renounced the throne, years after the great war described in the *Mahabharata*, Pariksit, grandson of Arjuna, assumed sovereignty, becoming the *kali yuga*'s first king. Jibanananda had previously employed the two symbols of both the Buddha's death and the Soviet Revolution (here, Lenin's death) to indicate the end of an age. None of these symbols bodes well for the times to come. Following just such a sunset began the *kali yuga*, the last and most degraded of the four great ages, and the one in which we are presently living.[73]

As birds pursue the light though richly colored clouds, mankind ceases to fight against the darkness, relaxing, as one relaxes after the threat of bombardment has passed. Instead of struggling to assure its own survival, mankind drifts off into night's cacophony—cacophony described above as the sound of dodo birds, portending extinction for the species. The poet warns that man may have forgotten the dodo's fate, their "extinct conscience." Man, if he exhibits similar behavior, may follow the dodos to oblivion.

5

For all his love of nature, Jibanananda appears unable to go home again. The man who wrote *Bengal the Beautiful* and "Banalata Sen" could no longer see the world quite as he saw it then. "Various Choruses" from *Kavita* begins, but for one sentence, with a statement to this effect:

> Once I had thought
> The ear might find pleasure in foul times
> With a wink to the heart, lulling it asleep.
> But that darkness has drawn much closer, denser today.

Jibanananda could not now live in his natural, fanciful world, nor write "Banalata Sen." But he could, of course, publish in book or booklet form what had already appeared in magazines during the previous decade. In December 1942, *Banalata Sen* joined the "One for a Pice" series. The twelve poems—belying the series' name from which one would expect sixteen poems—all had come out in *Kavita* during 1935–37.[74]

Caturanga's ("The Four Arts") reviewer, Abul Hosen, noted in passing that Jibanananda had written little if any political poetry.[75] Compared to the political poems of Subhas Mukherjee, it is true Jibanananda's verse strikes one as apolitical.[76] However, in contrast to the *Banalata Sen* volume, much of Jibanananda's poetry published in 1942 did indeed display a political tinge. Though previously he sought pleasure in his own physical and folk-tale world of Bengal, the darkness had grown much closer, much denser by 1942. Possibly forced by circumstances, Jibanananda had entered the human world around him.

Still relatively unknown to the public at large, Jibanananda had become recognized as one of the established poets of the day, his work appearing with some regularity in various and sundry journals. In May 1943, *Desh* published "Song of the Meek, Tired, and Introverted" (*niriha, klanta o marmanwesider gan*), the first poem of Jibanananda's printed in what has become today the most widely read Bengali periodical.

SONG OF THE MEEK, TIRED, AND INTROVERTED

We want nothing in particular now.
Our dark light
Has brought much that is trifling, undistinguished.
We have spent many days like this—yet
Wish to spend many more this very same way.
In late autumn an amazing pithy pulp coalesces in black waters, in
   water chestnuts, in rice gruel;
Or perhaps, nothing coalesces at all to fruition.
An elder brother, though ailing, yet scolds his sister-in-law on sight;
With eyes open, with eyes closed we have seen many times such sickly
   famine.
And when it grew much colder that evening, we finally went inside;
Let such an autumn silence
Come once again—
For as the stars in the sky revolve meekly,
Just so separation, death, fear spin around like gears of some machine,
All of us—every one of us—
In just such a silence,
Insipidly.

By luster, might, by the songs of both lion and dog
We are hindered.
But in the song of the owl as he descends to a thatched roof in
 December midnight
There is peace—finality—death, I know,
Yet that song is good.
The years from nineteen thirty to nineteen forty were good years;
Today in this December of forty-one there is a kind of apathy.
Swatting mosquitoes, husking rice, chasing away mice,
Borrowing from moneylenders—devouring the loan—forgetting that
 loan,
Going to quack doctors with frosty white bottles—
Taking—what is to be taken from everyone,
Giving—what is to be given to everyone,
In turn, we walk along and shall walk our children and children's
 children along upon the earth.
And when it grew much colder that evening, inside the *hariyal* dove's
 home
Or on one's doorstep, a couple of those virtuous doves tread—[77]
There we shall go feeling isolated; let such an autumn silence
Come once again.
For as the stars in the sky rise and set meekly,
Just so separation, death, fear turn us around like gears of some
 machine,
All of us—everyone.

Nothing in particular has happened here for a long time.
Men continue to die.
The poor, the wretched, the old, the crippled, great courtiers all
Are somehow reduced to rubble and ruin.
And I watched, indifferent, tired—closely.
I would have watched and watched, returning exhausted in darkness—
Had not dawn, at night's end, the sun, that filtering hand of time
Wiped away all.
Besides all this
Nothing in particular has happened here for a long time.
Sighs, as countless as bubbles in the ocean,
And as strong, wanted something—got something?—and at night
Returned detached to calm a society of sons and moderate woman.
Did they not return?
We too turned about: our hearts' inclinations
Call to restless base genius of our lives
As the doe in heat amid creation's moonglow
Called patiently, enduringly,
Calls fully—
In that very tone.
At times in the river's waters first clouds, then swans float by,
Once again clouds—waters—the month of September,
All was flooded—everything seemed to have vanished:

As how one tone, touching another, strives meaninglessly for alliteration.
At times paddy fields are empty of rice.
At other times the fields are full of peasants' joyous clamor,
Jabbering like mean mother-in-law mice in granary and storeroom;
A harbor wireless picks up all.
Sometimes fields of jute reeds bob and weave like snakes,
These cobra fangs biting peasants all over;
At other times the Accountant of Death claims these lands of jute,
Not missing a root, oh no.
But there's *carak* puja and *bhadu* puja—and how many songs of the *gajan* festival have come and gone;
How many moons have grown full behind thatched roofs at night, then waned once more;
Householder and peasant together have drunk the sweet toddy,
Eaten the new rice flour sweets of January—the greenish purple water chestnuts from misty waters.
All these festivities,[78] though, are dead history;
All these festivities are nothing.
There's always excitement alive in each approaching festival,
Suppressing anxiety over death—ever more subtly.
Each takes his proper place,
Dwelling only on life, sex, despair, lust, possessions.
Yet he thinks of but one thing after that
Due to his mental mannerism.
The middle-aged are now older,
The young have become middle-aged,
Children are now youths;
Many women are being lost from the land of women;
All is now the land of salaried servants.
And this all is quite natural, quite commonplace.
Yet when man proceeded to think quite naturally,
Where has he been effective?
If today, in the face of these limitations, real conviction exists in our hearts,
Then, like the doe in heat to the deer of life, toward that moonlight—
It calls to the ghostly moonlight.
Does it not?
If some utterly frightful fear
Creeps up on us slowly today,
Still then we would be slow to recognize it as fear—
The slower, the better.
We got sunlight in the morning,
We got lamps at night.
All those subtle couplets Ganesa once deliberated upon
Had burst forth spontaneously, oh Vyasa, born within your heart.[79]
Upon the sidewalks one night gas lamps had flared up
Like innate joy—or so it seemed.
We all

Each absorbed in his own birth, complacency, death,
Revolve in ignorance;
We talk and talk ourselves into an exhausted,
Glum populace.
But no one troubles to find out, to know
Through and through our narrow-mindedness.
Utter malice has descended upon us today;
Sometimes in the paddy fields—sometimes in the river's false waters
The starving years descend.
Great tumultuous confusion befell
The ranks of tenant farmers—moneylenders—tenants;
Local sharecropping—city bank drafts—contractors
Haunts of old crows—spirits of the twelve Bhuiya princes[80]—
    morgues—
Corpses—quack doctors—
Whispering intrigues—alleyways—
This hot sand under foot feels hotter than the sun.[81]
They all create tumultuous confusion.
Some middle-aged fellows are tyrannizing others.
A mass of uncountable youths has nothing to do—worries are
    well-off—
All-devouring poverty is all about.
On humanity's face is seen each private, grief-filled tale.
Each housewife is the merciless power for her own home.
A land of fools, a land of women, a land of lords, a land of servants,
    a land of lunatics yet remains,
A land of sand.
The philosophers' dilemma—the love of intellectual hearts
Draws lines upon all that sand and builds endless dream castles
Heartlessly near the wily sea,
Among the excrement of pigeons and plovers.
Everyone's individual sorrows remain.
These specks of individual sorrow, linked mile upon mile,
Are held together—are they not, by the pain of another?
Had all our sorrows wished to mesh and mingle—
Or had each in his own heart wished—had each attained frightful,
    independent darkness?
We don't see—don't know—but feel if we were to attain something
    beyond death in some sun-bright world,
We would have once again perhaps found the world of dawn in life,
Would we not?
But many a dawn has come and gone throughout history—dawn is not
    everything.
Today our individual hearts, as common man,
Have learned much—still when all the countless revolutions have
    begun and ended
The men of this universe will seek and receive from mankind
Conviction and the beauty of routine:
If not, what shall become of man—with his knowledge of doubt,
    experience and wisdom?[82]

Desultorily, Jibanananda mulls over mankind's sorry plight and the prospects for improvement. Though I have not seen the notebook(s) containing the manuscript for this poem, I suspect the poem's two parts were separate lyrics. If we accept the date given by the poet, he composed or conceived of the first section in December 1941; the latter one may be more contemporaneous with the date of its publication, April 1943. Both, of course, deal with much the same concerns.

Man, apathetic and resigned to a fate of confusion, seems headed nowhere. Social relationships turn caustic. Silence and cold set in, and man simply retreats inside—or goes his own lonely way, when his home is destroyed, living meekly, motivated by fear. Both the majestic lion and the scurrilous dog keep man at bay. Death terminates all this for the individual, but provides mankind no respite, for children and children's children will follow their forefathers. The 1930s had been better years. Jibanananda enjoyed his Bengal then. Now, in the early 1940s, political and social pressures impinge.

In the second section, Jibanananda reintroduces the decade-old image of a doe in heat. Man's heart is that *ghai harini,* calling and appealing to life's baser instincts, wooing patiently, persistently the deer of life. In "In Camp," she called those deer of life to the hunter's gun. In "Song," it is the heart that may well succumb to whims and fancies, thus luring the restless baser instincts.

> ... our hearts' inclinations
> Call to restless base genius of our lives
> As the doe in heat amid creation's moonglow
> Called patiently, enduringly,

Or, if true conviction or self-confidence in fact exists in our hearts today, then let those hearts call to the deer of life with the patience and the resolve of that doe in heat. It will not be the base genius which responds.

> If today, in the face of these limitations, real conviction exists in our hearts,
> Then, like the doe in heat to the deer of life, toward that moonlight—
> It calls to the ghostly moonlight.

Conviction, self-confidence is so positive an attribute that it is what generations to come will seek and receive as their heritage from present mankind. Jibanananda reiterates in the last six lines what he had said repeatedly during the early 1940s.

> But many a dawn has come and gone throughout history—dawn is not everything.
> Today our individual hearts, as common man,

> Have learned much—still when all the countless revolutions have begun and ended
> The men of this universe will seek and receive from mankind
> Conviction and the beauty of routine:
> If not, what shall become of man—with his knowledge of doubt, experience and wisdom?

Many a dawn—many a fresh start—has come and gone in human history. Revolutions, various cataclysmic changes have occurred throughout human time. But a fresh start is not an end in itself, for mankind has not necessarily benefited from revolutions or new days—world war or an impending proletarian revolution will not necessarily solve man's problems. Man's legacy to tomorrow's world is his conviction and the beauty of routine. Jibanananda has used the English word "routine" here; "order" or "continuity" or "stability" might be a better choice, since routine seems much too prosaic as it is presently understood in American English. Jibanananda suggests that man should proceed with order, for revolution solves nothing. Mankind, evolving into a better society, sets an example of stability and continuity, which, coupled with the strength of our convictions, men will look back on with pride. Mankind cannot continue to start afresh with another revolution whenever society seems imperfect. The new society envisioned by revolutionary theorists often remains totally unrealized.

> The philosophers' dilemma—the love of intellectual hearts
> Draws lines upon all that sand and builds endless dream castles
> Heartlessly near the wily sea,
> Among the excrement of pigeons and plovers.
> Everyone's individual sorrows remain.

More striking than his political philosophy are the poem's several images. Buddhadeva Bose and Abul Hosen called attention to Jibanananda's wonderful similes—the essence of his verse—in their reviews of his earlier poetry. One can hear peasants in the field "jabbering like mean mother-in-law mice in granary and storeroom." One can see the tips of jute stalks as they blow in the wind, appearing to be cobras striking again and again, first one place and then another on a peasant's body. Jibanananda produced better imagery than philosophy. As a poet, he remains known for how he sensuously perceived life and how he conveyed that perception through language.

6

In June 1943, *Nirukta*'s final issue came out, completing three full years for the quarterly. Though it contained no contribution by Jibanananda, this issue did carry the article by Sanjay, previously cited, on the poetry of Jibanananda Das.[83] Entitled simply "Jibanananda Das," that article was the first on his poetry since Buddhadeva Bose's two editorials in *Pragati* (1927–29) about the then relatively unknown poet. Reviews of *Gray Manuscripts* and *Banalata Sen* had appeared since, of course, but this piece examined Jibanananda's poetry from *Fallen Feathers* through poems in *Nirukta*. The essay represented a labor of love, for Sanjay thought highly of his fellow poet's work.[84]

Nirukta's demise did not signal the end of Sanjay's efforts to save Bengali poetry from the disease of Stalinism. On the contrary, Sanjay and Satyaprasanna resumed publication in 1943 of *Purvasa,* and continued the treatment that *Nirukta* had been administering. According to Satyaprasanna, he and Sanjay concluded that there was indeed scope for nationalism in India—as opposed to the internationalism of communism, a conclusion they reached just after Gandhi's Quit India movement commenced.

The Communist Party of India, legalized in June 1942 (illegal since 1934), now supported the British war effort and thus found itself cast in the role of collaborator with the imperialists. According to Satyaprasanna, the Communists had predicted that the country would go communist after the war. With the anticommunist feelings generated by the "Quit India" stance, Sanjay and Satyaprasanna became convinced that nationalism could prevail over communism. In furtherance of nationalism and in opposition to Stalinism in literature, the *Purvasa* management reaffirmed its support of romanticism in poetry. Bengali poetry needed a transfusion to survive the malady of Stalinism, and Jibanananda's poetry seemed just what the doctor ordered.

In the meantime, Jibanananda himself would collaborate with what Sanjay undoubtedly considered the enemy. Jibanananda did not, as noted earlier, participate actively in politics, even though Sanjay may have used Jibanananda's poetry in *Nirukta* and *Purvasa* for his own quasi-political reasons. However, Jibanananda did not refuse to contribute an essay, solicited by Subhas Mukherjee, for publication in a volume sponsored by the Anti-Fascist Writers' and Artists' Association, a group undeniably political in its motivation. Bishnu Dey apparently added his weight to the solicitation, for Jibanananda sent the essay to his long-time friend along with a letter.

      Sarbananda Bhavan
      Barisal
      19.12.43

[salutations]
 Today, after such a long time, I was extremely happy to receive your letter. Many old memories come to mind. Subhas and group had written

to my college address—and that letter, too, was forwarded to me today. I really can't think of what to write on such short notice on this topic—Why I Write. Subhas wrote that I should send without delay a three or four page essay. So just now I hastily dashed off three plus pages. From tomorrow on there won't be any time—I'll have to be going through piles and piles of examination notebooks. I am sending the essay to your address. I almost never write essays, just don't get the opportunity. Moreover, my handwriting is somewhat illegible, so I'd be happy if you could direct them to examine the proofs carefully.

During last summer vacation I was in Calcutta for two months. Were you in Calcutta during that time? If I had known, I could have come see you. I spent a few days of the Durga puja vacation also in Calcutta, but due to various tasks I had to tend to, I was unable to visit anyone. Won't be able to go for the Christmas holidays. But I know your address. When I next get to Calcutta, I'll definitely look you up.

I haven't answered Subhas's letter yet. Shall get around to it in a day or two.

Hope you are well. [salutations]

Jibanananda Das[85]

Jibanananda titled his essay "Responsibility of the Writer and Writing" (*lekha, lekhaker dayitwa*) and, in the main, reiterated his ideas on what makes for good poetry—ideas that ran counter to those espoused by his more politically minded colleagues who would bring out the volume.

> There are those who think that poetry may be created at any time because poetry is just like expository prose or an editorial statement based on direct experience ... hence we find everywhere genuine editorial commentary passing itself off as poetry. But is poetry really such? Any healthy, rational mind, confronting an unhealthy or otherwise different society, can set forth the above-mentioned type of statements—and may do so regularly. It does not seem to these people necessary to await that particular instant when one's unselfconscious emotions and the flash of imagination optimally coalesce. Because, in these persons' opinion, the flash of imagination and emotions of the heart have no bearing on the composition of poetry.

But further on, he starts to sound almost defensive:

> Besides the poetry of desiccated human life, the poetry of revolution emanating from that life, and the poetry of hopes and expectations of society at the conclusion of that revolution—besides these subjects, poetry made of many other things can also be truly great.[86]

Jibanananda has said before what he says here about poetic creativity. Now, however, he concedes some validity to opinions running counter to his. He could hardly have been unaware of the probable audience for a volume published by the Anti-Fascist Writers' and Artists' Association, for the benefit of which Jibanananda seems to entertain opinions on both sides of poetry's fence: The "poetry of desiccated human life," of revolution, of a future society, now qualifies for inclusion within the canon of great literature.

Nevertheless, Jibanananda adheres in the main to the earlier stance he had assumed in "On Poetry" (1938) and "Rabindranath and Modern Bengali Poetry" (1941). Regarding a poet's apprehension of the flash of imagination:

> At a moment of startling integration of this flash of imagination of his, he gains the chance to discover and to proclaim anew humanity's most worthwhile ideas. All such moments represent the creation of poetry or art.[87]

In "On Poetry" he declared poets are poets because

> in their hearts there is the autonomous substance of imagination, and within imagination, thought and experience, and because behind them are the past centuries to help them, and with them the new poetic radiations of the modern world. ... The moment this wonderful experience abandons our hearts, poetry ceases to be born—written, instead, is verse.[88]

In "Responsibility of the Writer and Writing," Jibanananda allows human life, even society as a whole, to be a stimulus to poetic composition. But all his essays, "Responsibility" no exception, emphasize that without inspiration, poetry is impossible—journalistic copy resulting in its stead. The copy may be well-written by an astutely observant writer, but the end product will be verse (here the term is used disparagingly) or *reportage,* not poetry:

> I do not wish to say that poetry inlaid with social or national or human problems cannot be an embodiment of beauty. There is nothing to prevent this from happening, and this has indeed happened in many outstanding poems. . . . [but] thoughts and conclusions and problems and ideology remain hidden in true poetry. . . .[89]

Poetry can do many things, says Jibanananda, but cannot transform "men's present condition into a better social life in the immediate future."[90] And he holds firm to his conviction that poets are poets, not economists, sociologists, or political scientists. Minimally effective, if at all, in improving and reconstructing life in the practical world, they compose poetry—period. Jibanananda seems to have anticipated opposition to this statement, from the communist writers, for he adds the following one-sentence paragraph: "My contemporary poet-friends must judge whether I am in fact uninformed when I make the above statements."[91]

Bishnu Dey, in his contribution to *Why I Write,* styled the writer as master and agent, both initiator of social change and conduit for the change, the revolution. The passive observer's writings, suggested Bishnu Dey, are destined to fail.[92] Jibanananda, however, earlier had asseverated that social science was not the work of the poet. Poetry aimed at the heart and the mind, not the body politic, as far as Jibanananda was concerned. Nearly a year after "Responsibility of the Writer and Writing," in December 1944, he restated his feelings—in somewhat different terms—that the poet did not write for the political system or for anybody in particular.

> ... the question of appropriate societal benefit, or nonbenefit, does not even cast a shadow upon the poet's greater consciousness when creating that poem. His consciousness and subconsciousness work single-mindedly to elevate the poem justly and successfully. Even the matter of for whom is this poem being written and whether or not those persons will be able to accept what is written—or whether if they fail to comprehend the essence, they will be offended or estranged—all these questions are of little significance to the poet's purpose.[93]

Why I Write came out in January 1944. In July Jibanananda's fourth book of poetry, *The World at Large* (*mahaprithibi*), was published by Sanjay and Satyaprasanna as part of their "romanticism" campaign. Since *Nirukta* and then *Purvasa* served that same cause, it is strange that only one (albeit in four parts—"Various Choruses") of the thirteen poems published in *Nirukta* during its three-year life span ended up in *The World at Large.* A majority of the thirty-five poems in this volume, thirty to be exact, first appeared in *Kavita* between 1936 and 1939. Twelve of these thirty-five, moreover, had been republished less than two years earlier in the "One for a Pice" booklet, *Banalata Sen,* brought out by Buddhadeva Bose's publishing concern, Kavita Bhavan. Stranger still, Kavita Bhavan's edition of *Banalata Sen* was still in print when *The World at Large* appeared.

According to Satyaprasanna, Jibanananda himself chose the volume's title, but it remains unclear who selected the poetry to be included, Jibanananda or Sanjay. In a letter to Sanjay, Jibanananda indicates that during the summer of 1951 he contemplated a second edition of *The World at Large* for which he need not be consulted in the selection of its poems.

                    183, Lansdowne Road
                    Calcutta 26
                    10.8.51

[salutations]
    It would be good if *The World at Large* appeared before the puja.

There would be considerable sales immediately, it seems to me. You yourself can decide which poems will be in this edition. Wouldn't it be best if the printing began right away?
 I shall be delighted to hear from you. Hope you are well.
[salutations]
Jibanananda Das[94]

The first edition of *The World at Large* contained poems composed between 1929 and 1942 and was dedicated to Premendra Mitra and Sanjay Bhattacharya, joint editors of *Nirukta*. The twelve *Banalata Sen* lyrics (Kavita Bhavan edition) and the poem "A Day Eight Years Ago" dominated this book. Among other poetry chosen for inclusion was a lyrical prayer, a phrase from which gave the volume its name.

PRAYER
(*prarthana*)

Give us vision, lord: Are we to die for the sake of the world at large?
Those who built pyramids once—and who tear down—and build—
Those who would put to the torch—like Genghis, if they stand today
Like intoxicating shadows—in countless bits of immature brain matter—
And all that journeying begun in Marco Polo's time only—
As we gaze toward the sky, we too realize that all that light
Is not so much a match—but Orion on the move.
What can we do if dynamite does not move mountains—
Don't abandon us, lord; in age after age in this house of carnal pleasures
Give us seed for thought: They build pyramids—tear down pyramids and build.[95]

Give us understanding, the supplicant poet prays, of the cycle of creation and destruction.[96] Give us thought anew as we carnally procreate. As mankind, heir to Marco Polo, journeys far guiding itself by the stars, let it realize that those stars are the constellation Orion, not just some harmless flickering flames. (Orion is *kalapurus,* the attendant of Yama, god of death.) Dynamite cannot destroy all barriers. Ultimately, mankind must rely on the mind of man.
 As even this short lyric, first published in *Kavita,* December 1938, shows, the poet who wrote "Banalata Sen" (*Kavita,* December 1935) had changed, displaying signs of a turbidity which marked (and marred) some of his efforts during the war years. The world at large, of which he speaks, was moving steadily toward that second great war.
 Buddhadeva Bose, irritated at seeing the *Banalata Sen* poems in print

again so soon, damned with faint praise the book and its author in his *Kavita* review.

> The first poem in *The World at Large* is "Banalata Sen." Moreover, all the poems of the "One for a Pice" series' *Banalata Sen* have been included in this book despite the fact that the *Banalata Sen* book is not yet out of circulation. And so, those who open *The World at Large* in hopes of reading new poetry by Jibanananda will be particularly disappointed. For that same reason, when this reviewer addresses himself to the book, he must repeat much of what he has already said. It is my opinion that, subsequent to *Gray Manuscripts,* the most characteristic of all the poetry Jibanananda has written and published had been gathered together in *Banalata Sen*. *The World at Large* contains no new melody; in fact, this book is a second edition of *Banalata Sen,* enlarged and under a different name.
>
> If one were to exclude the *Banalata Sen* poems, the most noteworthy poem in the book would be "A Day Eight Years Ago," published seven years ago, in *Kavita*. At that time the poem utterly enchanted me; that enchantment has not faded even today.

So much for the praise. Next came the criticism, not of Jibanananda's lack of lucidity but of his lack of originality.

> The latter poems in *The World at Large* appear to be merely the variegated and extraordinary arrangements of just so many stock expressions. Each individual expression is indeed beautiful, yet all of them taken together yield nothing as a whole. If we are not to call this repetition, then we must call it self-imitation. And the Muses heave a deep sigh whenever a poet starts imitating himself. It seems that Jibanananda has become a captive of his own milieu. I pray that he will extricate himself from that.[97]

Buddhadeva's charge of repetition can undoubtedly be supported by citing certain of the *The World at Large* poems, such as "A Moment" (*muhurta*), which echoes "In Camp."

A MOMENT

A sky of moonlight—the cheetah's scent on a forest trail,
And my heart, a deer:
Which way have I gone amidst this silence of night!
Shadows of silvered leaves cover my body,
And no other deer anywhere around.
Wherever I go the sickle-shaped moon
Seems to have harvested the last of the golden deer-crop.
Then slowly it sinks
Into darkness of hundreds of sleeping deer's eyes.[98]

Other poems in this volume have the feel of earlier compositions, but are intrinsically different. Himani Banerjee described that difference as follows:

> Most noticeable in the first [sort of poetry] ... is the Jibanananda of the soft, gray surroundings—whose appeal is generally to our senses and whose characteristic is lilting, lingering melody. The change reflected in the second ... is that, rather than startling us through our senses, Jibanananda wishes to jar our minds, our mental faculties.[99]

This latter poetry depends far less on imagery and more on "message" expressed through "conceptual" language. Furthermore,

> ... sometimes even when imagery is present, there is no opportunity for us to pause and enjoy just the image—because we are trying frantically to follow Jibanananda's train of thought or message.[100]

As Jibanananda begins to live less in his own personal world of lush Bengal and fantasy women and more in the real world with all its political and social complexities, his poetic voice shifts perceptibly from the sensuous to the cerebral. In one self-conscious lyric from *The World at Large,* resonating with word paintings, the poet muses on the change of venue from beautiful, rural Bengal to bleak Calcutta, and permits us a glimpse into the lonely torment of his chosen physical and poetic exile.

ON THE SIDEWALKS
(*phut pathe*)

It is late—so very late at night.
From one Calcutta sidewalk to another, from sidewalk to sidewalk,
As I walk along, my life's blood feels the vapid, venomous touch
Of tram tracks stretched out beneath my feet like a pair of primordial
    serpent sisters.
A soft rain is falling, the wind slightly chilling.
Of what far land of green grass, rivers, fireflies am I thinking?
Where are the stars?
Have those stars been lost?
Beneath my feet the slender tram track—above my head a mesh of
    tangled wires
Chastises me.
A soft rain falls, and the wind seems lightly chilling.
But you'll not see a single mallard's nest quiver in the face of this cold
    Calcutta wind so very late at night.
No dove will come to tell you of its broken sleep's soft bluish flavor,
    broken by olive leaves.
You'll not mistake a yellowed papaya leaf for an unexpected bird,
Nor will your eyes grow large with recognition as you comprehend
    creation as thick fog.

Nor will an owl rub her gray wings on an *amlaki* branch here,
Nor from that limb will sapphire dewdrops fall,
Nor will her call bring forth here stars like subtle fireflies,
Nor make the night even bluer.
You'll not see here green grass strewn with countless dying *dewali* moths,
Nor will the world here seem to you like a soft and gorgeous dead green moth,
Nor life itself a cold yet gorgeous, dead green moth.
The owl's call will not here bring forth stars like subtle fireflies,
Nor will the call of dewdrops bring forth stars like subtle fireflies,
Nor will your eyes grow large with recognition as you comprehend creation as thick fog.[101]

During the early 1940s Jibanananda's contributions to *Kavita* decreased in number. One reason for this was the publication of *Nirukta* and other magazines, such as *Caturanga*. Quite simply, he had more places where he could publish. Due to the exposure and to the eloquently laudatory criticism provided by Buddhadeva in *Pragati* and *Kavita,* Jibanananda's poetry had become more widely appreciated and more readily solicited by magazine editors. Even *Paricay,* which back in 1932 grudgingly published "In Camp," in 1939 printed three of Jibanananda's poems in one issue and continued to publish at least one of his poems a year for the next three years.

Another reason for Jibanananda's fewer contributions to *Kavita* undoubtedly stems from the nature of his poetry itself. In Jibanananda's own words:

> *Kallol* and *Kali-Kalam* were gradually waning. Buddhadeva Bose's *Pragati* brought with it new opportunities and enthusiasm. From a personal standpoint, my poetry received much more encouragement from Buddhadeva Bose and *Pragati* [than from the other literary journals]. My poems were perhaps, in Buddhadeva's opinion, not external to my own personal world nor outside a universe familiar to him—they were stars born of clarity. I was particularly gratified to have that opportunity to witness such courage and integrity—of Buddhadeva's critical acumen and sensitivity. He gave my poetry a position of prominence in *Pragati* and, after that, in the initial period of *Kavita.* Then later—in my post-*Banalata Sen* poetry—he felt I had become a stranger to his world and had even ventured outside my own universe.
>
> *Nirukta* and *Purvasa* editor Sanjay Bhattacharya feels that an awareness of my environment has achieved maturity in my later poetry. This environment is, of course, comprised of society and history.[102]

Still, Jibanananda's concept of the creative process had not changed, nor had his vocabulary. Later in the letter he speaks of the "aid of genius" and the "independent glow," both expressions used in "On Poetry." Only now his poetry takes its inspiration more from his societal and historical environment and less from a personal, fantasized stimulus or Bengal's physical-folklore milieu. For his part, Buddhadeva considered that new awareness unbecoming to Jibanananda's poetry.

During the first half of the 1940s, Jibanananda resided in Barisal. He traveled to Calcutta from time to time, staying with his brother, Asokananda. His sister, Sucarita, taught and then became headmistress at Tamluk Girls' School in Midnapur district, southwest of Calcutta. In Barisal Jibanananda lived with his wife, two children, and the rest of the Das family in Sarbananda Bhavan. Satyananda, his father, died in 1942, in Barisal; his mother, Kusum Kumari, following her husband's death, spent much time with her younger son and daughter-in-law in Calcutta, where she died in 1948.[103]

By the middle of the decade, Jibanananda considered a change of both career and place of residence. He did not really like the teaching profession, as he explained in a 1942 letter to his sister-in-law, Nalini:

What you wrote concerning the present situation as regards teaching and educational institutions is quite correct. However, I've never ever enjoyed teaching very much. I have little confidence in the way education is administered or in the substance of that education. Such work does not stimulate my mind, though I admit that at certain times it does interest me more than some other of my inclinations. You experience much greater enthusiasm and joy in this field than I do. That is wonderful, and I sincerely respect you for it.[104]

He voiced much the same sentiment four years later in a letter to an as yet unidentified person. "I must still teach," he wrote, after running through a partial list of the colleges where he had taught. "However, I feel I ought not stay in this line of work much longer. Are not the substance and manner in which education is administered all just narcosis by another name? It is time to effect a new contextual framework."[105]

Jibanananda, ever apart from the literary mainstream, was moreover a painfully private person whose very nature in certain respects ill suited him for academics. One of his B.M. College colleagues observed:

Our poet by nature did not like to socialize very much. I never saw him become close to anyone in the town of Barisal itself. He even seemed to avoid the various functions and festivities of his own family's Brahmo Samaj. Never was he seen at the gatherings of fellow professors or literature buffs. ... He used to take the path along the edge of a field to get to the college. In the classroom he would teach quietly, even somberly; in between classes he sat like a stone statue in one corner of the teachers' room. Later he would take that deserted path back to his solitary home. Before dark it was his habit to pace briskly about the grassy yard, his eyes downcast. I have seldom seen such an introverted, lonely life style. ... I saw him fall silent in a crowd. Even among his students in the classroom his mouth would go dry. Were he not to lick his parched lips repeatedly, he could barely get out a sentence. I am not a literary critic, not even an appreciative reader. I have heard he is called "the loneliest of poets."[106] If human problems are not central to his poetry, it must be understood that that itself was a part of his nature.[107]

Fellow poet and friend from the *Kallol* days, Acintya Kumar Sengupta characterized Jibanananda in like fashion:

Alone, detached, melancholy, gray, taciturn, weary—with just such a list of attributes have people tried all these years to convey this point: Jibanananda was not a particularly social being. A soft smile painted upon his lips, he did not know how to laugh; he did not know how to pour himself into a conversation; if he spotted someone he knew on the street, he would avoid him and slip away.[108]

On 6 August 1946, according to "Proceedings of the College Council, B.M. College," it was "[r]esolved that Prof. J. Das be granted leave with full pay from 8.7.46 to 14.9.46 under Rule XII(1)."[109] He spent the leave period in Calcutta, with his brother.[110] While there, he probably made arrangements to join the staff of the daily newspaper *Swaraj,* due to begin publication in November or December.[111] Those were momentous times in Calcutta; 16 August 1946, called Direct Action Day, witnessed ghastly rioting between Hindus and Muslims, harbinger of the bloodshed to come a year hence with the partition of Bengal. Despite his claim in July of that year that "At present I am in a bind; I have no urge to write,"[112] Jibanananda composed lyrics while in Calcutta, as well as after his sojourn there.[113] True, perhaps, to his dictum that poets should not be reporters, he forbids the riots' gore to overwhelm his verse.

Another entry in the Proceedings of the College Council of B.M. College pertained to a meeting held 23 December 1946: "leave application of Prof. J. Das. It is to allow him leave without pay from 11.11.46 to end of our summer vacation." A note in the margin read: "ask him to return all library books by the first week of January."

Independence, with the possibility of concomitant partitioning of Bengal, was in the air. Some Hindu professors at B.M. College left around the time of Partition and Independence, 14/15 August 1947.[114] Jibanananda, though a Brahmo and technically not a Hindu at all, may have felt uncertain about the post-Independence situation in Barisal. According to his wife, the local Bengali Muslims warned them that the "up-country" Muslims (i.e., Muslims from the Bihar province in India, primarily) would be coming to Pakistan and that Hindus would not be safe.[115] Couple this uncertainty with his expressed disaffection with the teaching profession and it becomes explicable why, when the opportunity presented itself for a job in Calcutta, Jibanananda chose to leave academics and Barisal—the latter for good.[116]

Those times involving internecine strife between Muslim and Hindu brethren, preparation for the subcontinent's partition, and anticipation of independence did find their way into his poetry.

1946–47

There's a rather indistinct human anxiety all around in the day's light:
On streets, in alleys, on tram line tracks and sidewalks;
Somewhere just now another's home is to be auctioned—it seems,
Dirt cheap.
Everyone is going to take advantage of everyone else and
Thereby get to heaven ahead of all.
Many must be out of breath, but
A couple or even one person may buy, through deceiving many,
The house and furniture on auction—or even all the things
That aren't up for sale.
In this world, interest accrues: but not for everyone.
Indescribable bank notes in the hands of one or two persons.
And these high-ranking persons of the world demand
And take everything, even women.
The rest of mankind, like profuse leaves of late autumn in darkness,
Wish to fly off toward a river somewhere,
Or toward the ground—and mix in with some germinating seed
Of the earth. Even knowing that many births have been destroyed, still
The proprietress must take possession of the familiar waters, partial light,
When again she returns in the smell of sunshine, in immortality of dust, grass, flowers:
And considering this, they blend into the darkness.

They disappeared then—dead.
The dead never return to this world.
Are the dead nowhere; are they somewhere?
It seems the dead are nowhere except in the hearts
Of peaceful men pacing some November path;
In that case, it would be well calmly to enjoy
Light, food, sky, and woman somewhat before death.

Thousands of Bengali villages, silent and powerless, sink into hopelessness and lightlessness.
When the sun sets, a certain lovely haired darkness
Comes to fix her hair in a bun—but by whose hands?

But it remains loose and flowing as she gazes out—but for whom?
There are no hands—no person anywhere; one of the thousand Bengali village
Nights, smiling, like a picture on some scroll, some floral decoration,
Had almost become a beautifully wife-eyed woman; then all was extinguished.

Here that day too they caught the scent of newly harvested rice;
Many crows, in the sunlight and flavor of the new rice,
At the conch-shell calls blown by the eldest and so on in this neighborhood—by lower-caste women of that neighborhood,
Flew in and ate of the nectar, then left;
Now there's no sound not even of all those crows;
Human skulls and bones do not finitely enumerate man;
In time's hand he is limitless.

Over there in the field on a moonlight night the peasants used to dance,
After drinking strange rice wine, prior to the wedding
Of a boatman with the little goddess daughter of a low-caste fisherman—
And after the marriage—and before the birth of their child.
And those children today are nearly trampled to death
In the exhausted, ignorant crowded human community
Of this age's evil nation-states; the great grandfathers of all these present
Village children have laughed, played, and loved—and now gone to sleep
In darkness after raising permanently the zemindars' hook-swinging tree.[117]
They were not much better then; still,
Compared with the blind and tattered village beings
Of today's famines and riots and sorrows and illiteracy,
They were the inhabitants of some separate, obvious world.

Is everything today hazy? It is now difficult to think clearly;
The rule is to keep everyone informed with half-truths in darkness;
And then alone in that darkness it has become the practice
To surmise the other half of the truth; and everyone
Looks at everyone else out of the corner of his eye.

The inner thoughts of creation are—enmity.
The inner thoughts of creation: the dragging of a shadow of
Our doubts over our sincerity and thus bringing us pain.
We see a fountain of water gush forth from nature's
Mountains and stones and then we gaze into our hearts
And see that because the first water is red with the blood of the slain,
The tiger is still today chasing after the deer;
I have killed man—my body is filled with his
Blood; I am the brother of this fallen brother

On the paths of the world; he considered me his younger brother
Yet the heart hardened and he felled me, and I lie
Sleeping beside the bloody swells in this river, having slain
The ignorant one who was like an elder sibling—burying their heads
In his narrow chest, they appeal to all who
Have taken the affectionate vow of life,
Yet since there is no light anywhere, they sleep on.

They sleep on.
If I were to call, then from the river of blood as it
Billowed up, coming close by, he would say, "I am Yasin,
Hanif Mahammad Makbul Karim Aziz—
And you?" placing a hand upon my chest and
Raising up those eyes from his dead face, he would
Ask—that blood river welling up would say,
"Gagan, Bipin, Sasi, of Pathuria Ghata;
Of Manik Tala, of Syam Bazar, or Galif Street, of Entaly—"[118]
Who knew from where; they are all men of
Life's low classes; ragged shoes on their feet
They purchase the bug-damaged articles in the market;
Through creation's relentless drive
All these tiny beings awoke—and in the rays of the afternoon sun
Suddenly all these atomlike neglected lives of the
Luminous world had appeared beautiful in the bright
Eyes of some of the intellectuals.
The sounds that arise in the stream of the sun's light,
In the titillated bodies of these particles, in the collision of these
    particles,
There time, in the music of its incomparable voice,
Speaks; to whom does it speak? Yasin, Makbul, Sasi
Suddenly came near and before saying anything
Spoke at length as if from the interior of a half-fragmented eternity;
    yet—
Eternity is not fragmented; thus that dream, effort, speech
Have vanished within the unfragmented eternity;
There is no one, nothing—the sun has gone out.

In this age there's much less light everywhere, however.
We have now squeezed out a value from the fabricated stories
About dignity of thought, determination, mistakes, pain, work, tales
Of this world's many days and collected it
In sentence, word, language, and incomparable style of speech.
Man's language, however, is merely an exercise if it does not receive
    light
From outside of immediate experience; attributes; a skeleton of
Scattered helpless words far distant from knowledge.
Though we've inherited much learning, yet
The science of this century of ours is merely a crowd of
Collected things—which merely grows larger;

However, because it has no heart at all, there is not
Meaningful knowledge in the world today; without knowledge there's no love.

In this age nowhere is there any light—no gracious light
Before the eyes of the travelers; nothing like the mother of
Radiated dark night: washing away all faults
Of man's overwhelmed body—of man's overwhelmed mind,
Hidden in the solitary darkness, devoid of human gatherings
No one is asked any more—answers to previously
Asked questions are no longer wanted—simply surrounded by noiseless,
Deathless darkness, all faults, weariness, fear, mistakes, sins
Become passionless—this life gradually becomes devoid of sorrow,
A refreshing cool fills the heart; as though at the edges of the direction-marked
Sea, beloved voices of wind come merging
Into several *devadaru* trees—that incessant, sure-flowing wind
Upon the bloody soul of man—man's life is without stain.
Today is there not in this world such a pervasive darkness?
Is there no sweet breeze, no profundity, no purity?
Yet man, as he turns from the blind state of adversity toward soothing darkness,
From darkness toward the celebration of his new cities and villages
Where degradation has not set in even today—an area of self-awareness,
Transcending the sources of error and sin in his heart,
Does remain, it seems to me.[119]
Come forward, oh knowledge, humility, unclouded vision, peace, light, love.

5
Another Fling at Fiction

"If he can make his way in Calcutta, so much the better. Let him do it. He needn't return. That obsession or infatuation or illusion—call it what you will—under which he spent the past twenty-three or so years here, that's over, dead. It would be hard to recapture once again that special feeling for this place. These sorts of persons do not stir easily. But once they waver ever so slightly, were they not to find some new haven to their liking, they would prefer death itself rather than go on living."

—Jibanananda Das, *Jalpaihati*

1

On 26 January 1947, the daily paper *Swaraj* began publication in Calcutta.[1] Bengali newspapers include, as a rule, a special literary-cultural section in their Sunday editions. Sanjay Bhattacharya arranged for Jibanananda to be hired as that section's editor.[2] Jibanananda went to Calcutta, joining the *Swaraj* staff toward the end of January 1947.[3] It was at the Lahore meeting of the Indian National Congress (December–January, 1929–30), with Jawaharlal Nehru as president, that the Independence Resolution had been adopted. Nehru then designated the coming twenty-sixth of the month as Purna Swaraj (complete self-government) day; 26 January continues to be celebrated in India as Swaraj or Independence Day.[4]

This affiliation with the *Swaraj* should not be taken to imply that Jibanananda had now become politically active. He remained essentially aloof from politics. And, as time progressed, it became clear that he did not have the makings of a newspaperman. Nirendranath Chakravarty recalled how toward afternoon Jibanananda would grow restless and wander over to his desk, suggesting that the two of them visit Sanjay Bhattacharya at the *Purvasa* office, a few minute's walk away from the *Swaraj*'s Creek Row offices.[5] Jibanananda was out of his element, remarked Niren. And before long, Jibanananda and the *Swaraj* parted company.

Had he stayed on, Jibanananda would have been the editor of the *Swaraj*'s puja issue, which he worked on prior to leaving the paper. A perusal of contributors suggests that Jibanananda himself probably solicited much of the writing which appeared therein. The initial entry, a novel by Narayan Ganguly, without question had been requested by Jibanananda personally.

Narayan Ganguly recalled that the *Swaraj* came to him for a story for its first puja special. He wrote one and sent it off, only to have it returned. Narayan Ganguly was somewhat taken aback. There comes a time, he explained, when an author's work no longer meets with rejection. He thought he had reached that plateau some time back. Incredulous, he read the unsigned note accompanying the returned manuscript, addressed informally to "Narayan," asking him to come to the *Swaraj* office. Complying, he found, much to his surprise, Jibanananda behind the desk. The two knew each other from Barisal where the younger Narayan had been one of Jibanananda's students at B.M. College. Following an exchange of pleasantries, Jibanananda wanted to know what had crossed Narayan's mind when his story came back, to which the ex-student replied demurely that he accepted his teacher's opinion and was withdrawing the work. No, no, Jibanananda protested, saying he did not dislike it but needed a full-length novel within a matter of weeks to meet the puja issue's deadline. Narayan, being his former student, was the only person Jibanananda felt free to impose upon, on such short notice. Obligingly, Narayan Ganguly, in less than three weeks, dashed off *The Flattering Bard* (*baitalik*), published in the *Swaraj* puja number for 1947.[6]

Besides the special puja issue, Jibanananda's responsibilities lay with the Sunday magazine section. To one of his features, a column entitled "Rustlings of the Mind" (*mana-marmar*), Jibanananda invited colleagues and acquaintances to contribute. Any topic would do as long as the writing was lively. Niren, for instance, responded with a short article dealing with the distinctive characteristics of novelists and short story writers.[7] Years later, just a few months before his death, Jibanananda would reciprocate with a poem entitled, "Rustlings of the Mind," in response to Niren's request for a contribution to the *Ananda Bazar Patrika*'s puja issue of 1954.[8]

Newspaper work did not suit Jibanananda. Narayan Ganguly recalled asking why he had forgone teaching for such a job. Jibanananda cited salary. Apprehensive about his former professor's well-being, he warned Jibanananda that, given the instability of periodical publications, his job could cease to exist at any moment. The *Swaraj,* in fact, survived for several more years, before it finally fell into financial difficulties. But Jibanananda had relinquished his post well before then, probably by midyear of 1947. Not until September 1949, at the age of fifty, did he again have a salaried position, once more as a college professor.

In the meantime, his immediate family, which had followed him to Calcutta, managed to survive. But Calcutta was not like Barisal where one and all shared the ancestral home as part of the joint family's collective household—the way Jibanananda and wife and daughter had done during the early 1930s when he found himself similarly unemployed. Calcutta was not without its attraction, but Jibanananda's feelings toward the city seem always to display reserve, even ambivalence. One of his short stories, estimated to have been written in 1946, probably well before he moved to Calcutta, begins as follows:

> It was not that he passed every day comfortably—there was no happiness, no tranquility, not even comfort. But then, where else could Santisekhar go, were he to leave Calcutta? And it wasn't that he didn't want to go, but in this world whose wishes are ever fulfilled, and to what extent?
> But it wasn't that he despised living in Calcutta either. Yet where was that financial independence, that place of residence he had sought? Many seek just that; how many attain it? Of course, the mind can experience its own comfort—the body is not the only receptor of feeling. There are those folks who, though their bodies are racked with pain, though they feel exhausted and put upon, still seem somehow mentally to maintain their distance, unaffected. Santisekhar had, certainly, seen such persons. It would have been nice had he himself, at age 44, been able to be like them. But as yet, he couldn't.[9]

During the first half of 1947, Jibanananda, his wife, and their two children shared quarters with Asokananda and his family in their flat at 183 Lansdowne Road in south Calcutta. Later in 1947 Asokananda was transferred to Delhi. The Jibanananda Das family continued to reside at that address—for better and for worse—until Jibanananda's death some seven years later.

From that address, just two weeks before Britain turned over power to an independent India, Jibanananda wrote a fatherly letter to his daughter Manju, then sixteen years old, who was vacationing with her aunt and uncle in Jubbulpore, a sizable town in the central Indian province of Madhya Pradesh:

> 183, Lansdowne Road
> First floor
> P.O. Kalighat
> Calcutta 26
> 30.7.47

Manju,
    I was happy to get your letter. Earlier I had worried when I received news of your fever. Perhaps the fever resulted from a cold. Be very

careful now. We become very concerned when you fall ill away from home.

I was quite delighted to read all that description of Jubbulpore which you included in your letter. It seems you've seen just about everything there is to see. Does it rain a lot in Jubbulpore these days? I suppose it may be hard to be out-of-doors then. How do you pass your day? Are there many books and such to read there? I imagine you spend quite a bit of time talking with Aunt Chutu and Uncle and Srijay. It's been raining a great deal here recently. A few days ago Auntie [Sucarita Das] and Aunt Nani visited here. They will be coming again during their vacation. Uncle [Asokananda Das] and family are moving from this place to his father-in-law's house on August 3rd. We shall remain here in this flat for the month of August. Currently housing is not available anywhere else. You might want to come back to Calcutta toward the end of August. Is Aunt Chutu going to come to Calcutta then? If you don't care to stay in Jubbulpore any longer, write me just as soon as you find some traveling companion. I'll send you the money to return to Calcutta.

It will still be some time before the Matric examination results come out; even the I.A. exam results are not out yet. I hope all of you are well. We are all so-so these days.

No more for today. Love and affection to both you and Srijay, and my best wishes to everyone else.

Father[10]

Jibanananda's brother planned to move to his wife's (Nalini Das's) parents' home at 172/3 Rashbehari Avenue—a few minutes' walk away—before transferring to Delhi. The scarcity of housing, at least in the price range Jibanananda could afford, persisted. With Independence came the partition of Bengal and an influx of Bengali Hindu refugees from East Pakistan, many of whom proceeded directly to Calcutta, exacerbating the housing problem even more. Jibanananda and family eventually moved from the first floor down to the ground floor at 183 Lansdowne Road, after some conflict with the landlord and a court case to boot. According to Asokananda Das, the case was settled amicably, with the landlord agreeing to rent Jibanananda the ground floor flat. Matters, however, do not seem to have ended there. The last page of one of Jibanananda's poetry notebooks contains a note penciled in English, in Jibanananda's hand.

7.7

In 1947 I was the petitioner & Mr. J. Das was the defendant for standardization of the rent of the ground floor occupied by Mr. J. Das. And the rent has been standardized by the R.C. [Rent Control] at Rs. 110/-. I don't remember the case no.[11]

Both housing and employment concerns harried Jibanananda from the time he came to Calcutta right up until his death. By late 1947, he had no job and little means of supporting himself and his family. Certainly his poetry did not provide an adequate income. Asokananda helped out, but, as he learned later from his brother's diary (as yet not made public), Jibanananda felt uncomfortable about accepting financial assistance. Labanya Das, who had taught school in Barisal, again taught in Calcutta, first at the Kamala Girls' School during 1948–49. Later, after attending the David Hare Institution during 1950–51, she taught for a few months in 1952 at the Deshapran School. Her B.T. (Bachelor of Teaching) degree conferred in November of 1952, she joined the staff of the Sisu Bidyapith school.[12]

Sisu Bidyapith (now called Srimati Jahar Nandy School) is located in the Park Circus neighborhood of Calcutta. Ramesh Chandra Sen, Jibanananda's former colleague from B.M. College, had since immigrated to Calcutta and was living in that area. He, by chance, sat on the governing board of Sisu Bidyapith. Ramesh Sen recalled that Jibanananda wrote him regarding a teaching position for Labanya Das. Ramesh Sen did write some sort of letter of recommendation. Once Labanya Das had secured the position, Jibanananda sent his former colleague and one-time critic a letter of thanks.[13] But all that came later and did not solve the immediate problems of 1947.

In order to ease the rent burden, Jibanananda sublet part of his apartment to three different persons at three different times. The first such sublessee was Major H.K. Majumdar, husband of Aunt Nani's sister. Major Majumdar stayed for six or seven months at the Lansdowne Road flat, beginning sometime in August of 1947. During this period, Jibanananda tried his hand at selling insurance—requesting his tenant, among others, to purchase a policy.[14] He may also have earned a little money by giving "tuitions," private tutoring of students. Still, it was difficult to make ends meet without a regular job.

2

During this period of unemployment, specifically the latter part of 1947 through the first half of 1948, Jibanananda tried his hand at writing novels. No one in Bengal makes a decent living from poetry, but successful fiction writers can earn a respectable livelihood. His immediate motivation for turning once again to prose (he had written, but never published, a considerable number of short stories and one novel during the early 1930s) may have been monetary, but Jibanananda's interest in fiction predates the move to Calcutta and his financial difficulties there. "From childhood on," he stated in 1946, "I have read a considerable number of stories and novels—both from here and abroad. I once aspired to become a novelist, and those hopes have not as yet been dashed."[15] Three novels have been published to date: *Malyaban* (1973), *Sutirtha* (1977), and *Jalpaihati* (1985).

Jibanananda wrote all three around 1947–48, as far as we know,[16] setting them in or around that period.

Nearly two decades intervened between his death and *Malyaban*'s release for publication. Jibanananda's brother, who served as the book's editor and publisher, held the opinion that *Malyaban* may be a thinly disguised autobiographical work.[17] In his introductory comments to the 1981–82 serialized publication of *Jalpaihati,* Asokananda further explains the timing of these publications:

> Following Jibanananda's sudden and unexpected death, all of his manuscripts came into my possession. . . . For some reason, my sister-in-law [Labanya Das] did not consent to have these novels published. Many years later, after her permission had been obtained, first *Malyaban* went into print. Then came *Sutirtha,* brought out in *Desh* and, later, in book form. Now the third novel, *Jalpaihati* is about to be published, in the periodical *Siladitya.*[18]

Ironically, it is *Malyaban,* published during Labanya's lifetime, which focuses upon conjugal disharmony and which, of the three novels, should have been potentially the most embarrassing to the novelist's wife.

One cannot say with any certainty why Jibanananda himself published none of his fiction. Though quite different in many ways from *Bengal the Beautiful,* his prose may have represented for him, like those sonnets, something extremely personal, unmitigated by poetic embellishments such as surrealistic imagery or allusions to exotic times and places. In both those early sonnets and short stories and in the later novels, he may have wished to externalize his feelings on paper but may not have been quite ready for a reading public's scrutiny.

Certainly Jibanananda felt a need to earn more money. Based on available evidence, it appears that he hoped to do so by writing and publishing fiction. In mid-1950 he wrote to Sanjay for funds:

> I am in a rather bad way financially, and for that reason must disturb you. I need four to five hundred rupees immediately; please make some arrangements for that.
>
> I am enclosing five poems herewith. Later I shall send essays, etc. (nothing written just now). You may print a novel of mine (under a pseudonym, not my real name) in *Purvasa;* if you think it is necessary, I can send it along. I shall write my *Reminiscences* [*jiban-smriti*] month by month in *Purvasa,* starting in September or October.[19]

The redundancy—"under a pseudonym, not my real name"—announces plainly an extreme reticence to making public what he had penned in a work like *Malyaban.*

Jibanananda never abandoned the idea of publishing his fiction, however. At some point he approached the editor of *Desh* about the prospects of getting his prose published there. *Desh* is one among the few publications that can pay regularly for literary contributions. Editor Sagarmay Ghosh agreed to publish Jibanananda, who, however, never submitted any fiction.[20] Jibanananda also paid a visit to Protiva Bose, wife of Buddhadeva and respected author in her own right, whose novels sold well. They talked about prose writing and about the market for literature, Jibanananda eager for any suggestions she might offer a novice.[21] Ajit Datta, former joint editor with Buddhadeva of *Pragati* back in the 1920s and later sole editor of his own journal and publishing house, recollected:

I had established a book publishing concern then by the name of Diganta ["Horizon"]. I don't know exactly what Jibanananda had in mind, but he approached me one day during that period—"I have a couple of novels I've written, could you take a look at them sometime." But since he died just a few days later, I never got to see those pieces.[22]

Outside of stray references in the few surviving personal letters, his fiction—particularly the novels—was the closest Jibanananda came to commenting on events in his life. But even when a novel seems autobiographical, readers interested in an author's life must be wary of accepting fiction as fact. "Candid" autobiography may be an obfuscating apologia, the telling of lies about lives. The biographer confronting autobiographies and seemingly autobiographical works of fiction must become like the famed geese of the Sanskrit poetic conceit, who can sip milk in water, deftly separating the prized former from the plain latter. Such a ganderlike reader will discover much biographical milk in two of Jibanananda's three novels, *Malyaban* and *Jalpaihati*. As biographical source material, these two works and their main characters—the eponymous antihero of the first and Nishith in *Jalpaihati*—strike resonances in anyone who knows something of Jibanananda's life.

Malyaban is a character study or, more precisely, a study of the relationship between a particular middle-class, middle-aged Bengali couple. Malyaban, who carries the Dasgupta family name (as did Jibanananda originally), and his wife Utpala and daughter Manu (the name suggests a correspondence with Jibanananda's real daughter Manjusri) occupy a two-storied flat in north-central Calcutta. Utpala and Manu sleep on the large bed in the upstairs room—the room with all the light and fresh air during the day. Malyaban, now forty-two years old, has been relegated to the sitting room on the ground floor, where he reads, works, and sleeps. In the course of this two-hundred-page novel, Malyaban spends but one night with Utpala in the upstairs bed.

Utpala, however, is not cold to everyone. In fact, she conducts almost nightly her own little soiree in that upstairs room. Malyaban takes note of what transpires but shows himself too weak a person to prevent it.

> Of those who frequented this house, some stayed only fifteen minutes, some for two to three hours. Nearly all of them would go right upstairs to Utpala. Malyaban might be sitting in the downstairs room reading the newspaper, smoking his cigar. And whether they looked in or not, they saw everything, assuming him to be either aloof or fatigued or just a bit odd. But no one really felt obliged to introduce himself fully to Malyaban. Some of them knew quite simply that this man's wife paid no attention to him. . . . Never ever did he follow those folks up the stairs. Never said anything to any one of them, either. He hesitated to go up when the sessions were in full swing there. And late at night, when only a few people remained in Utpala's room—one or two—probably just one—he most certainly never went up then. Though he imagined things, he didn't want to uncover with his own eyes the sediment that lay at the bottom of those lives.[23]

Malyaban decides to solve his problem by waiting until age takes its toll on human passions, having resigned himself to let bygones by bygones. For the time being, he copes by fantasizing his and Utpala's life some twenty years hence.

Nonetheless, the present occasionally overwhelms Malyaban, his awareness of reality subconsciously making him physically ill. Utpala had been entertaining late one night, and he, downstairs, dozes off, then suddenly awakes:

> The upstairs room seemed as silent as stone all right. Malyaban was just about to head on up.
> "The mistress and your daughter are asleep," the cook volunteered.
> "Oh, I see. You're here very late tonight, cook. What's the matter? Didn't they eat?"
> "They've eaten."
> "When?"
> "They had dinner with two of the gentlemen—"
> Malyaban fell silent for a moment, then asked, "Is there some rice for me?"
> "Yes, there is. Shall I serve you in here?"
> "Don't give me much. I feel rather queasy—"
> He got up after eating only a few mouthfuls. The serving woman wiped up what had spilt and took his plate away. Then she and the cook went home.
> Malyaban felt as if he were about to vomit. He closed the door, spread out some paper and threw up, again and again, for quite some time—everything came up.
> All he could think about was his mother. Confused, he thought to

himself: she is in this room—I feel as though she's standing in this very darkness—perhaps sitting beside my bed, stroking my chest, my back, perhaps—

Gradually it subsided—then finally that urge to vomit left Malyaban altogether. A bit startled and befuddled, he stared straight ahead: there stood Utpala.

"The cook told me as he was leaving that you were feeling sick to your stomach. What made you throw up?"

"Who knows."

"What did you have to eat?"

"Nothing much, just rice."

"Any food from outside?"

"No."

Utpala observed, "It doesn't look like you're going to be sick any more."

"I guess not."

"Does your stomach hurt?"

"No, I didn't have a stomach ache."

"All right, lie down, now go to bed. I'll fan you."

Malyaban laid his head down on the pillow, enjoying the breeze for a moment. "I feel better now."[24]

A short while later Malyaban perceives that Utpala, who wasn't fanning him with much enthusiasm anyway, grows gradually less attentive to the task at hand, her concern a fleeting, not heartfelt one.

Early in the book, one of Utpala's relatives writes that he and his family plan to come for a visit. Malyaban and Utpala consider moving to a larger flat, a plan that never materializes. Ultimately, Utpala insists that Malyaban move into a boarding house (called "mess" in Bengali) for the duration of the relatives' stay, a stay which lasts some seven months. Malyaban's feeble arguments to the contrary prove unpersuasive, and he takes up residence in nearby temporary quarters. Unhappy with his living arrangements, Malyaban at one point tries reasoning with Utpala to be allowed back into his own home—but once again to no avail.

That very day Malyaban went directly from the office to Utpala. As soon as he arrived, he protested, "No. No more of that boarding house nonsense."

"Why?"

"I tell you—I'm coming back here today."

"Well, where do you plan to stay, if I might ask?"

"Where I always stayed—downstairs."

"But there's no room there."

Malyaban replied, "I'll just squeeze myself into some nook or cranny around here. You don't have to concern yourself about that."

"Are you out of your mind?" responded Utpala, displaying a bit of temper. "There's absolutely no place to put you in this house. You're fine where you are. We simply don't have enough room here. You have got to stay at that boarding house for now. After all, I can't drive them out, now can I?"

"But, this is my house."

"If you're going to be that way, then I'm afraid I'll have to take my brother and his family with me and go rent ourselves another apartment."

"No, no. That's not what I meant at all," said Malyaban, sensing that the conversation had gotten out of hand. "What's the point in my coming back here if you leave. That would be just like back in the boarding house."

And because he felt compelled to say something more, he added, "As I lie there on my bed in the boarding house night after night, I keep losing confidence, losing hope. I think, 'If I should die, I would never again see you—'"

But as he glanced at Utpala's face, Malyaban felt rather awkward. Without finishing what he was saying, he added, "Enough. You did pay my life insurance policy premium, I trust. I left the money with you—"[25]

But she hadn't paid the premium, instead spending the money on herself. Unembarrassed, Utpala tells him her brother advises Malyaban to take out another policy—for which, of course, they have no money.

The book ends with a scene that takes place well after the relatives have departed. It is night. Another of Utpala's male visitors having just left, Malyaban goes upstairs to take his meal with his wife and daughter. As the action develops, Malyaban seems headed for a confrontation with Utpala regarding her evening liaisons, while Utpala herself appears to be softening in her attitude toward her husband. The two lie down together and speak of how nice the long winter nights are—how nice it would be if this night should never end. A real change appears to have taken place in the marriage. But then we come to know that Malyaban has fallen asleep at the dinner table, just when, and therefore how much of the preceding conversation was real and how much a dream, is uncertain. Obviously, nothing has really changed at all. He may get to move back into his own flat, now that Utpala's relatives have vacated it. Those yearned-for qualities in woman, sympathy and support and love and companionship, however, will continue to elude Malyaban.

Unlike Malyaban, Sutirtha, in the second posthumously published novel, possesses a character difficult to know and even more difficult with which to sympathize. Jibanananda has created neither a shy Malyaban-like individual nor a strong persona but instead a hodgepodge of the two, an inconsistent characterization which makes for an unengaging protagonist.

When we first meet him, Sutirtha is alone but has been hailed by a group of more gregarious men, Birupaksa, the black marketeer among them. Sutirtha, a sometime poet who now finds himself unable to write, initially comes across as a relatively quiet, mild-mannered sort, though a bit eccentric.

> "Sutirtha, what's the news from your father-in-law's? I heard your wife is very ill. What's the matter?"
> "Nothing. She's fine."
> "Still those two kids, or more now?"
> "They say there haven't been any others." Sutirtha spoke while working over his toast and cake—breaking, squeezing, dunking, chewing—and sipping his coffee.
> At that, Bijan, Birupaksa, and Asit, catching each other's eye, now took a good look at Sutirtha. But no one said a thing. They sipped their coffee, made more, poured again, and continued to drink.

His current vexation has to do with housing—Sutirtha seeks a modest but comfortable place to live, an obsession that exercised Jibanananda from the moment he moved to Calcutta in 1946 until his death.

> "Where's Sutirtha live?" Bijan inquired of Birupaksa.
> "Nearby. Lake Road, or is it Lake View Road. Where's your place, Sutirtha?"
> "I was making do quite nicely, away from all the ruckus, but now they want to kick me out."
> "But of course they do, given the going rate for finder's-fee surety these days. On top of that, you've got to pay two to three hundred rupees a flat in these parts. How much do you pay? Twenty or so? Take my advice, Sutirtha, ..." Birupaksa didn't finish his sentence.
> "Where's your family?"
> "In Pashgan."
> "Why don't you bring them to Calcutta? What is your father-in-law, a rich guy?"
> "He was a big *talukdar* [owner of a sizable estate] once, it's true, but he's come down in the world. ..."

Then, we see a manifestation of the eccentricity—which never really occurs again in the novel:

> "It wouldn't be impossible to bring her to Calcutta. I'll bring the children one of these days. My wife is very much in love with me. ..." With these words, Sutirtha put his arms around Birupaksa, holding him in a firm embrace.
> "This fellow's gone crazy. ..."
> As he gradually, with considerable effort, was about to extricate himself from the solid grip of Sutirtha's billowing wave of a body, Birupaksa fell back even more engulfed, saying again and again, "For goodness' sake, for goodness' sake. Of course your wife loves you.

What's so unusual about that, please tell me. It's your wife—no one else's. This is ridiculous. Why are you falling all over me this way, bellowing like some unweaned calf! Is he laughing or crying, listen you—hey, Bijan, Asit—let go of me, let go, Sutirtha! LET—GO—OF—ME!" With a sudden and powerful push, Birupaksa sprang free, falling back onto the cabinet, taking everything, teapoy, coffee cups and saucers, with him. Sutirtha raised his tall, large-boned body and stood there a few moments, his hair all tousled, shocks sticking out like blackbirds' legs, wings flapping. He stared in the direction of the three men. Then, shaking like a man besieged by a chill, he left the room.[26]

Histrionics aside, Sutirtha, a man in his early forties, has lied to these acquaintances as well as to his landlady, for no apparent reason, about his marital status. And he continues to prevaricate, telling others of his nonexistent family. Some three-fourths of the way through the novel, when his landlady questions him again on the matter, Sutirtha admits he has never been married.

"You're not married?"
"When did I marry?"
"But you've been saying all along that your father-in-law in Pashgan. ..."
"Does any such place called Pashgan exist on the face of this earth?"
"Doesn't it?"
"You know it doesn't."
"You mean, no wife, no daughter, no mother-in-law?"
"No."[27]

And the matter is dropped there for good, with no consequences from that gratuitous falsehood—except to suggest, perhaps, that Sutirtha might be an inveterate liar.

After Sutirtha has been shown to be an irresponsible character, on the edge of penury (ten months behind in his rent by novel's end), we see him in the office of the British commercial firm where he quite competently works, when in attendance—which seems not to be very often. There he stands up to and in fact attempts to humiliate his rather pathetic Bengali boss. Later Sutirtha once again absents himself from that office to sleep on the picket line alongside factory laborers, with whom he has little in common—more a gesture than commitment, for later he easily deserts their cause. Finally, Sutirtha gets bought off for Rs.5,000/- by the manager of the struck factory, who had threatened to frame him for the murder of one of the striking employees.

We last see impetuous Sutirtha heading off for "the village" with the sincerest intentions of doing an unspecified good. At the same time, he leaves his landlady, and the reader, in the lurch. He had asked Jayati, wife of Birupaksa, to accompany him. She has now renounced her husband but not her coveted share of his black-market spoils.

Jayati responded, "I'll go with you."

"Not just a sight-seeing trip. There's a lot of hard work to do out there in the village. You find plenty of stupid people in the city. You're going to find even denser folks in the village. But just because they're a bit thick doesn't mean they're corrupt. They have people above them who are even worse. And above them—there's a sort of senseless lack of discipline which pervades the entire country."[28]

Though at first agreeing to go with him on his mission, she ultimately remains behind, leaving Sutirtha to go off by himself, presumably to set the world aright.

Sutirtha has many redeeming qualities, not the least of which are the frequent brilliant passages, particularly dialogue, displaying an impressive range of vocabulary and—in contradistinction to his poetry of this same decade—lucidity. All his fiction possesses that same clarity, revealing a side of Jibanananda almost inconceivable to the reader of his poetry or essays only. *Sutirtha,* a strangely poetic novel, contains many lyrical interludes which transport the reader to rural Bengal. In chapter 5 of this twenty-six-chapter narrative, Sutirtha inexplicably finds himself at midday on Calcutta's north side, a fair distance from where he lives in Ballygunge toward the south of the city. ("Who knows what I was thinking today that I should end up in Shova Bazar, Madhumangal. It seems some ghost dragged me here."[29]) He has stepped into Madhumangal's barber shop for a haircut and shave, where the barber recognizes his customer as a former grammar school classmate. It only dawns on Sutirtha later that he and Madhumangal actually went to school together, an inconsequential realization as far as the plot is concerned, for the two never meet again. But while Sutirtha sits in the barber chair, his conversation provides one of the novel's many, albeit brief, poetic swatches of color.

> "You can call me an idiot, but lately I can't seem to concentrate on anything. Come on, why don't you take me somewhere—come on, I'll handle all the expenses. Is it possible to bathe around here?" [It is the custom in Bengal to bathe before taking one's midday meal.]
> "Of course. No problem."
> "Do you have some decent soap? I'm getting hungry—how about having a bite to eat, then going some place and spending the rest of the day, the night too. Even better if we could stay two or three days. I insist it be very dark—utterly quiet. As though life were just a sleep-inducing winter's night, nothing more—date palms, fog, an owl, crowded in upon a rural winter—and night shall never be exhausted. The taste—of waking just a little now and then, on one's way from sleep to other sleep—and but for that, sleep never ends. All this—all this I crave—if you could only give me that, for several days."[30]

More so than in the other two novels, Jibanananda's poetry resonates throughout *Sutirtha.* For example, in the poem "1946–47" cited above, we read:

> They sleep on.
> If I were to call, then from the river of blood as it
> Billowed up, coming close by, he would say, "I am Yasin,
> Hanif Mahammad Makbul Karim Aziz—
> And you?" placing a hand upon my chest and
> Raising up those eyes from his dead face, he would
> Ask—that blood river welling up would say,
> "Gagan, Bipin, Sasi, of Pathuria Ghata;
> Of Manik Tala, of Syam Bazar, of Galif Street, of Entaly—"
> Who knew from where; they are all men of
> Life's low classes; ragged shoes on their feet
> They purchase the bug-damaged articles in the market;
> Through creation's relentless drive
> All these tiny beings awoke—and in the rays of the afternoon sun
> Suddenly all these atomlike neglected lives of the
> Luminous world had appeared beautiful in the bright
> Eyes of some of the intellectuals.

In front of the struck factory, Sutirtha joins those on the picket line:

> Sutirtha had stood up—he paced. Now he sat down on a tree stump. No sooner had he done this than it occurred to him: they all were seated on the ground—it wasn't proper for him to sit upon a stump. Maybe they would think that this Sutirtha Babu [the term of respect affixed to a Hindu Bengali gentleman's name] was setting himself apart just this much. He went and sat on the ground, rubbing shoulders with Ananta and Golam Mahammad.
>
> Sutirtha said, "Hamid, Yasin, Makbul, Bipin, listen. Banku contends that *babus* like us are buying a name for ourselves, taking advantage of this strike."[31]

Though the names vary, here is the mix of Hindus (Ananta, Bipin, Banku) and Muslims (Golam Mahammad, Hamid, Yasin, Makbul),[32] all laborers, all "Life's low classes," all suffering the same plight. Yet, because of man's innate ability to hate what is different, these Bengalis will continue butchering each other, in the name of their sacred religions.

During another scene, while Sutirtha and Manika, his landlady, converse, the narrator calls to our attention the sounds of a hawk in the skies over Calcutta.

> Amid the sunshine from far-off skies there could even be heard the cry of a hawk. Man's heart becomes so agitated, yet nature herself keeps calm throughout her vast domain, and is so amazingly, so vivaciously well-governed, large-hearted.[33]

Early on in Jibanananda's poetry a similar hawk was heard to cry beside a *mofussil* river:

O hawk, golden winged hawk, in this afternoon of damp clouds
Cry no more, soaring beside the Dhansiri river!
Her languid eyes, like cane reed fruit, come to mind through your
   lamenting melody!

Further on in the narrative, Manika and Sutirtha—their quasi-familial relationship now transformed into a blend of subconscious sexual attraction and adversarial reserve—verbally spar, discussing the strike in which Sutirtha had briefly participated.

> "You'll have to submit a letter. I'll write it for you," appended Manika.
> "What sort of letter?"
> "To your boss. I'll say: 'The dog will stay here, take his meals here—he'll bite his fleas—spread his foul odors—so let him—there's nothing one can do.'"
> "Write it. I'll send you a puppy next winter."
> With gravity added to her voice, Manika said, "You've got money in your cash box, but you're not going to give me any? [He's now ten months behind in his rent.] What are you going to do with that money?"
> "I'm going to give it to those whom I must."
> "To the families of those strikers? But the strike has been broken—"
> "They're in jail. Still, the strike must go on, and those families have to eat and clothe themselves," Sutirtha, like a cheetah on the far bank of the canal, stared over at Manika.
> On this side of the stream, like a doe alert, Manika stared back and said, "Of course they do. But are you going to feed them on my charity? I'm for Mukherjee [management]. Why should I give money to buy a bowl of watery rice for all those men and their women folk who go against Mukherjee?"
> Manika's gaze grew keen. As when a golden-bodied creature, striped in black, spies within the forest, by a river on a moonlit night not her favorite but a common jungle cat, just so Manika set tight her disdainful lips.[34]

First, Jibanananda presents his often exploited image of cheetah and deer, of sexual and predatory attraction, which he so beautifully developed in "A Tale of the Sundarban Jungles." Then, with a subtle, telling twist, he gives the woman's perspective in a developed simile of the breadth of those Michael Madhusudan Dutt deployed in his epic poem *The Slaying of Meghanada*—she becomes a black-striped, golden-bodied creature. We don't know whether she's one of the many striped deer of the Sundarban, as she was in the previous pair of similes, until this golden beauty looks upon the common jungle cat with scorn: no deer, this, we realize, but a Royal Bengal tigress.

Toward the end of the novel, Sutirtha contemplates leaving for the village, proffering his invitation to Jayati to accompany him.

"Have you decided then to come to the village?"
"Do you think I haven't been speaking frankly, Sutirtha?"
"If you accompany us, there are a couple of stipulations, though."
"But you already told me those."
"Have I told you about all the terms?"
"Why? Is it really necessary? This is a mutual matter."
"Then you understand completely," responded Sutirtha with great trust. And from Jayati's chest there heaved a sigh, like a pair of wild ducks, escaping man's gunfire, off in the boundless safety of the skies.[35]

The poems entitled "Wild Ducks" (*buno hans*) and "If I Were" (*ami yadi hotam*) formed part of the original *Banalata Sen* "One for a Pice" booklet. Closing lines for the former read:

> Let them fly, silently, in December's moonlight.
>
> Imaginary ducks—once all the world's sound and color ceases
> Let them fly, in the silent moonlight of the heart.[36]

The latter in its entirety:

> If I were a wild duck,
> If you were my mate,
> On some faraway Jalasiri river bank
> Beside a paddy field
> Among the slender reeds
> In a secluded nest,
>
> Then on this February night,
> As we watch a moon rise behind *jhau* tree branches
> We would leave behind the marshy lowland smells and
> Float our bodies upon the sky's silver harvest—
> My feathers upon your wing, your blood pulsating on my wing—
> In a blue sky numberless stars, like golden flowers of a puffed-rice field,
> And the February moon
> Like a golden egg
> In the woolly green nest of a *siris* grove.
> Then maybe the sound of a bullet:
> Our flight zigzags,
> There's the thrill of pistons in our wings,
> The song of the north wind in our voices!
>
> Perhaps the sound of a bullet again:
> Our calm,
> Our peace.
>
> There would not be this gradual death, bit by bit, of life these days.

Nor would there be the darkness, the little failures of life these days.
If I were a wild duck,
If you were my mate,
On some faraway Jalasiri river bank
Beside a paddy field.[37]

And apropos of *Banalata Sen,* we find that Jibanananda has his characters expatiate on time and distance, dimensions he himself explored to the fullest, particularly in that volume, as in "Banalata Sen" itself:

> For thousands of years I roamed the paths of this earth,
> From waters round Ceylon in dead of night to Malayan seas.
> Much have I wandered. I was there in the gray world of Asoka

And in "The Hunt":

> A single star lingers in the sky
> Like the most twilight-intoxicated girl in some village bridal chamber,
> Or that pearl from her bosom the Egyptian dipped into my glass of
>   Nile-blue wine
> One night some thousands of years ago—

And in "Walking" (*path hanta*):

> I shut my eyes, move aside. Withered leaves, brown, are blown
>
> From trees. In Babylon just so I walked alone at night for some such Reason. Why, I have no idea today, thousands of hectic years later.

In *Sutirtha,* Sutirtha and Manika converse about time:

> Sutirtha got up to shut one of the windows that faced east.
> "Why did you close those shutters?"
> "The sun's too harsh."
> "Is it hitting you in the eyes?"
> "Your face was getting flushed—as if you had a fever."
> "Good. So be it," replied Manika, eyes closed. The mild burning sensation from the sun's rays felt nice. "I was enjoying it. Why did you have to go and pull those shutters to?"
> "All but one of the windows are wide open," said Sutirtha, savoring his own impressions, rather lost in a nascent reverie. "I see in my mind's eye young women of ancient Egypt. This too seems to be the blue sky of that Egypt. I am sitting on the bank of the Nile in the last sunlight of winter's cool." Sutirtha remained motionless, staring blankly out the window.
> "And me?"
> "You? You seem to be sitting there too, beside that statue at El Giza."
> Sutirtha swallowed hard, pausing. But in the next instant, his voice as

though rich with the calling birds in Egypt's sun, he spoke: "I can feel the breeze of some dawn, some Nile—a breeze like what would waft by if that sun that set three thousand years ago should return again—how deep the blue of that sky, incredibly blue—orgasmic sunshine, wondrous river, fertile, fallow fields, that light like endless blood spilled by births and deaths—far beneath the blue, blue patches here and there, among the many hundred bogus efforts that have failed, of pain, of all the gloom of all the many simple folks. Do you hear the fans, Manika? Are they date palms singing? Water rushing everywhere, tumultuous, has flowed into the present day, accompanied by the sunlight of three thousand years ago." Sutirtha kept staring out at the sky, toward Calcutta—the world.

"This three-thousand-year-old day today, you say," spoke Manika. Then, returning her focus from that oneness of spirit where, far, far off, two people's vision fuses at a point the size of a sesame seed, she said, "I too sometimes think that there is nothing called time."

"Time goes by, yet stands still?"

"No, no. It's not that. It seems to me that past time, present time, the history of all time is of one time."

The idea played like a shaft of lightning through Sutirtha's thoughts. He looked hard at Manika, then said, "I often have that same idea. But how can one reconcile such thoughts with mathematics?"

"I have no idea what mathematics would say. You are the mathematician. You are even more than that, Sutirtha—as you just said, in this day today of three thousand years ago. In that case, all time is contemporaneous. You yourself just said as much."

Later, in this same conversation, Manika asks Sutirtha:

"What do you see?"

"The radiance of this shining universe daily exposes birth and death, suffering, slums, fresh white sheets, mansions, the minars of this city, blue skies, and this sunshine. You said so yourself one day—it was thus in Babylon also. I was in Babylon, and we saw it. But together we had little time to drink in the sight."[38]

With *Jalpaihati,* the author takes firmer command of his subject matter and characters, for they evolve in large part from him and his experiences. The protagonist, Nishith Sen, resides in Jalpaihati (literally, "Olive Mart"), the name of a fictive town located on "the far side of the Padma," in other words, in eastern Bengal—then the east wing of Pakistan, now Bangladesh. (The manuscript bore no name, so Asokananda, as he had done with *Bengal the Beautiful,* titled the published work—choosing the town's name. He could just as easily have picked "Nishith," in keeping with the previous two novels, named for their main characters.)

Jibanananda sweetens *Jalpaihati,* an extremely powerful and bitter novel, with some fascinating individuals. But the anger which the main character—middle-aged, thwarted in his search for a teaching position in

Calcutta—feels toward certain persons, the teaching profession ("—in this godforsaken country it would be best if there were neither schools nor colleges. Let everyone become policemen, or join the military!"),[39] and contemporary society ("There's no point faulting the students, professors, or college governing boards. The fault lies with that worm of destruction which eats its way through Bengal's twentieth century—and grows fatter day by day."),[40] provides much of the book's dominant rasa or emotion. But that rage—actually seldom expressed—never causes overt, violent behavior, but rather seethes subcutaneously. It is a rage born of frustration in a man whose means of earning a living, meager as it may be, has now been jeopardized.

This novel also explores the dilemma confronting Hindus in Pakistan (and Muslims in India) once British India became two separate nations. Was it right to leave one's home for India? Did such a move show cowardice or common sense? On this issue, Jibanananda is far more than just a disinterested artist, for he, in Calcutta, had already made his decision. Moreover, he wrote *Jalpaihati* when these concerns weighed heavily on many minds.

The *mofussil* town of Jalpaihati looks much like Barisal. Both border on a river. Both can claim status as government headquarters of some sort: Jalpaihati has a Collector in residence. There is a hospital in both Jalpaihati and Barisal, and, more significantly, each town can boast a local nongovernment college. The name Nishith Sen—his full name used to be Sengupta, just as Jibanananda Das was once Dasgupta—indicates a Hindu of the Vaidya caste, the same as Jibanananda by ancestry.

"I remember your name."
"You do? I have come to see you several times before."
"Yes, yes. I remember everything now." Jayanath picked up a sheet of paper from the carpeted floor, placed it on a wicker stool, then said, "Your name is Nishith Sengupta, isn't it?"
"Yes, Nishith Sen."
"Sen? You think you're being sophisticated by cutting off the Gupta? 'Sen' could be a lowly Kayastha, a Sudra, a Sonar Bene—"
"I don't care a whit about all that caste stuff. They're all equal. At least they all should have the same opportunities. What's the point of keeping somebody down by declaring him to be of a lower caste?"[41]

(All of Jibanananda's protagonists, by the way, have been Vaidyas: Malyaban Dasgupta, Sutirtha Gupta—referred to as Dasgupta once[42]—and now Nishith Sen, formerly Sengupta.)

Nishith is nearly fifty years old in 1948, the same year that Jibanananda turned forty-nine. He teaches English at the Jalpaihati college, and, despite a score of years of service, still holds the rank of lecturer, one rung in the academic ladder below professor. By 1948 Jibanananda had already been residing in Calcutta for a year, having taken leave from—never to return to—his post of some thirteen years in the English Department at Barisal's B.M. College. Other, more major discrepancies, alert us not to presume complete congruence between Jibanananda and the fictional Nishith Sen. Comparisons, however, beg our attention.

Unlike that of *Malyaban* and *Sutirtha,* both set in Calcutta exclusively, *Jalpaihati*'s action takes place at two locales, Calcutta and Jalpaihati. The year is 1948, with British India already divided into Pakistan and what Jibanananda consistently refers to in this novel as the Indian Union, or just "the Union." When the novel opens, Nishith has only that evening arrived in Calcutta from Jalpaihati, proceeding straight to the door of his longtime friend with whom he will stay while seeking a teaching job in the city. During the time Jibanananda wrote this novel, he himself pursued that same quest for the elusive post at a Calcutta college.

Our narrator quickly delineates the situation. Jiten Dasgupta, the college buddy, recently married charming and sensual Namita—whose blood line includes a mother named Ma Thin (called Mr. Martin in jest by Jiten), herself the child of a Burmese father and Norwegian mother. Husband Jiten, for all practical purposes the boss of his British firm now that the former executives and their more official compatriots have quit India, suddenly gets called out of town on business. Nishith finds himself alone in the house with Namita, and the couple's several, ubiquitous servants. The scene involving Nishith and Namita, played with restraint, is laced with a subtle sexual tension, the woman slightly more the aggressor.

Toward evening, there comes a phone call from her father's residence—Jiten and Namita live in Ballygunge, the very middle-class Hindu Bengali neighborhood (where Sutirtha and, in reality, Jibanananda himself resided). Her parents' home lay a mile or so to the north, in the Park Circus area, a mixed neighborhood of both Muslims and Hindus and one which suffered mightily during and after the riots of August 1946. Namita's father has been ill for some time, paralyzed on one side of his body. Her mother, though mobile, suffers from a recurring problem that requires Namita's immediate attention. She might return late, she tells Nishith, or perhaps spend the night at her parents'—or at a gentleman friend's (for Namita, though married, has not stopped seeing old acquaintances).

Nishith takes his meal and later retires for the night, sleeping in the upstairs room Jiten uses as his office at home. Fast asleep, Nishith is unaware of Namita's return. Not sleepy, she decides to take a late-night shower. Stepping out of the shower, she throws over her shoulders a large turkish towel, letting it hang open. Still dripping wet, she marches stark naked (but for the towel) into Nishith's room. There she drinks a glass of water, slightly giddy from thinking about what his reaction would be were he to awake and see her in that condition standing before him.

Nishith does not wake. Namita returns to her room and lies down. Unable to fall asleep, she gets up again and puts on her Women's Auxiliary Corps uniform, complete with military shoes. She had served in World War II, liked the uniform, and continued to have her tailor make facsimile WAC outfits for her to wear at her pleasure. Now fully dressed, she returns to Nishith's room, to find him still asleep. She turns off the fan, reasoning that the hot humid air will undoubtedly rouse him. But, having done this, as she returns from the window, she catches her foot on the teapoy, the crash bringing Nishith abruptly awake. The two pass the remainder of the night chatting—she telling him, among other things, that her parents suffer from syphilis. She herself undergoes treatment for incipient syphilis, for her father had contracted the disease prior to her birth. Dawn breaks before they can venture up to the roof and stargaze. The night has passed without incident—that anomalous puddle of water in the middle of Nishith's room neither questioned nor explained. Namita retires to her own room, tells her servant to call her if she is not up by noon, closes the door, draws the curtains, divests herself of the WAC attire, and sprawls bare-skinned abed. Nishith, after a cup of tea, steps out to face the new day, in search of that teaching job.

The episode is noteworthy for its frank sensuality. Although nothing really happens, the candor with which Jibanananda treats the female body shows us a facet of this poet-cum-novelist which his poetry obscured. True, we find references to breasts in his earlier verse—verse which so agitated Sajani Kanta—but "harvest's breast" or even a "doe in heat" are a far cry from references to the actual female physique. Shy he may have been, but prudish, even circumspect, he was not. However, up to this point the language itself remains seemly, even reserved. Later on, in a quite different context, we see that Jibanananda does not shy from blatantly scurrilous language, if such language helps delineate character.

Nishith's pursuit of a job takes him that day to a number of old classmates and acquaintances, some of whom have risen to positions of power and could, if they so chose, provide him with a teaching position. One such a person, Kuladaprasad, a man shown to be of questionable scruples, Nishith visits at his home. His wife is away and her younger widowed sister flirtatiously plays with Kulada's hair. His two-storied flat costs a mere Rs.30/- per month, absurdly low for Calcutta rents in 1948.[43] Kulada had also built his own house—then and now the cherished goal of most middle-class Bengalis—but that home he rents out for Rs.350/-, preferring the cash income to creature comforts for himself and his family. (He also pocketed a finder's-fee surety of Rs.5,000/- for allowing the present tenants to rent his place.)

Kulada has risen to the post of vice-principal at his Calcutta college, a position that yields both status and reasonable remuneration—reasonable enough so that he need not earn extra (he does it out of greed) money by performing the odious task of correcting examination papers. And how very important the scores on those examinations are! An error in totaling points on a given exam might mean the difference between a first- and a second-class, or a second- and a third-class degree—which might in turn make a world of difference to the recipient of that score, spelling success in life or struggle and even failure. Kulada, we learn, has been lax in performing this duty for which he garners extra pay. His sister-in-law checked several examination notebooks and found, she tells him pouting coyly, errors of addition.

In the course of their conversation Kuladaprasad, whose reddened eyes, slurred speech, and noticeable drowsiness imply *ganja*,[44] describes to Nishith the fine art of what he calls crudely "fuckin' around."

> Kuladaprasad cocked his head to one side, dragged on his cigarette for a time—then exhaling the smoke through his nostrils and mouth, he said, "Teachers in the *mofussil* have to live the part twenty-four hours a day. And that's a horrendous imposition. I'd find it stifling. Calcutta, on the other hand, forms a vast continent in its own right. Nobody keeps tabs on who's doing what down which dim alleyway. No, I certainly could not have survived in the *mofussil*. They offered me five hundred fifty—"
>
> "Where?"
>
> "A principal's post—they were going to throw in quarters—and this, and that—but I didn't go. Who in his right mind is going to leave Calcutta? To sit upon a dais twenty-four hours a day, in my venerable teacher's garb? I suppose I'd have to watch out for who was being naughty where, so as to set him or her straight. Who says rich foods, like ghee, make your hair fall out? They'd expect you to take castor oil, but not touch the widow ladies, high class or no, not even just once in a while?"
>
> "Prostitutes?"
>
> "None of that nonsense around here, my friend. But all you have to do is cross that Maginot Line at Dharmatala Street, even in the middle of the day, and, with a hearty 'Victory, Hind!', head north—that's it—who's going to check on which Calcutta you, in your Gandhi cap and Nehru jacket, are patronizing—"
>
> "You mean the black market?"
>
> "I mean all sorts of fuckin' around."
>
> "You do that? How long have you been carrying on like this?"
>
> "Always have. Karaya Road, China Town, Free School Street—"
>
> "What do you do, leave your shoes outside the doorway before entering those carnal temples? Don't your boys ever recognize their teacher's shoes? Free School Street, China Town—you like those Mongoloid-type noses and eyes?"
>
> "I like 'em all, want to try them all. That's what our University's Khoda Baks Shaheb used to say."
>
> Lalita entered the room, bringing in a tray of rolled betel leaves.
>
> "Sixteen different nationalities." The words were English.

"What's that, Kulada, what did you just say?" asked Lalita, her sari, like a breeze through the leaves of a betel grove, rippling over her body.

"I said, 'Sixteen different nationalities,'" roared out Kulada, his eyes hard cast.

With the loose end of the sari drawn across her mouth, Lalita, giggling, left the room. So even she knew about Khoda Baks's predilections?[45]

Despite his "exalted" position as vice-principal, Kulada is vulgar. It takes a vulgar man to use such an unseemly expression as "fuckin' around," the Bengali original of which is even more obscene. Jibanananda has written *bancoti,* quite literally "sister-fucking."

Some Bengalis would claim that the Bengali language has no swear words, that they all come from Hindi.[46] No matter its origin, profanity is heard in Bengali, but seldom in polite company. Kulada's activities and his language characterize him as crass. Though appropriate in this context, such profanity would undoubtedly have given Sajani Kanta apoplexy and, I venture to say, would have been condemned by a large portion of the Bengali reading public in 1948.[47] (Even Norman Mailer—or his publisher—felt constrained to have American GIs in *The Naked and the Dead* [1948] utter a quaint "fug.")

As a source for the biographer-gander, *Jalpaihati* is rich with biographical milk. Besides the surprising daring with which Jibanananda exploits sexuality and profanity in this novel, *Jalpaihati* gives us a much fuller understanding of what it must have been like for a man in his late forties—a professor at a small *mofussil* college where salaries were low and prospects for advancement ranged from "slim to fat to none"—to conclude that it was best to leave his beloved bucolic homeland and move to Calcutta.

At a meeting called by Harilal, secretary of the college's governing board, we get another slant on concerns—realistic or not—that exercised Hindus who found themselves living in a Muslim-majority nation.

"Hey, you little monkey, bring out another sofa, quick." Sibanlal, the servant's son, went back into the inner quarters of the house to fetch one.

"There are sofas and settees all over the place. Why sit in one of those hard chairs, Kali Babu?"

"Bedbugs. They're fierce, Harilal Babu," said Himangshu Chakravarti.

"You can say that again. Terrible bedbugs, Harilal Babu. Tough to stay seated," added Brajamadhab.

"These new wooden chairs are bug-free. Kali Babu is sitting pretty." And the laughter began.

"Vicious bugs. Don't even think about shifting to a sofa. You're just fine where you are, Kali Babu," volunteered Bankim Datta, attorney for the Ghosh-Mallik estate.

No sooner did Sibanlal and Purna, pushing and tugging, position a beautiful new sofa in that upstairs sitting room than Wazed Ali Shaheb [a term of address for a Muslim man], having just entered the room, marched a bit arrogantly to it and sat down with authority. Kalisankar Babu had the previous moment arisen from his chair and was heading toward the same sofa. On catching sight of Ali Mia [a term of address for a Muslim man, often implying that of a devout Muslim], he returned to his wooden chair. And the room once again erupted in a burst of laughter.

"What happened—what's so funny?" questioned Wazed Ali.

"Nothing at all."[48]

The Hindu Kalisankar's reluctance even to sit on the same sofa with a Muslim shows clearly the Hindu-Muslim tension rife in Pakistan following Independence.

The meeting proceeds, though the conversation tends toward the discursive. And at one point an obviously sensitive subject surfaces:

"The Muslim League [the party of Mohammad Ali Jinnah, then the dominant political force in Pakistan] talks about whether or not to administer the nation according to Shariat canons."

"There you go with politics again!" rebuked Harilal Babu, becoming slightly flustered. Actually it was Wazed Ali who, rather sotto voce, had brought up the Shariat issue—two or three different tones emanate from Wazed's mouth. Harilal Babu, eyes closed, had been puffing on his cigar. He concluded that Brajamadhab Babu, showing signs of getting agitated, had brought up the matter of Shariat-based rule. Tactless Brajamadhab. With the intention of putting Brajamadhab in his place, Harilal Babu opened his eyes wide. Wazed Ali, still talking, flashed Harilal a set of hard, snowy white teeth, then fell silent.

"Brajamadhab Babu, you shall not speak about this Shariat! The Muslim League leaders know best in these matters. If they wish to say something, we shall listen. Wazed Ali Shaheb, would you like to say a thing or two about administrative policy? We're listening. We're all ears. What does Brajamadhab Babu, or Kalisankar Babu, know about Shariat law? And why should they go meddling?" said Harilal Babu in a measured voice, reprimanding both Brajamadhab Babu and Kalisankar Babu, then, like an obsequious junior lawyer, slowly turned his gaze to Wazed Ali.

Without questioning the sincerity of Harilal's earnest stare, Wazed decided he enjoyed it, and gushed. "No, no, Brajamadhab didn't say a thing. I was the one who brought up the Shariat."

"I had no intention of mentioning the Shariat or administrative policy, Harilal Babu," blurted out Kalisankar, getting defensive. "Why did you—"

But Kalisankar's words were snatched from his mouth as though by a hawk—go ahead, feast on them. Paying those words no need, Harilal Babu, pulled up short, seemed only now to have heard what Wazed Ali had said.

"Oh, it was you! You were mentioning the Shariat. I thought it was

Brajamadhab's voice, or maybe Kalisankar's. I was just thinking, here's this college principal [Kalisankar], 'Hey, stick to your students. Of what concern is all this minister-magistrate business to you?' Oh, you were speaking, Wazed Ali Shaheb! You were discussing Koranic, Shariat administrative law! Please go on, please do. I'd like to hear, we all would like to hear what you have to say. It's all still rather murky in our minds. I'm sure you will make the whole thing clear as water." It never occurred to Wazed Ali that Harilal Babu might be forcing himself to spew out this cant.

Wazed Shaheb felt flattered. With palms pressed together in supplication, he addressed Harilal Babu, "Not now. Things have become a bit higgledy-piggledy today, rather 'communal,' I should say. Another day, perhaps. I'll bring along Imam Hosen Shaheb, Mustak Shaheb, and Rafiq Shaheb."

"Fine, do that. You let us know when you're coming. We all definitely will want to hear what you have to say," said Harilal Babu.[49]

Pakistan never did invoke strict Islamic law (that contained in the *Shari'a*), although conservatives then and still today, in both Pakistan and Bangladesh, have advocated such measures. A literal interpretation of Shariat law would view Hindus as *kafirs,* infidels. That nervous exchange and lack of real comprehension represent an atmosphere which must have been not uncommon in Barisal and other towns in Pakistan's eastern wing in the late 1940s. Note, too, the ratio of Hindus to Muslims on the college governing board. But for Wazed Ali Shaheb, a highly educated barrister, all those in attendance are Hindu (four to five Muslim members, however, are said to be absent),[50] though the population of East Pakistan had a Muslim majority. B.M. College's faculty prior to Independence would have been, except for the Arabic and Persian teachers, totally Hindu (or Brahmo or Christian).[51] Today that ratio would be just the reverse, with all but the Sanskrit professor being Muslim. Bangladesh's population is even more lopsidedly Muslim now than then—90 percent, with less than 10 percent Hindu. Whether to stay in the land of their birth posed a most difficult choice for Hindu Bengalis of that region. Obviously many, in fact most, chose to start life anew in West Bengal, often in Calcutta itself.

Here in Jalpaihati the uncomprehending and savvy alike wander about, in some sort of strange uncertainty, as though dispossessed forever of what was theirs. Many of them have already left the country. They leave every day—are still leaving. Harit has told them to stay—he makes the rounds daily, telling them to stay put. But they are not of a mind to listen to Harit. Their hearts are already fleeing westward. Given that, are they then going to continue to dwell upon the banks of the Padma? What an incredible, indescribable richness there is in this land of the Padma and Meghna rivers. If only men would shake off their fears and try calmly, clearheadedly for understanding, if only they would begin the task, to appreciate not this nation's or that nation's but the world's wondrous human-life-affirming drama. But do such people exist? When they hear the lion's roar, they throw on their shirt and vest of chintz, and—just see—they raise a cloud of dust, like striped zebras. No, not like wild zebras, these—that's the way, in highest spirits, those vigorous American, Australian colonists galloped off—no, these, like moths, beat their wings from flame to greater fire. There's not adequate housing in Calcutta, no jobs, no food. Death lurks there—and still they go and fall flat on their faces like babies suffering rickets, upon the sidewalks, down the alleys of Calcutta.[52]

Calcutta had her own problems, compounded by the refugees from eastern Bengal. Housing became expensive and in short supply. Jobs, though many were created by the increased population, could not always be had by the newcomers when needed most. Jibanananda, who had come to Calcutta with a job on the newspaper *Swaraj,* found himself job hunting once again by late 1947. He may have searched earnestly for a teaching position off and on prior to 1946, as the Nishith character affirms he did, denying that his decision to leave East Pakistan stemmed from the new political realities there.

Why did Nishith want a job in Calcutta? If not in Jalpaihati, he could at least try to find work in some other *mofussil* college. There's a much better chance there. But no. He loved the natural beauty of the *mofussil,* and the people, too. But now he had come to Calcutta and wanted to immerse himself in all manner of that which exuded life and that which had been inaccessible. For many a day he had lived relatively isolated, one could even say alone. Now he would shunt aside the man he was and become a willing witness to the roiling, boiling, churning, perturbation of mankind—if he were able. He would attempt to respect that intangible something, wherever the opportunity arose, wherever possible, and might even learn a thing or two perhaps from that something's innate beauty and intelligence.[53]

Nishith's son proves most understanding of his father, explaining, even justifying, his father's actions. To Sulekha, committed to remaining in Pakistan, Harit says:

"It was we who discovered that Nishith Babu had left Pakistan and gone to the Union. He himself had no idea he had done this, nor even that he had been in Pakistan. Not Pakistan, not the Union, not politics—it was something else that motivated him. From before the creation of Pakistan, for some four or five years, he had been trying to secure a position in Calcutta. His college here withheld from him what was rightfully his. Even his family cheated him. About all these matters he had, toward the end, begun to feel resentment. In Calcutta no one is going to run his life for him. Sitting here, we think of him as the Union's pawn and thus decry his actions. But these sorts of folks seek, though often fail to find, their way through today's world, not to speak of finding what is due them. He earned a salary of one hundred fifty rupees a month. He asked for two hundred. Could not he have demanded seven hundred? What would have been the wrong in that? But those in this world who are the benefactors are without question decent men. And that is why a hundred fifty rupees was bestowed on him. Did he childishly refuse such largess and go off to the Union in hopes of getting even more money? Or, is it not money but more a sense of dignity that he seeks?"[54]

Just how hard it could be for a middle-aged English professor from the *mofussil* to secure a teaching job in Calcutta in 1947–48 we see through Nishith's eyes. The frustration, humiliation, and anger Nishith feels in Calcutta comes through in all but the initial episode with Namita. Yet in the very first scene, in Jiten's house prior to his making Namita's acquaintance, silent resentment shows through. Nishith—feeling slighted by his host, this well-to-do, former classmate of his, who does not insist Nishith have something to eat but instead accepts at face value Nishith's decorous, but false, claim to have dined earlier—raids Jiten's refrigerator after his host has gone to sleep, deliberately consuming what Jiten had said he would have for his breakfast. The following morning, Jiten, finding his cupboard bare, has to go to work on an empty stomach. Nishith feels no guilt.

After leaving Namita's company on the morning subsequent of their all-night session, Nishith encounters (but for a single exception) venal, vulgar, mean, small-minded men who demonstrate both that life is indeed unfair and that the mediocre have inherited the earth.

Jibanananda guards against letting Nishith be pathetic but virtuous and the only injured party. Even so, Nishith has his share of foibles. He quit his job, in effect, at the college in Jalpaihati, having gone to Calcutta after applying for leave and knowing full well the request stood little chance of being granted.

Harit, his son, who has some problems dealing with his father, has for some time been living in Calcutta, engaged in small-time political organizing and philosophizing, of the socialistic persuasion. With Independence achieved and thus the prior *raison d'être* for his activities vitiated, he and his cohorts have formed a party—our narrator displaying some drollery here—with no name.

"Have you become a Communist, Harit?"
Harit had opened several windows, and, now seated on the edge of the bed, was rocking slightly in the breeze. He hadn't heard all that his mother said.
"Harit. Hey there. Harit."
"What is it?"

"I asked you if you had become a Communist."
"Communist? No. Our party is separate."
"What's its name?"
"It doesn't have a name," Harit replied. "You can call it socialist, but not Congress-socialist. About eight or ten types of socialist parties have sprung up. Every letter in the English alphabet from A to Z has been gobbled up naming these parties. And we have no intention of using some other alphabet—just not giving our party a name, that's all—"[55]

Harit's anonymous party works generally, though with no apparent urgency, toward that revolution which eventually must come to India. The day Nishith leaves Jalpaihati for Calcutta, Harit returns home. Some say he must have been living furtively in Jalpaihati all along and showed himself only after his father had gone, but Harit denies that.

Nishith has two other children, both unmarried daughters, neither living at home. The eldest, Ranu, mysteriously disappeared. There is reason to believe that one of the more unsavory (Hindu) characters in Jalpaihati had either abducted her or enticed her to go to Calcutta with him. No one knows. Officially nothing is being done. Nishith himself makes some inquiries that yield little. With only rumor to go on, he deems searching for her in Calcutta a pointless task.

The second daughter, Bhanu, suffers from tuberculosis and has been sent to his wife's brother, who lives in a town with a sanatorium. During Nishith's first full day in Calcutta, as he and Namita are chatting, the servant announces a visitor who wishes to speak with Nishith Sen. A young doctor appears, saying he has just returned to Calcutta and has been informed by the brother-in-law that Nishith would stay with his friend Jiten Dasgupta when in Calcutta. We learn that Bhanu has not been admitted to the sanatorium—no beds available—and that Nishith had neither visited his daughter nor so much as written a single letter inquiring how she was faring. Nishith excuses himself, claiming illness, despite his apparently decent health at present. The brother-in-law, who has been keeping Bhanu at his place, will no longer do so. The facility at Jadavpur in south Calcutta, the other major tuberculosis hospital in Bengal, likewise has no available beds. But the doctor, a very compassionate young man, declares that he and his mother, with whom he lives, would be willing to minister to Bhanu in their own Calcutta home. Nishith eagerly shifts the burden of his daughter's care to this very caring and probably romantically inclined young physician.

Whatever we might think of Nishith, as family man (a character very unlike Jibanananda who, from what we know of his actual family life, resembles more a Malyaban than a Nishith), we meet in *Jalpaihati* an individual seeking to earn a livelihood who, if he does not gain our sympathy, at least causes us to understand the anger he himself feels toward an unjust system as well as toward individuals who perpetuate the injustice.

At the entranceway to the residence of the first person he goes to meet, a Professor Ghosh, Nishith is confronted by a young man, Nripan, who insists on knowing Nishith's business with the professor before he will let him proceed upstairs to the sitting room. At his wit's end, Nishith adopts a ruse, assuming the persona of the physician who had visited him that morning concerning his tubercular daughter. The officious snip becomes apologetic, even deferential. But Nishith retreats from his dissembling, and the youth resumes his condescending stance. The professor's wife, Mohita, happens upon the scene and recognizes Nishith from the several visits he has made over the last four or five years. She treats him with cordiality, and the two converse, Nishith telling her of his desire to obtain a teaching position in Calcutta. No problem, she assures him. After all, Professor Ghosh placed Nripan in three different colleges. Of course, he was dismissed from all three posts, but still no matter; the professor, with his ties to the present state and federal ruling powers, can place his people.

Professor Ghosh, who has spitefully arranged to give his library to Benaras Hindu University instead of Calcutta's National Library (Bengalis in general and Calcutta University in particular had not bestowed on him the honors he feels his due), exits his office and comes face to face with his wife and Nishith. Though they were classmates at Scottish Church College, Professor Ghosh consistently fails to recognize Nishith, each time they meet, this time being no exception. Mrs. Ghosh pleads Nishith's case, but her husband demurs, asking rhetorically and with feigned humility who is he to secure another person a teaching post. Nishith volunteers the information that he has only a second-class M.A. degree.

About to get up from where he was sitting, the professor spoke. "If you want to teach at the college level, a first-class degree from our university is requisite. Moreover—"

Mohita, in an effort to counter what the professor was saying, interjected, "You certainly are not so indolent in your thinking as to judge the quality of a teacher by what class of degree he earned."

Obstinate, the professor replied, "Yes, I am."

"You are?"

"I am."

Offended, Mohita continued, "Nishith Babu has twenty-five years of college teaching experience—"

Without letting her finish her sentence, the professor countered, "That's all well and good, but it would be better if he had a first-class degree."

"What sort of talk is that? Where does that get us?"

"He'd have done fine had he gotten a first-class degree," said the professor. "Twenty-five years of experience by itself doesn't get us anywhere in particular."

"What's the value of all these university first-classes?" It was as though—like goddess Durga—Mohita had leapt upon her lion mount to speak from there, and all these university first-class degrees were collectively the buffalo demon Mahisasura.

The professor smiled and said, "There is none? A second-class, I guess, shines equally bright?"

"There's no appreciation of real value in this country of ours."

The professor spoke with gravity, "I have work to do inside."

"But you didn't say anything to Nishith Babu."

"Nishith Babu should get another M.A. He's an English teacher. Then let him take another M.A. in English. Let him secure a first-class this time. Even if it's not the very top score in first-class, it won't matter." All this the professor uttered looking at no one, staring toward the variegated carpets which ornamented this house of his, constructed in the spirit of wisdom and decorum, gazing at the celestial geometry of lines upon his floor.

Before returning to his inner office, Professor Ghosh sagely advises his contemporary:

"These days the importance of English is waning," said the professor. "In a few years there won't be much need for English. Bengali has become the state language of West Bengal. If Nishith Babu wishes to remain in the teaching profession, he ought to get an M.A. in Bengali, preferably a first-class."[56]

Mrs. Ghosh, quite out of character for a typical Bengali wife, continues to side with the visitor against her husband. As Professor Ghosh heads for his office, she asks again what he plans to do for Nishith. Says the professor:

"But Nishith Babu is a second-class."

"Of course, you too are a second-class," Mohita blurted out rashly.

"But Nishith Babu is a second-class," the professor's shoulders bouncing ever so slightly as he, chortling, disappeared into his office.[57]

From the Ghosh residence, Nishith goes to see Kuladaprasad, Nishith's junior by a couple of years, but a longtime acquaintance. Not to be outdone by this contemporary, Nishith claims he is due to become vice-principal of the *mofussil* college where he teaches, at a salary of Rs.300/- plus Rs.50/- for what goes by the name of D.A. ("dearness allowance")—then he asks bluntly for a job.

"You've got to get me a job in a Calcutta college, Kulada."

"After all these years, and at your age? You know, if you take a job in Calcutta, you're going to have to start all over again, Nishith. It'll be too much of a strain."

"How do you mean 'all over again'?"

"You're a vice-principal in the *mofussil,* right?"

"That's right."

"You draw a salary of three hundred fifty. How much are you hoping for here?"

"How much will they pay?"

"What class M.A. are you?"

"Second-class."

Kulada, sounding a bit disheartened, responded, "Second-class—"

"You're also a second-class, Kulada—"

Slightly amused, Kulada looked in Nishith's direction. "I entered this college twenty-four years ago with my second-class degree. Today I'm a first-class elder. But you really are second-class—"

"Well, why haven't I become a first-class elder? I too have taught college for twenty-four years."

"That's true, but not in our college."

"Oh for cryin' out loud, aren't you the potentate at this college of yours?"

"You got that right," said Kulada, exhaling thick cigarette smoke.

"How about at Ripon, or Presidency, or Scottish, then?"

"They've got their own potentates at all those places."

"With second-class degrees?"

"Second-class—third-class—more than just a few first-classes also."

"So—that's the way it is, is it," said Nishith. "Could have been a whole lot better, but I suppose the system serves its purpose."

Nishith worked a cigarette out of the tin and was groping for a match. Lighting up, he continued, "When some elder brother-in-law from this college goes to that college to take a job, they let the younger sisters-in-law there care for him, I guess."

"That they do. And it's the young brides in the household who waylay any bumpkin brothers-in-law from the *mofussil*. You still want to teach in a Calcutta college?"

"What's the pay scale like?"

"You interested in mornings or nights?"

"What do you mean?"

"I mean, I'm talking about our Commerce section."

Kulada took a rolled-up betel leaf from the tray, tucked it in his mouth, and said, "There are no vacancies in our General section. And even if there were, we don't take anyone without a first-class, a foreign degree, or a doctorate."

"Not even ex-students of the college?"

"Not without a first-class—"

"Not even a governing board member's wife's brother, or the husband of his wife's sister?"

"You mean, with a second-class?"

"Do you care if it's a third-class?"

"Sure, we'll take him. There are several different 'codes' at the college. A college is not a place without its rules, you know. It would create all sorts of complications if I were to slip you into our college now at two hundred a month."

"Why?"

"You're a second-class M.A., Nishith."

"You're also a second-class, Kulada."

"Oh, you bloody idiot!" Kulada added a little pungency to his words. "What have I been explaining to you all this time?"

Nishith picked out a rolled betel leaf, removed the clove, popped it in his mouth, then said, "What you mean is you've become head matron of the collegiate joint family, and I'm still one of the unmarried daughters—that's what you're saying."

Kulada, chewing on his betel, now got out a cigar and lit it. "That's what I'm saying. Besides, you have no connections with Lady Chatterjee or Lord Mukherjee or Goofus Doofusjee of the college's governing board, now do you. Or do you?"

"Of course not. Who am I to them?"

"Then how in the world am I supposed to put you on the payroll at two hundred rupees?"

"At what salary could you get me on it?"

"At a hundred."

"They'll pay that, for sure? In General?"

"No. At night, in Commerce. On a temporary basis."

Nishith let out a sigh, remained silent a moment, then asked, "Is it like this everywhere, Kulada? At all colleges in Calcutta?"

"All colleges. Why should I be less than candid with you. Hey, we come from the same place. I make my living in Calcutta. You twist your mustache and try to find your way. You're not going to find it in the college line—Nishith, you're not really prepared to abase yourself for a job in Commerce, at a hundred a month, are you?"

Kulada took another rolled betel leaf and started to chew. Lalita really knew how to prepare betel. Lalita's big sister—Kulada's wife—had gone to north Calcutta, to her brother's house. She probably wouldn't be back tonight. So, he'd have to entertain his little sissie-in-law half the night tonight, would he? Kulada's mind was wandering. A good head of ash had built up on his cigar.

"Check out the newspaper offices, Nishith. If they offer you a hundred fifty or two hundred, take it. What are you going to do back there in Pakistan? Stay in Calcutta. Stay in Calcutta."[58]

Proper credentials are invoked to exclude those not already a part of the academic clique, but not to rusticate those, competent or no, who had previously joined that fraternity when standards were not so high.

After leaving Kulada's, Nishith in desperation makes one last attempt, calling on a college administrator by the name of Jayanath. He had paid him visits a number of times over the past several years, always for the same reason and always with the same result: disappointment. Jayanath along with his father and uncles had actually founded a college. Now with the influx of Hindus from Pakistan, new colleges were starting up, and already functioning ones were expanding (enrollment increased, but Jayanath kept the number of his staff the same, thus enhancing his profits). Jayanath, also a Scottish Church student though three years Nishith's senior, happens to be a Vaidya by caste (like Nishith and Jibanananda) whose father became a Brahmo (like Jibanananda's grandfather). Nishith's grandfather befriended Jayanath's father when many years ago he had entered the Brahmo Samaj.

"When Gayanath Babu with wife joined the Brahmo Samaj, his Hindu relatives threw him out of the family. No sooner did the couple set foot on the street of the outside world than Hindus of that day shouted derisively at them. He was unemployed, had no means of livelihood, and possessed only the clothes on their backs. My grandfather worked in the town of Halisahar at that time. From Father I heard how Gayanath Babu went to live with Grandfather. Gayanath Babu's people chased after him all the way to Halisahar. Their several rooms at Grandfather's came under siege, literally. Those relatives would run menacingly at Gayanath Babu and throw rotten eggs in his face to try to shame him. They shouted, 'Bemmo, bemmo. Eat buzzard eggs!' One day they gave him a pseudo Hindu purification 'bath in the Ganges,' using a hundred rotten eggs. He bore it all, standing erect. That particular day Grandfather was not at home. A truly amazing individual, of real fiber, that Gayanath. Nonviolence, forgiveness, patience Gandhiji preached, also. The Brahmos of that period likewise demonstrated all of those qualities through their very own lives."[59]

Jayanath expresses annoyance at being reminded of what should be a debt of gratitude. When pressed by Nishith about his casual offer last year of a job, Jayanath retorts:

"I had to give that post to Matimohan Babu's son."
"Who's Matimohan Babu?"
"My goodness. He was one of the most influential men at the time of the Suhrawardy ministry. Now, of course, he's fallen. Sank a full ten fathoms under water."
"And you ensconced Matimohan Babu's kid in your college?"
"No, no. We gave him the boot, even before the fifteenth of August, just as the shadow ministry was forming."
"You booted him out!" Nishith remarked, a bit mortified.
"A second-class, after all."
"What did he do, pass himself off as first-class?"
"Certainly not. My eyes were wide open when I hired him. But it was the shadow ministry's reign then. We had to take another chap, to make his mother-in-law happy."
"Mother-in-law?" Nishith seemed to be speaking not to Jayanath but to himself—not requiring a reply—"What's the connection between the shadow ministry and a mother-in-law?"
"Well, how about with his father-in-law, then?" Jayanath drew slowly on his cigar, then continued, "You've always got the husbands of the sisters of the father-in-law standing tall, right behind the sisters on the mother-in-law's side."[60]

Politics and paternalism carried to the extreme! Pressed even further, Jayanath retaliates with the specter that haunts Nishith:

> "You've got to give me a job in your college."
> "But you're a second-class M.A., Nishith Babu."
> "There are scads of second-classes, working as principals even—"
> "Those gentlemen joined the faculty many years ago. Would you take a post in our Commerce section?"
> "What sort of pay, Jayanath Babu? Can I get two hundred?"
> "Oh no, we couldn't pay more than a hundred, on a temporary basis. But there aren't any vacancies just now. Maybe later. Check back with us before all the fledgling vultures alight, OK?"[61]

Following the interview with Jayanath, the locus of action, which has moved back and forth from Calcutta to Jalpaihati to Calcutta, shifts back to the *mofussil* town for the remainder of the novel. Nishith returns home in the final scene, only moments before his wife dies. He hears the news that his daughter Bhanu also has succumbed to her TB. Though the subject is never broached, we assume he has found no job. Jibanananda in the late 1940s had about as much success finding another teaching job in Calcutta as had Nishith, although, to be sure, his family suffered none of the dramatic, ever romantic, vicissitudes presented in *Jalpaihati*. What the novel does emphatically reveal is the struggle Jibanananda, and others like him, had to endure in a blithely corrupt system. Moreover, given the known facts of his life and of the situation in post-Independence Calcutta, the novel is the closest we have to those reminiscences Jibanananda promised one day to publish in Sanjay's *Purvasa*.

What we notice in his poetry over the years—he shifted from concentrating on his inner life to an attempt to comprehend the outside world—we observe again in the three novels published thus far. When he creates a character like Malyaban, who in terms of personality verges on being Jibanananda himself, the novel succeeds. And when he writes of the concerns he had over leaving his ancestral home and the frustrations he knew as a forty-eight-year-old college English professor holding a second-class M.A. degree, recently come to Calcutta, trying without much luck to find a job, his fiction becomes engaging, believable, powerful. In short, *Sutirtha*, somewhat outside the sphere of Jibanananda's own experience, never achieves coherence or credibility, while *Malyaban* and *Jalpaihati*, in many ways fashioned out of the truth of his own life, succeed wonderfully.

6
The Poetry of Politics

> I have heard that the respect given to literature in France is somewhat comparable to the importance rendered politics by the educated of England. I do not know whether this is in fact true. To be sure, from reading the newspapers one gets the impression that in France, too, as in other countries, there is very little else except ubiquitous politics. But perhaps literature garners true respect there—even contemporary literature. In that case, France must be commended.
>
> —Jibanananda Das, in a letter to the organizing secretary of the Contemporary Writers' Association

1

Despite his preoccupation with prose, Jibanananda managed to turn his mind to the business of poetry, publishing his fifth book, *Darkness of Seven Stars* (*satati tarar timir*) in late 1948. From a letter, we learn that he had tried since mid-1946 to get another collection into print:

> At present four books of my poetry have been published. My fifth book—in which many "representative" poems of the later period will be found—has not yet come out. I have none of the manuscripts—they are at the "press." It will be quite some time before the book appears.[1]

Whoever had those manuscripts in mid-1946, Ataur Rahman eventually brought out *Darkness of Seven Stars* under the publishing house name of Gupta, Rahman and Gupta.[2] Ataur Rahman recalled that Jibanananda himself initiated the publishing process, giving him (Ataur Rahman) the manuscripts when both men worked on the *Swaraj* staff, and that Satyaprasanna Datta urged publication of Jibanananda's book.[3] Jibanananda dedicated *Darkness of Seven Stars* to Humayun Kabir, fellow poet and one of the considerable number of Bengali Muslims opting to stay in secular India rather than emigrate to East Pakistan.

Those seven stars in the title almost certainly allude to the Big Dipper of Ursa Major. Jibanananda had referred to these stars previously, in a letter to Rabindranath.

> One or two questions come to mind concerning the points you raised in your letter. We see in many of the better works of literature driving passions of either joy or sorrow. Poets sometimes effusively raise their faces skyward to embrace the seven sages—at other moments, embittered, they roam the dark recesses of the netherworld. But it does not seem to me that within such bitterness or darkness, or even in fountains of light, that serenity is necessarily expressed. The ancient Greeks were most partial to that something called "serenity." Its melody waxes strong in much of their poetry. Yet I do not consider a poem flawed when some other melody resounds. "Serenity" does not make its presence felt in Dante's "Divine Comedy" or in Shelley. But I would not conclude that their compositions lack for abiding poetry.[4]

The "seven sages" (*saptarsi*), or more fully "the ring of seven sages" (*saptarsi mandal*), denotes both the "seven sages" and the constellation Big Dipper. In this letter from 1930, the seven sages are a synecdoche for the heavens and light: "Poets sometimes effusively raise their faces skyward to embrace the seven sages—" That seemingly natural association of stars with light is then perverted, in the late 1940s, into a puzzling oxymoron.

The fifth volume's oxymoronic title has prompted several critics to speculate on its significance. Most cogently, Nirendranath Chakravarty points out that the Big Dipper resembles a question mark. Ancient India's seven wise seers symbolically comprise this interrogatory note: Marici, Atri, Angiras, Pulaha, Pulastya, Kratu, and Vasistha. Even these exceptional pundits, suggests Nirendranath, cannot shed light on the contemporary world's enigmatic condition.[5] And indeed many of *Darkness of Seven Stars'* forty poems deal with the uncertainties precipitated by World War II.

The poetry in *Darkness of Seven Stars* and the earlier *The World at Large* (1944) come from approximately the same period of time: 1929–42 for *The World at Large* and 1928–44 for *Darkness of Seven Stars,* with most of the *The World at Large* poetry appearing prior to 1940, whereas the vast majority of *Darkness of Seven Stars'* poems came out in the 1940s. However, the tenor of the two books differs substantially: *The World at Large* depends heavily on sensuous imagery, turning cerebral only in the latter parts of that collection. *Darkness of Seven Stars* relies heavily on Jibanananda's intellectualized perception of the world around him.

Darkness of Seven Stars' pre-1940s poems allude to little of the "darkness" found later on in the book. For example, "Merged into the Skies" (*akasalina*) (1937):

MERGED INTO THE SKIES

> Suranjana, do not go over there,
> Do not speak with that young man.
> Come back, Suranjana,
> In this night silvered by starfire.

The Poetry of Politics

> Come back to these fields, these waves,
> Come back to my heart.
> Do not go further and further,
> Yet further with the young man.
>
> What have you to say to him, with him?
> In sky behind skies
> You today are like the earth,
> His love, the grass.
> Suranjana,
> Today your heart is grass—
> Wind beyond winds,
> Sky beyond the farther shores of sky.[6]

Suranjana, or Haimantika, as she was first called in the *Kavita* magazine version, represents once again one of Jibanananda's imaginary lovers. He beseeches the woman not to leave him but to return to his fanciful world amid Bengal's environs. She, likened to the earth out of which grows love, becomes one with that love, symbolized by grass, merging, in the poet's imagination, with grass, wind, sky.

The "darkness" of the volume's title begins its encroachment in a poem like "Wristwatch" (*ristoyac*), published toward the end of 1938.

WRISTWATCH

> Reduced to rubble by the cannon's quake
> Tonight many a sacrificial offering lies strewn about, cold,
> Below a mountain—wristwatches on some of them.
> And perhaps those hands of time yet slowly circle.
> Beneath the moon's glow all these strange timekeepers
> Will talk for a while—
> And tripping as if with the gladdened desires of their mechanical hearts,
> Will sip bright starlight.
> Puddles of dewdrops fallen from olive leaves,
> Sounds of a distant sea,
> The wailing of wind—desolate, like white sheets,
> Their life's story will spin on a few moments more.
> Dim, and growing ever dimmer,
> They will wake to the unending darkness of inexhaustible sunlight.[7]

Watches on the wrists of dead men shine with phosphorescent hour-minute hands. Sunlight rejuvenates the inevitable fading glow in the "darkness of ... sunlight," phosphorescence not being visible in sunlight. The focus is on wristwatches, the dead to whom they belong being almost—but not completely—ignored. Not mere figments of imagination, like a Suranjana or Haimantika, the dead, although nameless, are real.

As for man's navigating the darkness of the present age, Jibanananda uses the sailor for his metaphor. He used that image earlier, in a more personal way, in "Banalata Sen": "As the helmsman, /His rudder broken, far out upon the sea adrift, /Sees the grass-green land of a cinnamon isle, just so/Through the darkness I saw her." In the 1940s the sailor took on the attributes of mankind. Jibanananda published during this period two poems entitled "Sailor" (*nabik* and *nabiki* respectively—the first, published initially in 1940, the latter, in 1944), both included in *Darkness of Seven Stars*.[8] Jibanananda rendered the 1940 poem into English himself:

SAILOR

The sailor has a sense of defeat as he gets up with a start
And finds that instead of taking his post at the helm
He had dozed off hoping that his ship at mid sea
Would take care of itself.
He pulls himself together, resumes his position of watch and toil.

Sun—the din and hurry of a port nearby
And the row of palms hail him.
His ship moves on.

To the priestess with a shock of golden hair
The evening sun seems like the egg of the bird of paradise,
To the farmer a plaything amid his acres of ripening wheat.
Human heads huddled together in dark
Have a glimpse of Sunray's slant
Piercing like a lance into their hovel;
They look, rapt, at the golden beam and the motes in it
Rapidly throbbing and flying—flying and throbbing; why? to what end?

O Sailor, you press on, keep pace with the Sun;
You have been caught awhile in the mirrors of Babylon, Nineveh, Egypt, China and Ur;
Loosened yourself and headed for other shores,
The impulse from Vaishali, Byzantium and Alexandria
Has been to you like thin, straight candles glowing on remembered beaches.
They are good, but whet the quest;
You want deeper knowledge, completer experience.

As long as honeybees, with wings sparkling like spray fly in the sun
And the heron with a surer touch than the jet plane
Brings home the virgin vastness of the blue
Man will not rest content;

Purged of follies, sin and tragic mistakes
His sailor-soul will fare forward
To move into a better discovery of life on this planet,
A greater joy—a deeper communion.[9]

(Trans. by the poet)

In the second and later "Sailor" poem from *Darkness of Seven Stars,* that sailor becomes even more generalized into everyman of human society:

As afternoon passes today, everyone, like wayfarers on an ocean
Of dark night,
Searching the horizon for good sailors and ships,
Like helpless representatives of the various nations of the world,
Call out to one another, "O, sailor, O you sailor—
The sea has turned so pure, so blue—but yet a great desert,
And even we are nobody—"
Men and women both high and low have become today so indifferent to
Their class, their origins, and debts and blood and lust and fraud
That the utter sailor is far better off
Alone, like human society.
O, sailor, sailor, is life not limitless?[10]

The utter or absolute sailor—the sailor-soul in Jibanananda's own translation of the previous lyric—that metaphor for questing man—he is better off, says Jibanananda in 1944, to proceed alone. Alone, common man must advance—like a stainless sailor—he asserts yet again in *Darkness of Seven Stars*:

Do not suppressed concerns simply increase—not calm down?
O sea of time
O man—even if he, recognizing the pure fraud
Of the sea of time, must become alone like an immaculate sailor,
Then he would become such—yet in the world's great sunshine—in even dearer humanity
He wishes to spread joy, victorious over feelings of "there is not."[11]

More emblematic of this volume than the lonely sailor is the oxymoron conceit itself. The title, as noted, is an oxymoron. A similar image pervades the poetry in this book: "darkness of sunshine" (or the obverse, "bright rays of night").[12] Unfathomable, "darkness of sunshine" defies nature and thus is both frightening and hostile to man and his natural, physical world.

From another point of view, "darkness of sunshine" simply stands for the Japanese, whose flag displayed the rising sun, a Japanese sun which brought the darkness of war. Such a reading certainly facilitates an understanding of some of the *Darkness of Seven Stars'* poetry. But the volume's title indicates that even if the Japanese flag initially inspired this oxymoron, Jibanananda extracted the more general antinomic connotation and transferred it to other images: Not only the sun but starlight too now loses its main property—light. And, as mentioned earlier, the title carries an even richer set of connotations when the seven stars are associated with the Big Dipper and the seven ancient Indian sages. Ignorance, confusion, and losing one's way are here attributed to the Big Dipper (which should help a navigator or lonely sailor locate the pole star) and to the wisdom of the ancient sages.

Oxymoronic imagery signals the poet's loss or potential loss of contact with his sensorially perceivable universe. In fact much of *Darkness of Seven Stars* lacks Jibanananda's so familiar physical and folk-tale Bengal. Around 1940, forced out of his natural world—some say by the communists or simply by World War II—he tried to comprehend that seemingly inexplicable one into which he had been thrust. Turned topsy-turvy, Jibanananda's world contains, for example, a deer that "has ripped out and eaten the heart of his carnivorous hunter" ("On the Shores of Creation" [*sristir tire*, 1943]).

Understanding that Jibanananda would lose his grasp on a universe heretofore familiar to him leads to a profitable rereading of transitional poetry, written when he still stood in his own world but was losing contact with it. In "Merged into the Skies" (1937), the initial poem in *Darkness of Seven Stars,* the poet struggles to maintain his fantasy woman, along with his entire personal universe as he bids Suranjana: "Come back to this field, these waves. /Come back to my heart." In "Septet" (*saptak,* 1939) he writes of the uncertain whereabouts of Sarojini: "Here lies Sarojini—I don't know whether she is lying here or not. /She had lain long—then one day she went away into some distant cloud." Jibanananda tells us more about himself and his own perceptions of his environment than about any Suranjana or Sarojini. It is his world that is receding "into some distant cloud."

In his new world, Jibanananda appeared almost phototropic—seeming to crave light. Even the titles of poems indicate this obsession: "Perihelion's Song" (*anusuryer gan*), "A Song of Slaying Darkness" (*timirahananer gan*), "Solar Brightness" (*saurakarojjwal*), "Darkness of the Sun" (*suryatamasi*), "Luster" (*dipti*), and "In the Likeness of the Sun" (*suryapratim*). Not only did he concern himself with sunshine but also with the distance from the sun to the earth, the perihelion being that point in a planet's orbit closest to the sun. The titles of two other poems, which appear consecutively in *Darkness of Seven Stars,* also allude to distances between the narrator and the sun. "On the Night of the Winter Solstice" (*makarasamkrantir rate*) precedes the poem "New Entrance" (*uttaraprabes*).

Uttaraprabes is a word that Jibanananda coined. *"Prabes"* glosses as entrance; *"uttara"* has a number of denotative meanings, one of which is the direction north. So *"uttaraprabes"* or "northern entrance" implies the return of the sun to the northern hemisphere. However, Qazi Abdul Mannan convincingly argues that *"uttara"* here is analogous in meaning to the *"uttara"* in *"uttarapurus"* (successor, descendant).[13] *"Uttarapurus"* pairs with its antonym *"purbapurus"* (ancestor). Thus if *"purba"* denotes precedent or former or past, then *"uttara"* would denote subsequent or latter or future—*"uttaraprabes"* thus connoting an entrance into the future or into some place or some time which is subsequent or, by extension, new. And Jibanananda seems to have intended just such a meaning as one of the connotations for his neologism. The poem "New Entrance" was published in August 1945. In a letter written in 1946, Jibanananda made use of this word again:

> Perhaps my poetry has displayed an awareness of history and society, has sought a new entrance (*uttaraprabes*) into an even higher level of awareness; but has it gained that insight which could direct society to a new path?[14]

All of these poems whose titles are listed above were published during 1943–45. By then the oxymoron had become a standard poetic conceit for Jibanananda. In "A Song of Slaying Darkness" (*timitahananer gan* [first pub. 1943]) he decries customs that "are like dead eyes today—/Gazing toward the lightless light of stars." In "Sailor" (*nabiki* [1944]), the poet notes "the darkness of this endless sunshine." "In the Likeness of the Sun" (*suryapratim* [n.d.]) ends with the same words, in slightly different order, which are found in "Sailor" and which, in fact, conclude the poem "Wristwatch": "They wake through nineteen forty-three, forty-four, forever's dark of endless sunlight." And employing the obverse image, the "bright rays of night," Jibanananda wrote in "Darkness of the Sun" (*suryatamasi* [1944]), "But there instead of dawn are the bright rays of night/Vienna, Tokyo, Rome, Munich—you?" and in "Night Chorus" (*ratrir koras* [n.d.]), "... and knowing this/Yet the ocean bird is bright in beams of night."

Oxymora are frequently employed to convey the ineffable (*jyante mora* or "dead while alive," a desirable state for Bengali Baul mystics, for instance) but also to mirror chaos in nature and society. Jibanananda uses this particular trope in the latter sense, to convey a sense of apprehension about the chaotic present.

The darkness of night symbolizes the present temporary state of human civilization, for dawn will come and sunshine will shed its present darkness. But Jibanananda vacillates between optimism and pessimism on the matter of the coming dawn of light, his "Darkness of the Sun" displaying that uncertainty as to mankind's fate:

> Somewhere I hear a bird's call,
> Someplace an ocean's melody.
> Somewhere the dawn has appeared—however.
> Though countless men have died—in darkness, the hearts of both living
> And dead gaze forth astonished.
> What ocean's melody is this?
> Of death—of life?
> What dawn is this?
> Yet it seems like endless night.

His optimism strengthens in "To Time" (*samayer kache* [n.d.]):

> On the shores of the sea of time
> In the dawn of tomorrow and in this darkness of today
> Like huge white seabirds
> With wings spread, someone believes
> Somewhere, flame in heart flaring,
> There is courage, desire, the dream.
> So let him believe—it is the living symbol of youth: hail to it!
> And though the intellectual age of the world is advancing
> Toward middle-age, what bird of light has he seen?
> Hail, hail to it, praise be to it age after age!
> It is no dodo bird.

The dodo, noted earlier, functioned as Jibanananda's symbol for the extinction of human civilization. In "To Time" he forthrightly states that mankind's demise has not arrived, but, he adds, for all his efforts man has yet to establish a utopia.

> Men have been born again and again in the life-span of this world.
> They have crowded in upon the beaches of ever new history.
> Yet is there anywhere that indescribable
> Dream's fruition—that freshness—the bright dawn of humanity?

But a dawn breaks, so "Hail to the setting sun, hail to the unseen sunrise, hail" ("To Time"). Or, as he wrote in "What Sea Breeze Is This" (*ei ki sindhur haoya* [1946]), "There is no light, but it is approaching." As World War II drew to a close, Jibanananda seems to have been regaining, maybe simply gaining for the first time, faith in his fellow human beings.

2

Kavita, still then Bengal's premier poetry journal, carried a review of *Darkness of Seven Stars.* Buddhadeva Bose chose not to do the critique himself. Instead, Asok Mitra's evaluation appeared in the September–

The Poetry of Politics 243

December 1949, issue—a year after the book's publication (November 1948). Following several paragraphs of high praise for the poet and reminiscences about Jibanananda's earlier, endearing poetry—particularly that which *Kavita* had printed during its first few years—the reviewer shifted to a different voice:

> Jibanananda's poetry, it seems to me, is calling forth some new self. Looking back on all his verse published in various periodicals over the last several years, it becomes obvious that the grass has been receding from under his feet. There was ample lucidity of meaning in his *Banalata Sen* and earlier poetry and, for a while, in what followed. That gift at present is gone. We very often observe these days a troubling abstruseness in his poetic constructions. I have tried again and again to attune myself to the inner suggestive meaning of many of the poems in *Darkness of Seven Stars*. But, and I say this with some self-pity, each and every effort proved futile. He repeats himself here extensively, in his imagery and his use of both individual words and whole sentences. He most certainly intended some depth of meaning through this reiteration. However, sadly enough, that meaning remains as if concealed within some philosophic code language. Consequently, the infatuating mist that his lyrics used to exude seems here like a disconcerting smoke screen. Though syntax is compact, the thoughts are quite diffuse, and here and there even his sentence structure itself reveals a certain debility. What does he want to say? What is his present intellectual bias? What convictions does he now hold? All these questions buzz about in my head.
> I shall attempt to become somewhat analytical for the moment. Jibanananda is the original poet of feeling. The pulsating of his poetry emanates from the gray footfalls of heartfelt sorrows. Sometimes with the vision of an astonished child and sometimes with the loneliness of a weary traveler, he has approached life; he has viewed nature, the universe, the world of living beings, the life of man. There was a faultless clarity to his language, a simple style—this latter quality being the primary reason for the impact of his poetry. Yet in *Darkness of Seven Stars* this pure utterance of the heart has gone almost mute. Obversely, Jibanananda has come to rely primarily on intellectual concepts and finds himself entangled in the complexities of some personal philosophy. This reliance on ideas, it strikes me, results in an obliquity of language and, conjointly, a dearth of his former gift. Had he been able to combine naturally concepts with emotions, that would have been another matter; clearly here, however, that conjugal tale is a sorrowful one. The poetry of this volume has in many places taken on an utterly philosophical character, and the philosophy itself is, moreover, unintelligible.[15]

Following Buddhadeva Bose's earlier, somewhat negative review of *The World at Large* (March 1945), Jibanananda's poetry seldom graced the pages of *Kavita*. The September 1945 issue carried one Jibanananda poem ("On the Night of the Winter Solstice" [*makarasamkrantir rate*]) with three and a half years elapsing before any more of his poetry appeared in that journal. Given the review of *Darkness of Seven Stars,* and considering the infrequency of Jibanananda's poetry following the review of *The World at Large,* one might expect that now his poems would disappear altogether from *Kavita.* This, however, did not happen. The very next issue carried "Darkness" (*andhakar*)—accompanied by a rather lengthy prefatory remark:

> The poem "Darkness" was written about seventeen years ago (1933). Quite likely I gave it to *Kavita* in 1935 or 1936. It was not published then, and later the manuscript got lost. At the time I had thought that I did not have a copy. One day, while searching through some old notebooks, I came across one. I no longer possess that particular mentality of seventeen years back; it is not possible for me to write such poetry today.[16]

Much later, Jibanananda translated this poem—one of his prose-poetry experiments from the 1930s—for inclusion in a bilingual number of *Kavita* (1953). But prior to publication, Buddhadeva suggested several revisions, receiving by postcard a somewhat curt reply. Jibanananda not only questioned the specific emendations but challenged the reasoning behind the proposed changes:

Calcutta
19.7.53

[salutations]

I received your letter and the copy. It seems to me that just as we had to learn the significance of "Lethe" etc., so the readers in the West ought to learn gradually the deeper meaning of Vaitarani, Kirtinasa, and so forth. Kirtinasa carries with it a special suggestion—that particular meaning does not arise in the Ganges, Yamuna or "waters of the earth." I don't believe that the poets in China ever translate specific rivers into English.

If you change "Paus" into "December," then are you going to change "Magh" (O kokil of Magh night) into "January"? Let the foreign readers learn that Paus and Magh are our winter season; let their ears get accustomed to our rivers, seasons, and various other things. Later they can make the connections. For the time being, how about putting in a footnote?

"Planning, aplomb" may be deleted. It seems to me that if you change "I am too full of sleep" to "But I am too full of sleep," it becomes too "logical." "Never see how Never have I known," etc. sound a little too much like exuberant oaths or vows. It doesn't seem to me that a "plain statement" contains "simple and direct force." But be that as it may, your revisions are perhaps an improvement. You may make changes according to your various suggestions; I do not withhold my consent. I was not satisfied frantically translating a poem and racing to post it on the very last [of the month] "Air Mail."

[salutations]
Jibanananda Das[17]

"December" and "January" are used instead of Paus and Magh; Vaitarani and Kirtinasa appear once transliterated and once "translated"—"River of Death" and "River of Mutability," respectively. "I am too full of sleep" remained as it was, and "Never have I known" ended up "I have never known." Jibanananda's admonition that one rendition would be "too 'logical'" must amuse all those readers who have struggled with his more opaque poems.

DARKNESS

In deep darkness
I awoke once more
Distracted by the splash and fret of the river flowing by.
I saw the pale moon wont to gleam on Vaitarani
Had caught Kirtinasha in its still noose of shade.
I had slept by Dhansiri river on a cold December night,
And had never thought of waking again.

O Moon, dimmed to a faint blue disc,
Day's light you are not, you are not enterprise, ambition, or dream;
The quiet and peace of death,
Its sleep—so dear to our heart
Is like a holy tryst
Which you moon have no means to spoil.

Do you not know, O Moon,
Do you not know, O Night,
I have gone to bed with Darkness,
And slept with her
For long, silent ages;
And then all of a sudden on a morning
I have found myself awake in the horrid crack of this earth's light—
So loud, so foolish!

The sun from a red sky, in a dry level tone, has called on me as a soldier
To range against foes I have never known.
The vast belt of the sun-bedeviled earth
Has shrieked and squealed like millions of pigs in merriment.
Ah, mirth! ... a penumbra in my soul radiating darkness—darkness
    ever more.

O Man, O Woman,
I have never known your level;
Nor am I a wanderer from another star.
Only this I have known that wherever there is movement, desire, work and thought
There are divisions of friends, families, nations, the whole range of day-time madnesses.

I am too full of sleep, of enveloping nescience;
Why should you keep me awake?
To Time, O Sun, O Kokil of January night, O Memory, O Winter wind,
Why stir to announce me to the day?

Never more shall I waken
By the river's ruthless gurgling.
I shall not see how the dim, assorted moon
Divides the flickering between the River of Death and the River of Mutability.
By the waters of Dhansiri
I shall go to bed with Darkness that never ends,
The sleep that never abates.[18]

(Trans. by the poet)

Jibanananda's postcard of 1953 notwithstanding, the final statement in his prefatory remarks shows great humility. Neither bitter nor vindictive, Jibanananda states simply that he can no longer write as he did when his poetry so enthralled Buddhadeva. His mental or emotional nature was no longer what it had been. He had changed. His statement reveals a sense of lack. He might like to feel what he felt then, see what he saw then and thus express what he expressed then—but he cannot. During the early 1950s a dozen of his poems appeared in *Kavita,* about half similarly identified as "from the mid-1930s, revised."

For the most part, Jibanananda made an effort in the 1950s to accommodate *Kavita*'s expectations of him. And he had in his notebooks a considerable quantity of unpublished poetry from the mid-1930s upon which to draw. The entire *Bengal the Beautiful* collection with its sixty-odd sonnets, for instance, languished yet unpublished.

3

Pressure from the Left had been discernible since the late 1930s. Sanjay Bhattacharya, it will be recalled, was reacting to what he perceived as Stalinist incursions into Bengali literature when he and Premendra Mitra inaugurated *Nirukta* in 1940. Then in 1945, the Anti-Fascist Writers' and

Artists' Association became the Progressive Writers' and Artists' Association, finally losing many of the non-Leftist literati in the process.[19] *Paricay,* begun by Sudhindranath Datta in the early 1930s, during the 1940s turned into the mouthpiece for the Progressive Writers or, in other words, for the Communist writers. And as the decade drew to a close, the Communist Party's line became much more critical with respect to literature, recalled Abu Sayeed Ayyub. From 1948, due to the Ranadive Doctrine, the CPI pursued an exclusive rather than inclusive (popular front) organizational policy.[20]

The Communists convened in Calcutta the second All-India Party Congress in February 1948. Bhowani Sen delivered a major address in which he called for the use of force to achieve goals. The historians Overstreet and Windmiller write:

> This speech represented a crucial revision of the nationality policy which the Party had pursued from 1942 to 1948; now the CPI declared that self-determination must be accomplished, not by the whole population of a given nationality, but by revolutionary action of the working class and its allies.[21]

In response to this new political thesis, the government of West Bengal, citing the Public Safety Act, outlawed its local Communist Party in March 1948 and suppressed the official party newspaper.[22]

Later that same year, a quasi-underground magazine entitled *Marksbadi* ("The Marxist") surfaced. Though not clandestine (*Marksbadi* listed its publisher, the same as that for *Paricay*),[23] the journal gave no person's name as editor, and contributors used pseudonyms. Bhowani Sen undoubtedly wrote for *Marksbadi,* though his name does not appear there. Both *Marksbadi* and *Paricay* were Marxist in orientation, but the former reflected the more virulently critical literary doctrine of which Ayyub spoke.

Marksbadi's first issue, which came out in October 1948, or thereabouts,[24] contained two articles on literature: "Several Trends in Bengali Literature" (*bamla sahityer kayekati dhara*), signed by one Satyajit Das, and "The Marxist Method of Literary Criticism" (*sahitya bicarer marksiya paddhati*), signed by an Urmila Guha. "Several Trends" attacked, albeit mildly, Rabindranath Tagore, a large and always favorite target. "Individualism was Rabindranath's main creation," declared Satyajit Das. "The victory of this individualism became a weapon for the capitalists. ..."[25] But he conceded that what Rabindranath (and Sarat Chandra Chatterjee) did to combat certain evil social practices had indeed benefited his society. The truth that Rabindranath found had been but a partial truth, however.[26]

Satyajit Das singled out some living writers for scrutiny, among them Tarasankar Banerjee and Manik Banerjee, both taken to task for their "pessimism,"[27] although the critic conceded that a portion of Tarasankar's and Manik's writings qualified as "progressive literature," somewhat dated. Their fictional characters, too, lacked the ability to help build a new society, capable only of tearing down the old.[28] Bishnu Dey, by certain criteria a Marxist, came under reproach as "a skilled artist but not a Marxist—his artistic skillfulness itself stifles Marxism."[29]

Then this writer named Satyajit Das set out some guidelines for the Marxist author. He must: (1) follow the class struggle; (2) express only the words, thoughts, and feelings of the proletariat; (3) attack reactionaries; (4) awaken the common man; and (5)

> paint a picture of the breaking down and the building up everywhere, in the family, in one's personal life, in the struggle, in the world, in love— one must point out what is old and what is new, what is dead and what probably is to be born. ...[30]

Urmila Guha's article stated that literature should not be a facsimile or mimesis of life, nor a passive criticism of it. Literature is or must become a weapon with which to strike the enemy.[31] Both Buddhadeva Bose's book, *An Acre of Green Grass,* and Bishnu Dey's *Sahitya Patra* ("The Literary Journal") drew the writer's fire.[32] *Sahitya Patra* debuted July 1948; *An Acre of Green Grass* had come out early that same year. Though both were the target of *Marksbadi*'s salvos, the two publications reflected quite disparate literary philosophies. In fact, one impetus for bringing out *Sahitya Patra* had been, Bishnu Dey told me, that he himself wanted a forum for his criticism of Buddhadeva's book.[33]

An Acre of Green Grass, written in English, takes its title from a line in W. B. Yeats's poem, "An Acre of Grass." Buddhadeva somewhat ebulliently reviews much of modern Bengali literature from Rabindranath through Jibanananda and beyond. But it was not so much the manner in which he expounded his ideas and his judgments of Rabindranath and others, but more his statements vis-à-vis politics and literature at which Bishnu Dey took umbrage. Buddhadeva spoke of the "political cacophony" into which poets had fallen, of the "parrot-politics" that demanded art serve its will. He noted that the *Kallol* writers had been criticized for doing little with literature to gain India's independence. Such attacks had a "disarming naïveté," but lately "the same trend of thought has reappeared in an insidious form, being clothed in the pretentious language of political schools." The press of current events had forced writers into assuming the role of reporters or editorialists, with the lamentable result that recent works of so-called literature "are made mostly of newspaper stuff, descriptions of latest events and comments on current topics, dressed up, now flashily and now shabbily, as fiction or verse."[34] And, comments Buddhadeva:

Bishnu Dey's poetry, since his conversion to Marxism, seems to have lost its "champagne flavour"; what is more, and more distressing, Jibanananda, by nature the loneliest of our poets, is stuffing his recent work with "war and war's alarms," lest some should figure him out as an incorrigible "escapist."[35]

Sometime in February 1949, the second issue of *Marksbadi,* subtitled "an anthology of critical essays in Marxist culture," appeared, with an article entitled "The Struggle in the Fields of Literature and Philosophy" (*sahitya o darsaner ksetre samgram*) signed by one Satyajit Ray (not the movie director). It defended in essence the two articles printed in the first issue.[36] That issue of *Marksbadi* also carried an advertisement for *Paricay*:

Throughout the entire world today the struggle is going on—the invincible struggle of life against death, of peace against war, of humanity against barbarism. *Paricay* is the cultural mouthpiece of those who are in the forefront of this struggle, of those who tear through the veil of darkness and bring forth the new dawn. The cultural voices of those who struggle in all countries of the world are echoed in *Paricay*.

While *Paricay* and *Marksbadi* espoused similar political views, *Marksbadi* did so more loudly. Its fourth issue carried a particularly acerbic attack on Bengali literature and, apparently (this issue is unavailable), on Rabindranath specifically. The article set *Paricay* and *Marksbadi* at odds, at least for the time being. Nirendranath Ray, joint editor of *Paricay* in 1949 along with Gopal Haldar, protested the criticism of Rabindranath, recalled Abu Sayeed Ayyub, which caused Niren Ray to fall into disfavor with the Party.[37]

For *Marksbadi*'s fifth issue, which came out September 1949 or thereabouts, a Rabindra Gupta contributed a lengthy article entitled "Self-criticism of Bengali Progressive Literature" (*bamla pragati sahityer atmasamalocana*).[38]

The editorial board of *Paricay* and several prominent writers have raised a strong protest against the self-criticism of Bengali progressive literature which appeared in the fourth issue of *Marksbadi*. Two basic points of opposition are apparent among these protests.
It was stated in the essay that if one searches for the inspirational source of progressiveness, it is to be found within the various popular rebellions such as the Sepoy Rebellion, the Indigo Rebellion, and the Santal Rebellion. A few writers objected to that essay saying that the source is to be found within Bankim, Vivekananda, and Rabindranath. And there the writers deny the revolutionary character of the above-mentioned rebellions. They are of the opinion that this line of argument by *Marksbadi* is "too Left wing" and thus in opposition to Marxism. *Marksbadi* proclaims that these writers' ideas are bourgeois—revisionist and Hindu "revivalist." What Prakash Ray wrote in the fourth issue of

Marksbadi (in "Self-criticism of Bengali Progressive Literature") may not have been without error in some of the details, but the major verifiable points are absolutely correct.[39]

This Rabindra Gupta then mentions two "progressive" authors, Kaliprasanna Simha (1840–76) and Dinabandhu Mitra (1829–74).[40] Another nineteenth-century author also fell among the progressives: "Like them, Michael Madhusudan Dutt, too, has written realistic and progressive literature."[41] Madhusudan's play *Down on the Nape of the Old Bird's Neck* (*buro saliker ghare ron*), he argued, stripped the zemindars naked, something similar to what Kaliprasanna accomplished in *Mr. Owl's Sketch Book* (*hutom pencar nakasa*). He also applauded Madhusudan's poetry, for it opposed the Sanskrit literary tradition in two meaningful ways: first, the ancient gods and goddesses were rendered more human and more modern, and second, Madhusudan disregarded ancient literary rules and conventions and produced such innovations as blank verse.

> Progressive bourgeois culture was forthrightly revealed in their writings; Hindu-Muslim unity, equal rights for both women and men and opposition to foreign rule—these were the significant characteristics of their literature.[42]

The remainder of this lengthy article concentrates mostly on refuting the initial point raised by the *Paricay* writers, i.e., that Bankim, Vivekananda, and Rabindranath were in fact the sources of progressivism.

The seventh issue of *Marksbadi*—possibly the last one to be issued—came out around March 1950. This number contained no articles on literature, but it did carry another advertisement for *Paricay,* an indication of a rapprochement between the two communist journals.

4

Politicizing the arts was to spawn yet another literary organization, the Contemporary Writers' Association (*samakalin sahitya-kendra*). The mere presence of an identifiable communist literary group, replete with mouthpiece in the form of *Paricay,* motivated noncommunist writers to form their own opposing literary cliques. One such faction coalesced around the familiar figure of Sajani Kanta Das and came to be known as the Sani Circle (*sani cakra*).[43] The Contemporary Writers' Association was to consider itself a third political-literary force in West Bengal (in opposition to both the Progressive Writers' and Artists' Association and the Sani Circle).

Not all literature in West Bengal had become self-consciously political. *Kavita* was still going strong; *Purvasa,* too, had resumed publication in

1943; *Caturanga* came out regularly. The editors of these three literary journals, Buddhadeva Bose, Sanjay Bhattacharya, and Humayun Kabir, all had their political views, but their magazines assumed no particular political stance. Nevertheless, active, aggressive pursuance of politics through literature, as exemplified by *Marksbadi* and *Paricay,* caused some Calcutta writers concern, which ultimately led to the formation of the Contemporary Writers' Association.

Abu Sayeed Ayyub had joined, by invitation, *Paricay*'s editorial board during the 1940s. Around 1948, as he recalled, he resigned. About that same time, the communists solicited an article on literature from him, doubtless with the hope that this fine critical mind could be enlisted to advance their cause. Ayyub chose as topic what he called the "final" and "instrumental" values of literature. He identified two forms of literature: one, in and of itself the final, supreme object; the other, a vehicle for effecting social change. Arguing that two categories of literature existed, pure and applied—just as there were two types of science—he stated that applied literature had little value as art per se. Ayyub concluded that the communists produced applied literature, such writing being of no "final" literary value. Since the article had been solicited, it was published in *Paricay*. However, along with his essay, remembered Ayyub, were juxtaposed two rebuttals.

Around this time, with the communist literati exceedingly vociferous, Ayyub came to the conclusion that there should be a third force in literature. Essentially, as Ayyub described it, these third-force writers should be aware of their social milieu along with all the contemporary problems; they should, nonetheless, write as individual, independent persons, not as anticommunists and not as writers lacking awareness of their sociopolitical surroundings. These third-force writers were not to produce "applied" or "instrumental" literature of the communist sort but works bearing "final" literary value.[44]

June of 1950 began the fourth year for a monthly by the name of *Dwandwa* ("Conflict"), listing as editors Abu Sayeed Ayyub, Jibanananda Das, and Narendranath Mitra.[45] An advertisement for *An Anthology of Contemporary Bengali Poetry* (*samakalin bamla kabita samkalan*), published by Suhrid Rudra, was carried on the penultimate page of this particular issue. *Dwandwa* had been started three years earlier by that same Suhrid Rudra along with Biswanath Bhattacharya, both of them bona fide socialists. Through the efforts of Anandagopal Sengupta, Secretary of the Cultural Committee of the Socialist Party,[46] *Dwandwa* became in 1950 the mouthpiece of the Contemporary Writers' Association.[47]

Neither the Contemporary Writers' Association nor *Dwandwa* was recognized officially by the Socialist Party, however. Many of the members of the Association did not even belong to the Socialist Party.[48] Jibanananda, in particular, according to Anandagopal, was probably a member of the Association only and not of the party. It goes without saying, though, that members of the Association generally sympathized with Socialist ideas. How much Jibanananda avowed socialism remains unclear. Ayyub recalled with certainty, however, that Jibanananda had been keen on the idea of a third force in literature.[49]

Toward the end of 1949, Jibanananda published an essay in English entitled "Bengali Poetry Today," commenting upon the contemporary Bengali poetry scene. And though the word *Marxist* appears only once—and *communist* not at all—it is clear that the monolithic nature of communist philosophy bothered him. A true poet must be free, he argued, for he "arrives at his own philosophy and builds his own world." But, he conceded, social and political realities may "demand of the age a perspicuous confession of what it believes," which may in turn require a new literature as well as a new attitude toward literature. Nevertheless, when poets become obsessed with social and political realities and try "to make a poetic success, or so they think, of dialectical materialism," then they fail to produce anything of enduring value.[50]

Shortly after the publication of Jibanananda's article, the Contemporary Writers' Association officially came into being; Abu Sayeed Ayyub was chairman, Santosh Kumar Ghosh, general secretary, and Anandagopal Sengupta, organizing secretary.[51] By mid-1950, the Association not only held meetings but also produced its monthly magazine. At one such meeting, presided over by Ayyub, Narendra Deo, head of the Socialist Party of India, addressed the group, the event being reported in the Socialist newspaper *Janata* under the heading: "Advocate Democracy, Internationalism and Social Justice: Acharya Narendra Deo's Call to Writers." There followed a summary of Narendra Deo's speech wherein he called for the establishment of Socialism and spoke against communalism. "This is an age of democracy, internationalism and social justice. Through their literature our writers should convey these new values."[52]

Jibanananda was unable to attend the Association's first meeting.[53] Instead, he sent Anandagopal a letter setting out some of his ideas regarding the relationship of literature to politics—which read in part:

> For the major civilized countries of the world, the word literature almost always connotes more or less ancient literature. Yet no attempt is made to understand clearly what value it has in relation to life's needs. And they do not even care to consider contemporary literature. Today's writers may think and write whatever they wish; the "state" could not care less, for literature is deemed of no significance. This represents the picture from one perspective. From another, we have instances of a

completely different attitude toward literature in one or two rather important nations. In those places the government runs everything—even the literature. It is their opinion that if the writer possesses any independence of thought, the authority of the government diminishes. This is untrue—and unjust. It seems to me that Bengal has not yet concluded that the "state" is imperiled by a requisite independence of literature. Yet she may do so very soon. I am pleased to learn that the Contemporary Writers' Association is proceeding with humility, intelligence, and patience in the task of preserving as far as possible the freedom of literature from the hands of illegitimate domination—on the one hand, from the befuddled indifference of the people and society, on the other, from the inequities of government. You all have assembled for the advancement and the realization of literature; I wish you complete success.

Jibanananda Das[54]

Just how advancement and realization of literature would be effected, the Association outlined in its "manifesto." An essay by Abu Sayeed Ayyub, entitled "The Path of Contemporary Literature" (*samakalin sahityer path*), appeared in the June 1950 issue of *Dwandwa* as the introductory editorial. Having been written much earlier and, in fact, published previously (*Desh*, December 1949),[55] this essay's contents were well-known to Association members.

The Renaissance, wrote Ayyub, liberated the mind from the Church. But today there is a new attempt to control thought, a "second phase of medieval stricture upon the mind."

To the advocates of this political philosophy, literature and art have no value if that literature et alia is not of value as a weapon in their political struggle. They forget that the very purpose of the political struggle is the establishment of a classless society wherein the material needs of the populace will be met and in which their lives can be liberated and expressed through art, through literature, through culture in ever new forms.

After criticizing an official Communist Party proclamation regarding controls to be placed on "artistic production," Ayyub called attention to the local manifestation of such a philosophy, quoting the *Marksbadi* essay that stated that Bengali literary and cultural heritage from Ram Mohan Ray through Rabindranath is "the garbage from a bourgeois cultural tradition, its proper place being in history's dustbin" (*Marksbadi,* no. 4, p. 119).[56]

Despite their outlandish statements, Ayyub gave Marxists their due:

Just because we have our differences of opinion with the Marxist literary maxims, let us not forget that, through their literature, they have stimulated a new social awareness and have broadened and deepened the previously existing one. This social awareness has lasting literary and societal value.

But, he pointed out, the vicious attacks on contemporary literature cause many writers to shun politics and expunge from their writings any semblance of social awareness—reactions neither natural (for man is a social animal) nor desirable. Ayyub met the Marxists more than halfway when he stated:

> The writers will obtain from the revolutionary leaders and workers their own philosophy of life in a more practical, tested, and materialistic form. But the responsibility for depicting that through thought and imagination falls within their [the writers'] purview; there their own authority reigns supreme, and "their own authority" is, of course, another was of saying no authority.

The writer must freely express his individuality. Social awareness and political philosophy should naturally be manifested in literature. Art should remain art and not become a political weapon.[57]

The Contemporary Writers, according to Ayyub, were for political democracy, economic planning, and absolute artistic freedom. With such a conservative agenda, one must wonder why Jibanananda wrote a rather cautious and cautioning letter to the Association via Anandagopal Sengupta. In March of 1948, it will be recalled, the West Bengal Communist Party had been banned, its paper suppressed. Was he afraid of such action when he wrote: "It seems to me that Bengal [the government] has not yet begun to think that the 'state' is imperiled by a requisite independence of literature. Yet she may do so very soon." Was he also worried that Ayyub or others might become more radical, when he declared with more hope than assurance: "I am pleased to learn that the Contemporary Writers' Association is proceeding with humility, intelligence and patience. . . ."

Jibanananda contributed little to the magazine that named him an editor. The first issue contained a poem of his, "Hope and Faith" (*asa bharasa*), and the fourth issue, September 1950 (designated as the puja issue), carried his essay "Modern Poetry" (*adhunik kabita*) in which he identifies his subject:[58] "Modern literature or modern poetry may be defined as that poetry or literature in which the enduring intrinsic worth of man's mind is made manifest distinctively through the hands of truly great writers."[59] According to this definition, as Jibanananda admits, many great writings, from Sanskrit and Greek literature on up to the present, may be designated modern.[60] But he speaks of another more commonly understood meaning of the term "modern literature," the "first" meaning of modernity: "The first type of modern poetry is saturated with all the vulgar markings of its own era; concluded within that era, it may very well wither away."[61] The rebellion against Rabindranath and his kind of literature, which ignited the *Kallol* generation, resulted, Jibanananda concluded, in this type of modern, ephemeral poetry. The structural experiments with prose meter during the 1930s ended up as period pieces, interesting but not necessarily noteworthy for their literary value. Topical concerns permeated much of that verse from the 1920s right up into 1950, but these topical poems were examples of modern poetry of the first (inferior) variety.

Then Jibanananda noted modern poetry's lack of conviction. The *Marksbadi* writers had pointed out and condemned a pessimism in the novels of Tarasankar Banerjee and Manik Banerjee. Jibanananda, too, had doubts about a literature whose poets were without firm, positive belief:

> It may be hoped that the results of modern science (I am not speaking about applied science here) will not be simply to lend indulgence to pessimism. . . . A poet, firm in his belief—once he concludes for himself that the resolves of science (or of any other truth or intuition) are true—can write poetry; yet even without this belief, good poetry—even great poetry—might be written. This is so not because of the inherent nobility within disbelief or uncertainty but because any material—including disbelief and uncertainty—may perhaps achieve artistic perfection in the hands of a particular poet. However, I find little evidence in the history of literature of many such poets—or the likelihood of the attainment of such [poets].[62]

By the time this essay, which may be a revision of a talk delivered at an Association meeting,[63] appeared, Jibanananda had temporarily left Calcutta to take a teaching post in a *mofussil* college. The Contemporary Writers' Association itself proved short-lived. Two of *Dwandwa*'s three editors left Calcutta after about three or four issues of the magazine—Abu Sayeed Ayyub to Santiniketan[64] and Jibanananda to Kharagpur in Midnapur district, some seventy-five miles due west of Calcutta. To Amlan Datta, the subeditor of *Dwandwa* in charge of essays, Jibanananda wrote concerning this major contribution of his:

183, Lansdowne Road
Calcutta 26
15.9.50

[salutations]

Amlan Babu, in keeping with your suggestion, I have prepared the piece, "Modern Poetry" [*adhunik kabita*] for the Aswin issue of *Dwandwa* and have sent it along with this.

You had spoken of using this piece as the editorial for the Aswin number. It may be better, however, to use it as the first essay instead.

I definitely want to have a look at the final proof. Can't say whether I'll be coming to Calcutta this coming weekend; but even if I come later, I would hope that I'll get a chance to look at the proof copy.

[salutations]
Jibanananda Das[65]

His membership in the Association represents the closest this most private of poets ever came to taking an active role in anything political. Jibanananda had certainly not become, in 1950, an avid supporter of the Socialist Party or of socialism. He contributed to magazines of various political persuasions. For instance, in October 1950, his poem "Today" (*aj*)[66] appeared in *Nirnay* ("Discernment")—a cultural publication connected with West Bengal's Congress Party—not because he had any political sympathy for the Congress Party but because he knew personally the editor, Amiya Kumar Ganguly.[67]

TODAY

With the speed of blind oceans, in a churning like the upheaval of
Night, toward some dearer direction of man
Today the path of discernment stands blocked. Yet somewhere
New shores of stainless time, country, posterity:
Perhaps the human heart may attain them.
In these days of total collapse, today must take heed.

And though with restless glances man has moved through darkness
Through destruction, hope, sorrow,
Through blue fog of wild swanlike consciousness,
As the haze lifts from the path of man's tale
Radiance appears now and again
Upon a world like the crystalline ecliptic.

It seems that man, a suckling babe of great midnight,
Is yet a child of the infant sun.
More resolute worldly is he—
Though in his heart, his blood, yet today flows the false song of a
    shoreless sea.[68]

Jibanananda appears determined to exhibit that conviction which he spoke of in his essay. The path of "discernment" (*nirnay,* also the name of the magazine) may be blocked or at least seem so today, but this blind sea's far shores of midtwentieth-century civilization can yet perhaps be reached. Seemingly a child of darkness, man in reality sprang from the dawning sun. Nevertheless, pessimism reigns: man yet sings that "false song of a shoreless sea." Jibanananda has faith that new shores will be found. The path of his own life, too, seemed to have taken a temporary turn for the better in the fall of 1950, though not without some earlier moments of utter desperation.

5

Back in mid-1949, Jibanananda did not display undue concern with his financial situation, or at least did not wish to convey such concern to Acintya Kumar Sengupta, whom he wrote:

> I am not doing anything in particular these days. I manage with what little income I get from writing and some teaching. I had applied for a job, and they wanted a "reference"—so I put down your name. But none of those jobs will come through. It would be nice if I could give up everything and just write. That hasn't been possible for a long time now.[69]

His wife, employed as a teacher for the year 1948–49, would be unemployed the following year and then attend the David Hare teachers' training institute in 1950–51, straining further the Das family budget.

A year to the day after writing Acintya Kumar, he sent a rather plaintive letter to his close friend Sanjay Bhattacharya.

> 183, Lansdowne Road
> Calcutta 26
> 13.6.50
>
> [salutations]
>
> I hope you are well.
>
> I am in a rather bad way financially, and for that reason must disturb you. I need four to five hundred rupees immediately; please make some arrangements for that.
>
> I am enclosing five poems herewith. Later I shall send essays, etc. (nothing written just now). You may print a novel of mine (under a pseudonym, not my real name) in *Purvasa*; if you think it is necessary, I can send it along. I shall write my *Reminiscences* [*jiban-smriti*] month by month in *Purvasa*, starting in Aswin or Kartik. That is all in the future, but I would like the money right away. For a long time now you have been receptive to these sorts of importunities by the several of us writers who have been in difficulty—and for that I am deeply appreciative.
>
> I shall repay all of your money with writings, or in cash. If I am to repay in cash, it may take six or seven months (no more). The poetry is not all of the same period. I have picked these poems out; but if you don't like any of them, you may return them to me. You may publish this poetry at your convenience in *Purvasa* or in some other decent magazine (provided they pay appropriately and maintain high standards). Urgent. I am expecting the money in a matter of days.
>
> [salutations]
> Jibanananda Das[70]

A month later he wrote to Haraprasad Mitra, in search of a teaching position:

> 183, Lansdowne Road
> Calcutta 26
> 11.7.50
>
> [salutations]
>
> I have written you previously. But I just noticed in the papers that a Lecturer in English will be hired at Serampore. If the salary is at least two hundred rupees, I would submit an application. Some sort of permanent income is utterly essential. You certainly can arrange something at Serampore College.
>
> In today's (and in Sunday's) *Amrita Bazaar* I saw that some First Grade College in Calcutta has a Lecturer's post vacant; they didn't indicate which college it was, the advertisement listed a Box No. I can't figure out whether it is Scottish Church College or maybe City—. What news do you have about Women's College?
>
> I'd be very happy if you would kindly drop by here one of these days. I'm sure you will come.
>
> How is your own writing progressing? Hope you are well.
>
> [salutations]
> Jibanananda Das[71]

Nothing materialized at any of the colleges mentioned in the letter, but within a matter of weeks, Jibanananda did manage to secure employment. At the beginning of September 1950, he joined the recently established (1949) Kharagpur College, an intermediate-degree-granting institution, as a member of the English department. Kharagpur town, too far to commute from Calcutta, required him to live there, but he returned to Calcutta for weekends or whenever feasible. Some of the college staff recalled that Jibanananda made rather frequent trips to Calcutta. Moreover, his absence from the college sometimes extended over several days, interfering occasionally with his teaching responsibilities. Labanya Das fell ill during this period, and Jibanananda was caring for her. He remained on the college staff only five and a half months, until 15 February 1951.[72]

At one point Jibanananda approached Narayan Ganguly, who then taught at City College, and inquired rather pitifully, Narayan thought, whether he might not get a teaching post at that college where he had begun his career some three decades earlier. He wondered out loud whether Narayan realized he had once been dismissed from there, then added that he would need to earn at least Rs.5/- more in salary than what his former student earned—in order to maintain the respect inherent in the student-teacher relationship. Narayan protested that Jibanananda should receive at least Rs.100/- more than his own salary but questioned what he, a junior faculty member of the college, could do on behalf of his former professor. The matter ended there.[73]

About this time (1950–51) Jibanananda sublet part of his Lansdowne flat for the third and last time.[74] This particular tenant became an obsession with Jibanananda; he would later want her out of the flat, or, in lieu of that, want out of the flat himself. The major complaint seems to have been that she, like the Utpala character in his novel *Malyaban,* had visitors who sang and laughed and talked rather loudly—all of which disturbed him. He tried to get her to leave, but she refused. A number of persons, even casual acquaintances of the last several years of his life were requested by Jibanananda to help him solve his problem, one way or another.

Housing had become a major preoccupation. In the early 1950s Jibanananda approached Kiran Sankar Sengupta, then working for the Refugee Relief and Rehabilitation Department. Jibanananda inquired about the possibility of securing a plot of residential land. Unfortunately, as Kiran Sankar explained, Jibanananda could not qualify as a refugee, since he had come to Calcutta prior to Partition/Independence.[75] One of his very close friends during his last few years, Subodh Ray, tells of a room that Jibanananda rented for six months but then, oddly enough, never occupied even a single night.[76]

A notice appeared in the newspaper in 1951 about a research assistant's post at the Asiatic Society in Calcutta. Jibanananda applied but was never called for an interview. Another item announced an opening for an English professor at Charu Chandra College in Calcutta. Jibanananda contacted both Naresh Guha, then an English professor there (as well as assistant editor of *Kavita*), and Suddha Sattwa Bose, poet and a Bengali professor at the same college, but nothing came of this effort. At one point, he thought seriously about starting up a business of some sort and may even have tried his hand at it once, very briefly.[77]

Jibanananda also approached one of his former Braja Mohan College colleagues, Narendralal Ganguly, founder and principal of Dum Dum Motijhil College located just north of Calcutta, which had advertised for an English professor. Some months previously, N.L.G. (as he was known from the Barisal days) visited Jibanananda at his Lansdowne residence. Jibanananda was unemployed at the time, recalled Naren Ganguly. After the ad appeared, Jibanananda went straight to Naren Ganguly's house with job application in hand. Naren tried to dissuade him, arguing that the pay was low. Upon leaving, Jibanananda shook a finger, admonishing Naren to give him the position. He was writing his autobiography, Naren remembered Jibanananda saying, and would, with the mention of his name, make N.L.G. "immortal."[78] Jibanananda, however, was not given the post.

In his ever more frantic search for a livelihood, Jibanananda did not limit himself to friends and acquaintances, as this letter to a total stranger illustrates:

183, Lansdowne Road
Calcutta 26
23.12.51

[salutations]

I was delighted to receive this letter and your new book of poetry, *Footfalls* [*padadhwani*]. Many thanks. I really enjoyed quite a few of the poems in *Footfalls;* as yet I haven't finished reading all of them. And I must read carefully all the poems once again.

I gave up doing book reviews a long time ago. I don't feel I have much ability in that field. Anyway, your book is with me; if I am able to write something, I shall of course do so. You'll have to give me some time, however.

From your letter I realize I've had the pleasure of becoming acquainted with a talented, sensitive individual. I would be very happy if, when you are in Calcutta, you would come to visit one day.

At present, I am in serious difficulty; I am seeking employment. There is simply nothing available in Calcutta. Can you suggest anything? In yesterday's paper I noticed the Jangipur College (Murshidabad) is looking for a lecturer in English. My present situation is such that I cannot afford to hesitate about taking even such a job as this. You are in Murshidabad; perhaps you could arrange something.

I hope you are well.

[salutations]
Jibanananda Das[79]

He at one time considered working in a bank. Satyaprasanna Datta and Sanjay Bhattacharya maintained close connections with N. C. and B. K. Datta of the Comilla Banking Corporation—all four men hailing from the district of Comilla. A position had been arranged for Jibanananda, but, apparently, he never accepted it.[80] Not until sometime in November 1952 did Jibanananda actually find another college teaching position, at Barisha College in the suburbs just south of Calcutta. The post had been a temporary appointment from the outset. By one account, an English professor resigned from the college unexpectedly in late 1952. Bani Ray, sister of the principal and good friend of Jibanananda, managed to secure for her fellow poet this particular job, which lasted till February 1953.[81]

In February or March of 1953, Jibanananda submitted his application for a position being offered at Fakir Chand College in Diamond Harbor, about thirty miles south of Calcutta. Gopal Chandra Ray knew some of the college officials and just happened to run into one of them. The man invited him to the interviews, which were being held in Calcutta, and mentioned that the poet Jibanananda would be among those interviewed. Gopal Ray had never met Jibanananda. A friend of Gopal Ray's, a highly qualified professor, had also applied and asked Gopal Ray personally if he would recommend him. Gopal Ray replied that he was going to see to it that

Jibanananda got the post—which he did. In the end, however, Jibanananda turned down the position, arguing that to commute daily by train would be difficult and to reside there in some dormitory—as he had in Kharagpur—would be out of the question. Also, he mentioned that he did not want to relinquish his private tutoring.[82]

Jibanananda immediately requested his most recent benefactor to find him another teaching position, which again Gopal Ray did, this time at Howrah Girls' College, just across the river from Calcutta. Gopal Ray approached the founder and principal of the college, Bijay Krishna Bhattacharya, showing him some of Jibanananda's articles on education that had been published during the previous couple of years. Jibanananda was very reluctant to meet with the principal and asked Gopal Ray to arrange everything. When Jibanananda did finally speak with the principal, Bijay Krishna simply asked him to fill out an application and told him he would be hired. According to Gopal Ray's account, Jibanananda was made head of the department immediately, surpassing the four or five then present English department members, even replacing the current department head.[83] At the time of his death, little over a year later, Jibanananda was being considered for the post of vice-principal, according to Gopal Ray.[84]

Theoretically, both men should have been quite content. Jibanananda found dignified employment close to home; the principal could boast of having a known poet on the faculty. But this was not to be—at least not right away. Gopal Ray writes that one day when he met with Principal Bhattacharya soon after Jibanananda had joined the staff of Howrah Girls' College, the principal expressed some displeasure over his new faculty member. Jibanananda, it seems, had been scheduled to teach a particular class, when, without a word to anyone, he disappeared, staying away several days. Upon his return, being asked where he had been, Jibanananda replied sheepishly that he had gone off to Delhi. At the principal's request, Gopal Ray spoke to Jibanananda about this blatant indiscretion. Jibanananda told him to relay the message to the principal that such a thing would not happen again. Then, as Gopal Ray recalled, he blurted out his boyish, embarrassed, peculiarly Jibananandian laugh.[85]

In the arena of mundane concerns, problems of employment rivaled but did not supersede, in his mind, those of domicile. From the very outset upon moving his family permanently to Calcutta, housing commensurate with his means and expectations eluded him. Subletting part of his apartment only added to his vexation. Just prior to the puja holidays in 1953, Jibanananda, his job seemingly secure, once again prepared to move—this time but a few blocks. Earlier he sent Sanjay a postcard, announcing the impending event:

Calcutta 26
12.9.53

[salutations]

After the 30th of this month I am changing my address. My new address is:

Jibanananda Das
c/o Sri A.N. Chakravarty
172/3 Rashbehari Avenue
(first floor)
Calcutta 29

Kindly notify the others of this. What is Ataur Rahman's address? I'll come to see you one day very soon. Hope you are well.

[salutations]
Jibanananda Das[86]

The address was that of Asokananda Das's father-in-law. For some reason, Jibanananda changed his mind and did not move.

He left Bengal but a few times in his entire life, once during the puja vacation in the fall of 1953 when he took his family to Delhi to visit his brother, Asokananada.[87] It may have been either then or on the short, unsanctioned trip about which Gopal Ray spoke that Jibanananda met with Humayun Kabir and Ataur Rahman in Delhi. Humayun Kabir, still nominal editor of *Caturanga,* at that time held the post of secretary to the central government's Minister for Education and Natural Resources and Scientific Research, Maulana Abul Kalam Azad. Ataur Rahman remembered Jibanananda asking Humayun Kabir about a possible job. Kabir, feeling very sympathetic toward Jibanananda, arranged for one in a Delhi college. But Jibanananda chose not to leave Calcutta.[88] Later Kabir requested Parimal Ray, then Director of Public Instruction for West Bengal, to assist Jibanananda in securing a teaching position. Parimal Ray did find Jibanananda a position at the Krishnagar Government College; again Jibanananda declined, because he did not want to move to Krishnagar, fifty-plus miles north of Calcutta. Jibanananda importuned Humayun Kabir to obtain for him a post at Calcutta's prestigious Presidency College. Kabir broached the subject with Parimal Ray, but no vacancy existed.[89]

For at least part of the period when these efforts were afoot, Professor Jibanananda Das was gainfully employed at Howrah Girls' College. The following letter, directed to both Sanjay Bhattacharya and Satyaprasanna Datta, alludes to his earlier request to Humayun Kabir:

183, Lansdowne Road
Calcutta 26
17.5.54

[salutations]

I received your letter and the Baisakh issue of *Purvasa*. Many thanks.

I've read your *Verses* [*padabali*] and liked it very much. It seems to be radically new material; these poems are really quite different from your previous work. Your erudition, the breadth and depth of your mind is obvious in a number of places throughout these compositions.

I have enclosed a poem for *Purvasa*. When I get the chance, I hope to be able to drop by one of these days. I dearly love *Purvasa*. Both the paper and the printing turned out fine this time.

Did the two of you speak to Kabir Shaheb about me? I am in a terrible fix concerning my flat, too. Shall I get in touch with Tarasankar Babu? I could go with you two and discuss all these matters, or you could even write a letter and explain. It's urgent.

Hope you are well.

[salutations]
Jibanananda Das[90]

The Kabir reference pertained to a job, recalled Satyaprasanna, while the references to Tarasankar Banerjee and to Jibanananda's flat bespoke his obsession with the female boarder he tried unsuccessfully to evict.[91]

6

In July 1952, Signet Press brought out a new and enlarged edition of *Banalata Sen*. The now famous film director Satyajit Ray then earned his living as a commercial artist, and it was he who designed the cover—a multi-line portrait of a woman's face.[92] He had also done the cover layout for Jibanananda's previous book, *Darkness of Seven Stars*. The Signet Press edition of *Banalata Sen* contained, first and foremost, the twelve poems from the Kavita Bhavan edition of *Banalata Sen* (1942). To this original core—which had also been the core of *The World at Large* (1944)—were added eighteen other poems. Most of the additional poetry came from around the early 1930s, the same period as the original twelve. A few had been composed either earlier or later, for Jibanananda indicates at the front of the book that the poetry in this *Banalata Sen* edition spanned the period between 1925 and 1940.

A number of these additional poems in *Banalata Sen* (Signet Press) had appeared in the fifteenth and sixteenth years of *Kavita* (1950–51), most with a note to the effect that they had been composed some time around the mid-1930s. Among the additions is "Sudarsana" (*sudarsana*), like "Banalata Sen" the title a woman's name:

SUDARSANA

One day beside a woman such as you
Wanly smiling I,
About to be absorbed in the collected merit of the age,
Pausing suddenly inside a ring of fire,

> Heard some heavenly voice in a *devadaru* tree,
> Saw the immortal sun there.
>
> Best is a night of chrysanthemums, grass, stars, and sky.
> Yet time does not stand still:
> It sought another more profound and final beauty,
> Then gazed upon your bangles.
>
> Your body is like the earth's
> Familiar sunshine—you did not offer it, however.
> And because widowers bestow upon you all time,
> Sudarsana, today you are dead.[93]

Apostrophes to four other women accompany "Sudarsana": "Syamali" (*syamali*), "Suranjana" (*suranjana*), "Sabita" (*sabita*), and "Sucetana" (*sucetana*). Unlike Banalata Sen, none of these five women could give to the narrator that coveted moment's respite. Though now dead, Sudarsana seems closest to such a peaceful woman, which may explain why Jibanananda published only "Sudarsana" in *Kavita,* given that magazine's partiality to "Banalata Sen" and poetry of that period.

The latter women, each in her turn, recede further and further from Banalata Sen, though much of the same imagery pervades these poems. The narrator wandered long and far in "Banalata Sen"; in "Suranjana," he wandered with Mahendra (son of Asoka) upon a sea similar to those Malayan and Sri Lankan seas from "Banalata Sen":

> I recall long ago in a star-filled night of wind
> Along with Dharma Asoka's son, Mahendra,
> Upon the path of a vast tumultuous sea with ultimate desire in heart

Man had known civilizations on the Mediterranean shores—the narrator tells Sabita. But they—Christian nations about to wage or already waging war—know the waters of darkness and the ocean's night. And we, who had progressed halfway toward another and newer world, were—in times of war—again cast adrift on a shoreless sea:

> Now another light shines in the world;
> Some sort of extravagant, tireless fire!

This fire, suggests Dipti Tripathi, symbolizes the destructive fire of World War II,[94] but the woman to whom the narrator speaks stands for hope—her face resembling the rising of a sun (*sabita* means "sun") from within the darkness brought on by war.

In the initial lines of "Sucetana," we again find "Banalata-Sen"-type imagery, an island of cinnamon trees where peace holds sway:

> Sucetana, you are a far-off isle
> Near the star of early evening;
> There among cinnamon groves lies solitude.

But the poet sees

> ... brother sister
> Friend and relative sprawled about, slain perhaps
> By my own hand.

This is not the weary poet of "Banalata Sen" who sought darkness rather than his own flesh and blood. Then he tells Sucetana of the road to life that requires much effort and many years to traverse:

> Sucetana, by lighting the light on this path—by this very path will the world one day be free;
> But that is a task for many centuries of learned men.

Pulled back to earth, perhaps weary of life's struggles, he rejoices in sensuous pleasure as he once again touches "the dew on a bright morn." He knows the past and the future, a blend, he tells us, of eternal night and endless sunrise. More to the point, life for the poet presents a continual tug-of-war between optimism and pessimism:

> When did I, pulled by the very soil of this earth, take human birth,
> Feeling it would have been better had I not;
> But then I realized it was worth my while to come
> Once my body touched the dew on a bright morn.

"Sucetana" may have been composed far closer to 1940 than to 1925—or at least extensively revised when Jibanananda wavered in his view of the future of human civilization.

One of the additional eighteen poems in the Signet Press edition, "Walking" (*path hanta*), displays the terza rima sonnet structure found in *Gray Manuscripts* (1936).

WALKING

> As if beckoned by a memory alone, I have walked many a sidewalk
> Of the city. I often watched bus and tram plying their designated ways,
> Finally to leave their route and calmly enter a world of sleep.
>
> The whole night through, gaslights perform their appointed task, burning brightly.
> None errs: bricks, buildings, billboards, windows, doors, roofs,

All quietly observe their need for sleep beneath the sky.

As I walked alone I sensed a peace profound within their hearts.
It was late then, many lonely stars surrounding
Monument and minaret, and I wondered if I'd ever seen anything

So natural, uncomplicated as that monument- and star-filled Calcutta?
I glance down: cigar burns silently, a gust full of chaff and dust.
I shut my eyes, move aside. Withered leaves, brown, are blown

From trees. In Babylon just so I walked alone at night for some such
Reason. Why, I have no idea today, thousands of hectic years later.[95]

From such a slant he viewed Calcutta in the 1920s—before worries about living quarters and making a living in post-Independence West Bengal: a simpler, "natural, uncomplicated . . . monument- and star-filled Calcutta."

7

Signet Press's *Banalata Sen* established Jibanananda's popular appeal and public reputation. He had been, for the previous two decades, well-known, well-read, and well-criticized—at least orally, if not in print—by his fellow poets. Now he began to receive substantial recognition for his poetic achievements.

The 1953 All-Bengal Rabindra Literary Conference (*nikhil banga rabindra sahitya sammelan*), awarded *Banalata Sen* (Signet edition) its annual literary prize for poetry. This conference, founded in 1945, had in the 1950s connections with *Dwandwa*. Conference festivities extended over a seven-day period centering around Rabindranath Tagore's birthday, the twenty-fifth of Baisakh (approximately 10 May). That year marked the first time the conference awarded a prize (later, Sudhindranath Datta and Amiya Chakravarty were so honored).[96]

The award consisted of Rs.101/- (numbers that end in zero are inauspicious, hence the extra rupee), a coconut (an auspicious symbol), and a shawl (a quintessentially Indian article of clothing).[97] Younger brother of Arun Kumar Sarkar, conference secretary Alok Sarkar remembered that Jibanananda dropped by the Sarkar residence soon after receiving the prize. Jibanananda had been told by Sanjay Bhattacharya, Alok recollected learning, that such a small prize as Rs.101/- somehow did not befit a poet of his stature. Arun Sarkar and the others present explained to Jibanananda that they had originally intended to make the prize simply a *haritaki* fruit, for the idea had been just to honor him publicly. The prize itself, in their estimation, carried no importance whatsoever. Instead of a mere token (a *haritaki*), they had decided upon Rs.101/-, a coconut, and a shawl. And Jibanananda seemed mollified with that explanation.[98]

The All-Bengal Rabindra Literary award had been presented at a public meeting. Moreover, *Banalata Sen* (Signet edition) was meeting with popular acclaim. Communist writers could not let this go unchallenged. Subhas Mukherjee reviewed the book in the July 1953 issue of *Paricay*. Entitling his article "The Most Lonely of Poets" (*nirjanatama kabi*), Subhas described in Marxist terms what occurred during the decades between the world wars:

> The people of a vast area of the world, straddling two hemispheres, have arisen free of shackles. . . . In country after country enchained peoples are awaking with the promise of victory. The flames of struggle are raging from the ocean to the Himalayas. . . . This progression of the people, through the complex interrelationship of victory and defeat, of agony and joy, draws before the poet a glorious, splendiferous panorama—that which today's man with pride and tomorrow's man with awe will gaze upon.

And, asks Subhas rhetorically, what has "Banalata Sen's Jibanananda Das" shown us at this momentous time in man's history? He quotes the first stanza of the poem "Banalata Sen," adding:

> Jibanananda informs us loud and clear in his poetry that he is not bound by the limits of time. To him, "thousands of years merely played." Is it surprising then that someone who demarcates time by thousand-year intervals should consider two slender decades between the wars as mere bubbles that will fall back into the great sea?

While people struggled for independence, even sacrificing their lives, Subhas's fellow poet confused reality and fantasy, spreading "a heavy net of illusion." Exploiting this revolutionary imagery to the hilt, he speaks of Jibanananda as "a very competent general" who "strikes a forceful blow where the opposition is weak, unprepared, disorganized. He overcomes the reader by distracting his attention in another direction."[99]

Subhas chose to confine his criticism to Jibanananda's writing between the world wars, quite justified since the *Banalata Sen* (Signet Press) poetry concentrated on that period. At one point in the review, he depicts Jibanananda as an escapist.[100] Had the reviewer taken into consideration poetry appearing since the beginning of World War II, he would have had less reason to so categorize Jibanananda. Subhas, however, intended not so much to explicate Jibanananda's work as to discredit the poet of *Banalata Sen*. The honor afforded the volume by the All-Bengal Rabindra Literary Conference had to be countered, if the literary tastes of the populace were to be properly cultivated. But Jibanananda's poetic reputation suffered not a whit from Marxist criticism. He had figuratively come of age, as that negative review itself bears witness to, in a perverse sort of way.

In January 1954, a Poets' Conference (*kabi sammelan*) was held at the (old) Senate Hall of Calcutta University. Most of West Bengal's noteworthy practicing poets had been invited to recite one of their compositions at this two-day affair.[101] On the morning of first day, the following news item appeared in the English-language daily *Amrita Bazar Patrika:*[102]

POET'S CONFERENCE BEGINS AT SENATE HALL TODAY

A conference of modern Bengalee poets, will be held in the Senate Hall, Calcutta, today (Thursday) and to-morrow (Friday). It has been convened by Dr. Nihar Ranjan Roy, Prof. Abu Sayed [sic] and Sri Dilip Kumar Gupta.[103] Poets, some sixty in number, will recite their own poems. The conference seeks to establish the great communication power of proper recitation. In smaller groups than this, poets often read out their poems to select audience; but never before has such a big conference been thought of. Adequate arrangements have been made to make this attempt a success. The preparatory committee has also been trying to bring out a booklet that will contain short biographical sketches of the participating poets. Everyone, interested in poetry, may attend, but those who want definitely to be present, may enquire at the Signet Book Shop (12, Bamkin Chatterjee Street and 142/1 Rashbehari Avenue) and also at 10/2 Elgin Road. The poets who have been invited to recite their poems include: Sudhindranath Datta, Jibanananda Dash, Bishnu De, Premendra Mitra, Annadashankar Ray, Ajit Datta, Jatindranath Sengupta, Ashokebijay Raha, Samar Sen, Subhas Mukhopadhyaya, Bimalcandra Ghosh.[104]

The program listed sixty-nine poets in all—Jibanananda as the last of those to recite on the first day and Sudhindranath Datta to conclude the second day's session. Jibanananda, when he discovered his position on the program, took it as an affront. Once it was explained that last had been reserved for him as a place of honor, that many in the audience would surely attend solely to hear his recitation, he seemed not only appeased but flattered.[105]

Amrita Bazar Patrika reported the first day's session as follows:

POETS' FORUM
INTERESTING FUNCTION HELD IN SENATE HALL
(by Our Staff Correspondent)

A very interesting literary gathering of modern Bengali poets was held on Thursday evening in the Senate Hall. The poets will again appear before the gathering at the same place this evening. About thirty poets who took part in the function read selected verses from their own writings, and a well-attended house listened with absorbing interest. Dr. Nihar Ranjan Roy speaking on behalf of the organizers said that the principal aim of the gathering, which he claimed as the first of its kind in modern Bengal, was to make people in general interested in the poets and their creations of the post-Tagore era. Besides such a platform would also help the poets and their readers to come closer. He added in old days in the country there were various platforms where the poets could appear in person and read their own verses before an appreciative gathering. But such things were coming to be antiquities in the modern society, particularly in Bengal. Among the Hindi, Urdu and Tamil poets such a tradition was still continuing. He expressed high hope that the present efforts of the organisers would break new ground. Among the poets who evoked much interest in the audience by their recitals were Shri Ajit Datta, Shri Jibananda [sic] Das, Shri Achintya Kumar Sen Gupta, Dinesh Dutt, Shri Niren Chakravorty and others. Among the younger section Shri Sunil Gangopadhyaya, Shri Dipak Majumdar deserve special mention. Among the prominent absentees in the day's function were Shri Bishnu Dey, Shri Bimal Chandra Ghose and Shri Samar Sen.[106]

And on this day Jibanananda recited his most famous poem, "Banalata Sen." The assembled, however, would not settle for just one offering, and so he, the audience's favorite that day, recalled Bani Ray, proceeded to recite several more of his compositions before the program finally came to an end.[107]

8

In this same year two books, each in its own way, paid additional homage to the poet who was at long last becoming publicly recognized for his poetic talents. A new edition of the anthology, *Modern Bengali Poetry,* appeared in March 1954, edited this time by Buddhadeva Bose himself. Very much in response to Rabindranath's anthology, *An Introduction to Bengali Verse* (1938)—about which many had doubts as to who actually did the editing[108]—Kavita Bhavan, or in other words Buddhadeva Bose, had undertaken to publish an anthology of modern Bengali poetry, enlisting Abu Sayeed Ayyub as editor, along with Hirendranath Mukherjee. The first edition (1940) of *Modern Bengali Poetry* included only four poems by Jibanananda. Ajit Datta and Nazrul Islam were represented by five poems each, Bishnu Dey and Buddhadeva Bose by seven apiece, Samar Sen by eight, and Sudhindranath Datta by nine. Twelve poems by Rabindranath appeared in that anthology. Ayyub, as noted earlier, did not think highly of Jibanananda's poetry. Buddhadeva resolved to edit anew a second edition of *Modern Bengali Poetry* in order to redress what he felt was the slighting of Jibanananda's poetry in the collection.[109]

In the second edition, Jibanananda was represented by fifteen poems, as was Buddhadeva himself. Sixteen poems by Rabindranath and an equal number by Amiya Chakravarty appeared in this edition of the anthology.[110] Samar Sen was represented by thirteen poems, Ajit Datta and Bishnu Dey by eight each, Sudhin Datta by seven, and Nazrul Islam still by only five. In his introduction to the second edition, Buddhadeva wrote of the Bengali poetry anthologies previously published as either meant "to accommodate school syllabi or intended as wedding presents." He compiled his, meaning both the first edition and the present one, "solely for enjoyment." He admitted his edition differed considerably from the Ayyub-Hirendranath collection and suggested that he was expanding the one aspect of Bengali poetry they, in response to the demands of that day, had curtailed: "Poetry of feeling, poetry of the emotions did not receive their just recognition."[111]

Buddhadeva had redressed the imbalance, with Jibanananda, in his opinion, now afforded his proper place in comparison to Rabindranath and the post-Rabindranath poets. Amiya Chakravarty also received his due. Subsequent anthologies have maintained essentially the same relative position of Jibanananda vis-à-vis the other Bengali poets of this century.[112]

In April 1954, Navana published *Jibanananda Das's Best Poems,* the seventh and last volume to appear during his lifetime. Only two in this series of "Best Poems"—*Buddhadeva Bose's Best Poems* and *Premendra Mitra's Best Poems*—had preceded Jibanananda's, indicative of his standing with regard to his fellow poets. Bishnu Dey's would be the fourth in this series.[113] For the most part, *Jibanananda Das's Best Poems* anthologizes selected poems from all of his already published works, plus some poetry which had not appeared in any previous book.

About a week before his death, Jibanananda would have one further indication of his popularity. He was invited to take part in another poets' conference, only this time on radio, with far fewer participants, including, of all people, the *Kallol* writers' old nemesis Sajani Kanta Das.[114] Jibanananda would bask in the warmth of all this belated recognition but a short while. On the evening following that radio broadcast, he was struck by a tram and died eight days later.

Jibanananda had been in the habit of going for a walk, often by himself. Just south of his Lansdowne flat is a park with a lake, a favorite spot for such ambulations. On the fateful evening, Jibanananda was returning home, heading north. Rashbehari Avenue, a major thoroughfare, had to be crossed before he could proceed the hundred yards or so back to his flat. Down the center of Rashbehari run two tram lines. Of just such tram lines he had written some sixteen years earlier:

It is late—so very late at night.
From one Calcutta sidewalk to another, from sidewalk to sidewalk
As I walk along, my life's blood feels the vapid, venomous touch
Of tram tracks stretched out beneath my feet like a pair of primordial
    serpent sisters.
A soft rain is falling, the wind slightly chilling.

Of what far land of green grass, rivers, fireflies am I thinking?
Where are the stars?
Have those stars been lost?
Beneath my feet the slender tram track—above my head a mesh of tangled wires
Chastises me.

A streetcar approached from the west as Jibanananda began to cross the road, and, for some reason oblivious, he stepped in front of it. Taken by taxi to Shambhunath Pandit Hospital, Jibanananda was treated for several broken ribs, a fractured clavicle, and one shattered leg. While at the hospital, Dr. Bhumendra Guha, then a medical student, and some of his fellow students from the Medical College were constantly at Jibanananda's side. Satyaprasanna Datta telephoned Sajani Kanta Das who, showing great and very genuine concern, arranged for Dr. Bidhan Chandra Ray, then Chief Minister of West Bengal, to see personally to Jibanananda's care; Dr. Ray came to the hospital the following day. Every effort was made to save his life. But Jibanananda contracted pneumonia, and on 22 October 1954, eight days after the accident, he died. Cremation took place the next day at Keoratola burning grounds near south Calcutta's famed Kalighat temple.[115]

7
Posthumous Jibanananda

> One poet now dead, killed near his fiftieth year on Rashbehari Avenue run over by a tramcar, Jivananda [sic] Das, did introduce what for India would be "the modern spirit"—bitterness, self-doubt, sex, street diction, personal confession, frankness, Calcutta beggars etc—into Bengali letters.
>
> —Allen Ginsberg, in *City Lights Journal,* number two

Calcutta's three Bengali daily newspapers, *Ananda Bazar Patrika, Jungantar,* and *Basumati,* ran notices of Jibanananda's death.[1] And a week later, the *Ananda Bazar Patrika,* in its Sunday, 31 October edition, printed a lengthy article by Ajit Datta.[2] Along with it came a poem by Jibanananda—the first line a fitting epitaph.

TODAY
(aj)

Always another path you seek: today I seek no more.
I found in that void on the far shore something to hold at last
In my heart, my own: beneath Bengal's fearful blue
A small straw hut—beside which flows the Banajhiri river.

Its turbid pale whirlpool is like a constant relative
Which sometimes comes to rest.
Fields, paddy, stands of betel, the unrest of kingfishers
Embraced and then unfurled her woman's body.

The hut stands vacant—but for a book or two
And exquisite pictures—of four or five accomplished artists:
Of France, Italy, Bengal, Kangra—in *nim, jam, nageswar* tree
Sit nests for countless birds.

Still, the unrest of the larger world impounds the mind
And this world's endless doubt hate love and war
Sought to slay the ancient Raktabija demon through our own blood,
Will end up paying the price in full.

The days of this century are all but spent today.
New hope's message, afloat through the blue unsheltered void,
That which man had sought, that very woman shall bestow the sun and that society
When once his suicidal battleground finally falls silent.³

Even *The Times of India,* as far away as Bombay, carried a notice of the poet's death:

> The premature death after an accident of Mr. Jibanand [*sic*] Das removes from the field of Bengali literature a poet who, though never in the limelight of publicity and popularity, made a significant contribution to modern Bengali poetry by his prose-poems and free verse.
>   Born in 1898 [*sic*], the son of a Barisal teacher, Jibanand followed his father's profession and taught English at a Calcutta college. Not for very long, however. His peculiar diction and the originality of his themes, which marked a departure from the prevailing traditions, and his defence of these deviations soon cost him his job. . . . Jibanand Das was known not so much for the social content of his poetry as for his bold imagination and the concreteness of his images. To a literary world dazzled by Tagore's glory, Das showed how to remain true to the poet's vocation without basking in its reflection.⁴

A number of gatherings were held to mourn his death and eulogize his contribution to Bengali poetry. The *sraddha* ceremony was held on 31 October, at 8:00 A.M. at Asokananda's residence, 172/3 Rashbehari Avenue. Friends and fellow writers were invited. In the evening on that same Sunday, another memorial offering to Jibanananda was arranged by a local cultural and literary society, the Calormi Cultural Center (*calormi samskriti kendra*). One of Jibanananda's fellow poets and friends, Gopal Bhaumik, was its secretary for literary affairs. Discussion of Jibanananda's poetry, and recitations by Buddhadeva Bose, Ajit Datta, Sanjay Bhattacharya, Bani Ray, Naresh Guha, and Rana Bose were advertised in the notice. A news item appeared in the *Ananda Bazar Patrika,* 28 October 1954, reporting that there had been a gathering the previous Tuesday, 26 October at the office of Our Gang (*amader dal*) in order to honor Jibanananda. The meeting was chaired by the editor of *Pandulipi Patrika* ("The Manuscript Magazine"), one Pratap Mukherjee (M.A.); a Rabindranath Mandal had spoken about Jibanananda the person, and a discussion of his poetry had been conducted by Ram Sankar Patra, Ramanath Chatterjee, and Tarun Kumar Datta.⁵

Several literary journals brought out special issues devoted to Jibanananda. *Usha* ("Dawn," edited by Sudhir Sarkar and Pran Sen) appeared first, in October 1954. Then in December, *Kavita* printed its special Jibanananda issue containing essays about the poet and his poetry along with eight of his poems, seven hitherto unpublished, taken from two of Jibanananda's poetry notebooks.[6] *Uttarsuri* ("Future Poets," edited by Arun Bhattacharya), a relatively new magazine, devoted the second issue of its second year (December–February 1954–55) to articles on Jibanananda by divers hands; a poem, an essay, and a letter by Jibanananda were also included in this issue. Another fairly new magazine at that time, *Mayukh* ("Luster," edited by Snehakar Bhattacharya, Samar Chakravarty, and Jagadindra Mandal), in a very ambitious and excellent Jibanananda issue dated December–May 1954–55, listed nearly two hundred of Jibanananda's poems published previously in periodicals only. *Ekak* ("Unaccompanied," edited by Suddha Sattwa Bose) brought out a combined special issue devoted to both Jibanananda and the poet Yatindranath Sengupta, who had also recently died. And the Howrah Girls' College, where Jibanananda was employed at the time of his death, dedicated its eighth annual magazine (1954–55) to his memory (edited by Asit Kumar Banerjee); articles on teacher and colleague Jibanananda Das were included therein.

Any number of periodicals carried poetry on or by Jibanananda. More yet ran essays about the man and his works. Even *Sanibarer Cithi*'s Sajani Kanta Das could not but print a few words about the deceased poet, in the "News-Literature" (*sambad-sahitya*) part of his journal. That same section of the very same journal, back in the late 1920s and 1930s, had carried many of the more vitriolic attacks on Jibanananda Das. Somewhat sheepishly, Sajani Kanta apologized for those earlier excesses in negative criticism:

> In our youth we tried to ridicule poet Jibanananda's poetry. And we did not cease and desist from trying to make him a laughing-stock by quoting line after line and by mocking his obscurantism. He was primarily a writer of the *Kallol-Pragati* clique. And so, having cast him into that opposing camp, we took delight in attacking—as is in keeping with the spirit of battle. Today, following the trend of the age, our ideas and attitudes have changed, and he has passed on, superseding all criticism and acclaim. Despite that earlier unbecoming opposition, we feel it our duty to acknowledge today that he was indeed one of the most important figures in the post-Rabindric field of poetry. He sincerely and with firm resolve served poetry's muse [Saraswati]. Though his manner of expression lacked clarity, there was nothing whatsoever fraudulent in his efforts. ... Sensitive persons who found the key to his message were pleasantly rewarded; those who did not turned away from him. We were among the latter group. Yet what we did does not invalidate any of Jibanananda's poetic contributions. On the contrary, it is we who, cultivating a greater sensitivity, are endeavoring to understand him.[7]

Sajani Kanta, apparently feeling yet inadequate to the task of discussing Jibanananda's poetry, devoted over half of the *Sanibarer Cithi* piece to a direct quotation from the Ajit Datta article on Jibanananda that had been published in the *Ananda Bazar Patrika*.[8]

In the year following Jibanananda's death, his book *Jibanananda Das's Best Poems* was awarded the first Bengali language prize by the recently formed Sahitya Akademi. The purpose of the Akademi had been put forth by S. Radhakrishnan, vice-president of India, on the occasion of the Akademi's inauguration, 12 March 1954: "It is the purpose of this Akademi to recognise men of achievement in letters, to encourage men of promise in letters, to educate public taste and to improve standards of literature and literary criticism."[9] Recognition by the Akademi was in the form of Rs.5,000/- prizes awarded for the outstanding books of literary merit in the various Indian languages. The first such awards were bestowed in 1955 for books published from Independence through the year 1954. And the Bengali language prize went—not without opposition, however—to the "(late) Jeevanananda Das" for his "Sreshtha Kavita (poems)."[10]

This Sahitya Akademi prize conferred upon Jibanananda even greater public recognition than that which had accompanied the All-Bengal Rabindra Literary Conference's award for *Banalata Sen* (Signet Press). And as in that previous situation, here again the Marxist literary critics could not let this affirmation of Jibanananda's poetry go unchallenged. Manindra Ray contributed an article to *Paricay* in which he did what Subhas Mukherjee had chosen not to do in his review of *Banalata Sen* (Signet Press), that is, examine all of Jibanananda's books of poetry.[11] Manindra Ray quoted Jibanananda from his introduction to *Best Poems* as to how varied the critical statements about him had been and why:

> My poems, or rather the composer of this poetry, has been depicted as lonely, even the most lonely. Some have said this poetry is primarily about nature or primarily about a consciousness of society and history; other opinions are that it reflects no awareness at all. According to the determination of others, this poetry is excessively imagistic, totally from the subconscious, surrealistic. Various other descriptions, also, have come to my attention. Nearly all of them are partially correct—applicable to certain phases of the poetry or certain poems. These are not depictions of the total corpus of the poetry, however. ...
>
> The creation of poetry and the reading of poetry are both in the final analysis matters of the individual mind; that is why there is such disparity in perceptions and conclusions among readers and critics.[12]

Manindra Ray concurred in part, agreeing that the hopes and desires of the "individual mind" are more pronounced in lyric poetry than in other forms of literature. But he argued that even there the individual mind interacts with what he called the societal mind. Critical judgment, he concluded, should be made by holding up the poet's work against the social background of the times.[13]

Having set forth his tenets of criticism, Manindra Ray proceeded to consider Jibanananda's books and the social context in which each book was composed, taking cognizance of the message of these books and the relevance of that message for the period in question. The volumes from *Fallen Feathers* through *The World at Large* were deemed failures, for want of a relevant message or because of the poet's inability to integrate some fundamental belief with his poetic strength, i.e., sensory perception.[14]

According to Manindra Ray, one of Jibanananda's volumes of poetry was fairly successful: *Darkness of Seven Stars* finally commented upon the social environment.

> Jibanananda became conscious of the realities of society much later—in the forties—against a background of war, famine, riots, and partition of the country. Most of these poems were included in *Darkness of Seven Stars*. And from the point of a message, this volume is Jibanananda's most illustrious composition.[15]

The 1940s had been the crucial period in Jibanananda's development, Manindra Ray concluded. His particular situation, however, had been a case of too little too late. Jibanananda could not effectively coordinate the message with the poetic medium.

> From the literary point of view, Jibanananda's greatest asset is his sense-perception. And this quality is present in greater quantity in the poet's earlier poetry. In the forties, when through the influence of his surroundings he was forced to turn his attention to the material, real world, he was unable to transplant his previous strengths into the soil of new perceptions. From time to time, certainly, we are transfixed by his exquisite endeavors. However, since he never consciously strove for an integrated organization, the vast majority of his poems appear as fragmentary entities incapable of a unified intent.[16]

Had he lived longer, Manindra Ray believed, Jibanananda might have become a truly great poet.[17]

While Manindra Ray's analysis is quite perceptive and essentially correct, his premise and therefore his conclusion are subject to dispute. Contrary to Manindra Ray's opinion, Jibanananda rightfully has been recognized as a truly great poet, the greatest Bengali poet since Rabindranath Tagore. He has received this recognition for, among other reasons, his ability to transfer his keen sense perception into verbal poetic expression. Manindra Ray's contention, that great art must possess some message of social truth, has not been acknowledged by subsequent Bengali literary commentators. But his observation that Jibanananda in *Darkness of Seven Stars* failed to integrate or "transplant" his literary strengths into his newly acquired social consciousness has validity. For that very reason, some of the poetry in *Darkness of Seven Stars* becomes vitiated. But Manindra Ray's—and Subhas Mukherjee's—condemnation of the poetry in *Gray Manuscripts* and *Banalata Sen* seems unwarranted: while the poetry in these two volumes might lack a social message, its value as literature has stood the test of time to date.

By the latter half of the 1950s, the Marxist critics had withdrawn from the attack on Jibanananda. Two factors may account for this retreat. First, Jibanananda was not alive, and though his poetry continued to appear posthumously both in magazines and in book form, even the Marxist critics may have turned sympathetic to the deceased poet simply because he was no more. Secondly, some of the communist literati had become rather disillusioned when in 1956 the Soviet Union announced to the world the atrocities committed by Josef Stalin. According to Abu Sayeed Ayyub, the faith of many a Leftist poet was terribly shaken after Stalin's image had thus been tarnished.[18] Following that brief flurry of attacks in the 1950s by Marxists, Jibanananda has received sustained acclaim. And though some critics laud several lines here and there from various poems of the 1940s and 1950s, most of the attention and praise has been directed toward Jibanananda's compositions from the late 1920s and the decade of the 1930s, when such poem as "Sensation," "Banalata Sen," and "A Day Eight Years Ago" were written and published.

Today Jibanananda is not merely a respected poet, but one of the most—if not the most—influential poets of Bengal. As Alokeranjan Dasgupta expressed it, Jibanananda has become dangerously influential to the Bengali poets presently writing, as dangerously influential as Rabindranath had been in the earlier part of this century. Jibanananda's contemporaries felt they had to be ever alert lest they fall under the influence of the master poet (Rabindranath), thereby losing their own individuality. Today, according to Alokeranjan, poets must be vigilant in order that they not succumb to a Jibananandian style and become imitators rather than creators.[19] Just following Jibanananda's death, Bani Ray wrote, referring to the 1954 Poets' Conference at the Senate Hall of Calcutta University when more than sixty poets read from their own works, "The best proof of his popularity is found in much of the compositions read. Among the young poets today, eighty percent are attempting to write poetry along Jibanandian lines."[20] Pranabendu Dasgupta observed that in the forties "it was Bishnu Dey, Jibanananda, Sudhindranath, Amiya Chakravarty, Buddhadeva Bose (particularly Jibanananda) who were the sources of inspiration for today's poets."[21] Sarat Kumar Mukherjee, concurring, pushed the positive assessment of Jibanananda even farther:

It is my opinion that in Bengal today there is not a single hale and hearty poet who writes poetry free of Jibanananda Das's influence. A few will not admit it, perhaps, because the word "influence" belittles man. We who are prideful do not wish to become influenced. Just a few days back at an informal gathering, I witnessed the storm of protest that arose immediately upon raising this very point. Perhaps it is best to say "illuminated" [*alokita*], because Jibanananda's influence is a pale yellow, somewhat like the light of the moon; his writings are a lexicon of our feelings of melancholy, aloofness, vulnerability, etc. In a word, Jibanananda was the destiny of this decade.[22]

Whereas much of his influence may subtly "illuminate," some of that Jibananandian quality blatantly shines out in a poem such as Krishna Dhar's "In Haiku Style" (*haiku dharane*):

(1)

moonlit night
falling waters
deer in heat,

(2)

deep forest
tiger's eyes
intimate.[23]

And though Krishna Dhar has depicted a male deer (*ghai harin*)—whereas Jibanananda's deer was female (*ghai harini*)—the reference to "In Camp" from *Gray Manuscripts* is patent.

In "This Calcutta & My Lonely Bed," Samser Anwar pays homage to "Banalata Sen" and "Naked Lonely Hand" when he laments that "no Vidarbha rises in my dreams," "I am not aware of sorrowless Ashok or a palace beside the Sea of Tyre/No Banalata Sen waits beside my bed." Affecting Jibanananda's bashful demeanor, he muses, "I laugh nervously when I try to search for Bidisha's darkness/In the foul smell of cheap hair-oil."[24] And it was during the 1960s that an iconoclastic group of angry young poets styled itself the "Hungry Generation," claiming Jibanananda as father-preceptor. One "Hungry," Malay Roy Choudhury, refers directly to Jibanananda in his denunciatory "Against Freedom of Art":

He who demands Freedom of Art is a fool.
I am against the Freedom of the Artist.
Only the slave henchmen of the Establishment are Freed because they
    are not Artists but liars larceners & diseased robots.
Only insane cultures need Artists.

Art is prophecy because dooms require warning.
Sane civilizations need folk culture which is not Art but Nature.
Sane governments have not yet appeared.
No Artist can compromise because he is He.
Art is healer of wounds.
I do not want wounds to humanity because I am against doom.
The Artist should fight single-handed because he is the healer.
The Artist should make his own way.
He should not beg & bargain for Freedom.
He should not have the weakling sobbings to have Freedom from Outside.
Egypt diluted down the Nile.
Van Gogh through the *iron wall* he mentioned in a letter.
Calcutta will be shattered into dust.
But Jibanananda Das will live for ever, in me & in you.
I am against Freedom of Art
Free Artist is an impossibility in a sick barbarous order.
Art is sacrifice at the altar of Humanity.
So I say shackles for the Artist
Dungeons breathing venomous blue vapour for him
Electric chairs for him
Gibbets for him
Auto-da-fe for him
Black sweaty damp jails for him
Loonybins for him
Because Franco & Salazar's graves are to become grave-yards of future
Lorca will sleep with Pasternak in eternity & I'll be there.
And I do not need any guarantee of Freedom from anybody.
I will write whatever I please.
Wherever I am I will write whatever I like
I listen to the tidal murmurs of my blood cataclysmed by moon.
I do not demand my Freedom from anybody.
Poetry will blow down million governments.
All insane civilizations will groan on their knees before the Artist.
No nuclear explosion can threaten the divinity of Time which is Poetry.

(Trans. by the poet)[25]

Malay, who lived in Patna, probably did not attend the festivities himself when some of his fellow Hungries celebrated Jibanananda's birthday in 1968 at Khalashi Tola, "the sailors' bar":

POETS' PUB

Last Monday (February 19th) was a big day for a score of Calcutta's young "rebel" poets of the "Hungry Generation." It was the birthday of their "guru and inspirer," Jibanananda Das, with whom however, they had never come in contact. The celebration was a complete departure from the usual pattern of anniversaries; its organizers planned it so. The venue was not any of the city's cultural *sadans* [halls] but a popular and rumbustious Desi (country liquor) pub in central Calcutta. There were no special invitees. The "unseen but pervading spirit of Jibanananda Das" was the evening's chief guest.

As soon as the "Hungry Gs," as they are affectionately called, occupied a wobbly corner table, the celebration began. It started with a minute's memorial silence, which was shattered by the audience's earsplitting cachinnation. Saileshwar Ghosh, a "budding poet" to his colleagues, then followed with a discourse on why this celebration was here. "Simply because this is the place where Jibanananda was inspired day after day. So we follow suit." The thin bespectacled poet then launched on reading "Janmaniantran" (Birth Control), his latest work dealing with such diverse subjects as creation and the culinary art. This time too the audience was unkind. The poet's voice was drowned in the ceaseless din.

Next came another "Hungry G" poet, who lamented the hardships of his tribe. "We are broke, our works remain unpublished; and our comrades are constantly shadowed by Special Branch men for reasons unknown." Suddenly he erupted: "We damn those poets who think we can't write. We have freedom. Our minds can think everything and our pens can write anything." He concluded, "Our works will be read by the whole Bengali community one day." Not surprisingly, when the celebration ended, about a dozen bottles and glasses had been shattered.[26]

Jibanananda most assuredly never saw the inside of Khalashi Tola, much less drink there night after night. It is extremely doubtful that Jibanananda ever took so much as a drink of liquor in his entire life. But, as the above item indicates, he has influenced poets of all walks of life in many and varied ways.[27]

More gentle than Malay Roy Choudhury's "Hungry" verse is Abdul Mannan Syed's lyric entitled "Jibanananda" (*jibananda*), a lyric that expresses metaphorically what many poets in Bengal feel today—that Jibanananda in essence remains a part of the Bengali landscape, vividly and ever present:

> I observe Jibanananda from time to time on the street.
> Stout of body, a somewhat soiled *kurta,* stained *dhoti*
> Hitched up to his knees, nondescript sandals,
> Or maybe moccasins on his feet; in his eyes
> Shine two shards of a green prism
> From my childhood, now lost.
> I saw him one day at the head of Greene Road.
> Another day, it was in a bookstore, second floor, outside the stadium.
> As I headed up the stairs, he brushed by me on his hurried way down.
> Still another day I saw him pacing by the lake,

Absorbed in his own thoughts.
And yet another time, through the fish market's raucous din, making
   the rounds.
Hopeful, I started,
But he disappeared among the crowd, before my very eyes,
Slipped into that human void.
Just once, as he walked by,
He cast a momentary, distracted glance my way,
Seeming to convey those words of welcome,
"Where have you been so long?"
But not waiting for an answer
He blended into stark reality.
On another day—it was after dark—I saw him
Standing chagrined, like a captured star,
In Dhaka's most deserted spot—
I was on a rickshaw, going by that field—
I see the night, caught in his hair.
From within green prism eyes grasshoppers leap.
His feet, held fast by pins of autumn dewdrops
Like gray men knelt before some primal god.
I see his *kurta,* his *dhoti,* threaded of fog.
I see that from his mumbled words of welcome
Come all the evening stars.
I watch the moon peek out from loose and flowing pockets of his
   kurta.
Then Bliss-of-Life began to walk away
Nonchalantly, aimlessly
Away from my life's sorrows—far, far away.[28]

A number of magazines the names of which display some link with Jibanananda have appeared throughout West Bengal, names such as *Dhanasiri* ("*Dhansiri*"), after the river mentioned in several of Jibanananda's poems, *Bibhinna Koras* ("Various Choruses") and *Sindhusaras* ("Sea Storks"), titles for Jibanananda's poems, *Bela Abela* ("Time, Untime"), whose name approximates the title of Jibanananda's posthumously published volume *Time, Untime and Time Apart* (*bela abela kalabela*). One book on Jibanananda lists as many as thirty such little magazines sporting Jibanananda-related titles, including one forthrightly called *Jibanananda.*[29] The editor of this slim publication explained, "Another name for *jibanananda* ("bliss of life") IS poetry."[30] From Bangladesh the first issue of a small publication named *Parampara* ("Authoritative Ancestry") came out in December 1980, containing only poems dedicated to Jibanananda and some translations of his work into English. Many of the contributors play quite self-consciously with characters, phrases, and settings found throughout Jibanananda's poetry. From West Bengal, again, comes *Jibanananda Akademi Patrika* ("The Jibanananda Academy

Journal"), an irregular publication devoted to literature and scholarship on Jibanananda.

In the "letters to the editor" section of the newspaper came a suggestion that a street in Calcutta should be renamed in honor of Jibanananda:

> ... we are in favor of making South Calcutta's "Southern Avenue" into "Jibanananda Avenue." To date we have not been able to set up in the city of Calcutta this sort of memento for the most overpoweringly influential poet of the past three decades. ... And it is not hard to uncover Jibanananda's ties with Southern Avenue and the adjacent Rabindra Lake.[31]

In one way or another, nearly every Bengali critic in the latter half of the twentieth century has acknowledged Jibanananda Das as the greatest of the Bengali poets to succeed Rabindranath Tagore. Bani Ray spoke of Jibanananda as the "father of modern poetry,"[32] "modern poetry" being defined for Bengali as that poetry which came into existence during the two decades between the wars.[33]

As previously noted, T. S. Eliot made the following observation on the language poets use:

> The immediacy of poetry to conversation is not a matter on which we can lay down exact laws. Every revolution in poetry is apt to be, and sometimes to announce itself to be, a return to common speech. ... The followers of a revolution develop the new poetic idiom in one direction or another; they polish and perfect it; meanwhile the spoken language goes on changing, and the poetic idiom goes out of date.[34]

It is to the language poets use that we turn in order to understand Bengali modernity in poetry. Unfortunately, this aspect of the poetry is least perceptible in translation. Buddhadeva Bose, early on, characterizing Jibanananda as one who "has been able to create a separate language for his own use," wrote just following Jibanananda's death:

> ... the truth is that no other Bengali poet before Jibanananda used indigenous and foreign lexical items so extensively, reasonably, and comfortably in poetry of a serious nature. ... These examples [from Jibanananda's poetry] had caused us to be more bold in our own writings.[35]

What should be noted in the statements by Buddhadeva is that he makes no mention of the immediacy of Jibanananda's poetry to conversation or of any return to common speech. Dipti Tripathi sees it somewhat differently:

Needless to say, one of the goals of the modern poets was to eliminate the division between the spoken language and the language of poetry. They all attempted to bring poetry naturally and directly within the basic linguistic idiom, that is, within the peculiar indigenous manner of using the language. But no one else was able to use [the language] so extensively and comfortably as Jibanananda.[36]

Though some of Dipti Tripathi's comments are reiterations of Buddhadeva's observations, she does add to Jibanananda's accomplishments the ability to use the spoken language in his poetry. This however must be qualified. As Buddhadeva pointed out, Jibanananda created a separate language, one for his own use.

Ambuj Bose writes, "The language of Jibanananda's poetry is definitely not the common poetic language of Bengali, nor is it even his own spoken idiom."[37] Sarat Kumar spoke of Jibanananda as creating "an uneasiness by deliberately mixing together the *sadhu* with colloquial [*kathya*] speech." And, he adds wryly, "Of course—thanks to our civility—as we read it, we caused it to become accepted. We didn't despise it. And now, I would say, it has become one of the poet's main characteristics." Furthermore:

> Does a line written in mixed *sadhu* and *kathya* diction sound so terrible? But he alone was afforded this courtesy by us readers. It is not that subsequent poets did not try [this diction], yet readers never gazed upon them with an approving eye. Jibanananda perpetrated metrical irregularities. He employed in many places obsolete verbs of the *charateche* type ["he strews"—the form is neither *sadhu* nor *calit* but something in between]; he imported the metallic sounds of words like *bhanr* ["jester"], *gunacat* ["coarse jute fibre"], *haidrant* ["hydrant"], *bephans* ["slip of the tongue"], etc., to vex his audience. Mercilessly outraging the reader, he then passed on to that other shore.[38]

We have noted above how outraged such readers as Sajani Kanta Das were by such language.

But Jibanananda Das will not take his place alongside Rabindranath Tagore and other great poets simply because he inadvertently led a revolution in Bengali poetry wherein the poet's lexicon was given new freedoms. Even without the ability to read Bengali, Allen Ginsberg, in talking with the "Hungries," grasped much of Jibanananda's contribution: "bitterness, self-doubt, sex, street diction, personal confession, frankness, Calcutta beggars." As Ginsberg himself and, say, Dylan Thomas stand with regard to T. S. Eliot in modern English poetry, so may Jibanananda, alone, be said to stand contraposed to Rabindranath in Bengali.

Energetic manipulation of language, intensely sensuous images, daring displays of personal revelation, analytically unwieldy doubts and insecurities—this is the stuff of Jibanananda's poetry and of his greatness. And while his fellow poets and those who came after him cite his innovative use of language and the superb quality of his rural poetry as evidences of the enduring value of Jibanananda's art, it is, in fact, the loneliness and despair, and his atomistic immersion in nature, that most communicate Jibanananda to those outside the borders of the Bengali-speaking world. As he himself wrote, "The creation of poetry and the reading of poetry are both in the final analysis matters of the individual mind." The barrier of language notwithstanding, Jibanananda's poetry has the capability to speak volumes to all of us about the finely tuned, passionately involved imagination of an ordinary man who also happened to be a poet apart.

Notes

Chapter 1. Roots

1. I would like to thank my colleague from the Department of Geophysical Sciences, Robert C. Newton, for his fascinating lecture on the geology of India. For further information, see Philipe Patriat and José Achache, "India-Eurasia Collision Chronology Has Implications for Crustal Shortening and Driving Mechanism of Plates," *Nature* 311 (18 October 1984): 615-21.

2. There are any number of informative books in both Bengali and English on the prelude to independence, the war itself, and independent Bangladesh. The reader might profitably consult the following: Rounaq Jahan, *Pakistan: Failure in National Integration* (New York: Columbia University Press, 1972); Jyoti Sen Gupta, *History of Freedom Movement in Bangladesh, 1947-1973: Some Involvement* (Calcutta: Naya Prokash, 1974); A. M. A. Muhith, *Bangladesh: Emergence of a Nation* (Dhaka: Bangladesh Books International, 1978); and Charles Peter O'Donnell, *Bangladesh: Biography of a Muslim Nation* (Boulder, Col., and London: Westview Press, 1984). The definitive collection of documents, generated from both within and outside of Bangladesh and pertaining to the war of independence, is contained in thirteen volumes published by the government of Bangladesh; Hasan Hafizur Rahman, ed., *Bamladeser swadhinata yuddha: dalilapatra* (Bangladesh's independence war: Documents), 13 vols. (Dhaka: Ganaprajatantri Bangladesh Sarkar; Tathya Mantranalay, 1982).

3. Nazimuddin Ahmed, *Mahasthan: A Preliminary Report on Archaeological Excavations,* 2d ed. (Karachi: Department of Archaeology and Museums; Ministry of Education & Scientific Research; Government of Pakistan, 1971); Barrie M. Morrison, *Lalmai, a Cultural Center of Early Bengal: An Archaeological Report and Historical Analysis* (Seattle and London: University of Washington Press, 1974).

4. R. C. Majumdar, ed. *Hindu Period,* vol. 1 of *The History of Bengal* (Dhaka: The University of Dhaka, 1943); Himangshu Mohan Chattopadhyay, comp., *Bikramapur* (Bikrampur), 2 vols. (Narayanganj, Dhaka: Bikrampur-Pratibha Karyalay, 1931).

5. Jadunath Sarkar, ed., *Muslim Period, 1200-1757,* vol. 2 of *The History of Bengal* (Dhaka: The University of Dhaka, 1948) and J. J. A. Campos, *A History of the Portuguese in Bengal* (Calcutta and London: Butterworth & Co., 1919). (Campos deflects blame from the pirates of Portuguese ancestry and places it upon the Arakanese Mogs instead.)

6. For an informative and delightful account of the tea industry in British India, see Percival Griffiths, *The History of the Indian Tea Industry* (London: Weidenfeld and Nicolson, 1967).

7. See Begum Rokeya Sakhawat Hossain, *Rokeya-racanabali* (The collected works of Rokeya), ed. Abdul Kadir (Dhaka: Bangla Academy, 1973). Although

most of her writings are yet untranslated, one piece, "Sultana's Dream," a short fantasy of what life would be with men secluded in the zenana and only women allowed to appear in public, was originally written in English. One of her works, "The Secluded Ones" (*abarodhabasini*), dealing with the purdah system and seclusion of women, has been translated and sensitively introduced; see Roushan Jahan, ed. and trans., *Inside Seclusion: The Avarodhbasini of Rokeya Sakhawat Hossain* (Dhaka: Women for Women, 1981).

8. For a brief account in English of this event and its ramifications, see Rangalal Sen, "A Study of Political Elites in Bangladesh 1947–1970" (Ph.D. diss., University of Sussex, 1977), 124–47; the definitive work in Bengali remains Badruddin Umar, *Purbabangalar bhasa andolan o tatkalin rajaniti* (The language movement of East Bengal and politics of that time) (Dhaka: Maola Brothers, 1970).

9. Satyananda Das, "Amar jyestha bhrata" (My elder brother), *Brahmabadi*, Bhadra–Aswin 1325, 78–79.

10. Asokananda Das, "Balyasmriti" (Childhood reminiscences), *Mayukh,* Paus–Jyaistha 1361–62.

11. Jibanananda Das, *Rupasi Bamla* (Bengal the beautiful), 4th ed. (Calcutta: Signet Press, 1968), 44.

12. Though the Hindu *varnas* are four (Brahman, Ksatriya, Vaisya, and Sudra—often referred to by the Portuguese-derived word "caste"), medieval and modern India's "castes" are many and do not necessarily conform to the *varnas*. Bengal has but two *varnas,* Brahman and Sudra. However, the three "high castes" in Bengal, in ranked order, are Brahman, Vaidya, and Kayastha, the latter two being Sudras, technically. For more information regarding caste and the history of castes in Bengal, see Ronald B. Inden, *Marriage and Rank in Bengali Culture: A History of Caste and Clan in Middle Period Bengal* (Berkeley and Los Angeles: University of California Press, 1976).

13. Sucarita Das, "Kacher Jibanananda" (Intimate Jibanananda), *Mayukh,* Paus–Jyaistha 1361–62, 172.

14. For an introduction to the Brahmo Samaj, see David Kopf, *The Brahmo Samaj and the Shaping of the Modern Indian Mind* (Princeton: Princeton University Press, 1979).

15. Satyananda Das, "Amar jyestha bhrata," 79.

16. For an account of the founding of the Barisal Brahmo Samaj, see Sivanath Sastri, *History of the Brahmo Samaj* (Calcutta: R. Chatterjee, 1912), 2: 358–77. Manmatha Mohan Das, *Barisal Brahmasamajer samksipta itihas* (A short history of the Barisal Brahmo Samaj) ([Barisal]: Manmatha Mohan Das, 1927) includes Sarbananda's brief history of the local Samaj, published on the occasion of its sixth anniversary (1867).

17. Satyananda Das, "Amar jyestha bhrata," 80–81.

18. Yogendranath Gupta, *Banger mahila kabi* (Women poets of Bengal), 2d ed. (Calcutta: A. Mukherjee and Co., 1953), 316–17.

19. Sumita Chakravarti, in an excellent article on Kusum Kumari, quotes citations pertaining to Kusum Kumari from a brief biography of the girls' father by Kusum Kumari's youngest sister, Hemanta Kumari; S. Chakravarti, "Kusumakumari Das—sei chele'r ma" (Kusum Kumari Das—'that boy's' mother), *Desh,* 11 Asarh 1389, 11.

20. Jibanananda Das, "Amar ma baba" (My parents), *Uttarsuri,* Paus–Falgun 1361, 7.

21. Shanta Chatterjee, *Ramananda Cattopadhyay o arddhasatabdir Bamla* (Ramananda Chatterjee and a half century of Bengali) (Calcutta: Prabasi Press, n.d.), 48.

22. *Mukul,* Caitra 1302.
23. *Mukul,* Paus 1302.
24. Manomohan Chakravarty, "Barisale pamyatallis batsar" (Forty-five years in Barisal), *Brahmabadi,* Caitra 1342, 273.
25. There is some controversy over which of three journals published that year should be honored as first; see Smarajit Chakraborti, *The Bengali Press (1818–1868): A Study in the Growth of Public Opinion* (Calcutta: Firma KLM Private Limited, 1976), 16–19. The passion for periodicals continues; a fairly recent index of West Bengal magazines presently in print (or recently in print) lists as many as 1,143 titles; see Asok Kumar Kundu, *Patrika-panji* (Periodical index), vol. 1 (Calcutta: Banglabhasa Sahitya o Samskriti Gabesana Samstha, 1982).
26. Yogendranath Gupta, *Banger mahila kabi,* 317–18.
27. Jibanananda Das, "Amar ma baba," 11–12. A slightly different version of the last paragraph is given in Asokananda Das, "Amar dada Jibanananda Das" (My elder brother Jibanananda Das), *Girls' College Magazine, Howrah* (1955): 12.
28. Asokananda Das, "Jibanananda Das" (Jibanananda Das), *Purvasa,* Falgun 1371, 91.
29. Sucarita Das, "Kacher Jibanananda," 176.
30. Asokananda Das, "Jibanananda Das," 91.
31. Asokananda Das, "Balyasmriti," 129.
32. The Admission Register lists his name as Jibananda, the first but not the last such misspelling.
33. Quoted in Krishna Kripalani, *Tagore: A Life* (Calcutta: published by the author, 1971), 157.
34. *The Cambridge History of India,* vol. 6, edited by H. H. Dodwell with additional chapters by R. R. Sethi (Delhi, Jullundur, and Lucknow: S. Chand & Co., 1958), 611; R. C. Majumdar, H. C. Raychaudhuri, and Kalikinkar Datta, *An Advanced History of India,* 3d ed. (London, Melbourne, and Toronto: Macmillan; New York: St Martin's Press, 1967), 981; and Percival Spear, *A History of India,* vol. 2 (Baltimore: Penguin Books, 1965), 191–92.
35. For more on the subject, see Syed Nurullah and J. P. Naik, *A History of Education in India (during the British Period),* 2d ed. (Bombay, Calcutta, Madras, and London: Macmillan and Co., 1951), 567–72; P. C. Bamford, *Histories of the Non-Cooperation and Khilafat Movements* (Delhi: Government of India Press, 1925; Delhi: Deep Publications, 1974), 17, 22, 101–8; and Leonard A. Gordon, "Subhas Bose in Indian Politics, 1921 to 1928," *The Oracle* (1984): 3–4.
36. On this initial phase of the movement, see Haridas and Uma Mukherjee, *The Origins of the National Education Movement (1905–1910)* (Jadavpur, Calcutta: Jadavpur University, 1957).
37. Hiralal Dasgupta, *Jananayak Aswinikumar* (Aswini Kumar, leader of the people) (Calcutta: Dasgupta and Co., [1969]), 51–59. Due to the violence, the separate literary conference never convened, and Rabindranath returned earlier than expected to Santiniketan. The impetus for that literary conference emanated from fears that partition would not only divide Bengal physically but, unless efforts were made to the contrary, would also foster a literary and linguistic schism between the two Bengali-speaking halves of the province; see Probhat Kumar Mukherji, *Rabindrajibani o rabindrasahitya-prabesak* (The life of Rabindranath and a guide to his literature), rev. ed. (Calcutta: Visvabharati Granthalay, 1949), 2: 138–39.
38. *Aswinikumar racanasambhar* (The collected works of Aswini Kumar) (Calcutta: Adhyayan, [1968]), 16 of "Lectures."
39. Ibid., 8–9.
40. Ibid., 12.

41. Local News, *Brahmabadi,* Magh 1327.
42. Local News, *Brahmabadi,* Falgun–Caitra 1327.
43. Local News, *Brahmabadi,* Baisakh 1328. Chitta Ranjan Das had called on students everywhere to boycott educational institutions, to which students in Barisal responded, demanding "national education." Hiralal Dasgupta, *Jananayak Aswinikumar,* 94–95.
44. Local News, *Brahmabadi,* Baisakh 1328; and interview with Asokananda Das.
45. Local News, *Brahmabadi,* Asarh 1328.
46. Quoted by Asokananda Das in his essay, "Amar dada Jibanananda Das," 8–9; only the first third of this paragraph appears in Jibanananda's essay "Amar ma baba."
47. Jayanta Kumar Dasgupta, editorial, *Brajamohan Bidyalay Patrika,* 1968–69, v.
48. Percival Spear, *A History of India,* 191.
49. *Jubilee* (Barisal), 1934, 19.
50. Interview with Jayanta Kumar Dasgupta.
51. Local News, *Brahmabadi,* Bhadra–Aswin 1334.
52. Satyananda also published a book entitled *Santanasiksa niti o dharmma* (Education of children: Moral and religious) (Dhaka: East Bengal Brahmo Conference, 1917).
53. Jibanananda Das, "Amar ma baba," 10.
54. Interview with Asokananda Das.
55. Interviews with Father Carelton of the Oxford Mission and with Dr. Bhupen Mukherjee, originally from Barisal and former resident of the hostel.
56. Interview with Asokananda Das.
57. Local News, *Brahmabadi,* Sravan 1326.
58. A program began in 1917 whereby Presidency College students enrolled at Calcutta University through Presidency College; see *The Presidency College Magazine* 4, no. 1 (September 1917).
59. *University Law College List of Students from 1913–1914 to 1920–1921.*
60. Local News, *Brahmabadi,* Sravan 1329.
61. Interview with Sucarita Das.
62. The following item appeared in *The Presidency College Magazine* 7, no. 1 (October 1920): 55: "UNIVERSITY NOTES—The MA and MSc Exam commenced on the 30th August 1920. In all there were 735 candidates. . . . This is the first time in the history of an Indian University that arrangements have been made for the institution of an MA Exam in Indian Vernaculars." There were sixteen candidates for "vernacular" degrees, all non-collegiate (i.e., not full-time students of the University) the first two candidates, college professors of English.
63. Cited in Abdul Mannan Syed, *Suddhatama kabi* (The purest of poets), 2d ed. (Dhaka: Knowledge Home, 1977), 250.
64. Letter dated 2 July 1946, in *Mayukh,* Paus–Jyaistha 1361–62, 227.
65. *Brahmabadi,* Baisakh 1326, 1.
66. Jibanananda Das, "Amar ma baba," 4–13.
67. Jayakanta Mishra, *History of Maithili Literature* (New Delhi: Sahitya Akademi, 1976), 26; Birinchi Kumar Barua, *History of Assamese Literature* (New Delhi: Sahitya Akademi, 1964), 7; and Mayadhar Mansinha, *History of Oriya Literature* (New Delhi: Sahitya Akademi, 1962), 22ff.

68. Sukumar Sen, *History of Bengali Literature* (New Delhi: Sahitya Akademi, 1960), 70ff; and Baru Candidasa, *Singing the Glory of Lord Krishna; the Srikrsnakirtana,* trans. and annotated by M. H. Klaiman (Chico, Calif.: Scholars Press, 1984), 18–20.
69. *Rupasi Bamla,* 31.
70. Harekrishna Mukherjee, ed., *Vaisnava-padabali* (Vaishnava lyrics) (Calcutta: Sahitya Samsad, 1961), 639. For more translations of Vaishnava lyrics, see Edward C. Dimock, Jr., and Denise Levertov, trans., *In Praise of Krishna: Songs from the Bengali* (Garden City, N.Y.: Anchor Books; Doubleday & Co., 1967).
71. Leonard Nathan and Clinton Seely, trans., *Grace and Mercy in Her Wild Hair: Selected Poems to the Mother Goddess* (Boulder, Col.: Great Eastern; Shambhala Publications, 1982), 35.
72. *Rupasi Bamla,* 13.
73. An English translation of this tale can be found in Edward C. Dimock, Jr., *The Thief of Love: Bengali Tales from Court and Village* (Chicago and London: University of Chicago Press, 1963), 209ff.
74. *Rupasi Bamla,* 12.
75. Qazi Abdul Mannan, *Literary Heritage of Bangladesh: Medieval Period* (New York: Learning Resources in International Studies, 1974), 4–8. Qazi Abdul Mannan and Clinton B. Seely, trans. *Iusuf Jalikha by Md. Sagir* (New York: Learning Resources in International Studies, 1974). Qazi Abdul Mannan and Clinton B. Seely, trans. *Padmabati by Alaol* (New York: Learning Resources in International Studies, 1974). The latter two consist of introductory comments, and very brief excerpts from the respective narratives.
76. Sushil Kumar De, *Bengali Literature in the Nineteenth Century (1757–1857),* 2d ed. (Calcutta: Firma K. L. Mukhopadhyay, 1962), 106ff.
77. See Anisuzzaman, *Purono Bamla gadya* (Old Bengali prose) (Dhaka: Bangla Academy, 1984).
78. See, e.g., Maturin M. Ballou, *Due West, or Round the World in Ten Months,* 11th ed. (Boston: Houghton, Mifflin and Co., 1895), 169; Nirad C. Chaudhuri, *The Autobiography of an Unknown Indian* (New York: Macmillan Co., 1951), 255; and Dominique Lapierre, *The City of Joy* (Garden City, N.Y.: Doubleday & Co., 1985), 32.
79. Sushil Kumar De, *Bengali Literature in the Nineteenth Century (1757–1857),* 480, 488.
80. Thomas Babington Macaulay, "Minute on Indian Education," in *Selected Writings,* ed. and with an introd. by John Clive and Thomas Pinney (Chicago and London: University of Chicago Press, 1972), 241.
81. Letter dated 7 October 1842, in Ksetra Gupta, ed., *Kabi Madhusudan o tanr patrabali* (Poet Madhusudan and his letters) (Calcutta: Grantha Nilay, 1963), 77–78.
82. Ibid., 113; letter dated 18 August 1849.
83. Ibid., 133–34; letter dated 1 July 1860.
84. Bankim Chandra Chatterjee, *Bangadarsan* 1, no. 1 (April 1872): 1.
85. Probhat Kumar Mukherji, *Rabindrajibani o rabindrasahitya-prabesak* 2: 125, 489ff.
86. Mary M. Lago, *Imperfect Encounter: Letters of William Rothenstein and Rabindranath Tagore, 1911–1941* (Cambridge: Harvard University Press, 1972).
87. See Nabaneeta Sen, "The 'Foreign Reincarnation' of Rabindranath Tagore,"

Journal of Asian Studies 25, no. 2 (February 1966): 275–86; and Sujit Mukherjee, *Passage to America: The Reception of Rabindranath Tagore in the United States, 1921–1941* (Calcutta, Patna, and Allahabad: Bookland Pvt., 1964).

88. Ezra Pound, "Rabindranath Tagore," *Fortnightly Review* 43 (January–June 1913): 575.

Chapter 2. The Kallol Era

1. Interview with Asokananda Das. One had to make application for membership in the Sadharan Brahmo Samaj, which was open to persons eighteen years of age and older.

2. Jibanananda Das, "Amar ma baba," 6.

3. Jibanananda Das, *Jhara palak* (Fallen feathers) (Calcutta: Sudhir Chandra Sarkar, 1927), 51–52; appeared in *Bangabani,* Aghran 1332.

4. This excerpt comes from my translation, with slight modification, as published in Qazi Abdul Mannan and Clinton B. Seely, trans., *Lyric Poetry* (New York: Learning Resources in International Studies, 1974), 5–6.

5. Jaroslav Prusek and Dusan Zbavitel, eds., *Dictionary of Oriental Literatures* (New York: Basic Books, 1974), 107.

6. Nazrul Islam's "A Chronicle of the Heart" (*cittanama*) (the title plays on Chitta [*citta*] Ranjan Das's name and the genre of eulogistic histories [*nama*] of Muslim kings), published in July 1925, contained lyrics and poems in honor of C. R. Das, one of which carried the footnote: "a song for Deshabandhu's funeral procession." *Najarul racana-sambhar* (The collected works of Nazrul Islam), vol. 2, 2d ed. (Calcutta: Haraph Prakasani, 1970), 241.

7. Asokananda Das, "Amar dada Jibanananda Das," 4.

8. Jibanananda Das, "Amar ma baba," 13.

9. Swami Vivekananda, "My Master," in *The Complete Works of Swami Vivekananda,* vol. 4 (Mayavati Memorial 10th ed.; Calcutta: Advaita Ashrama, 1972), 156.

10. Leonard A. Gordon quotes Chaudhri Muhammad Ali, a prime minister of Pakistan: "[C. R. Das was] the one Hindu leader who inspired unreserved confidence among Muslims; never again was Hindu leadership to rise to his height." Gordon, *Bengal: The Nationalist Movement, 1876–1940* (New York and London: Columbia University Press, 1974), 219.

11. *Jhara palak,* 56–59; appeared in *Bangabani,* Asarh 1333.

12. Jibendra Simha Ray, in his *Kalloler kal* (The Kallol times) (Calcutta: Kathasilpa, 1973), gives a good account of the Four Arts Club.

13. *Jhara palak,* 33–34.

14. *Mayukh,* Paus–Jyaistha 1361–62, 122–23.

15. Interviews with Premendra Mitra and Buddhadeva Bose.

16. Ajit Datta, "Kabita lekhar katha" (About writing poetry), *Desh,* special literary number, 1379, 202.

17. *Sanibarer Cithi* began in July 1924 as a weekly but lasted only until February 1925. Then in August 1927 it started up again as a monthly. The weekly had been edited officially by Yogananda Das, and published through the efforts of Asok Chatterjee, Ramananda's son. The monthly was first edited by Yogananda with Sajani Kanta as assistant editor. From January of the following year Nirad C. Chaudhuri had taken over as editor, but left the editorship in September 1928, allowing Sajani Kanta to assume full responsibility for editing and publishing the magazine.

18. Debajyoti Das, *Sajanikanta Das* (Sajani Kanta Das) (Calcutta: Bangiya Sahitya Parishat, 1970), 51.
19. There is no publication date in the book. Jibanananda's own brief introduction bears the date Aswin 1334 (September–October 1927). A review of the book appeared in the November–December issue of *Kallol* that same year.
20. *Mayukh,* Paus–Jyaistha 1361–62, 226.
21. *Jhara palak,* 68–70.
22. Ibid., 71–74.
23. Ibid., 87–89.
24. *Kallol,* Aghran 1334, 623.
25. Interview with Sarojendranath Ray.
26. In April 1925, Sajani Kanta became the assistant editor of both *Prabasi* and *Modern Review.* By May 1928, he had been promoted to manager of the Prabasi Press. Debajyoti Das, *Sajanikanta Das,* 6–7.
27. Letter dated 5 March 1936, cited in Abdul Mannan Syed, *Suddhatama kabi,* 253–54.
28. As far as I know, Sunil Ganguly fashioned the epithet "literary goon" (*sahityer gunda*), with reference to *Sanibarer Cithi.*
29. Debajyoti Das, *Sajanikanta Das,* 31–32.
30. Mohitlal Majumdar, *Sahitya-katha* (On literature), 2d ed. (Santragachi, West Bengal: Banga Bharati Granthalay, 1959), 6–7. "The Literary Ideal" was first published in *Sanibarer Cithi,* Aswin 1334. For a fuller statement on Mohitlal's stance, see his "Adhunik Bamla sahitya" (Modern Bengali literature) published in July 1929 and included in his *Adhunik Bamla sahitya* (Modern Bengali literature), 5th ed. (Calcutta: General Printers and Publishers, 1959), 1–22.
31. Although Sajani Kanta wrote under many pseudonyms, this is not one of them. For a list of his noms de plume, see Debajyoti Das, *Sajanikanta Das,* 49–50.
32. *Sanibarer Cithi,* Kartik 1334, 119–20.
33. Sajani Kanta Das, *Atmasmriti* (Reminiscences) (Calcutta: D.M. Library, 1956) 2: 54–55.
34. In all fairness to Sajani Kanta, it should be noted that he had tried once to form an alliance with Rabindranath. Early in 1927 he wrote Rabindranath, citing specific complaints against certain of the *Kallol* writers and progressive literature in general. In that letter, he attempted unsuccessfully to draw Rabindranath into the fray on his side. Sajani Kanta's letter and Rabindranath's reply are cited in Acintya Kumar Sengupta, *Kallol yug* (The Kallol era), 5th ed. (Calcutta: M. C. Sarkar and Sons, 1965), 183–85.
35. Rabindranath Tagore, "Jiban smriti" (Reminiscences) in *Rabindra-racanabali* (The collected works of Rabindranath) (reprint; Calcutta: Visvabharati, 1965), 17: 375.
36. Rabindranath Tagore, "Sahityadharma" (The essence of literature) in *Rabindra-racanabali* (Calcutta: Visvabharati, 1958), 23: 407.
37. *Atma-Sakti,* Bhadra 9 to Aswin 27, 1334, carried Sajani Kanta's article, according to Debajyoti Das, *Sajanikanta Das,* 62.
38. Both letters are dated 13 December 1927, and are reprinted in Sajani Kanta Das, *Atmasmriti,* 2: 4–7. For an account of the multi-faceted relationship Sajani Kanta maintained with Rabindranath, see Jagadish Bhattacharya, *Rabindranath o Sajanikanta* (Rabindranath and Sajani Kanta) (Calcutta: Ranjan Publishing House, 1973).
39. Sajani Kanta Das, *Atmasmriti,* 6.
40. *Sanibarer Cithi,* Aghran 1334, 272.
41. *Sanibarer Cithi,* Asarh 1335.

42. *Sanibarer Cithi,* Aghran 1334, 280.
43. Sajani Kanta Das, *Atmasmriti* 1: 268. He proceeded to support his claim with a quote from Mohitlal's "The Literary Ideal" (*Sanibarer Cithi,* Aswin 1334). The selection quoted differs considerably from the essay as published subsequently in Mohitlal Majumdar, *Sahitya-katha,* 1ff.
44. Jibanananda Das, *Dhusar pandulipi* (Gray manuscripts), 3d Signet ed. (Calcutta: Signet Press, 1967), 73–76.
45. *Sanibarer Cithi,* Caitra 1334, 225.
46. Jibanananda Das, *Banalata Sen* (Banalata Sen), 8th Signet ed. (Calcutta: Signet Press, 1968), 28.
47. *Rupasi Bamla,* 24.
48. *Banalata Sen,* 15.
49. Sravan 1334. Rabindranath's *Lord of the Dance,* attacked by Sajani Kanta, had appeared in the maiden issue of *Bicitra.*
50. Aghran 1334. The essay originally appeared in *Prabasi* under the title of "A Traveler's Diary" (*yatrir dayari*).
51. It is worth noting that Rabindranath himself was to do—modestly to be sure—what he was condemning others for in print: borrowing from another culture. Upon returning from the archipelago, he revised his *Lord of the Dance,* added new songs, and staged it in Calcutta, December 1927, under the title of "Play of the Seasons" (*rituranga*). This time, notes Rabindranath's biographer, the dances had special characteristics: "The poet had had the opportunity, while in Bali and Java a few months earlier, to observe in detail the local dance form, the influence of which was now very apparent in the performance." Probhat Kumar Mukherji, *Rabindrajibani o rabindrasahitya-prabesak* (The life of Rabindranath and a guide to his literature) (Calcutta: Visvabharati Granthalay, 1952), 3: 229.
52. Rabindranath Tagore, "Sahitye nabattwa" (Literary innovation), in *Rabindra-racanabali,* 23: 411.
53. Acintya Kumar Sengupta, *Kallol yug,* 291.
54. Rabindranath Tagore, "Sahityasamalocana" (Literary criticism), in *Rabindra-racanabali,* 23: 509.
55. Krishna Kripalani has rendered this prose work into English under the title *Farewell, My Friend.* Serial publication began in August 1928, only months after the conference, of the novel, expanded from one of Rabindranath's short stories named "Mita."
56. Buddhadeva Bose, *Rabindranath: Kathasahitya* (Rabindranath: Fiction) (Calcutta: New Age Publishers, 1955), 125–26.
57. *Pragati,* Aswin 1335. Reprinted in Buddhadeva Bose, *Prabandha-samkalan* (Collected essays) (Calcutta: Bharabi, 1966), 96.
58. For a discussion of rasa and Sanskrit poetics, see S. K. De, *Sanskrit Poetics as a Study of Aesthetic,* with notes by Edwin Gerow (Berkeley and Los Angeles: University of California Press, 1963), 48ff.; and V. Raghavan and Nagendra, eds., *An Introduction to Indian Poetics* (Bombay, Calcutta, Madras, and London: Macmillan and Co., 1970), 36ff.
59. Buddhadeva Bose, *Prabandha-samkalan,* 96.
60. Ibid., 97.
61. *Dhusar pandulipi,* 41–44. First appeared in *Pragati,* Bhadra 1336.
62. Dipti Tripathi, *Adhunik Bamla kabyaparicay* (An introduction to modern Bengali poetry), 3d ed. (Calcutta: Navana, 1964), 182.
63. Ambuj Bose, *Ekati naksatra ase* (A star arrives) (Calcutta: Mausumi, 1965), 111–14.

64. Rabindranath Samanta, *Jibanananda pratibha* (The genius of Jibanananda) (Calcutta: Alpha Publishing Concern, 1972), 44.
65. Buddhadeva Bose, "Bamla kabyer bhabisyat" (The future of Bengali poetry), *Pragati,* Bhadra 1336; republished in part in his essay "Jibanananda Daser smarane" (In memory of Jibanananda Das), in *Prabandha-samkalan,* 100–101.
66. T. S. Eliot, "The Music of Poetry," in *Selected Prose of T. S. Eliot,* ed. Frank Kermode (London: Faber and Faber, 1975), 111.
67. *Dhusar pandulipi,* 77–78; appeared in *Kallol,* Baisakh 1336.
68. Sunil Ganguly, "Kabita ki" (What is poetry?), *Bela Abela,* Falgun 1376, unpaged.
69. English vocabulary, for instance, is said to be 80 percent foreign born; Robert McCrum, William Cran, and Robert MacNeil, *The Story of English* (New York: Elizabeth Sifton Books; Viking Penguin, 1986), 47.
70. Sajani Kanta Das, *Atmasmriti,* 2: 59, 64.
71. Jabez T. Sunderland, *India in Bondage,* rev. ed. (New York: Lewis Copeland Co., 1932), vii.
72. Sajani Kanta Das, *Atmasmriti,* 2: 64, 74.
73. Ibid., 73. The article in question was "The Muse of Meter" (*chanda-saraswati*), a treatise on metrics by the then deceased Satyendranath Datta (d. 1922).
74. Ibid., 87.
75. Acintya Kumar Sengupta, *Kallol yug,* 258.
76. April–June, 1929. Sajani Kanta Das, *Atmasmriti,* 2: 89.
77. Ibid., 92.
78. *Brahmabadi,* Aghran, Paus, Magh, 1333, 143–44.
79. Binod Bihari Banerjee, *Smriti katha* (Recollections) (Calcutta: Vidyasagar Book Stall, [1949]), 2: 68.
80. Ibid., 69.
81. Ibid., 68.
82. *Amrita Bazar Patrika,* 29 January 1928, 3. Other places in Bengal reported puja-related trouble at this time. Calcutta police stood in front of mosques on the day of the immersion processions, to guard against Hindu-Muslim confrontations. News from Barisal: "Saraswati Pujah Precautions—A Barisal Notification—Processions without License Prohibited"; ibid., 27 January 1928, 3.
83. Ibid., 12 February 1928, 4.
84. Ibid., 14 February 1928, 5.
85. Binod Bihari Banerjee, *Smriti katha,* vol. 2, 70.
86. *Sadharan Brahmo Samaj Annual Report, 1928,* 41.
87. *Sanibarer Cithi,* Asarh 1335, 309–14.
88. *Sadharan Brahmo Samaj Annual Report, 1928,* 42.
89. According to Sarojendranath Ray, the English department in 1928 consisted of the following members, in order of seniority: Heramba Maitra, Rajani Kanta Guha (head of department), Suresh Chandra Ray, then either Priyanath Chatterjee or Brajasundar Ray, followed by Binod Bihari Banerjee, Dhirendranath Mukherjee, Sarojendranath Ray, Nirmal Chandra Chakravarty, and finally Jibanananda Das.
90. People on both sides of the argument claim to have had verification from Jibanananda himself.
91. Acintya Kumar Sengupta, *Kallol yug,* 158. There is no poem entitled "Harvest." Acintya Kumar may have had in mind "Song of Thirst" (cited above) in which is found the phrase "harvest's breast" (*phasaler stan*), *phasal* and *sasya* both glossing as harvest.
92. *Mayukh,* Paus–Jyaistha 1361–62, 122–23. Acintya Kumar had written that

he dragged Jibanananda to *Kallol*'s office a couple of times but that Jibanananda felt uneasy. A second letter from Jibanananda to Acintya Kumar the following month carried no references at all to *Kallol yug;* ibid., 124.

93. Buddhadeva Bose, "Caram cikitsa" (The ultimate remedy), *Desh,* 28 Baisakh 1375, 237.
94. Interviews with Acintya Kumar Sengupta and Buddhadeva Bose.
95. *Desh,* 29 Asarh 1375, 1224.
96. Of Brahmos and prudish puritanism, Jibanananda's brother states: "Among the Brahmos of that day, many displayed 'Puritanism,' but though he was a devout Brahmo, we never saw any 'Puritanism' in our father—" Asokananda Das, "Balyasmriti," 130.
97. *Sadharan Brahmo Samaj Annual Report, 1923,* 24.
98. *Brahmabadi,* Magh 1339, 223.
99. Nirad C. Chaudhuri, *The Autobiography of an Unknown Indian,* 211.
100. Interview with Sarojendranath Ray.
101. Interviews with Manoranjan Kar, who succeeded Jibanananda at Prafulla Chandra College, and Prabhash Chandra Ghosh.
102. *Ramjas College Golden Jubilee, 1967; Souvenir,* 6.
103. Jibanananda Das, "Sudhirakumar" (Sudhir Kumar) in *Smriti-tarpan* (In memoriam), no editor ([Barisal]: no publisher, introd. dated April 1942), 137. Courtesy of Sunil Ganguly of Barisal. When the last of the Das family vacated Sarbananda Bhavan and left Barisal for good, part of their library was deposited with Sunil Ganguly.
104. Interview with Prabhash Chandra Ghosh.
105. Interview with Labanya Das.
106. Labanya Das, "Sahadharminir cokhe kabi Jibanananda" (Poet Jibanananda through the eyes of his wife), *Betar Jagat,* Saradiya, 1969, 139.
107. Labanya Das with Kabita Simha, "Amar swami Jibanananda Das" (My husband Jibanananda Das), *Dainik Kavita,* 25 Baisakh 1375, 2; Labanya Das, *Manus Jibanananda* (Jibanananda the man) (Calcutta: Bengal Publishers, 1971), 1–2.
108. Labanya Das, "Sahadharminir cokhe kabi Jibanananda," 139; Labanya Das with Kabita Simha, "Amar swami Jibanananda Das," 2; *Brahmabadi,* Jyaistha 1337, 47–48.
109. *Brahmabadi,* Asarh 1342, 71.
110. Ksetra Gupta, ed., *Madhusudan racanabali* (The collected works of Madhusudan) (Calcutta: Sahitya Samsad, 1965), 186.

Chapter 3. Back to Barisal

1. *Jubilee* [a publication to commemorate the fiftieth anniversary of B.M. Institution], Barisal, 1884–1934, 19.
2. Jibanananda's manuscripts are held in a special collection at the National Library of India, Calcutta. All but a few of the short-story notebooks bear a 1931 or 1932 date. Those few exceptions contain material dated 1936 and 1937. From one of the notebooks bearing the date 1931 comes a recently published story, "Desire's Dalliance" (*akanksa-kamanar bilas*), followed closely by "Company, Alone" (*sanga, nihsanga*). See Debesh Ray, ed., *Jibanananda samagra,* vol. 1. The first story was probably composed in 1931, the latter in 1933; ibid., 457–58. Three other stories Asokananda had released to the magazine *Anukta* ("Unspoken") in the

mid-1950s: "Chayanat" (the name of an Indian musical air), "A Story of Village and City" (*gram o saharer galpa*), and "Dalliance" (*bilas*). See Sukumar Ghosh and Subinay Mustaphi, eds., *Jibanananda Daser galpa* (Jibanananda Das's stories) (Calcutta: Dasgupta and Co., 1972). The dates of composition for the first and second of these have been estimated to be 1932 and 1936, based on stylistic comparison with Jibanananda's poetry of the same period. See introduction to *Jibanananda Daser galpa*, 14, 16. The third story, "Dalliance," may have been penned around 1946; see Sunil Kumar Nandy, *Anukta,* Sravan–Aswin, 1377, 139. In another thirty-six exercise books are five longer works of fiction, the untitled work (1933) and four others written in the late 1940s: "Malyaban" (*malyaban*) (1948), "Sutirtha" (*sutirtha*) (n.d.), "Jalpaihati" (*jalpaihati*) (1948), and "Basmati's Tale" (*basmatir upakhyan*) (1949).

3. From "1333" (A.D. 1926–27) in *Dhusar pandulipi,* 65–68; appeared in *Pragati,* Baisakh 1335.

4. From "Simplicity" (*sahaj*) in *Dhusar pandulipi,* 20–21; appeared in *Pragati,* Asarh 1335.

5. From "Sensation" (*bodh*) in *Dhusar pandulipi,* 41–44; appeared in *Pragati,* Bhadra 1336.

6. "Chayanat" (*chayanat*) in *Jibanananda Daser galpa,* ed. Sukumar Ghosh and Subinay Mustaphi, 32–35.

7. "A Tale of Village and City" (*gram o saharer galpa*) in *Jibanananda Daser galpa,* 61–64.

8. "Company, Alone" (*sanga, nihsanga*) in *Jibanananda samagra,* ed. Debesh Ray, 414–16.

9. On the page facing this introduction, Asokananda gives March 1932 as the period during which these sonnets were composed (*racanakal marc 1932*), and indeed twenty-five from 1957 would be 1932. The notebook itself, however, bears the date of "March 1934," in English and in Jibanananda's hand. See Jibanananda Das, *Rupasi Bamla: Prakasita-aprakasita pandulipi o pathantar samskaran* (Bengal the beautiful: Published and unpublished manuscripts and emended versions), ed. Debesh Ray (Calcutta: Pratiksan Prakasan Bibhag, 1984) for a photographic reproduction of all the pages of the notebook with transcription on the facing printed page.

10. Ksetra Gupta, ed., *Madhusudan racanabali,* xlii.

11. Sisir Kumar Das, "Michael Madhusudan Datta and the Sonnet in Bengal," *Mahfil* 3, no. 4 (1967): 102.

12. See Uttam Kumar Das, *Bamla sahitye sanet* (The sonnet in Bengali literature) (Calcutta: Kabi o Kabita, 1973). For a good anthology of Bengali sonnets, see Sisir Kumar Das, *Caturdasi* (Sonnets) (Calcutta: Sambodhi Publications, 1966).

13. *Mayukh,* Paus–Jyaistha 1361–62, 195.

14. Ibid., 195–96. Asokananda, who released the above sonnet to *Mayukh,* remains the sole source of information on Jibanananda's early English writing. He gives some other examples of poetry Jibanananda composed during his student days, including another English sonnet; see Asokananda Das, "Balyasmriti," 138–40. He also informs us that Jibanananda composed many songs during his school days but never published any of them; see Asokananda Das, "Amar dada Jibanananda Das," 5.

15. Courtesy of Bishnu Dey. Prabhash Chandra Ghosh was a fellow Bengali teaching at Ramjas College in Delhi; Jibanananda had left there in 1930. *Paricay* magazine, a quarterly, had begun publication in Sravan 1338 (July 1931); the second issue appeared in October 1931; Jibanananda's poem "In Camp" (*kyampe*) would come out in the third issue, January 1932.

16. *Rupasi Bamla,* 36.
17. Ibid., 38.
18. Ibid., 24.
19. Ibid., 17.
20. Kalidaha signifies various locales in mythology, e.g., in the Vaishnava tradition Krishna subdues Kaliya in the Yamuna river at Kalidaha.
21. Ibid., 29.
22. Ibid., 13.
23. Ibid., 22.
24. Alok Sarkar, "Jibanananda" (Jibanananda), *Dainik Kabita,* 20 Jyaistha 1373, 4.
25. Introduction to *Rupasi Bamla.* Unfortunately, Asokananda Das does not indicate the source of this quotation, thereby implying that it is included in the notebook itself, which is not the case.
26. Sanjay Bhattacharya, *Kabi Jibanananda Das* (Poet Jibanananda Das) (Calcutta: Bharabi, 1970), 49.
27. Poetry notebook #3, dated 1931, 16; Jibanananda Das collection, National Library of India.
28. Interview with Buddhadeva Bose.
29. Asru Kumar Sikdar writes in his article entitled "Caturtha dasak" (The fourth decade): "Sudhindranath's 'The Emancipation of Poetry' came out in 1930 [*sic*, 1931]. In that essay was heard throughout Bengal modern poetry's invocation—just as somewhat earlier, in the English language, it was heard in Eliot's 'Tradition and the Individual Talent.' " Alokeranjan Dasgupta and Debiprasad Banerjee, eds., *Adhunik kabitar itihas* (A history of modern poetry) (Calcutta: Vak-Sahitya, 1965), 80.
30. Sudhindranath Datta, *The World of Twilight,* trans. Edward C. Dimock, Jr., and A. T. M. Anisuzzaman (Calcutta: Oxford University Press, 1970), 132, 137, 145–46.
31. Interviews with Bishnu Dey and Hiran Kumar Sanyal.
32. Interview with Bishnu Dey.
33. Hayat Mamud, *Mrityucinta Rabindranath o anyanya jatilata* (Thanatopsis, Rabindranath, and other complexities) (Dhaka: Sahityika, 1968), 41.
34. Courtesy of Kalyan Kumar Bose and Satyaprasanna Datta. As far as I know, Sudhin Datta never put in writing his thoughts on Jibanananda's poetry.
35. Sanjay Bhattacharya wrote: "Despite their literary differences, Sajani Kanta displayed a genuine helping friendship till the end, and I saw Sudhindranath Datta's dumbfounded expression those last two days. I'll always remember that because these were persons upon whom Jibanananda had never depended." *Kabi Jibanananda Das,* 147–48.
36. Interview with Buddhadeva Bose.
37. Interviews with Satyaprasanna Datta and Paramananda Saraswati Sadhu (formerly Mrinal Kanti Das).
38. Harindranath Datta, "Gharer manus: Kabi Sudhindranath Datta" (A part of the family: Poet Sudhindranath Datta), *Kabita Bita,* Baisakh [1377], unpaged.
39. *Dhusar pandulipi,* 50–52; appeared in *Paricay,* Magh 1338.
40. Asokananda Das, "Balyasmriti," 134.
41. Ibid.
42. *Sanibarer Cithi,* Magh 1338, 669–72.
43. *Sajne* (the Indian horseradish) alludes quite obviously here to Sajani Kanta.

44. Sandip Datta, ed., *Jibanananda prasangiki* (Concerning Jibanananda) (Calcutta: Hardya, 1984), 158–59.
45. Buddhadeva Bose, *Kaler putul* (The puppet of time) (Calcutta: New Age Publishers, 1959), 145.
46. *Dhusar pandulipi,* 80–81; appeared in *Kavita,* Aswin 1342. The version published in *Dhusar pandulipi* differs considerably from what appeared in *Kavita* and also differs slightly from the version that was subsequently included in his *Jibanananda Daser srestha kabita* (Jibanananda Das's best poems), 2d ed. (Calcutta: Bharabi, 1968).
47. Jibanananda Das, *Kabitar katha* (On poetry), 2d ed. (Calcutta: Signet Press, 1963), 9.
48. Criticism here is directed toward T. S. Eliot and his "Tradition and the Individual Talent."
49. "On Poetry," in Buddhadeva Bose, ed., *An Anthology of Bengali Writing* (Bombay, Madras, Calcutta: Macmillan Company of India, 1971), 99–100.
50. Courtesy of Kiran Sankar Sengupta.
51. "On Poetry," in Buddhadeva Bose, *An Anthology of Bengali Writing,* 103–4.
52. Coincidentally, Kankabati, as the traditional folk-tale maiden, had been mentioned in passing in the initial section of Jasimuddin's modern narrative, *Sojan badiyar ghat* (Gipsy wharf), composed in folk meters and published two years earlier in 1933. In 1937, Buddhadeva Bose brought out a volume of poetry called *Kankabati,* containing a poem of the same name; Jibanananda reviewed Buddhadeva's book in *Kavita,* Paus 1344. (Buddhadeva's eldest granddaughter, herself a writer today, carries the name Kankabati.) Toward the end of the previous century, Trailokyanath Mukherjee had published a full-length book entitled *Kankabati* (1892) after the heroine, a little girl who, in the delirium of a fever, proceeds to some fanciful world.
53. We have Rabindranath's brief reply of December 1915 to Jibanananda and a December 1930 letter by Jibanananda to Rabindranath which, though it does not refer directly to any book of his, may have been part of an exchange of letters in connection with *Jhara palak*; see Abdul Mannan Syed, *Suddhatama kabi,* 250–52.
54. Rabindranath's letter to Buddhadeva was published in its entirety in the second issue of *Kavita,* Paus 1342.
55. *Kavita,* Caitra 1343, unpaged.
56. Reprinted in *Kavita,* Paus 1361, 152.
57. Nilratan Sen, "Chandakusali" (The metricist), in *Jibanananda smriti* (Remembering Jibanananda), ed. Deb Kumar Bose (Calcutta: Karuna Prakasani, 1971), 25.
58. *Dhusar pandulipi,* 79.
59. *Dhusar pandulipi,* 99.
60. Asokananda Das, introduction to *Dhusar pandulipi.*
61. *Dhusar pandulipi,* 101; appeared in *Kavita,* Aswin 1343. The poem was titled "River" (*nadi*) in *Kavita,* and "Rivers" (*nadira*) in *Dhusar pandulipi.* The manuscript is part of the same notebook in which "Vultures" is found, dated 1931–32.
62. Jibanananda Das, "Bengali Poetry Today," *Statesman* (Calcutta), 6 November 1949, 11, Sunday section.
63. Buddhadeva Bose, *Kaler putul,* 32.
64. Ibid., 27.

65. Ibid., 29.
66. Ibid., 31.
67. Ibid., 32, 33.
68. Review of *Dhusar pandulipi* by Girijapati Bhattacharya in *Paricay,* Baisakh 1344, 400.
69. Courtesy of Buddhadeva Bose.
70. Cited in Alokeranjan Dasgupta, "Response to Modernism," a reprint from *Modernity and Contemporary Indian Literature* (Simla: Transactions of the Indian Institute of Advanced Study, 1968), 9–10.
71. *Banalata Sen,* 9; appeared in *Kavita,* Paus 1342.
72. Dipti Tripathi, *Adhunik Bamla kabyaparicay,* 185.
73. "... *mukhe tar pakhir nirer mata aswas o asrayer,*" "Sudhir Kumar," in *Smriti-tarpan,* 136.
74. *Jibanananda Daser srestha kabita,* 65; appeared in *Kavita,* Aswin 1343.
75. *Banalata Sen,* 39.
76. *Rupasi Bamla,* 58.
77. *Banalata Sen,* 9; appeared in *Kavita,* Caitra 1342.
78. Rabindranath Tagore, *Rabindra-racanabali* (The collected works of Rabindranath) (reprint; Calcutta: Visvabharati, 1965), 16: 5.
79. The article, according to the editors of *Rabindra-racanabali,* was retitled "Kabya o chanda" (Poetry and meter) and published in his book *Sahityer swarupa* (The essence of literature) (1943); see *Rabindra-racanabali* (The collected works of Rabindranath) (Calcutta: Visvabharati, 1965), 27: 266–68, 614.
80. Sanjay Bhattacharya, "Amar kabita" (My poems), *Purvasa,* Asarh 1376, 262.
81. Ibid., 263; letter dated Sravan 21 [1344], addressed to Sanjay Bhattacharya.
82. *Banalata Sen,* 19–20.
83. *Rupasi Bamla,* 55.
84. *Banalata Sen,* 21–22.
85. *Caturanga,* Magh 1362.
86. *Banalata Sen,* 15. Two poems entitled "Grass" were published, both in *Kavita*—in December 1935 and in September 1941. The one cited here appeared in 1935.
87. *Banalata Sen,* 18; appeared in *Kavita,* Asarh 1343.
88. The four types of women are described in the Sanskrit text *The Koka Shastra* (*koka sastra*), trans. Alex Comfort (London: George Allen and Unwin, 1964), 103ff.
89. *Rupasi Bamla,* 47.
90. *Banalata Sen,* 16; appeared in *Kavita,* Caitra 1342.
91. Resemblances between "O Hawk" and W. B. Yeats's "He Reproves the Curlew," as Buddhadeva Bose pointed out, are too close to be coincidental: "O curlew, cry no more in the air, /Or only to the water in the West." Besides the specific correspondences of these two poems by Yeats and Jibanananda, Buddhadeva had called attention to influences, in general, upon Jibanananda from Shelley, Keats, the Pre-Raphaelites, and Yeats. More recently, Abdul Mannan Syed has shown us, in convincing fashion, parallel passages in Jibanananda, on the one hand, and Edgar Allan Poe, Shelley, Keats, Yeats, and Dylan Thomas, on the other—the greatest debt, as Abdul Mannan Syed sees it, is to Yeats. *Suddhatama kabi,* 78–87.
92. *Rupasi Bamla,* 30, 35, 43.
93. Ibid., 32.
94. Jibanananda Das, *Mahaprithibi* (The world at large), ed. Manabendra Banerjee (Calcutta: Signet Press, 1969), 26–29.
95. Jibanananda uses both the English word "morgue" and the term "*las kata*

ghar" ("corpse-cutting room"); the expressions are synonymous, at least in this particular poem.

96. Asokananda Das, "Balyasmriti," 137.
97. Dipti Tripathi has expressed essentially the same idea, though not linking new life with Sasthi; *Adhunik Bamla kabyaparicay,* 181.
98. *Rupasi Bamla,* 24.
99. *The Bhagavad Gita,* trans. and commentary by Swami Chidbhavananda (Tirupparaitturai: Sri Ramakrishna Tapovanam, 1972), 749.
100. *Mahaprithibi,* 25; appeared in *Kavita,* Aswin 1343.
101. "Sudhir Kumar," in *Smriti-tarpan,* 126–27.
102. Dipti Tripathi, *Adhunik Bamla kabyaparicay,* 182.
103. Rabindranath Samanta, *Jibanananda pratibha,* 45.
104. *Dhusar pandulipi,* 89–90.
105. *Rupasi Bamla,* 69–70. The printed version and the manuscript version differ in several places; I have followed the manuscript version. See Debesh Ray, *Rupasi Bamla: Prakasita-aprakasita pandulipi o pathantar samskaran,* 177–79.
106. Ibid., 49.
107. Edward C. Dimock, Jr., examines the relationship between life and death in this poem, but from a different perspective, in his "The Poet as Mouse and Owl: Reflections on a Poem by Jibanananda Das," *Journal of Asian Studies* 33, no. 4 (August 1974): 603–10.

Chapter 4. The War Years: Prelude and Aftermath

1. Gene D. Overstreet and Marshall Windmiller, *Communism in India* (Berkeley and Los Angeles: University of California Press, 1959), 157.
2. For an excellent study of the AIPWA, see Carlo Coppola, "Urdu Poetry, 1935–1970: The Progressive Episode" (Ph.D. diss., University of Chicago, 1975).
3. *Tribune* (Lahore), 15 April 1936, 13.
4. Pranabendu Dasgupta, "Pancam dasak" (The forties), in *Adhunik kabitar itihas,* ed. Dasgupta and Banerjee, 108.
5. Abu Sayeed Ayyub, "Tendencies in Modern Bengali Poetry," in *Longmans Miscellany, 1943* (Calcutta: Longmans, Green & Co., 1943), 46.
6. Both Sanjay and Satyaprasanna hailed from Comilla in the eastern part of Bengal, now in Bangladesh, from where they began publishing *Purvasa.* The name remained even after the two men moved to Calcutta, bringing their journal with them.
7. Sanjay's opinion was published posthumously in June 1969; Buddhadeva expressed to me his surprise at learning that his fellow poet had held such a notion.
8. Interview with Satyaprasanna Datta.
9. Interview with Satyaprasanna Datta.
10. *Purvasa,* Asarh 1376, 267–68.
11. Reprinted in *Purvasa,* Asarh 1376, 267.
12. *Purvasa,* Asarh 1376, 165 [*sic,* 265].
13. Sanjay Bhattacharya, *Kabi Jibanananda Das,* 73.
14. *Nirukta,* Aswin 1347.
15. Maitreyi, wife of an ancient sage, was a seeker after immortality; Nagarjuna, Buddhist teacher, a Bodhisattwa and main theorist of the Mahayana school; Kautilya, minister of Candragupta Maurya and reputed author of the *Arthasastra,* treatise on mundane success and how to achieve it.
16. *Nirukta,* Aswin 1347.

17. Sanjay Bhattacharya, *Adhunik kabitar bhumika* (An introduction to modern poetry), 2d ed. (Calcutta: Purvasa Publications, 1966), 42.

18. Narendralal Ganguly would disagree with this statement. He considered himself one of Jibanananda's closest friends—though he admitted no one seemed ever to get very close to Jibanananda.

19. Once Buddhadeva Bose had corrected the misspelling of Jibanananda's name, *Sanibarer Cithi* invariably would print Jibanananda's name correctly spelled adding in parentheses (not Jibananda).

20. Heramba Chakravarty, "Jibananandake yeman dekhechi" (Jibanananda as I saw him), *Girls' College Magazine, Howrah,* 1955, 17.

21. The two men had lived in the same dormitory during their college days. Sajani Kanta attended Ramesh Sen's wedding in Barisal; see Sajani Kanta Das, *Atmasmriti,* 1: 128.

22. *Saptak,* [Paus 1347]. Published in Barisal, *Saptak* came out in the late 1930s and lasted (estimates by those who edited it vary) for about ten years.

23. Jibanananda Das, *Satati tarar timir* (Darkness of seven stars) (Calcutta: Bharabi, 1969), 14–15; appeared in *Paricay,* Magh 1345–Asarh 1346.

24. Sunil Ganguly, in *Kavita-Paricay,* no. 3, n.d., unpaged.

25. Ibid.

26. Naresh Guha, in *Kavita-Paricay,* no. 4, 15.

27. Manabendra Banerjee, in *Kavita-Paricay,* nos. 5 and 6, 22.

28. Naresh Guha, in *Kavita-Paricay,* no. 4, 16.

29. Arun Kumar Sarkar, in *Kavita-Paricay,* nos. 5 and 6, 19.

30. Manabendra Banerjee, in *Kavita-Paricay,* nos. 5 and 6, 21.

31. Ibid., 19–20.

32. Sanjay Bhattacharya, *Kabi Jibanananda Das,* 115–26.

33. Ibid., 116 and 119.

34. Courtesy of Kalyan Kumar Bose, who is of the opinion that this letter was probably written during the *Nirukta* period, 1940–43.

35. Interview with Abu Sayeed Ayyub.

36. Sanjay Bhattacharya, *Adhunik kabitar bhumika,* 44–45. The quotation is from a letter written to Sanjay by Jibanananda; the article itself first appeared in *Nirukta,* Asarh 1350.

37. Ambuj Bose, *Ekati naksatra ase,* 212.

38. The smallest Indian coin.

39. *Nirukta,* Paus 1347; *Jibanananda Daser srestha kabita,* 63. Ahiritola, Badur Bagan, and Pathuria Ghata are all sections of Calcutta; Harrison Road, since renamed Mahatma Gandhi Road, is also a part of that city.

40. Subrata Ganguly discusses the advent of Calcutta into Jibanananda's compositions; see S. Ganguly, "Kabitay Kalakata: Jibanananda" (Calcutta in poetry: Jibanananda), *Kali-o-Kalam,* Magh 1379, 893–901.

41. *Nirukta,* Paus 1347.

42. *Satati tarar timir,* 25–26; appeared in *Kavita,* Paus 1347.

43. "Bengali Poetry Today," *Statesman* (Calcutta), 6 November 1949.

44. "Rabindranath o adhunik Bamla kabita" (Rabindranath and modern Bengali poetry), in *Kabitar katha,* 19.

45. The manuscript appears in one of his notebooks dated 1931–32 and has been published recently in Debesh Ray, *Jibanananda samagra,* 436–38.

46. Jibanananda Das, *Jibanananda Daser kabya sambhar* (Jibanananda Das's collected poetry), ed. Ranesh Dasgupta, 2d ed. (Dhaka: Khan Brothers and Co., 1970), 332; appeared in *Usha,* Jyaistha 1361.

47. See Ananda K. Coomaraswamy, *The Transformation of Nature in Art* (New York: Dover Publications, 1956; Harvard University Press, 1934), 178; and Heinrich Zimmer, *Myths and Symbols in Indian Art and Civilization,* ed. Joseph Campbell (New York and Evanston: Harper Torchbooks; Harper & Row, 1962), 152.

48. Rabindranath Tagore, *Gitanjali (Song Offerings): A Collection of Prose Translations Made by the Author from the Original Bengali,* with an introduction by W. B. Yeats (New York: Macmillan Publishing Co., 1913; paperback ed., 1971), 23 (song #1).

49. Rabindranath Tagore, *Personality: Lectures Delivered in America* (Calcutta, Bombay, Madras, London: Macmillan and Co., 1917; reprint, 1970), 54–55.

50. "On Poetry," in *An Anthology of Bengali Writing,* ed. Buddhadeva Bose, 102.

51. "Rabindranath o adhunik Bamla kabita," in *Kabitar katha,* 22–23.

52. *Nirukta,* Aswin 1348.

53. The possessive case ending on "world" was changed to an objective case ending in the version printed in *Mahaprithibi.*

54. *Mahaprithibi,* 72; appeared in *Kavita,* Aswin 1348.

55. *Jayasri,* Aswin 1348.

56. Allen Ginsberg, *Indian Journals: March 1962–May 1963* (San Francisco: Dave Haselwood Books & City Lights Books, 1970), 118–19.

57. *Satati tarar timir,* 33–35; appeared in *Nirukta,* Asarh 1349.

58. Satyajit Ray's film *Distant Thunder* presents a dramatization of the famine's effect in the West Bengal countryside—based on Bibhuti Bhusan Banerjee's novel *Asani sanket* (The hint of thunder); Tarasankar Banerjee's novel *Manwantar* (Epoch's end), trans. Hirendranath Mukherjee (Calcutta: Mitralaya, 1945) is set in Calcutta during that same period.

59. Then, the monetary system consisted of the rupee, the anna coin (16 annas to the rupee), and the pice coin (4 pice to the anna or 64 pice to the rupee). The present system has eliminated the anna altogether and, adopting a decimal system, has 100 pice (paisa) to the rupee.

60. *Satati tarar timir,* 40.

61. *Kavi-o-Kavita,* Mahalaya 1376.

62. Lila Ray, *A Challenging Decade: Bengali Literature in the Forties* (Calcutta: D.M. Library, 1953), 16.

63. Hiren Mukherjee, "Bengal Progressive Writers Getting Together for the People," in *Anti-Fascist Traditions of Bengal* (Calcutta: Indo-GDR Friendship Society, 1969), 67.

64. Pramatha Chaudhuri and Tarasankar Banerjee penned a denunciation of the slaying and a tribute to the young author; see Arun Bose and Khoka Rai, *Inside Bengal 1941–1944: Forward Bloc and Its Allies versus Communist Party* (Bombay: People's Publishing House, 1945), 56.

65. Lila Ray, *A Challenging Decade,* 16.

66. *Pratirodh,* Autumn 1942. Courtesy of Saralananda Sen.

67. What I translate as "something" is in Bengali *bacaknabi;* to date, no Bengali with whom I've consulted has understood the meaning of this word. Ranesh Dasgupta, in his edited collection, has made it *bacaklabi,* likewise a word no one understands.

68. *Mahaprithibi,* 50–54; appeared in *Nirukta,* Aswin 1349.

69. Vibhisana, brother of Raksasa king Ravana, advised his brother to return Sita to her rightful husband, Rama; Ravana refused and was defeated by Rama and

the monkey army in pitched battle. Nrisimha, the half man (*nri*) and half lion (*simha*) incarnation of Vishnu, thwarted the boon granted the impious Daitya, Hiranyakasipu, and tore him limb from limb.

70. *Satati tarar timir,* 36–39; appeared in *Kavita,* Kartik 1349.

71. *Nutan Lekha,* Kartik 1349. Courtesy of Sunil Ganguly of Barisal. Jibanananda had in his possession in Barisal some six issues of this journal. *Nutan Lekha* was published by Nihar Ranjan Raha from Calcutta. The quarterly began September 1941. Sanjay Bhattacharya and his brother Ajay published there, as did Buddhadeva Bose and Amiya Chakravarty.

72. Recounted in the *Mahabharata*; see J. A. B. van Buitenen, trans. and ed., *The Mahabharata: Book I: The Book of the Beginning* (Chicago: University of Chicago Press, 1973), 216.

73. In Hindu cosmology "the cosmos passes through cycles within cycles for all eternity. The basic cycle is the *kalpa,* a 'day of Brahma,' or 4,320 million earthly years." Each *kalpa* contains fourteen *manwantaras*; each *manwantara,* seventy-one *mahayugas*; each *mahayuga,* four *yugas,* the *krita, treta, dwapara,* and *kali.* As the fourth *yuga* draws to a close, there is "confusion of classes, the overthrow of established standards, the cessation of all religious rites, and the rule of cruel and alien kings. Soon after this the world is destroyed by flood and fire." A. L. Basham, *The Wonder That Was India* (New York: Grove Press; Evergreen, 1959), 320–21.

74. The twelve were: "Banalata Sen," "Twenty Years After" (*kuri bachar pare*), "Night of Wind" (*haoyar rat*), "If I Were" (*ami yadi hatam*), "Grass" (*ghas*), "O Hawk" (*hay cil*), "Wild Ducks" (*buno hans*), "Sankhamala," "Naked Lonely Hand" (*nagna nirjan hat*), "The Hunt" (*sikar*), "Deer" (*harinera*), and "Cat" (*beral*).

75. *Caturanga,* Caitra 1950, 219–22.

76. Unlike Jibanananda, Subhas in his political poetry is frequently hortatory, urging his readers on to some sort of action. His "A Song for All the People" (*sakaler gan*) calls on his "comrades" and exhorts them to usher in the new age, to draw into the fold of true believers the confused Trishanku. (Subhas Mukherjee, *Subhas Mukhopadhyayer srestha kabita* [Subhas Mukherjee's best poems] [Calcutta: Bharabi, 1970], 14.) Trishanku, an ancient sage, with the aid of Viswamitra, gained access to heaven but was tossed out, head first. Viswamitra arrested his fall to earth, but Trishanku remains suspended halfway between heaven and earth—in the form of the Southern Cross. Trishanku, in other words, is someone in between, someone as yet uncommitted.

77. Dove (*ghughu*) in Bengali, when used to modify a person, connotes a sly or wily or harmful individual. To cause a dove to tread upon someone's homestead is an idiom that means to ruin or render homeless that person.

78. *Carak* puja, sometimes called the "hook-swinging" ceremony, is a festival for worshiping Shiva and occurs at the end of the Bengali calendar year (mid-April). The larger festival, of which *carak* puja is a part, is called *gajan. Bhadu* is a goddess. The rice flour sweets of January are the sweetmeat offerings in the *paus parwan* festivities, which occur at the end of the month of Paus, i.e., mid-January.

79. Ganesa, the elephant-headed son of Shiva, serves as scribe (his broken tusk he uses as a pen) when the sage Vyasa composes and dictates the epic *Mahabharata.*

80. Between the decline of Pathan power and the advent of the Moguls to Bengal (1575), local zemindars in the eastern part of that region exerted the power of quasi-autonomous petty rajahs. Though there were probably more than twelve such "Bhuiya princes," folk wisdom has it that there were indeed precisely twelve of these independent Bengali rulers.

81. Hot sand compared to the sun is an idiom that means the immediate problem surrounding us, though not as monumental as some more distant concerns, does affect us more. The sun may be hotter than the hot sand under bare feet, but the sand feels as though it hurts more.

82. *Desh,* 17 Baisakh 1350.

83. *Nirukta,* Asarh 1350, 153–65.

84. The article, along with essays on Premendra Mitra and Buddhadeva, was published as a monograph, in 1351 (1944–45) under the title *Tinajan adhunik kabi* (Three modern poets) (Calcutta: Purvasa) and included in a later book, *Adhunik kabitar bhumika.*

85. Courtesy of Bishnu Dey.

86. Published in *Kena likhi* (Why I write), January 1944. Jibanananda's essay was reprinted in *Anukta,* Magh–Caitra 1363; Gopal Chandra Ray, *Jibanananda,* 53–56.

87. *Anukta,* Magh–Caitra 1363.

88. "On Poetry," in *An Anthology of Bengali Writing,* ed. Buddhadeva Bose, 99–100.

89. Ibid., 100.

90. "Lekha, lekhaker dayitwa" (Responsibility of the writer and writing), *Anukta,* Magh–Caitra 1363.

91. Ibid.

92. The Bengali original was reprinted in *Dainik Kavita,* Sarat 1376; this translation is by Dipendu Chakravarty, published in *Poetry Bengal: Bishnu Dey Special Number,* ed. Samir Dasgupta, Santi Lahiri, Stephen N. Hay, and Paresh Banerjee (Calcutta, April 1970), 74–76.

93. "Matracetana" (A sense of proportion), in *Kabitar katha,* 27; first published in *Prabhati,* Paus 1351.

94. Courtesy of Satyaprasanna Datta. During the Durga puja holidays, presents are purchased and exchanged in many families. Book sales, as a result, increase during this season (September–October).

95. *Mahaprithibi,* 40; appeared in *Kavita,* Paus 1345.

96. I am indebted to Qazi Abdul Mannan, then Head of the Department of Bengali, the University of Rajshahi and Visiting Professor at the University of Chicago, for discussions concerning this poem and his valued insights on Jibanananda's poetry in general.

97. *Kavita,* Caitra 1351, 62.

98. *Mahaprithibi,* 21; appeared in *Kavita,* Asarh 1344.

99. Himani Banerjee, "Jibanananda Daser *Mahaprithibi*" (Jibanananda Das's *The world at large*), *Saraswat,* Jyaistha 1375, 11.

100. Ibid., 11, 16.

101. *Mahaprithibi,* 38–39; appeared in *Caturanga,* Aswin 1345.

102. Letter dated 2 July 1946, printed in *Mayukh,* Paus–Jyaistha 1361–62, 229–30.

103. Asokananda Das was posted in or near Calcutta (Dum-Dum, Barrackpur, and Alipur) during 1942–46; interview with A. Das. Following their deaths, Jibanananda composed a short piece on each of his parents which he read out at their *sraddha* ceremonies. The two compositions were published after Jibanananda's own death, under the one title of "Amar ma baba" (My parents), in *Uttarsuri,* Paus–Falgun 1361, 4–13. Asokananda Das quotes portions of these two pieces in his article "Amar dada Jibanananda Das" (My elder brother Jibanananda Das), in *Girls' College Magazine, Howrah,* 1955, 3–14. Sumita

Chakravarty, in her previously cited article, "Kusumakumari Das—'sei chele'r ma" (Kusum Kumari—'that boy's' mother), gives a good, brief account of Jibanananda's mother's life and includes entries from Kusum Kumari's diary written in the 1940s; *Desh,* 11 Asarh 1389, 13–14.

104. Letter dated 31.10.42, printed in *Mayukh,* Paus–Jyaistha 1361–62, 233; reprinted in Gopal Chandra Ray, *Jibanananda,* vol. 1 (Calcutta: Sahitya Sadan, 1971). Nalini Das was to become principal of Bethune College, Calcutta.

105. Ibid., 227.

106. Buddhadeva Bose gave him this epithet.

107. Heramba Chakravarty, "Jibananandake yeman dekhechi," 17–19.

108. Acintya Kumar Sengupta, "Antaranga Jibanananda" (My close friend Jibanananda), *Mayukh,* Paus–Jyaistha 1361–62, 118.

109. I would like to thank the faculty and staff there who graciously assisted me during my brief return visit to Barisal in 1970.

110. Interview with Asokananda Das.

111. Interview with Nirendranath Chakravarty, who worked for the *Swaraj.* The paper did not actually come out until the following year.

112. Letter dated 2 July 1946, printed in *Mayukh,* Paus–Jyaistha 1361, 226.

113. For instance, the second section of one of his notebooks is labeled "songs; Calcutta, August–September, 1946" and contains fourteen "songs."

114. Heramba Chakravarty departed in October of that year. Narendralal Ganguly left B.M. College in 1949 for Munshigunge College, Dhaka, and then from there for West Bengal in 1950. Ramesh Chandra Sen also emigrated in 1950, a year that saw widespread Hindu-Muslim violence.

115. Interview with Labanya Das.

116. According to his brother, Jibanananda at least officially maintained his ties with B.M. College until 1948, though he never resumed his teaching chores there again.

117. A person or two people allowed themselves to be hooked under the shoulder blades, suspended, and then spun around—their blood dripping on the ground meant to bring fertility to the land.

118. Yasin, Hanif, Mahammad, Makbul, Karim, and Aziz are Muslim names; Gagan, Bipin, and Sasi are Hindu.

119. The version of this poem included in *Jibanananda Daser srestha kabita,* 135–39, ends here; the poem as printed in *Purvasa,* Kartik 1355, had the additional line.

Chapter 5. Another Fling at Fiction

1. Interview with Ataur Rahman. The paper, never deposited in an archive, is not now available.

2. Two sources, Amiya Kumar Ganguly and Nirendranath Chakravarty (see Nirendranath Chakravarty, "Sanjayada" [Sanjay], *Desh,* 3 Falgun 1375, 295–96) indicated that Sanjay was the moving force behind the Jibanananda appointment. Ataur Rahman stated that Satyaprasanna Datta, Sanjay's colleague, enticed Jibanananda to come to Calcutta and take the *Swaraj* job. According to Ataur Rahman, the governing board questioned the wisdom of Satyaprasanna's proposal to hire Jibanananda, but in the end consented.

3. Interview with Nirendranath Chakravarty.

4. Jagdish Saran Sharma, *India since the Advent of the British, a Descriptive*

Chronology from 1600 to Oct. 2, 1969 (Delhi: A. Chand and Co., 1970), 302-3.

5. Nirendranath Chakravarty, "Sanjayada," 295-96.

6. Interview with Narayan Ganguly. The student-teacher relationship, which involves absolute respect for the teacher, persists throughout life. Even if the former student were to become a high-ranking official in the government, he would still maintain the attitude of deference toward his former teacher whenever the two might chance to meet.

7. Interview with Nirendranath Chakravarty. The article, signed with his wife's name, "Susama Ray," appeared 4 Falgun 1353 (February 1947).

8. The manuscript was included in a letter dated 1 August 1954. For some reason, the poem never saw print.

9. "Dalliance" (*bilas*), in *Jibanananda Daser galpa,* ed. Sukumar Ghosh and Subinay Mustaphi, 65.

10. Courtesy of Manjusri Das. Aunt (*masi*) Chutu, Uncle (*mesomasay*), and Srijay are of the N. K. Ghosh family. Auntie (*pisimani*) is the poet's younger sister, Sucarita Das; Aunt (*pisi*) Nani is not technically a relative but simply Sucarita Das's good friend from Tamluk.

11. The notebook in which this appears contains three sections dated November 1951, June 1952, and 24 September 1952. The date "7.7" I assume translates into 7 July 1952, because of the presence of this note in a notebook dated that year. Jibanananda must have copied down a note written by the landlord. I examined some records at the Rent Control court but was unable to locate any case involving Jibanananda. I thank the Rent Control court for showing me those records. According to Asokananda Das, there was no case in 1952. The landlord, when I called on him, did not care to discuss the matter.

12. Interview with Labanya Das.

13. Interview with Ramesh Chandra Sen.

14. Interview with Major H. K. Majumdar.

15. Letter dated 2 July 1946, printed in *Mayukh,* Paus-Jyaistha 1361-62, 227-28.

16. Asokananda Das states categorically in a preface to *Malyaban* that his brother wrote it during the month of June 1948, while unemployed. That date probably appears on the notebook in which Jibanananda composed or copied his novel. Dates on Jibanananda's notebooks (unless two dates appear) most likely indicate only starting points or dates of completion. Asokananda, moreover, indicates that there are but three novels. (This assertion appears in the introductory material to the serialized publication of the third novel, in the journal *Siladitya* [1981-82], and is cited by Debesh Ray, editor and publisher of the first of several planned volumes containing Jibanananda's collected works.) There does seem to be yet another novel, possibly still inchoate. Debesh Ray, likewise, is of the opinion that, contrary to the brother's statement, one more of Jibanananda's novels remains to be published. Debesh Ray, *Jibanananda samagra,* 457.

17. None of his novels should be confused with the "autobiography" which Jibanananda told certain persons he would write and for which he kept a notebook of information (diary). To date, no one but members of the Das family has been allowed to read that diary.

18. Cited in Debesh Ray, *Jibanananda samagra,* 456.

19. Courtesy of Satyaprasanna Datta, who noted that this same letter had been printed in an article by Sanjay entitled "Purbbasar [purbacaler?] pane takai" (Gazing eastward), *Purvasa,* Falgun 1372.

20. Interview with Sunil Ganguly. According to Sunil, the conversation took place a year or so before Jibanananda's death.

21. Interview with Protiva Bose. As she recalled, Jibanananda came by sometime in the early 1950s. Buddhadeva was not there at the time. Since Buddhadeva spent the academic year 1953-54 teaching in the United States, it was probably in 1953 or early 1954 that this conversation took place.
22. Gopal Chandra Ray, *Jibananda,* 88.
23. Jibanananda Das, *Malyaban* (Calcutta: New Script, [1973]), 100-101.
24. Ibid., 124-26.
25. Ibid., 164-65.
26. Jibanananda Das, *Sutirtha* (Calcutta: Bengal Publishers, 1977), 9-11.
27. Ibid., 243-44.
28. Ibid., 273-74.
29. Ibid., 30.
30. Ibid., 28.
31. Ibid., 155.
32. Generally speaking, Bengali names reveal the religion of the bearer. Most Bengali Muslims will have Arabic names. Nearly all Bengali Hindus will have a Sanskritic name. Unaccounted for in this overgeneralized scheme are those more liberal Muslims in Bangladesh who have abjured the naming conventions and opted to give their children "Bengali," not Arabic names. "Bengali" names tend to be Sanskritic, viewed by the Pakistani government in 1971 as evidence that Bengali Muslims had become religiously corrupt and "Hinduized." This issue of names is nicely illustrated in the disturbingly brutal novel *Raiphel roti aurat* (Rifles, bread, and women), by Anwar Pasha (who died at the hands of the Pakistani army in 1971), whose protagonist, Sudipta Chaudhuri, is a bona fide Bengali Muslim with a "Bengali" first name ("sudipta" means "lustrous, radiant" in Sanskrit and Bengali).
33. Ibid., 148.
34. Ibid., 235.
35. Ibid., 274.
36. *Banalata Sen,* 17.
37. *Banalata Sen,* 14.
38. Ibid., 146-49.
39. *Jalpaihati,* in *Jibanananda samagra,* ed. Debesh Ray, 18.
40. Ibid., 17.
41. Ibid., 286-87.
42. *Sutirtha,* 174.
43. Such low rents resulted from the war. After the Japanese bombed Calcutta several times at the end of 1942—never to bomb it again, and inflicting greater psychological than physical damage—many Calcutta residents evacuated their city for the sanctuary of the countryside. Calcutta houses and apartments went begging for tenants, which perforce drove down rents. Those who rented then and maintained their place of residence continued to pay rents far under postwar fair prices.
44. This marijuana-like intoxicant is not normally used by any but certain holy men, and then theoretically only to obtain an ecstatic state.
45. *Jalpaihati,* 274-75.
46. Analogously but not equivalently, one hears English speakers say with feigned chagrin, "Excuse my French," before uttering some utterly English— usually Anglo-Saxon—profanity. Such words are, of course, not French at all. By calling them French, we merely shift the onus of guilt away from us and our language. The Bengali case is slightly different. Bengali swear words are almost exclusively borrowed from Hindi. (*Mairi,* a form of "Mary," and used as an

expletive, comes from English.) However, such borrowed words are now very much a part of the Bengali language, just as are the many "decent" words borrowed from Hindi, English, Sanskrit, Persian, and Portuguese.

47. Jibanananda had used the same expletive, applied to the person instead of the action, a couple of years earlier, if the estimated dating of his short story "Dalliance" is correct (placed in 1946 by Sunil Kumar Nandy, editor of *Anukta*; see *Anukta,* Sravan–Aswin 1377, 139). "... you have to pay Dr. Sen a visit—Dr. T. B. Sen. T. B. stands for—how should I say it—the Typical Bastard." *Jibanananda Daser galpa,* 78. The word I translate here as "bastard" is in the Bengali *bancot* ("sister-fucker").

48. *Jalpaihati,* 96.
49. Ibid., 101–2.
50. Ibid., 103.
51. Judging from names alone, it appears from the *Report on Braja Mohan College, Barisal, inspected March 25, 1936, for 1935–36* (probably a part of the *University of Calcutta, Minutes of the Syndicate for the year 1935–36,* though the *Report* I examined was bound as a separate publication) that when Jibanananda joined the B.M. College faculty in 1935, only the three members of the Arabic and Persian Department were Muslims, out of a faculty of forty-two.
52. Ibid., 301.
53. Ibid., 234–35.
54. Ibid., 379–80.
55. Ibid., 121–22.
56. Ibid., 259–60.
57. Ibid., 262.
58. Ibid., 278–81.
59. Ibid., 292.
60. Ibid., 295–96.
61. Ibid., 299.

Chapter 6. The Poetry of Politics

1. Letter dated 2 July 1946, printed in *Mayukh,* Paus–Jyaistha 1361–62, 226.
2. One of the Guptas, Dilip Kumar Gupta, established another company, Signet Press, which became the premier publishing house during the 1940s and 1950s. According to Ataur Rahman, D. K. Gupta allowed him to use the name of Gupta, Rahman and Gupta for publishing Jibanananda's book.
3. The two journals *Caturanga* (Humayun Kabir, nominal editor; Ataur Rahman, actual managing editor) and *Purvasa* (Sanjay Bhattacharya editor; Satyaprasanna Datta, publisher and printer) had offices in the same building. Satyaprasanna and Ataur Rahman would have been in constant contact with each other at this time.
4. Letter dated 3 Paus 1337 (December 1930), printed in *Mayukh,* Paus–Jyaistha 1361–62, 216–17.
5. Interview with Nirendranath Chakravarty.
6. *Satati tarar timir,* 9; appeared in *Kavita,* Aswin 1344, originally entitled "O Haimantika" (*o haimantika*).
7. *Satati tarar timir,* 13; appeared in *Kavita,* Paus 1345.
8. A third poem by the same name—but of a very different tone—appeared earlier in *Kallol,* Sravan 1333, and was included in *Jhara palak.*
9. *Satati tarar timir,* 24; appeared in *Paricay,* Falgun 1346. The translation was

published in *Green and Gold,* Humayun Kabir, ed., Tarasankar Banerjee and Premendra Mitra, assoc. eds. (Bombay: Asia Publishing House, 1957), later by New Directions, and now by Greenwood Publishers, Conn. (1970). This same poem appeared in *Poetry,* London and New York, and was also included in *Banalata Sen* (Calcutta: Writers Workshop, 1962). Jibanananda has taken several liberties in his translation, including substituting Byzantium for the original's Gethsemane.

10. *Satati tarar timir,* 62–63; appeared in *Baisakhi,* Baisakh 1351.
11. "The Insignificant Man" (*lokasamanya*), in *Satati tarar timir,* 66.
12. Haraprasad Mitra has written on *Satati tarar timir*'s (Omnipresent darkness—and its accompanying light) in "Jibananander alo—andhakar" (Jibanananda's light and darkness), *Kali-o-Kalam,* Aswin 1380, 125–32.
13. Interview with Qazi Abdul Mannan.
14. Letter dated 2 July 1946, printed in *Mayukh,* Paus–Jyaistha 1361–62, 230.
15. *Kavita,* Aswin–Paus 1356, 29–33.
16. *Kavita,* Caitra 1356, 60.
17. Courtesy of Buddhadeva Bose.
18. *Kavita,* June 1953, 237–39.
19. Tarasankar Banerjee, *Amar sahitya jiban* (My literary life), vol. 2 (Calcutta: Sundar Prakasan, 1962), 140.
20. Interview with Abu Sayeed Ayyub; see also Coppola, "Urdu Poetry, 1935–1970: The Progressive Episode," 273–74, 361, 370.
21. Overstreet and Windmiller, *Communism in India,* 272.
22. Ibid., 277.
23. Of the four issues (nos. 1, 2, 5, 7) in the National Library, the second number had been published by the National Book Agency, 12 Bankim Chatterjee St., Calcutta 12; an advertisement for *Paricay,* appearing in this issue, listed the same address for that magazine. The fifth and seventh issues were published by New Publishers, 6 Bankim Chatterjee St. The same address is listed in an advertisement for *Paricay,* appearing in the seventh number.
24. Dates written by hand appear on some of the copies of *Marksbadi* held in the National Library. It is unclear whether these reflect publication dates or dates of collection.
25. *Marksbadi,* no. 1, 76–77.
26. Ibid., 79.
27. Tarasankar's *Hansuli Banker upakatha* (The tale of Hansuli Bend) and Manik's *Putul nacer itikatha* (The puppet's tale) was said to purvey that negative, hopeless attitude.
28. *Marksbadi,* no. 1, 80; here Tarasankar's *Kalindi* (Kalindi) and *Manwantar* (Epoch's end) are cited.
29. Ibid., 93.
30. Ibid., 97.
31. Ibid., 137–47.
32. Chanchal Chatterjee, not Bishnu Dey, edited *Sahitya Patra.* However, Bishnu Dey worked closely with the magazine. It was in the second issue of *Sahitya Patra* (Kartik 1355) that Jibanananda's poem "This Consciousness" (*ei cetana*) appeared. A squabble over misspellings in the printed copy of this poem destroyed, by Bishnu Dey's own admission, what had been a longtime friendship between Jibanananda and Bishnu Dey.
33. Interview with Bishnu Dey.
34. Buddhadeva Bose, *An Acre of Green Grass* (Calcutta: Orient Longmans, 1948), 13, 101, 103.

35. Ibid., 57.
36. *Marksbadi,* no. 2, 165–70.
37. Interview with Abu Sayeed Ayyub.
38. *Marksbadi,* no. 5, 125–72.
39. Ibid., 125.
40. Ibid., 129. He cites Kaliprasanna's *Hutom pyancar naksa* (Mr. Owl's sketch book), a series of rather satirical sketches on various aspects of midnineteenth-century Bengali society, and Dinabandhu's *Nil darpan* (Mirror of indigo), a depiction of the inhumane treatment of Indian cultivators by the British planters and the local legal system during the same period.
41. *Marksbadi,* no. 5, 132.
42. Ibid.
43. Ayyub referred to Sajani Kanta as an anticommunist; Amlan Datta, an economist who was also part of the Contemporary Writers' Association, suggested that the Sani Circle was politically partial to Congress. Neither Ayyub nor Amlan Datta indicated that the Sani Circle held to a well-defined political line.
44. Interview with Abu Sayeed Ayyub.
45. The editors' names appeared in the above order for the first and second issues. Ayyub recalled that Jibanananda was displeased at being second on the list. From the third issue onward, the order became: Jibanananda Das, Abu Sayeed Ayyub, Narendranath Mitra.
46. Interview with Anandagopal Sengupta.
47. A magazine entitled *Samakalin,* edited by Anandagopal Sengupta, was begun in April 1953; it had no connection with the Contemporary Writers' Association.
48. Interview with Amlan Datta.
49. Interview with Abu Sayeed Ayyub.
50. Jibanananda Das, "Bengali Poetry Today," *Statesman* (Calcutta), 6 November 1949, 11, Sunday section.
51. Interview with Anandagopal Sengupta.
52. *Janata* (Bombay), 9 July 1950, 20.
53. Interview with Anandagopal Sengupta. Ayyub noted that Jibanananda never attended the meetings at his (Ayyub's) place and did little work on the magazine even though he was nominally an editor.
54. Courtesy of Anandagopal Sengupta. The letter, unfortunately, is undated.
55. According to Anandagopal Sengupta, the article was also published in the *Satyayug,* a daily newspaper similar to the *Swaraj.* Many of the same persons who had worked at the *Swaraj* when Jibanananda was there were in 1950 working for the *Satyayug.* Satyendranath Majumdar, the editor of the *Swaraj* in 1947, edited the *Satyayug.* Jibanananda's poem "The World Today" (*prithibi aj*) appeared in the 1950 puja issue of *Satyayug,* which was edited by Nirendranath Chakravarty, Gaur Kisor Ghosh, and Umaranjan Chakravarty. The first two had worked at the *Swaraj* and were also connected with *Dwandwa*; Niren served as the poetry section editor of *Dwandwa.*
56. *Dwandwa,* Asarh 1375, 1ff.
57. Ibid.
58. As far as I know, only one other contribution by Jibanananda might possibly have been published in *Dwandwa*: a poem entitled "On the Last Night of the Month of Magh" (*maghasamkrantir rate*). The bibliography published in *Mayukh* (Paus–Jyaistha 1361–62) lists this title and suggests that the poem may have appeared in *Dwandwa;* no date of publication is given in that bibliography. I have seen only the first six issues of *Dwandwa* and so am unable to confirm the *Mayukh* bibliographic

entry. This poem was posthumously published in two volumes of Jibanananda's poetry, in *Bela abela kalabela* (Time, untime and time apart) (Calcutta: New Script, 1961) and in the later editions of *Jibanananda Daser srestha kabita*. The same poem is also found in a section of Jibanananda's notebook labeled "Poetry, September, 1946, Barisal."

59. *Kabitar katha,* 101; appeared in *Dwandwa,* Aswin 1357.
60. Ibid.
61. Ibid., 105.
62. Ibid., 107.
63. Interview with Amlan Datta. Arun Dasgupta recalled he had attended a meeting of the Association at which Jibanananda gave a talk.
64. Interview with Abu Sayeed Ayyub.
65. Courtesy of Amlan Datta.
66. Jibanananda wrote four poems entitled "Today" (*aj*).
67. According to Amiya Kumar Ganguly, *Nirnay* had been published as a political weekly, brought out by Atulya Ghosh from 1353 (1946–47). Then in October 1950, Amiya Ganguly was appointed editor, a position he held for about six months. During that period, the magazine became a monthly literary and cultural journal.
68. *Nirnay,* Kartik 1357.
69. Letter dated 13.6.49, printed in *Mayukh,* Paus–Jyaistha 1361–62, 124.
70. Courtesy of Satyaprasanna Datta.
71. Courtesy of Haraprasad Mitra. This letter was addressed to him at Hooghly Mohsin College, Chinsura, where he taught. Along with Amiya Kumar Ganguly and Basanta Kumar Ganguly, Haraprasad Mitra brought out the booklet *Natun kabita* (New poems) from Serampore. Presumably Jibanananda felt Haraprasad Mitra had some influence with the Serampore College. The question about the Women's College refers to a previous request that Jibanananda had made of Haraprasad.
72. Dates of employment were obtained for me by an administrative assistant to the principal. The rest of this information comes from interviews with members of the college staff. Gopal Chandra Ray writes that Labanya's illness forced Jibanananda to resign from his position at Kharagpur College (*Jibanananda,* 61–62).
73. Interview with Narayan Ganguly.
74. Major Majumdar had sublet for six or seven months in 1947–48. The third person to sublet did not move in until 1950 or 1951. In between those two, a gentleman by the name of Amal Datta resided in part of Jibanananda's Lansdowne flat. Amal Datta contributed a short article to the special Jibanananda issue of *Usha* (Kartik 1361) in which he described his and Jibanananda's relationship. They apparently met through *Nirukta* in the early 1940s.
75. Interview with Kiran Sankar Sengupta.
76. Subodh Ray, "Amar cokhe kabi Jibanananda" (Poet Jibanananda in my eyes), *Usha,* Kartik 1361, 20.
77. Gopal Chandra Ray, *Jibanananda,* 62–65.
78. Interview with Narendralal Ganguly.
79. Courtesy of Kiran Sankar Sengupta. This letter was printed in *Samhita,* n.d. (editors Phanindranath Dasgupta, Kiran Sankar Sengupta, and Amitabha Gupta for the Tollygunge Cultural Association). It was written to Anil Biswas who, according to Kiran Sankar, was a district officer in Murshidabad at the time.
80. Gopal Chandra Ray writes that Sanjay suggested the bank job to Jibanananda and then worked out the details with the Dattas; another teaching

position materialized before Jibanananda had begun to work at the bank, and so he rejected the bank position in favor of the teaching post (*Jibanananda,* 65). Satyaprasanna Datta recalled that Jibanananda asked him to arrange for the bank position, but implied that the poet never actually worked there.

81. Ibid., 66.
82. Ibid., 157–60.
83. *Girls' College Magazine, Howrah* lists Jibanananda as Head of the Department in 1954.
84. Gopal Chandra Ray, *Jibanananda,* 161–64, 170.
85. Ibid., 169–70.
86. Courtesy of Satyaprasanna Datta.
87. Interview with Asokananda Das.
88. According to Ataur Rahman, this happened in 1953 or 1954, but he thought that it antedated the Howrah Girls' College appointment.
89. Interview with Ataur Rahman.
90. Cited in Sanjay Bhattacharya, *Kabi Jibanananda Das,* 141.
91. Ibid., 146. Gopal Chandra Ray interprets this letter quite differently. According to him, Jibanananda is requesting Sanjay to contact Humayun Kabir and Tarasankar so they might see to it that Jibanananda's recently published book, *Jibanananda Daser srestha kabita,* receive the newly established Sahitya Akademi prize; *Jibanananda,* 105–7. Abdul Mannan Syed likewise reads in this letter an effort by Jibanananda to secure the Sahitya Akademi prize; *Suddhatama kabi,* 224.
92. That Jibanananda took a dislike to the cover portraiture for *Banalata Sen* is a commonly heard story in Calcutta; see Gopal Chandra Ray, *Jibanananda,* 165.
93. *Banalata Sen,* 25; appeared in *Kavita,* Asarh 1358.
94. Dipti Tripathi, *Adhunik Bamla kabyaparicay,* 172.
95. *Banalata Sen,* 47.
96. Interview with Anandagopal Sengupta.
97. Interview with Arun Kumar Sarkar. Gopal Chandra Ray recalls visiting Jibanananda on the day after the presentation of the award; according to Gopal Ray, the prize consisted of Rs.101/- plus a basket of fruit—"an apple, a pomegranate, a coconut, a ripe papaya, etc."; *Jibanananda,* 166.
98. Interview with Alok Sarkar.
99. Subhas Mukherjee, "Nirjanatama kabi" (The loneliest of poets), *Paricay,* Sravan 1360, 51–55.
100. Ibid., 54.
101. Two major figures in Bengali poetry were absent. Buddhadeva Bose was teaching and lecturing in the United States at this time; Amiya Chakravarty was on the faculty of a college in the United States.
102. This esteemed paper, whose name glosses as "Journal of the Elixir Marketplace," began publication in 1868 in Bengali. Then "in 1878 it turned overnight into a full-fledged English newspaper to evade the clutches of Lord Lytton's infamous Vernacular Press Act." Smarajit Chakraborti, *The Bengali Press (1818–1868),* 177ff.
103. D. K. Gupta had founded the Signet Press which published Jibanananda's *Banalata Sen.*
104. *Amrita Bazar Patrika,* 28 January 1954, 5.
105. Interviews with Tarun Mitra and Sankar Chatterjee.
106. *Amrita Bazar Patrika,* 29 January 1954, 10.
107. Bani Ray, *Nihsanga bihanga* (A bird alone) (Calcutta: Mukherjee Book House, 1961), 9.

108. Though Rabindranath's name appears on the title page, it was thought by many (Buddhadeva included, as he states in his review of this work) that a "lesser light" selected the poems to be anthologized.

109. Interviews with Buddhadeva Bose and Abu Sayeed Ayyub.

110. The first edition had carried only four poems by Amiya Chakravarty.

111. Buddhadeva Bose, ed., *Adhunik Bamla kabita* (Modern Bengali poetry), 2d ed. (Calcutta: M. C. Sarkar and Sons, 1956), 5–6 of introd.

112. An anthology edited by Bishnu Dey, *Ekaler kabita* (Contemporary poetry) (Calcutta: Sambodhi Publications, 1963), includes fifteen poems by Rabindranath, fourteen poems by Jibanananda, eight poems each by Amiya Chakravarty, Sudhindranath Datta, and Premendra Mitra. Other poets are represented by fewer than eight poems, Buddhadeva Bose by six. Bishnu Dey includes five of his own poems only at the very end of the collection.

113. Biram Mukherjee had conceived of these "Best Poems" volumes; he also made the selection of poetry for Jibanananda's collection, according to Jibanananda's introduction.

114. *Ananda Bazar Patrika,* 13 October 1954, 3.

115. See Naresh Guha, in *Kavita,* Paus 1361, 150; Sanjay Bhattacharya, *Kabi Jibanananda Das,* 147; and Gopal Chandra Ray, *Jibanananda,* 100–101.

Chapter 7. Posthumous Jibanananda

1. The Sunday *Ananda Bazar Patrika* published a staff reporter's account of the funeral gathering—consisting of most of the important poets of the day—along with some biographical background material on Jibanananda. *Ananda Bazar Patrika,* 24 October 1954, 5.

2. "Kabi Jibanananda" (Poet Jibanananda), *Ananda Bazar Patrika,* 31 October 1954, 9. In the following week, there appeared an article by his friend and one-time colleague on the *Swaraj* newspaper staff; see Nirendranath Chakravarty, "Jibananander kabita" (Jibanananda's poetry), *Ananda Bazar Patrika,* 6 November 1954, 8.

3. Jibanananda Das, *Sudarsana* (Sudarsana), ed. Gopal Chandra Ray (Calcutta: Sahitya Sadan, 1973), 25; appeared in *Ananda Bazar Patrika,* 31 October 1954.

4. *Times of India* (Bombay), 1 November 1954, 6.

5. *Ananda Bazar Patrika,* 28 October 1954, 2.

6. One notebook was dated November 1951–January 1952 and the other dated May–June 1954.

7. *Sanibarer Cithi,* Kartik 1361, 101–2.

8. Ibid., 103–7.

9. *Annual Report, 1968: Sahitya Akademi,* back cover.

10. Ibid., 38. We are told by the editorial staff of *Mayukh* that there was indeed some resistance to awarding Jibanananda the first prize; see *Mayukh,* Paus–Jyaistha 1361–62, 268–69.

11. Manindra Ray, "Kabi Jibanananda Das" (Poet Jibanananda Das), *Paricay,* Sravan 1362, 1–11.

12. *Jibanananda Daser srestha kabita,* unpaged.

13. This essay by Manindra Ray has been republished in the volume Deb Kumar Bose, *Jibanananda smriti.* Other than one small revision— "nearly a year ago" has been changed to "nearly seventeen years ago"—the articles are, to the best of my knowledge, identical; ibid., 121–22.

14. Ibid., 123-27.
15. Ibid., 127.
16. Ibid., 130.
17. Interview with Manindra Ray.
18. Interview with Abu Sayeed Ayyub.
19. Interview with Alokeranjan Dasgupta.
20. Bani Ray, "Nihsanga bihanga" (A bird alone), *Mayukh,* Paus-Jyaistha 1361-62, 164.
21. Pranabendu Dasgupta, "Pancam dasak," in *Adhunik kabitar itihas,* ed. Dasgupta and Banerjee, 108.
22. Sarat Kumar Mukherjee, "Jibananander prabhab" (The genius of Jibanananda), *Dainik Kabita,* 20 Jyaistha 1373, 4.
23. *Patranu,* Caitra 1376, 6.
24. Subhoranjan Dasgupta and Sudeshna Chakravarty, eds. and trans., *Bengali Poems on Calcutta* (Calcutta: Writers Workshop, 1972), 121-22.
25. *Salted Feathers,* March 1967 (published from Portland, Oregon, by Dick Bakken and Lee Altman), unpaged. Malay Roy Choudhury was convicted in late December 1965 of having violated Section 292 (Obscenity law) of the Indian Penal Code and sentenced to one month in jail or a fine of Rs.200/- for his poem "Stark Electric Jesus," also printed in *Salted Feathers.*
26. *Statesman* (Calcutta), 26 February 1968, 10.
27. For those interested in the Hungry poets and their somewhat skewed view of Jibanananda and his poetry, see *City Lights Journal,* numbers 1, 2, and 3 (San Francisco: City Lights Books, 1963, 1964, 1965).
28. Abdul Mannan Syed, ed., *Jibanananda* (Jibanananda) (Dhaka: Caritra, 1984), 71-72.
29. Sandip Datta, *Jibanananda prasangiki,* 173.
30. *Jibanananda,* Baisakh 1377.
31. Jibanananda used to take walks along Southern Avenue and through the park in which is located Rabindra Sarobar (Lake). The letter was by Sobhan Mitra, Raja Chatterjee, and Partha Banerjee, in *Ananda Bazar Patrika,* 23 February 1970.
32. Both in Bani Ray, "The Modern Trend in Bengali Literature," in *Seminar of All India Women Writers: Souvenir* (Hyderabad: Andhra Pradesh Sahitya Akademi, 1965), unpaged; and Bani Ray, "A Survey of Bengali Poetry" (extract from an address delivered at Srinagar during the Nikhil Bharat Banga Sahitya Sammelan, [1969/1970]).
33. See Buddhadeva Bose, "Kabita: Bamla kabitar bhabisyat" (Poetry: The future of Bengali poetry), *Caturanga,* Aswin 1357, 29.
34. Eliot, "The Music of Poetry," 111-12.
35. Buddhadeva Bose, "Jibanananda Das" (Jibanananda Das), *Kavita,* Paus 1361, 69-70.
36. Dipti Tripathi, *Adhunik Bamla kabyaparicay,* 203.
37. Ambuj Bose, *Ekati naksatra ase,* 212.
38. Sarat Kumar Mukherjee, "Jibanananda prabhab," 4.

Select Bibliography

There are a number of bibliographies that deal specifically with published material written by or about Jibanananda: one each in the special Jibanananda issues of *Kavita* (Paus 1361) and *Mayukh* (Paus–Jyaistha 1361–62); a very extensive listing by Swapan Dasadhikari in *Jibanananda Das*, ed. Birendranath Bhattacharya (Calcutta: Anwista, 1973), 139–59; a survey of the major source material on Jibanananda, by Abdul Mannan Syed, "Jibanananda carca" (Research on Jibanananda), in Abdul Mannan Syed, ed., *Jibanananda* (Dhaka: Caritra, 1984), 19–57; and a list of journal articles published in "little magazines," in Sandip Datta, ed., *Jibanananda prasangiki* (Concerning Jibanananda) (Calcutta: Hardya, 1984), Appendix I.

The poet's prose and poetry manuscripts have been deposited in a special Jibanananda collection at the National Library of India in Calcutta.

For books listed below, the date of publication is given according to the Christian calendar. For periodicals, Bengali dates are given, unless—as in the case of daily newspapers—the Christian date was furnished.

Periodicals

Anukta. Jibanananda's fiction first appeared here, in the mid-1950s, after his death.

Anwista. In 1379 (1972–73), this Calcutta journal brought out a special Jibanananda issue.

Banga Bani. Founded in the early 1920s, this political-literary Calcutta magazine carried some of Jibanananda's earliest poetry.

Brahmabadi. Edited first by Jibanananda's father and then by his uncle, this mouthpiece for the Barisal Brahmo Samaj regularly published Jibanananda's mother's verse; Jibanananda's first published poem appeared here.

Caturanga. Initially edited jointly by Humayun Kabir and Buddhadeva Bose and then later by Kabir alone, this excellent literary and cultural magazine began publication in Calcutta in the late 1930s.

City Lights Journal. Allen Ginsberg contributed a few comments on Bengali poetry and some translations (reworked by Ginsberg) of verse from poets he had met in Calcutta, all of them in one way or another influenced by Jibanananda.

Desh. Published in Calcutta from the early 1930s, today *Desh* has the widest circulation of any Bengali magazine. It carried some of Jibanananda's writings toward the end of his life.

Dhupchaya. This was one of the avant-garde journals in Calcutta during the 1920s.

Dwandwa. This journal, published from Calcutta, became the mouthpiece for the Socialist writers' organization in 1950; Jibanananda, Abu Sayeed Ayyub, and Narendra Mitra were joint editors, at least in name.

Ekak. A Calcutta magazine, it carried a number of Jibanananda's poems and published a special Yatindranath Sengupta–Jibanananda Das issue following the deaths of these two writers.

Girls' College Magazine, Howrah. The college at which Jibanananda was teaching when he died devoted its annual magazine for 1955 to articles and poetry on, or dedicated to, the college's former professor.

Indian Literature. Begun after Jibanananda's death and published from Delhi by the Sahitya Akademi, India's academy of letters, this journal is essential reading for those interested in contemporary pan-Indian literature; from time to time, translations of Jibanananda's poetry appear here.

Jadavpur Journal of Comparative Literature. Started well after the death of Jibanananda by the first and still the only comparative literature department in all of South Asia, it carries articles of classical and modern literature from all over the world, including Bengal.

Jibanananda Smarak Patrika. This periodical publication, whose name means "Jibanananda Memorial Magazine," published a special issue in 1389 (1982–83).

Journal of South Asian Literature. Formerly called *Mahfil,* this journal from Michigan has carried translations and criticism of Jibanananda's poetry.

Jubilee (B.M. Institution). A special issue from Barisal's Braja Mohan Institution, where Jibanananda was a student and where his father taught, it was published in 1934.

Kali-Kalam. Published from Calcutta, this was one of the important avant-garde journals of the 1920s.

Kallol. This Calcutta-based magazine was the first and most influential of the avant-garde journals of the 1920s.

Kavita. Begun in Calcutta by Buddhadeva Bose, Premendra Mitra, and Samar Sen, later edited solely by Buddhadeva, then with Naresh Guha, *Kavita,* from its very first issue in 1935 right up to the final issues some two and a half decades later, set the standard for excellence in Bengali poetry. Much of Jibanananda's best work appeared here, some of it in translation in two special numbers—the bilingual issue, June 1953, and the special 100th issue, 1960.

Kavita-Paricay. A short-lived journal of literary criticism from the late 1960s, it printed a number of pieces on Jibanananda's poetry.

Kranti. Both the *Kranti* published from Dhaka and this one from Calcutta carried poetry by Jibanananda; the Calcutta *Kranti,* following the poet's death, brought out a special issue on him.

Mahfil (see *Journal of South Asian Literature*)

Marksbadi. Edited pseudonymously from Calcutta, this journal during the late 1940s carried the writings and literary criticism of the more radical Communists in West Bengal.

Masik Basumati. This Calcutta monthly and its sister daily newspaper carried poetry by Jibanananda and a number of articles on him, following his death.

Mayukh. A journal that had come out from Calcutta a year or so before Jibanananda's death, *Mayukh* published an excellent special issue in memory of the poet—with editorial help from the poet's sister, Sucarita Das, and Dr. Bhumendra Guha.

Mukul. A children's magazine, it carried Jibanananda's mother's poetry.

Nirukta. Begun by Sanjay Bhattacharya and Premendra Mitra from Calcutta, it was published during the early 1940s and featured Jibanananda's poetry as well as sympathetic criticism of it.

Paricay. An excellent and very sophisticated journal when it was started by Sudhindranath Datta in Calcutta in the early 1930s, *Paricay* later became the mouthpiece of the Communist writers.

Prabasi. This journal and its English-language counterpart, *Modern Review,* were both edited by Ramananda Chatterjee. *Prabasi* carried many of Rabindranath's writings; it also published some of Jibanananda's mother's poetry and a few of his own earlier compositions.

Pragati. Published from Dhaka by Buddhadeva Bose and Ajit Datta, this was one of the main avant-garde magazines of the 1920s; it carried much of Jibanananda's early poetry, and Buddhadeva, in two editorials, wrote the first literary criticism on Jibanananda's poetry.

Purvasa. Edited by Sanjay Bhattacharya first from Comilla and then in Calcutta through most of the 1930s, *Purvasa* resumed publication in the mid-1940s; Jibanananda contributed regularly to this journal from the 1940s.

Sanibarer Cithi. Sajani Kanta Das, editor and tireless critic, made fun of the avant-garde writers and their literature; Jibanananda was a favorite target for Sajani Kanta's ridicule.

Saptak. Though it probably carried nothing by Jibanananda, this was the one and only literary journal published from Barisal around the end of the 1930s and the beginning of the 1940s—a period when Jibanananda was living and teaching and writing in Barisal.

Swaraj. This daily newspaper began publication from Calcutta in 1947 with Jibanananda as editor of the Sunday literary and cultural section.

Usha. This Calcutta magazine carried poetry by Jibanananda and published a special commemorative number following the poet's death.

Uttarsuri. Begun shortly before Jibanananda's death, this Calcutta journal published his poetry and brought out a special Jibanananda issue after his death.

Books

BY JIBANANANDA, FIRST PUBLISHED DURING HIS LIFETIME

Banalata Sen (Banalata Sen). 8th Signet ed. Calcutta: Signet Press, 1968. Contains the twelve poems of the Kavita Bhavan edition, published 1942, plus eighteen additional lyrics. The first Signet Press edition appeared in 1952.

Dhusar pandulipi (Gray manuscripts). Edited by Asokananda Das. 3d Signet ed. Calcutta: Signet Press, 1967. First published in Calcutta by D.M. Library, 1936.

Jhara palak (Fallen feathers). Calcutta: Sudhir Chandra Sarkar, 1927.

Jibanananda Daser srestha kabita (Jibanananda Das's best poems). 1st Bharabi ed. Calcutta: Bharabi, 1966. First published in Calcutta by Nabhana, 1954; edited by Biram Mukherjee.

Mahaprithibi (The world at large). Edited by Manabendra Banerjee. 1st Signet ed. Calcutta: Signet Press, 1969. First published in Calcutta by Purvasa, 1944. The Purvasa edition contained all twelve poems published earlier in *Banalata Sen* (Kavita Bhavan edition, 1942).

Satati tarar timir (Darkness of seven stars). 1st Bharabi ed. Calcutta: Bharabi, 1969. First published in Calcutta by Gupta, Rahman and Gupta, 1948.

BY JIBANANANDA, PUBLISHED POSTHUMOUSLY

Aloprithibi (The world of light). Edited by Asokananda Das. Calcutta: Granthalay, 1982. Poems previously published in magazines, collected by the staff of the quarterly *Krittibas* and arranged for publication by the poet's brother.

Bela abela kalabela (Time, untime, and time apart). Edited by Asokananda Das. Calcutta: New Script, 1961.

Jibanananda Daser galpa (Jibanananda Das's stories). Edited by Sukumar Ghosh and Subinay Mustaphi. Calcutta: Dasgupta and Co., 1972. Contains three stories, "Chayanat" (Chayanat), "Gram o saharer galpa" (A tale of village and city), and "Bilas" (Dalliance), with introductory comments by Premendra Mitra, Sunil Kumar Nandy, and Amalendu Bose, respectively, along with a short note by Labanya Das.

Jibanananda Daser kabita (The poetry of Jibanananda Das). See Syed, Abdul Mannan.

Jibanananda Daser kabyagrantha (Jibanananda Das's books of poetry). Vol. 1. Calcutta: Bengal Publishers, 1970. Contains four previously published volumes: *Banalata Sen, Dhusar pandulipi, Mahaprithibi,* and *Rupasi Bamla,* along with a short introduction by Narayan Ganguly.

Jibanananda Daser kabyagrantha (Jibanananda Das's books of poetry). Vol. 2. Calcutta: Bengal Publishers, 1971. Contains three previously published volumes: *Satati tarar timir, Jhara palak,* and *Bela abela kalabela,* along with a short introduction by Sunil Ganguly.

Jibanananda Daser kabya sambhar (Jibanananda Das's collected poetry). Edited by Ranesh Dasgupta. Rev. ed. Dhaka: Khan Brothers, 1982. Introduction by the editor, who is a distant relative of Jibanananda.

Jibanananda Daser premer kabita (Jibanananda Das's love poems). Dhaka: Kathakali, n.d.

Jibanananda Daser srestha kabita (Jibanananda Das's best poems). Edited by Kazi Siraj. Dhaka: Sahitya Prakasani, 1970. The collection, quite different from the Calcutta edition, contains an introduction by the editor.

Jibanananda samagra (A Jibanananda collection). Vol. 1. Edited by Debesh Ray. Calcutta: Pratiksan Publications, 1985. Contains the novel *Jalapaihati* (Jalpaihati); two short stories, "Akanksa-kamanar bilas" (Dalliance from craving desire) and "Sanga, nihsanga" (Company, alone); and eleven poems—along with editorial comments by Debesh Ray.

Kabitar katha (On poetry). 2d ed. Calcutta: Signet Press, 1964. A collection of critical essays on poetry. First edition, 1956.

Malyaban (Malyaban). Calcutta: New Script, 1973. A novel.

Manabihangam (Birds of the mind). Calcutta: Bengal Publishers, 1979.

Rupasi Bamla (Bengal the beautiful). Edited by Asokananda Das. 4th ed. Calcutta: Signet Press, 1968. First published in 1957.

Rupasi Bamla (Bengal the beautiful). Edited by Debesh Ray. Calcutta: Pratiksan Prakasan, 1984. Includes photographic reproductions of all pages of the original notebook manuscript, with transcription on the facing printed page.

Samalocana samagra (A collection of criticism). Edited by Abdul Mannan Syed. Dhaka: Rupam Prakasani, 1983. A collection of reviews, all in Bengali, of the following books: Buddhadeva Bose's *Kankabati* (Kankabati); Krishna Dhar's *Angikar* (Promises); Ranjan's *Site upeksita* (Neglected in winter); Aldous Huxley's *The Gioconda Smile;* Thomas Mann's *Doctor Faustus;* Gide's *The Journals of André Gide;* and T. S. Eliot's *The Three Voices of Poetry.*

Sudarsana (Sudarsana). Edited by Gopal Chandra Ray. Calcutta: Sahitya Sadan, 1973.

Sutirtha (Sutirtha). Calcutta: Bengal Publishers, 1977. A novel.

ANTHOLOGIES IN TRANSLATION

Ahmed, Anwar, ed. *Selected Poems: Abdul Mannan Syed.* Dhaka: Rupam Prakasani, [1984]. Contains translations by divers hands.

Banalata Sen: Poems. Calcutta: Writers Workshop, 1962. Contains sixteen translations of Jibanananda's poetry by divers hands, including his own.

Bandyopadhyay, Pranab, ed. *The Voice of the Indian Poets: An Anthology of Indian Poetry.* Calcutta: United Writers, 1975. Contains Jibanananda's own translations of "Sailor," "Twenty Years After," and "Darkness."

Banerjee, Pradeep, ed. and trans. *Some Post-Independence Bengali Poems.* Calcutta: Writers Workshop, 1969.

Basu Majumdar, A. K., trans. *The Beauteous Bengal: Rupasi Bangla.* Delhi: Mittal Publications, 1987. A translation of Jibanananda's *Rupasi Bamla.*

Bengali Academy Journal. This English-language journal of the Bangla Academy, Bangladesh's national academy of letters, devoted its vol. 6, no. 11 (November 1977–March 1978) to a special poetry number, all translations by Kabir Chowdhury. Nearly every issue of this journal, begun in 1970, contains contemporary Bangladeshi Bengali poetry in English translation.

Bose, Buddhadeva, ed. *An Anthology of Bengali Writing.* Bombay, Madras, Calcutta: The Macmillan Company of India, 1971. Contains translations of the essay "On Poetry" and poems by Jibanananda.

Chakravarty, Prithvindra, and Ulli Beier, eds. and trans. *Playing a Thousand Years.* Papua, New Guinea: Department to English, University of Papua, New Guinea, 1971. An anthology of eighteen of Jibanananda's poems in translation.

Chatterjee, Debiprasad, ed., and Martin Kirkman, trans. *Modern Bengali Poems.* Calcutta: Signet Press, 1945. An anthology of modern Bengali poetry in translation; the poems entitled "If I Were," "O, Kite," "Banalata Sen," and "Meditation" are included.

Chowdhury, Kabir, ed. and trans. *Fifty Poems from Bangladesh.* Calcutta: United Writers, 1977.

Dasgupta, Samir, ed. *Bishnu Dey: Selected Poems.* Calcutta: Writers Workshop, 1972. Translated by various hands.

Dasgupta, Subhoranjan, and Sudeshna Chakravarti, eds. and trans. *Bengali Poems on Calcutta.* Calcutta: Writers Workshop, 1972.

De, Samir, and Abhijit Ghosh, eds. *Twentieth Century Bengali Poetry.* Vol. 1. Calcutta: Firma K. L. Mukhopadhyay, 1973.

Ghose, Sukumar, ed. *Contemporary Bengali Literature: Poetry.* Calcutta: Academic Publishers, [1972].
Jamal, Begum Yusuf, trans. *Poems from East Bengal: Selections from East Bengal Poetry of the Last Five Hundred Years (1389–1954).* [Karachi]: A Pakistan P.E.N. Publication, 1954.
Kabir, Humayun, ed., and Tarasankar Banerjee and Premendra Mitra, assoc. eds. *Green and Gold: Stories and Poems from Bengal.* Bombay: Asia Publishing House, 1957; New York: New Directions; Westport, Connecticut: Greenwood Press, Publishers, 1970. Contains Jibananda's translation of his poem "Sailor."
Khan, Sonia, trans. *Deep within the Heart.* Dhaka: Sabyasachi, 1984. Contains translations of sonnets composed by Syed Shamsul Haq.
Literary Review. The summer 1961 issue of this quarterly from New Jersey was devoted to Indian literature; Buddhadeva Bose's translation of Jibananda's "Grass" appeared there.
Nag, Ranju, ed. *Poems on Bangladesh.* Calcutta: Sm. Usha Chatterjee, 1971.
Nandy, Manish, trans. *Fifty Sonnets of Shakti Chattopadhyay: Translated from the Bengali.* Calcutta: Dialogue Publications, 1972.
Nandy, Pritish, trans. *Bangla Desh: A Voice of a New Nation.* Calcutta: Dialogue Publications, 1971. Subsequently published in London (1972) as *Poems from Bangladesh: The Voice of a New Nation.*
———. *The Complete Poems of Samar Sen.* Calcutta: Writers Workshop, 1970.
———. *Poet of the People: Poems of Subhas Mukhopadhyay.* Calcutta: Dialogue Publications, 1970.
Poetry. This Chicago-based journal, which was the first to publish Rabindranath's poetry in America (vol. 1, no. 3 [December 1912]), brought out a special Indian poetry number (vol. 43, no. 4 [January 1959]) that included Jibananda's "Twenty Years After."
Rashid, M. Harunur, ed. *Three Poets: Poems from Bangladesh Series: Shamsur Rahman, Al Mahmud, Shaheed Quaderi.* Dhaka: Bangladesh Books International, 1976.
Ray, Sibnarayan, and Marian Maddern, eds. and trans. *I Have Seen Bengal's Face.* Calcutta: Editions Indian, 1974. An anthology of modern Bengali poetry in translation.
Sengupta, Nandagopal, ed. *A Book of Bengali Verse: From the Tenth to the Twentieth Century.* Calcutta: Indian Publications, 1969.

SECONDARY SOURCES (BOOKS)

Anti-Fascist Traditions in Bengal. Calcutta: Indo-GDR Friendship Society, [1969]. Contains translations of some anti-Fascist poetry and writings on the anti-Fascist literature of the early 1940s.
Asaduzzaman. *Jiban silpi Jibananda Das* (Artist of life: Jibananda Das). Dhaka, Rajshahi, Jessore, Rangpur: Bangladesh Book Corporation, 1977. Criticism.
Ayyub, Abu Sayeed, and Hirendranath Mukherjee, eds. *Adhunik Bamla kabita* (Modern Bengali poetry). Calcutta: Kavita Bhavan, 1940. An anthology of modern Bengali poetry.

Banerjee, Binod Bihari. *Smriti katha* (Recollections). Vol. 2. Calcutta: Vidyasagar Book Stall, [1949].

Banerjee, Debiprasad. *Jibanananda Das: Bikas-pratisthar itibritta* (Jibanananda Das: A chronicle of his development). Calcutta: Bharat Book Agency, 1986. Collection of notices, reviews, and letters; the second section contains criticism.

Banerjee, Saroj. *Kabita kalpanalata* (A vine of poetic imagination). Calcutta: Esem Publications, 1972.

Banerjee, Sibaji. *Prasanga, Jibanananda* (For discussion: Jibanananda). Calcutta: Ayana, 1983. Criticism.

Banerjee, Tarasankar. *Amar sahitya jiban* (My literary life). 2 vols. 2d ed. Calcutta: Bengal Publishers, 1957; Calcutta: Sundar Prakasan, 1962.

Bhattacharya, Arun. *Kabitar dharma o Bamla kabitar ritubadal* (The nature of poetry and the change of Bengali poetic seasons). Calcutta: Jijnasa, 1958.

―――. *Tagore and the Moderns.* Calcutta: Renaissance Publishers, 1964.

Bhattacharya, Arun, ed. *Baro bacharer Bamla kabita* (Twelve years of Bengali poetry). Calcutta: Prantik, 1966. An anthology of modern Bengali poetry.

Bhattacharya, Birendranath, ed. *Jibanananda Das* (Jibanananda Das). Calcutta: Anwista, 1973. Contains critical essays by divers hands and an excellent bibliography compiled by Swapan Dasadhikari.

Bhattacharya, Sanjay. *Adhunik kabitar bhumika* (An introduction to modern poetry). 2d ed. Calcutta: Purvasa Publications, 1966. Includes Sanjay's earlier book, *Tinajan adhunik kabi* (Three modern poets). Calcutta: Purvasa, 1944.

―――. *Kabi Jibanananda Das* (Poet Jibanananda Das). Calcutta: Bharabi, 1970.

Bhattacharya, Tapodhir, and Swapna Bhattacharya. *Adhunikata, Jibanananda o parabastab* (Modernity, Jibanananda, and Surrealism). Calcutta: Nabarka, 1987.

Bose, Ambuj. *Ekati naksatra ase* (A star arrives). Calcutta: Mausumi, 1965. Criticism; contains an excellent introduction by Amalendu Bose. A second, expanded edition was published by De's Publishing, 1976.

Bose, Buddhadeva. *An Acre of Green Grass.* Calcutta: Orient Longmans, 1948. Criticism.

―――. *Prabandha-samkalan* (Collected essays). Calcutta: Bharabi, 1966.

―――. *Kaler putul* (The puppet of time). Calcutta: New Age Publishers, 1959.

―――. *Rabindranath: Kathasahitya* (Rabindranath: Fiction). Calcutta: New Age Publishers, 1955.

―――. *Tagore, Portrait of a Poet.* Bombay: University of Bombay Press, 1962.

Bose, Buddhadeva, ed. *Adhunik Bamla kabita* (Modern Bengali poetry). 2d ed. Calcutta: M. C. Sarkar and Sons, 1956. An anthology.

Bose, Deb Kumar, ed. *Jibanananda smriti* (Remembering Jibanananda). Calcutta: Karuna Prakasani, 1971.

Bose, Suddha Sattwa. *Kabi Jibanananda* (Poet Jibanananda). Calcutta: Sankha Prakasan, 1975. Criticism.

―――. *Adhunik Bamla kabyer gati prakriti* (The ways and means of modern Bengali poetry). Calcutta: Mandal Book House, 1973.

Bose, Suddha Sattwa, ed. *Satek kabita* (About a hundred poems). Calcutta: Signet Book Shop, 1970. An anthology of modern Bengali poetry.

Cevet, David, ed. *The Shell and the Rain.* London: George Allen and Unwin, 1973.

Chakraborti, Smarajit. *The Bengali Press (1818–1868): A Study in the Growth of Public Opinion.* Calcutta: Firma KLM, 1976.

Chakravarty, Sumita. *Jibanananda: Samaj o samakal* (Jibanananda: Society and the times). Calcutta: Sahityalok, 1987. Criticism; includes three essays by Jibanananda.

Chatterjee, Birendra, ed. *Jibanayan* (Jibanayana). Calcutta: Grantha Bitan, 1961. Collection of poems by divers poets dedicated to Jibanananda.

Chatterjee, Shanta. *Ramananda Cattopadhyay o arddhasatabdir Bamla* (Ramananda Chatterjee and a half century of Bengali). Calcutta: Prabasi Press, n.d.

Chaudhuri, Nirad C. *The Autobiography of an Unknown Indian.* New York: Macmillan Co., 1951.

Coppola, Carlo. "Urdu Poetry, 1935–1970: The Progressive Episode." Ph.D. diss., University of Chicago, 1975.

Das, Biswajit, and Rathindra Sanyal, eds. *Bodhi* (Realization). Kanchrapara (near Calcutta): Ritwik Prakasani, [1976]. An anthology of poems by divers hands on the theme of Jibanananda.

Das, Debajyoti. *Sajanikanta Das* (Sajani Kanta Das). Calcutta: Bangiya Sahitya Parishat, 1970.

Das, Labanya. *Manus Jibanananda* (Jibanananda the man). Calcutta: Bengal Publishers, 1971.

Das, Manmatha Mohan. *Barisal Brahmasamajer samksipta itihas* (A brief history of the Barisal Brahmo Samaj). [Barisal]: Manmatha Mohan Das, 1927.

Das, Sajani Kanta. *Atmasmriti* (Reminiscences). 2 vols. Calcutta: D.M. Library, 1954, 1956.

Das, Satyananda. *Santanasiksa niti o dharmma* (The principles and nature of educating children). Dhaka: East Bengal Brahmo Conference, 1917.

Das, Sisir Kumar. *Caturdasi* (Sonnets). Calcutta: Sambodhi Publications, 1966. This anthology of Bengali sonnets contains three of Jibanananda's poems.

Dasgupta, Alokeranjan, and Debiprasad Banerjee, eds. *Adhunik kabitar itihas* (A history of modern poetry). Calcutta: Vak-Sahitya, 1965.

Dasgupta, Chidananda. *Jibanananda Das.* New Delhi: Sahitya Akademi, 1972. Contains a brief biography, translations, and a bibliography on Jibanananda.

Dasgupta, Hiralal. *Jananayak Aswinikumar* (Aswini Kumar, leader of the people). Calcutta: Dasgupta and Co., [1969].

Datta, Aswini Kumar. *Aswinikumar racanasambhar* (The collected works of Aswini Kumar). Calcutta: Adhyayan, [1968].

Datta, Sandip, ed. *Jibanananda prasangiki* (Concerning Jibanananda). Calcutta: Hardya, 1984. A collection of criticism by divers hands, this volume also contains a listing of articles published in "little magazines," noted to be available at the Bengali Periodicals Library & Research Centre, Calcutta.

Datta, Sudhindranath. *The World of Twilight.* Translated by Edward C. Dimock, Jr., and A. T. M. Anisuzzaman. Calcutta: Oxford University Press, 1970.

Dey, Bishnu, ed. *Ekaler kabita* (Contemporary poetry). Calcutta: Sambodhi Publications, 1956. An anthology of modern Bengali poetry.

Fazal, Abul. *Sahitya o samskriti sadhana* (The practice of literature and culture). Dhaka: East Bengal Publishers, n.d. Contains "Dujan adhunik kabi:

Jibanananda Das o Sudhindranath Datta" (Two modern poets: Jibanananda Das and Sudhindranath Datta).

Ganguly, Narayan. *Sahitya o sahityik* (Literature and literati). 2d ed. Calcutta: D.M. Library, 1961.

Ghose, Nirmal, ed. *Studies in Modern Bengali Poetry*. Calcutta: Novela, 1968.

Gupta, Yogendranath. *Banger mahila kabi* (Women poets of Bengal). 2d ed. Calcutta: A. Mukherjee and Co., 1953.

Kabir, Humayun. *Studies in Bengali Poetry*. Bombay: Bharatiya Vidya Bhavan, 1962. This is a translation of his Bengali book: *Bamlar kabya* (Bengali poetry). Dhaka: Khan Brothers and Co., 1970.

Kopf, David. *The Brahmo Samaj and the Shaping of the Modern Indian Mind*. Princeton: Princeton University Press, 1979.

Kripalani, Krishna. *Tagore: A Life*. Calcutta: published by the author, 1971.

Maddern, Marian. *Bengali Poetry into English: An Impossible Dream?* Calcutta: Editions Indian, 1977.

Majumdar, Mohitlal. *Sahitya katha* (On literature). 2d ed. Howrah: Bangabharati Granthalay, 1959.

Mamud, Hayat. *Mrityucinta Rabindranath o anyanya jatilata* (Thanatopsis, Rabindranath, and other complexities). Dhaka: Sahityika, 1968.

Mitra, Haraprasad. *Kabitar bicitra katha* (On the variety of poetic expression). 2d ed. Calcutta: Rabindra Library, 1964.

Mitra, Pradyumna. *Jibananander cetanajagat* (Jibanananda's world of awareness). Calcutta: Sahityasri, 1983. Criticism.

Mukherjee, Basanti Kumar. *Adhunik Bamla kabitar ruparekha* (Form and design in modern Bengali poetry). Calcutta: Prakas Bhaban, 1969.

Mukherjee, Haridas, and Uma Mukherjee. *The Origins of the National Education Movement (1905–1910)*. Jadavpur, Calcutta: Jadavpur University Press, 1957.

Mukherji, Probhat Kumar. *Rabindrajibani o Rabindrasahitya-prabesak* (The life of Rabindranath and a guide to his literature). Vols. 2 and 3. Calcutta: Visvabharati Granthalay, 1949, 1952.

Nurullah, Syed, and J. P. Naik. *A History of Education in India (during the British Period)*. 2d ed. Bombay, Madras, Calcutta, and London: Macmillan and Co., 1951.

Overstreet, Gene D., and Marshall Windmiller. *Communism in India*. Berkeley and Los Angeles: University of California Press, 1959.

Patri, Purnendu. *Rupasi Bamlar dui kabi* (Two poets of Bengal the beautiful). Calcutta: Ananda Publishers, 1980.

Rahman, Hasan Hafizur. *Adhunik kabi o kabita* (Modern poets and poetry). Dhaka: Bangla Akademi, 1965.

Ray, Bani. *Nihsanga bihanga* (A bird alone). 2d ed. Calcutta: Mukherjee Book House, 1961.

Ray, Gopal Chandra. *Jibanananda* (Jibanananda). Vol. 1. Calcutta: Sahitya Sadan, 1971. This is the only book-length biography to date of Jibanananda; contains poetry and essays by the poet. Volume 2, according to the author's introduction to volume 1, will contain critical studies of Jibanananda's work. To date, that second volume has not been published.

Ray, Lila. *A Challenging Decade: Bengali Literature in the Forties.* Calcutta: D.M. Library, 1953.

Samanta, Rabindranath. *Jibanananda pratibha* (The genius of Jibanananda). Calcutta: Alpha Publishing Concern, 1972.

Sarkar, Bijan Kanti. *Rupasi Bamlar kabi Jibanananda Das* (Beautiful Bengal's poet Jibanananda Das). Calcutta: Bijaya Sahitya Mandir, 1973.

Sastri, Sivanath. *History of the Brahmo Samaj.* 2 vols. Calcutta: R. Chatterjee, 1911-12. Contains an account of *mofussil* Brahmo Samajs, including the founding of Barisal's.

Sen, Sukumar. *Bangala sahityer itihas* (A history of Bengali literature). Vol. 4. 2d ed. Calcutta: Eastern Publishers, 1963.

_____. *History of Bengali Literature.* New Delhi: Sahitya Akademi, 1960.

Sengupta, Acintya Kumar. *Kallol yug* (The Kallol era). 5th ed. Calcutta: M. C. Sarkar and Sons, 1965.

Sengupta, Kiran Sankar. *Swapna-kamana* (Dream-Desire). Calcutta: Sriharsa Pustak Bibhag, 1938. Jibanananda wrote the introduction to this volume of poetry.

Sengupta, Naresh Chandra. *Yugaparikrama* (Surveying the age). Vol. 1. Calcutta: Firma K. L. Mukhopadhyay, 1961.

Shils, Edward. *The Intellectual between Tradition and Modernity: The Indian Situation.* The Hague: Mouton & Co., 1961.

Sikdar, Asru Kumar. *Adhunik kabitar digbalay* (The horizons of modern poetry). Calcutta: Signet Book Shop, 1974.

Simha, Ranajit. *Sruti o pratisruti* (Hearsay and promises). Calcutta: Classic Press, 1964. Criticism; one chapter is devoted to Jibanananda.

Simha Ray, Jibendra. *Kalloler kal* (The Kallol times). Calcutta: Kathasilpa, 1973.

_____. *Kabitar simana* (Poetry's outer limits). Calcutta: Naya Prakas, 1973.

Syed, Abdul Mannan. *Jibanananda Daser kabita* (The poetry of Jibanananda Das). Dhaka: Knowledge Home, 1974. Awarded Bangladesh's Jatiya Granthakendra ("National Book Center") annual prize for 1974. Criticism; includes 65 poems by Jibanananda.

_____. *Suddhatama kabi* (The purest of poets). 2d ed. Dhaka: Knowledge Home, 1977. Criticism; includes a poem and four essays by Jibanananda plus four letters exchanged between Rabindranath and Jibanananda.

Syed, Abdul Mannan, ed. *Jibanananda* (Jibanananda). Dhaka: Caritra, 1984. This anthology contains previously published poetry written about Jibanananda, remembrances of the poet, critical pieces on his poetry, plus the two essays Jibanananda wrote concerning his parents, which appeared under the title "My Parents" *(amar ma baba).*

_____. *Jibanananda Daser patrabali* (Jibanananda Das's letters). Dhaka: Muktadhara, 1987. Contains 48 letters by Jibanananda and 5 to him.

Tagore, Rabindranath. *Rabindra-racanabali* (The collected works of Rabindranath). 29 vols. Calcutta: Visvabharati, 1939-65. Though this series represents the "collected works" of Rabindranath, it is not the "complete works."

_____. *Bamla kabya paricay* (An introduction to Bengali verse). Calcutta: Visvabharati, 1938. An anthology.

Tripathi, Dipti. *Adhunik Bamla kabyaparicay* (An introduction to modern Bengali poetry). 3d ed. Calcutta: Nabhana, 1964.

Articles

BY JIBANANANDA DAS
(See also his *Kabitar katha* and *Samalocana samagra*.)

"Amar ma baba" (My parents). *Uttarsuri,* Paus–Falgun 1361, 4–13. Republished in *Suddhatama kabi* (The purest of poets), by Abdul Mannan Syed. 2d ed. Dhaka: Knowledge Home, 1977.

"The Bengali Novel Today." *Hindustan Standard,* September 1950. Republished in *Jibanananda: Samaj o samakal* (Jibanananda: Society and the times), by Sumita Chakravarty. Calcutta: Sahityalok, 1987.

"Bengali Poetry Today." *Statesman* (Calcutta), Sunday section, 6 November 1949, 11. Republished in *Jibanananda,* by Gopal Chandra Ray. Vol. 1. Calcutta: Sahitya Sadan, 1971; and in *Jibanananda: Samaj o samakal* (Jibanananda: Society and the times), by Sumita Chakravarty. Calcutta: Sahityalok, 1987.

"Ekatukhani" (A bit). In *Jibanananda: Samaj o samakal* (Jibanananda: Society and the times), by Sumita Chakravarty. Calcutta: Sahityalok, 1987.

"Lekha, lekhaker dayitwa" (Responsibility of the writer and writing). In *Kena likhi* (Why I write). Calcutta: Anti-Fascist Writers' and Artists' Union, 1944. Republished in *Jibanananda*, by Gopal Chandra Ray. Vol. 1. Calcutta: Sahitya Sadan, 1971.

"Lekhar katha" (On writing). In *Suddhatama kabi* (The purest of poets), by Abdul Mannan Syed. 2d ed. Dhaka: Knowledge Home, 1977.

"Najaruler kabita" (The poetry of Nazrul). *Kavita,* Kartik–Paus 1351. Republished in *Jibanananda*, by Gopal Chandra Ray. Vol. 1. Calcutta: Sahitya Sadan, 1971; and in *Suddhatama kabi* (The purest of poets), by Abdul Mannan Syed. 2d ed. Dhaka: Knowledge Home, 1977.

"Prithibi o samay" (The world and the times). In *Suddhatama kabi* (The purest of poets), by Abdul Mannan Syed. 2d ed. Dhaka: Knowledge Home, 1977.

"Siksadiksa" (Education). *Desh,* 21 Bhadra 1359. Republished in *Jibanananda,* by Gopal Chandra Ray. Vol. 1. Calcutta: Sahitya Sadan, 1971.

"Siksa o lmraji" (Education and English). *Dainik Basumati,* Saradiya 1360. Republished in *Jibanananda,* by Gopal Chandra Ray. Vol. 1. Calcutta: Sahitya Sadan, 1971.

"Sudhirakumar" (Sudhir Kumar). *Smriti-tarpan* (In memoriam). [Barisal]: no publisher, introduction dated April 1942, unpaged.

"Swargiya Kalimohan Daser sraddhabasare" (At the late Kali Mohan Das's *sraddha* ceremony). In *Suddhatama kabi* (The purest of poets), by Abdul Mannan Syed. 2d ed. Dhaka: Knowledge Home, 1977.

SECONDARY SOURCES (ARTICLES)

Ayyub, Abu Sayeed. "Tendencies in Modern Bengali Poetry." In *Longmans Miscellany, 1943*. Calcutta: Longmans, Green & Co., 1943.

Select Bibliography

Banerjee, Himani. "Jibanananda Daser *Mahaprithibi*" (Jibanananda Das's *The world at large*). *Saraswat*, Jyaistha 1375, 10–19.

Banerjee, Manabendra. " 'Godhulisandhir nritya' " ('Dance of twilight'). *Kavita-Paricay*, 5th–6th combined issues, n.d., 19–22.

Bhattacharya, Sanjay. "Amar kabita" (My poetry). *Purvasa*, Asarh–Sravan 1376, 259–66 and 317–22.

———. "Sanjay Bhattacarya: Ekati saksatkar" (Sanjay Bhattacharya: An interview). *Saraswat*, Jyaistha 1375, 5–9.

Bose, Amalendu. "Jibanananda Das." In *Studies in Modern Bengali Poetry*, edited by Nirmal Ghose. Calcutta: Novela, 1968.

Bose, Buddhadeva. "Jibanananda Das" (Jibanananda Das). *Kavita*, Paus 1361, 61–81.

———. "Perspectives on Bengali Poetry: An Interview with Buddhadeva Bose." *Mahfil* 3, no. 4 (1967): 43–48.

———. "Kabita: Bamla kabitar bhabisyat" (Poetry: The future of Bengali poetry). *Caturanga*, Aswin 1357, 29–32.

———. "Caram cikitsa" (The ultimate remedy). *Desh*, 28 Baisakh 1375, 237–46.

Cevet, David. "A Note on Bengali Poetry." *Bengali Literature*, Winter 1969, 34–45.

Chakravarty, Heramba. "Jibananandake yeman dekhechi" (Jibanananda as I saw him). *Girls' College Magazine, Howrah*, 1955, 17–20.

Chakravarty, Jagannath. "The Spectrum of Modern Bengali Poetry." *Bengali Literature*, May 1967, 9–19.

Chakravarty, Manamohan. "Barisale pamyatallis batsar" (Forty-five years in Barisal). *Brahmabadi*. These reminiscences by Jibanananda's uncle were published over a period of many months, from Caitra 1342.

Chakravarty, Nirendranath. "Jibananander kabita" (Jibanananda's poetry). *Ananda Bazar Patrika*, 6 November 1954, 8.

———. "Sanjayada" (Sanjay). *Desh*, 3 Falgun 1375, 295–96. Written just after Sanjay Bhattacharya's death, this article in part describes the relationship between Sanjay and Jibanananda when the latter worked on the *Swaraj* newspaper staff.

Chakravarty, Sumita. "Kusumakumari Das—'sei chele'r ma" (Kusum Kumari Das—'that boy's' mother). *Desh*, 11 Asarh 1389, 10–16.

Chatterjee, Nirupam. "Rabindranath o Jibanananda: Du-jan asabarna kabi" (Rabindranath and Jibanananda: Poets of a different caste). *Kavita*, Aswin 1363, 19–35.

Chatterjee, Tirthankar. "Mrityur age: Jibanananda Das" (Before death: Jibanananda Das). *Kavita-Paricay*, Magh–Paus 1376, 2–6.

Das, Asokananda. "Balyasmriti" (Childhood reminiscences). *Mayukh*, Paus–Jyaistha 1361–62, 129–56.

———. "Jibanananda Das" (Jibanananda Das). *Purvasa*, Falgun 1371, 89ff.

———. "Jibananander prakritik o paribarik paribes" (Jibanananda's natural and familial surroundings). *Uttarsuri*, Paus–Falgun 1361, 14–17.

———. "Amar dada Jibanananda Das" (My elder brother Jibanananda Das). *Girls' College Magazine, Howrah*, 1955, 3–14.

Das, Labanya, with Kabita Simha. "Amar swami Jibanananda Das" (My husband,

Jibanananda Das). *Dainik Kavita,* Baisakh 1375, 2–4. An interview conducted by Kabita Simha.

———. "Smritir patay" (On a page from memory). *Betar Jagat,* 7 February 1970, 145–46. A talk broadcast over All-India Radio, Calcutta, 19 November 1969.

———. "Sahadharminir cokhe kabi Jibanananda" (Poet Jibanananda through the eyes of his wife). *Betar Jagat,* Saradiya 1969, 139–40. Republished in *Citrakas* (Bangladesh), 27 Sravan 1377.

Das, Satyananda. "Amar jyestha bhrata" (My elder brother). *Brahmabadi,* Bhadra–Aswin 1325, 78ff.

Das, Sucarita. "Kacher Jibanananda" (Intimate Jibanananda). *Mayukh,* Paus–Jyaistha 1361–62, 172–90.

Dasgupta, Alokeranjan. "Hajar bachar sudhu khela kare: Jibanananda Das" (A thousand years merely played: Jibanananda Das). *Kavita-Paricay,* Baisakh 1373, 4–5.

———. "Response to Modernism." In *Modernity and Contemporary Indian Literature.* Simla: Transactions of the Indian Institute of Advanced Study, 1968.

Dasgupta, Jayanta Kumar. Untitled editorial. *Brajamohan Bidyalay Patrika,* 1968–69, unpaged.

Dasgupta, Pranabendu. "Pancam dasak" (The forties). In *Adhunik kabitar itihas* (A history of modern poetry), edited by A. Dasgupta and D. Banerjee. Calcutta: Vak-Sahitya, 1965.

Datta, Ajit. "Kabita lekhar katha" (About writing poetry). *Desh,* special literary number, 1379, 195–202.

———. "Kabi Jibanananda" (Poet Jibanananda). *Ananda Bazar Patrika,* 31 October 1954, 9.

Datta, Jyotirmoy. "Jibanananda Das o Manik Bandyopadhyay" (Jibanananda Das and Manik Banerjee). *Kavita,* Aswin 1366, 24–52.

———. "A Note on Modern Bengali Poetry." *Kavita,* Paus 1366, 139–46.

Dey, Bishnu. "Kena likhi" (Why I write). *Dainik Kavita,* Sarat 1376, unpaged. First published in *Why I Write* (Calcutta: Anti-Fascist Writers' and Artists' Association, 1944).

Dimock, Edward C., Jr. "The Poet as Mouse and Owl: Reflections on a Poem by Jibanananda Das." *Journal of Asian Studies* 33, no. 4 (1974): 603–10.

Ganguly, Subrata. "Kabitay kalakata: Jibanananda" (Calcutta in poetry: Jibanananda). *Kali-o-Kalam,* Magh 1379, 893–901.

Ganguly, Sunil. "Godhulisandhir nritya: Jibanananda Das" (Dance of twilight: Jibanananda Das). *Kavita-Paricay,* Asarh 1373, 4–5.

———. "Kabita ki" (What is poetry?). *Bela Abela,* Falgun 1376, unpaged.

Guha, Naresh. "'Godhulisandhir nritya'" ("Dance of twilight"). *Kavita-Paricay,* Sravan 1373, 15–16.

———. "'Duhsamay' o anyanya" ('Untimely' and others). *Kavita-Paricay,* 8th issue, n.d., 9–10.

Gupta, Tarun, and Mary M. Lago. "Five Poems by Jivananda [*sic*] Das." *Literature East & West* 8, no. 4 (1964): 165–66.

Lago, Mary M., and Tarun Gupta. "Nine Poems by Jibanananda Das." *The Beloit Poetry Journal,* Fall 1965, 20–31.

———. "Pattern in the Imagery of Jivanananda Das." *Journal of Asian Studies* 24, no. 4 (1965): 637–44.

Majumdar, Binoy. "Adbhut andhar ek: Jibanananda Das" (A strange darkness: Jibanananda Das). *Kavita-Paricay,* Kartik 1373, 1–4.

Mitra, Haraprasad. "Jibananander alo—andhakar" (Jibanananda's light and darkness). *Kali-o-Kalam,* Aswin 1380, 125–32.

Mukherjee, Dhurjati. "Jibanananda—a World of New Sensibility." *Indian Literature* 20, no. 5 (1977), 97–100.

Mukherjee, Hiren. "Bengal Progressive Writers Getting Together for the People." In *Anti-Fascist Traditions of Bengal.* Calcutta: Indo-GDR Friendship Society, 1969.

Mukherjee, Sarat Kumar. "Jibananander prabhab" (The genius of Jibanananda). *Dainik Kavita,* 20 Jyaistha 1373, 4.

Mukherjee, Subhas. "Nirjanatama kabi" (The loneliest of poets). *Paricay,* Sravan 1360, 51ff.

Ray, Bani. "The Modern Trend in Bengali Literature." In *Seminar of All India Women Writers: Souvenir.* Hyderabad: Andhra Pradesh Sahitya Akademi, 1965, unpaged.

Ray, Manindra. "Kabi Jibanananda Das" (Poet Jibanananda Das). *Paricay,* Sravan 1362, 1–11.

Ray, Sarojendranath. "Alocana: Jibanananda sambandhe" (Discussion: Concerning Jibanananda). *Desh,* 29 Asarh 1375, 1228.

Ray, Subodh. "Amar cokhe kabi Jibanananda" (Poet Jibanananda in my eyes). *Usha,* Kartik 1361, 17–20.

Sarkar, Alok. "Ghora: Jibanananda Das" (Horses: Jibanananda Das). *Kavita-Paricay,* 8th issue, n.d., 1–3.

———. "Jibanananda" (Jibanananda). *Dainik Kavita,* 20 Jyaistha 1373, 4.

Sarkar, Arun Kumar. "'Godhulisandhir nritya'" ("Dance of twilight"). *Kavita-Paricay,* 5th–6th combined issues, n.d., 19.

Sengupta, Acintya Kumar. "Antaranga Jibanananda" (My close friend Jibanananda). *Mayukh,* Paus–Jyaistha 1361-62, 118–25.

Sikdar, Asru Kumar. "Caturtha dasak" (The thirties). In *Adhunik kabitar itithas* (A history of modern poetry), edited by A. Dasgupta and D. Banerjee. Calcutta: Vak-Sahitya, 1965.

Syed, Abdul Mannan. "Jibanananda carca" (Research on Jibanananda). *Sahitya Patrika* (University of Dhaka) 25, no. 1 (1388): 140–74. A revised version of this extensively annotated survey is included in *Jibanananda,* edited by Abdul Mannan Syed. Dhaka: Caritra, 1984.

Wadud, Kazi Abdul. "Bengali." In *The Indian Literatures of Today,* edited by Bharatam Kumarappa. Bombay: The P.E.N. All-India Centre, 1947.

Index

Acre of Green Grass, An: Buddhadeva Bose critical of political poetry, 248–49
All-Bengal Rabindra Literary Conference, 266–67, 275
All-India Progressive Writers' Association, 147; renamed Anti-Fascist Writers' and Artists' Association, 171
Andrews, Dinabandhu (C. F.): defends City College, 74–75.
Anti-Fascist Writers' and Artists' Association, 171
Anti-Imperialist People's Front in India, 147
Anwar, Samser: allusions to "Banalata Sen," 278
Asrukana Sanyal, 132
Ayyub, Abu Sayeed: and Anti-Fascist Writers' and Artists' Association, 171; chair of Contemporary Writers' Association, 252; coeditor of *Modern Bengali Poetry*, 269; joint editor of *Dwandwa*, 251; on Leftist literature, 147, 247; manifesto of Contemporary Writers' Association, 253–54; opinion of JD, 156; and *Paricay*, 251; and Poets' Conference, 268.

Bagerhat, 93
Bagerhat College. *See* Prafulla Chandra College
Banalata Sen, 122, 157; in other poetry, 122–23; significance of name, 120–21
"Banalata Sen" (*banalata sen*), 119–20; allusions to, in others' poetry, 278, 280–81; compared with JD's other poetry, 98–99, 124, 157, 164, 180, 181, 191, 264–65, 277; JD recites at Poets' Conference, 269

Banalata Sen (*banalata sen*): awarded All-Bengal Rabindra Literary Conference prize, 266; compared with later poetry, 164; critical opinion of, 277; in "One for a Pice" series (Kavita Bhavan edition of), 169, 181, 190, 263; Signet Press edition of, 123, 263
"Bande Mataram": early nationalist anthem, 26, 50, 72
Banerjee, Binod Bihari: on City College's Saraswati puja, 73
Banerjee, Himani: on *The World at Large*, 193
Banerjee, Manabendra: on JD's "Dance of Twilight," 154
Banerjee, Manik: and Anti-Fascist Writers' and Artists' Association, 171; criticized by *Marksbadi*, 247–48, 255
Banerjee, Tarasankar, 263; and Anti-Fascist Writers' and Artists' Association, 171; criticized by *Marksbadi*, 247–48, 255
Bangladesh: brief history of, 16–18; national anthem of, 38
Barisal: Brahmo Samaj in, 21; and City College, 40; geography of, 18–19; JD's love for, 91–92; JD's reasons for leaving, 196; similarity to fictional Jalpaihati, 219
Barisha College: JD on the faculty of, 260
Barricade, The (*pracir*): and Somen Chanda, 171
Bauls, 241
Bemmo: derogatory form of "Brahmo," 20, 76
Bengali: guru-*candali* error in, 54; literature, brief history of, 32–39; nonliterary diction in, 55; *sadhu* and *calit* forms of, 53–54, 68–69, 70,

82, 87, 283; and Sajani Kanta Das, 55; and Sanskrit, 63, 67–68
Bengal the Beautiful (*rupasi bamla*), 89–100; Asokananda's introduction to, 89; and death, 139; historical-geographic imagery in, 124; and JD's novels, 206; and JD's other poetry, 98–99, 121, 132, 134, 164, 180; literal meaning of, 90; public acceptance of, 97–98; unpublished during lifetime, 91, 100, 116, 246
Besant, Annie: defends City College, 75
Bethune School: JD's mother studied at, 22
Bhattacharya, Anil Krishna: designed cover for *Gray Manuscripts*, 113
Bhattacharya, Bijay Krishna: principal of Howrah Girls' College, 261
Bhattacharya, Biswanath: cofounder of *Dwandwa*, 251
Bhattacharya, Jagadish, 170
Bhattacharya, Sanjay: article "Jibanananda Das" (*jibanananda das*) by, 187; of assistance to JD in Calcutta, 201, 206, 257, 260, 262; and Communism and Stalinism in poetry, 147, 187; featured JD in *Nirukta*, 149; JD's comments on Sanjay's poetry, 262–63; on JD's poetry, 98–99, 146, 154–55, 156; and JD's *The World at Large*, 190–91; joint editor of *Nirukta*, 148; and memorial for JD, 273; opinion of JD, as perceived by JD, 194; opinion of *Kavita* and Buddhadeva Bose, 147, 149; and *Pratirodh*, 172; and *Purvasa*, 147, 187, 250–51; and romanticism, 147–48; and Sudhindranath Datta, 101–2
Bhaumik, Gopal: and memorial for JD, 273
Bicitra Bhavan conference, 61–62, 75
Blank verse. *See* Meter
B.M. College: JD joins faculty of, 81; JD leaves faculty of, 196, 220; JD studies at, 29; JD's colleagues at, 151–52, 225, 259; JD's wife earns B.A. degree at, 80
B.M. Institution: brief history of, 22, 25–28; JD's father teaches at, 22;
and national education, 27–28
Bose, Ambuj: on JD's poetic diction, 156–57, 283
Bose, Buddhadeva: and Anti-Fascist Writers' and Artists' Association, 171; and *Acre of Green Grass, An*, 248; attends JD's wedding, 79; and Best Poems series, 270; critical of political poetry, 248–49; criticizes Rabindranath's *An Introduction to Bengali Verse*, 126; inspiration for younger poets, 277; JD's comments on Buddhadeva's "Kokil, O Kokil" poem, 118; and JD's *Gray Manuscripts*, 113, 116–17; on JD's loss of his City College position, 76, 77; on JD's poetry, 40, 47, 62–64, 67–69, 186, 194, 249, 282; and JD's review of Buddhadeva's *Kankabati*, 109; and JD's translation of "Darkness," 244–45; and JD's *The World at Large*, 191–92, 243; and *Kavita*, 72, 108–9, 250–51; and Kavita Bhavan, 190; letter from JD concerning *Kavita*, 118–19; and *Mahakala*, 71; and memorial for JD, 273; and *Modern Bengali Poetry* (*adhunik bamla kabita*), 126, 269–70; opinion of JD, as perceived by JD, 194–95; and *Paricay*, 100; and *Pratirodh*, 172; protests killing of Somen Chanda, 171; on Rabindranath's *The Last Poem* (*seser kabita*), 62; writes JD's epitaph, 9
Bose, Protiva: JD sought advice from, 207
Bose, Rana: and memorial for JD, 273
Bose, Satyendranath, 18; and *Paricay*, 100
Bose, Subhas Chandra, 74, 179; and City College's Saraswati puja, 74
Bose, Suddha Sattwa: JD approaches for teaching position, 259
Brahmabadi: founding of, 23; JD's father editor of, 23; JD's mother contributes to, 24; JD's only contribution to, 31
Brahmo-Hindu relations, 21, 44, 72–78, 79, 233;
Brahmo Samaj: and Barisal, 21, 23;

Index

brief history of, 20; and caste, 20, 50, 79; and City College, 21, 72–78; JD never joined, 40; JD's father's upbringing in, 21; JD's grandfather's conversion to, 20; and morality, 76–77; opposed idol worship, 73
Braja Mohan College. See B.M. College
Braja Mohan Institution. See B.M. Institution
Browning, Robert, 108, 118
Buddha, the, 41, 94, 168, 169, 180; and JD's "A Day Eight Years Ago," 138, 140; and JD's "Sensation," 66, 67
Byron, George Gordon, Lord, 80

Calcutta University: and degrees in the vernaculars, 30; JD attends, 29
Calendar, Bengali, 15–16
Caliphate, 44
Calit. See Bengali: *sadhu* and *calit* forms of
Caste. *See* Vaidya
Caturanga, 194; review of JD's *Banalata Sen* in, 181
Chakravarty, Amiya: and All-Bengal Rabindra Literary Conference prize, 266; and Anti-Fascist Writers' and Artists' Association, 171; inspiration for younger poets, 277; and *Modern Bengali Poetry*, 269, 270; protests killing of Somen Chanda, 171
Chakravarty, Heramba: on JD, 151, 195–96
Chakravarty, Manomohan: cofounder and editor of *Brahmabadi*, 23, 24; officiates at JD's wedding, 79
Chakravarty, Nirendranath: and Poets' Conference, 269; contributes to JD's column "Rustlings of the Mind," 202; JD's colleague on the *Swaraj*, 201; on the meaning of *Darkness of Seven Stars*, 236
Chanda, Somen: slain Leftist writer, 171
Chandidasa, 95. Work: "On this dark night, thick with clouds," 33
Chandi Mangal, 34; allusions to, in JD's poetry, 94
Chatterjee, Bankim Chandra: and Bengali vs. English as medium for literature, 38; coined phrase "bande mataram," 50; in *Marksbadi*, 249; on plight of nineteenth-century Bengali writers, 38, 52
Chatterjee, Ramananda: and Anti-Fascist Writers' and Artists' Association, 171; defends City College, 74; founder of *Prabasi*, 24; and JD's mother, 22; and Sunderland's *India in Bondage*, 70–71
Chatterjee, Sarat Chandra, 44; attacked in *Sanibarer Cithi*, 71; criticized by *Marksbadi*, 247
Chaudhuri, Nirad C.: and Brahmo morality, 77
Chaudhuri, Pramatha: attacked in *Sanibarer Cithi*, 71; editor of *Sabuj Patra*, 53; and terza rima, 114
Choudhury, Malay Roy. Work: "Against Freedom of Art," 278–79
Church of England: JD's father translates for, 29
City College: and Barisal, 40; and Brahmo Samaj, 21, 40, 72–78; JD approaches Narayan Ganguly for teaching position at, 259; JD on faculty of, 40, 72, 75–78; JD's father attends, 21; and Saraswati puja, 73–78
City School, 21
Communalism. *See* Hindu-Muslim relations; Brahmo-Hindu relations
Communist Party of India, 146; legalized (1942), 187; outlawed (1934), 171; West Bengal outlaws (1948), 247, 254
Congress, Indian National: and Provincial Conference meeting in Barisal (1906), 26
Contemporary Writers' Association: brief history of, 250–56; JD joint editor of *Dwandwa*, 251; JD probably a member of, 252; manifesto of, by Abu Sayeed Ayyub, 253; and Socialist Party of India, 251
Creative process, 66–67, 110–12, 194–95

"Dance of Twilight" (*godhulisandhir*

nritya), 152–53; literary criticism of, by diverse hands, 153–55
Dante: sonnet by Michael Madhusudan Dutt on, 89; and terza rima, 114
"Darkness" (*andhakar*), 245–46; JD's prefatory comments to, 244
Darkness of Seven Stars (*satati tarar timir*), 235; critical opinion of, 276–77; JD's "Dance of Twilight" in, 155
Das, Asokananda (brother), 40, 42, 137, 195; introduction to second edition of JD's *Gray Manuscripts*, 115; on JD's *Bengal the Beautiful*, 89, 91; JD's family shares the residence of, 203, 204, 262; JD visits in Delhi, 262; on Muniruddin, Barisal hunter, 105; on publication of JD's novels, 206; titles JD's posthumously published books, 218
Das, Chitta Ranjan (C. R.): on death of, JD's reaction to, 40–41, 95; JD's poem on, 41; and national education, 26; and Subhas Chandra Bose, 74
Das, Dinesh Rajan: coeditor of *Kallol*, 45
Das, Jibanananda: autobiography (unpublished) of, 234, 257, 259; awards received by, 266, 275; birth of, 19; and Brahmo Samaj, 40, 195; called "father of modern poetry," 282; called "nature poet," 117; called "our most alone of poets," 9, 196; commemorative publications in honor of, 273–75; comments on his own poetry, 48, 90, 98, 107–8, 156, 194, 275; and Contemporary Writers' Association, 252–53, 254; his daughter, letter to, 203–4; death of, 9, 271; discomfort in the city, 46, 78, 203, 204–5, 206; *durbodhya* ("not easily intelligible"), 151, 152; education of, 25, 29; employment, 40, 72–78, 78–79, 81, 195, 196, 201–2, 255, 258, 260, 261; family background, 19–28; and fascination with death, 112, 139, 145; influence on younger writers, 277–82; joint editor of *Dwandwa*, 251; meets wife, 79; magazines on or inspired by his poetry, 281–82; memorial meetings in honor of, 273; in *Modern Bengali Poetry*, 269, 270; and his mother, 22, 24, 30, 31, 43; personality of, 151, 195–96; poetic diction of, 63, 67, 69–70, 126, 282–84; on poetic inspiration, 66–67, 110–12, 194–95; and Poets' Conference, 268–69; on prose fiction of, 81, 205, 206; on relationship between poetry and life, 111–12, 162, 194, 241; and "third force" in literature, 252

Das, Jibanananda. Works. *See also* Select Bibliography: Books
—poetry: "The afternoon grows damp with clouds" (*bhije haye ase meghe e-dupur*), 134; "Ah birds, were you not there at Kalidaha once?" (*hay pakhi, ekadin kalidahe chile na ki*), 93–94; "Ascertainment" (*nirdes*), 150; "As long as I might live I yearn to see the sky" (*yatadin bence achi akas caliya geche*), 96; "As I sat down to write all these poems" (*e-sab kabita ami yakhan likhechi ba'se*), 133; "Banalata Sen" (*banalata sen*) 119–20; "Before Death" (*mrityur age*), 109–10; "Beggar" (*bhikhiri*), 157; "Bird" (*pakhi*), 142–43; "Blue Skies" (*nilima*), 45–46; "Dance of Twilight" (*godhulisandhir nritya*), 152–53; "Darkness" (*andhakar*), 245–46; "A Day Eight Years Ago" (*at bachar ager ekadin*), 135–37; "Feeling" (*anubhab*), 172; "Glory" (*garima*), 163; "Grass" (*ghas*), 131–32; "Here life's current ebbs and flows" (*ekhane praner srot ase yay*), 144; "Hard Times" (*durddin*), 170; "The Hunt" (*sikar*), 129; "I have looked upon the face of Bengal" (*ami bamlar mukh dekhiyachi*), 35; "I have felt the breath of autumn wind," 89–90; "If I were" (*ami yadi hotam*), 216–17; "In Camp" (*kyampe*), 102–5; "In Fields Fertile and Fallow" (*khete prantare*), 167–68;

"Invocation for the New Year" (*barsa abahan*), 31; "I shall fall fast asleep one day within your starlit night," (*ghumaye pariba ami ekadin tomader naksatrer rate*), 97; "Merged into the Skies" (*akasalina*), 236–37; "A Moment" (*muhurta*), 192; "Movement" (*gatibidhi*), 149–50; "Naked Lonely Hand" (*nagna nirjan hat*), 126–27; "Night" (*ratri*), 158–59; "Night" (*ratri*), 159–60; "1946–47," 197–200; "No matter how new the poetry I invent," 99; "O Hawk" (*hay cil*), 134; "One day I grew upon the paths of the world" (*ekadin prithibir pathe ami phaliyachi*), 128; "One's Natural State (*swabhab*), 169–70; "On the Sidewalks" (*phut pathe*), 193–94; "Prayer" (*prarthana*), 191; "Rabindranath" (*rabindranath*), 161; "Rivers" (*nadi/nadira*), 115–16; "Said That Aswattha Tree" (*balila aswattha sei*), 138–39; "Sailor" (*nabik*), 238–39; "Sankhamala" (*sankhamala*), 132–33; "Sensation" (*bodh*), 64–66; "Shadowy" (*abachaya*), 165; "Some day no one will find me anymore in the foggy field" (*ekadin kuyasar ei mathe amare pabe na keu khunje ar*), 143–44; "Song of the Meek, Tired, and Introverted" (*niriha, klanta o marmanwesider gan*), 181–84; "Song of the Sea of Light" (*alosagarer gan*), 179–80; "Song of Thirst" (*pipasar gan*), 56–59; "Sudarsana" (*sudarsana*), 263–64; "A Tale of the Sundarban Jungles" (*sundar baner galpa*), 130–31; "Tangerine" (*kamala lebu*), 59; "There is a place in this world" (*ei prithibite ek sthan ache*), 91; "Thousands of Years Merely Play" (*hajar bachar sudhu khela kare*), 123; "Today" (*aj*), 272–73; "Today" (*aj*), 256; "Various Choruses" (*bibhinna koras*), 173–76; "Various Choruses" (*bibhinna koras*), 176–78; "Vultures" (*sakun*), 114; "Walking" (*path hanta*), 265–66; "When I return to the banks of the Dhansiri" (*abar asiba phire dhanasiritir tire*), 92–93; "Who would leave this delta" (*ei dana chere hay rup ke khunjite yay*), 92; "Windy Night" (*haoyar rat*), 124–25; "Wristwatch" (*ristoyac*), 237; "Your child will one day quit your bosom" (*tomar buker theke ekadin ca'le yabe tomar santan*), 95

—poetry (excerpts and references to): "Banalata Sen" (*banalata sen*), 11, 217, 238; "Back Then This Earth's" (*sedin e dharanir*), 48, 49–50; "Carelessly, the Kirtinasa crumbled Rajballabh's glory" (*tabu taha bhul jani—rajaballabher kirti bhane kirtinasa*), 20; "Birds" (*pakhira*), 69; "Darkness of the Sun" (*suryatamasi*), 240, 241–42; "A Day Eight Years Ago" (*at bachar ager ekadin*), 191, 192, 277; "Deer" (*harinera*), 132; "Egypt" (*misar*), 49; "Grass" (*ghas*), 60; "Grass" (*ghas*), 138; "Hindu-Muslim" (*hindu musalaman*), 44; "Hope and Faith" (*asa bharasa*), 254; "The Hunt" (*sikar*), 105, 217; "Invocation for the New Year" (*barsa abahan*), 90; "In the Likeness of the Sun" (*suryapratim*), 240, 241; "The Insignificant Man" (*lokasamanya*), 239; "Lighter Moments" (*laghu muhurta*), 166; "Luster" (*dipti*), 240; "Merged into the Skies" (*akasalina*), 132, 240; "Naked Lonely Hand" (*nagna nirjan hat*), 158; "New Entrance" (*uttaraprabes*), 240–41; "Night Chorus" (*ratrir koras*), 241; "1946–47," 214; "O hawk" (*hay cil*), 215; "On the Death of Deshabandhu" (*desabandhu prayane*), 41, 44; "On the sidewalks" (*phut pathe*), 270–71; "On the Shores of Creation" (*sristir tire*), 240; "On the Night of the Winter Solstice" (*makarasamkrantir rate*), 240, 243; "Perihelion's Song" (*anusuryer gan*), 240; "Pyramid" (*piramid*), 48, 49; "Rabindranath" (*rabindranath*), 160–61; "Ramdas" (*ramadas*), 43; "Rustlings of the Mind" (*mana-marmar*), 202; "Sabita" (*sabita*), 264; "Sailor" (*nabiki*), 239, 241; "Sensation" (*bodh*), 82; "Septet" (*saptak*), 240; "Shadowy" (*abachaya*), 169; "She" (*se*), 102; "Simplicity" (*sahaj*), 82; "Solar Brightness" (*saurakarojjwal*), 240; "Song of Leisure" (*abasarer gan*), 72; "A Song of Slaying Darkness" (*timirahananer gan*), 240, 241; "Sucetana" (*sucetana*), 264, 265; "Suranjana" (*suranjana*), 264; "Syamali" (*syamali*), 264; "A Tale of the Sundarban Jungles" (*sundar baner galpa*), 215; "1333," 82; "To Time" (*samayer kache*), 242; "Vaitarani" (*vaitarani*), 115; "Various Choruses" (*bibhinna koras*), 180; "Vivekananda" (*bibekananda*), 43; "Walking" (*path hanta*), 217; "What Sea Breeze Is This" (*ei ki sindhur haoya*), 242; "When I return to the banks of the Dhansiri" (*abar asiba phire dhanasiritir tire*), 59, 138; "Wild Ducks" (*buno hans*), 132, 216; "Wristwatch" (*ristoyac*), 241

—prose fiction: "Chayanat" (*chayanat*), 83–84; "Company, Alone" (*sanga, nihsanga*), 87–88; "Dalliance" (*bilas*), 203; *Jalpaihati* (*jalapaihati*), 201, 205–6, 218–34; *Malyaban* (*malyaban*), 205–6, 207–10; *Sutirtha* (*sutirtha*), 205–6, 210–18; " A Tale of Village and City" (*gram o saharer galpa*), 85–86

—essays: "Bengali Poetry Today," 252; "Modern Poetry" (*adhunik kabita*), 254–55; "On Poetry" (*kabitar katha*), 67, 109, 110–12, 162, 189, 194–95; "Rabindranath and Modern Bengali Poetry" (*rabindranath o adhunik bamla kabita*), 160, 162–63, 189; "Responsibility of the Writer and Writing" (*lekha, lekhaker dayitwa*), 188–90

Das, Kusum Kumari (mother), 19, 22–25, 31, 195; advice to son, 43; publications by, 24; saves son's life, 25. Work: "The Exemplary Boy" (*adarsa chele*), 23

Das, Labanya (wife), 88, 206, 258; attends teachers' training institute, 257; earns B.A. degree, 80; marries JD, 78–80; teaches school, 205

Das, Manjusri (daughter), 80; father's letter to, 203–4

Das, Nalini (sister-in-law): JD comments on educational system in letter to, 195

Das, Prasanna Kumari (paternal grandmother), 19; and hunting stories, 105

Das, Sajani Kanta: aids JD in hospital, 271; and Anti-Fascist Writers' and Artists' Association, 171; article by, following JD's death, 274–75; and B.M. College faculty, 151; charged with obscenity, 70; charged with sedition, 70–71; and City College's Saraswati puja, 75; criticism of JD's poetry, 59, 106–7; editor of *Sanibarer Cithi*, 48; and *Mahakala*, 71; "Nakur Thakur's Ashram" (*nakur thakurer asram*), satire by, 70; others' opinion of, 48; participant, with JD, in poetry reading on radio, 270; perception of himself, 55; and Rabindranath, 52–54; ridicules prose poetry, 52; and Sani Circle, 250; suppresses review of JD's *Fallen Feathers*, 50–51; threatened with legal action, 71

Das, Samarananda (son), 80

Das, Sarbananda (paternal grandfather), 20–21; conversion to Brahmo Samaj of, 21; founding of Barisal Brahmo Samaj by, 21

Das, Satyananda (father), 19, 21–22, 23, 25, 195; becomes a Brahmo, 21; cofounder of *Brahmabadi*, 23; founds English-medium high school (1921), 27; leaves post at B.M. Institution (1921), 27; political ideology of, as viewed by JD, 27–28; teaches at B.M. Institution, 25

Das, Sisir Kumar: on Bengali sonnet, 89
Das, Sucarita (sister), 40, 195, 204
Dasgupta: JD's surname, changed to Das, 50
Dasgupta, Alokeranjan: on JD's influence, 277
Dasgupta, Pranabendu: on JD's influence, 277; on poets of the 1940s, 147
Datta, Ajit: article on JD by, 272, 275; attends JD's wedding, 79; on JD's poetry in *Pragati*, 47–48; and JD's prose fiction, 207; and memorial for JD, 273; in *Modern Bengali Poetry*, 269; and Poets' Conference, 268, 269;
Datta, Amlan: and *Dwandwa*, 255
Datta, Aswini Kumar, 26–28; and B.M. Institution, 22, 25–29; high moral standards of, 77; and national education, 26–27; and Provincial Conference meeting in Barisal (1906), 26
Datta, Hirendranath: and *Paricay*, 107
Datta, Satyaprasanna: aids JD in hospital, 271; of assistance to JD in Calcutta, 260; and JD's *Darkness of Seven Stars*, 235; JD's letter to, 262–63; and JD's *The World at Large*, 147; and *Purvasa*, 147, 187
Datta, Satyendranath: JD's negative opinion of, 116; and poetic meter, 116
Datta, Sudhindranath: absent from JD's *sraddha*, 101–2; and All-Bengal Rabindra Literary Conference, 266; compared with JD, 102; editor of *Paricay*, 100; inspiration for younger poets, 277; in *Modern Bengali Poetry*, 269, 270; negative opinion of JD's poetry, 101–2; and Poets' Conference, 268; "The Emancipation of Poetry" (*kabyer mukti*), manifesto for modern poetry, 100–10
Datta, Sudhir Kumar, 78, 139; and "Banalata Sen" image, 122
Datta, Sukumar: nephew of Aswini Kumar Datta and vice-principal of Ramjas College, 78
"Day Eight Years Ago, A" (*at bachar ager ekadin*), 135–37, 192, 277; and the Buddha, 138; in JD's *The World at Large*, 191
Death, 40, 49, 90, 95–97, 109–10, 138–45
Delhi, 78, 95, 261, 262
Deo, Narendra: head of Socialist Party of India, 252
Deshabandhu: critical opinion of JD's poem on, 42; epithet for Chitta Ranjan Das, 41
Dey, Bishnu: and Anti-Fascist Writers' and Artists' Association, 171; and Best Poems series, 270; criticized by *Marksbadi*, 248; inspiration for younger poets, 277; and JD's "In Camp," 101, 102; and *Mahakala*, 71; in *Modern Bengali Poetry*, 269, 270; and opinion of JD's English poetry, 90; and *Paricay*, 100; and Poets' Conference, 268, 269; protests killing of Somen Chanda, 171; and Rabindranath, 118; and *Sahitya Patra*, 248; and *Why I Write*, 187–88, 190
Dhar, Krishna. Work: "In Haiku Style" (*haiku dharane*), 278
Dhupchaya: published some of JD's early poetry, 113
Dhusar pandulipi. See *Gray Manuscripts*
Dodo: as image of disaster for mankind, 179, 180, 242
Doe in heat, 76, 101, 106, 152, 182, 183, 185
Durbodhya ("intelligible with difficulty"), 148, 151, 156–57
Dutt, Dinesh: and Poets' Conference, 269
Dutt, Michael Madhusudan: called "progressive" by *Marksbadi*, 250; conversion to Christianity, 21; and his *The Slaying of Meghanada* (*meghanadavadha kavya*), 37, 215; and sonnet form, 89, 90; and writing in English and Bengali, 37. Work: "To Bengal" (*bangabhumir prati*), 80
Dutt-Bradley Thesis, 146
Dwandwa: and All-Bengal Rabindra Literary Conference, 266; JD joint editor of, 251; JD's essay to appear

in, 255; mouthpiece of the Contemporary Writers' Association, 251

Eliot, T. S., 283; on common speech and poetry, 68, 282
English: influence on Bengali, 38; and language of JD's poetry, 157; medium of education, 36; vs. Bengali as a medium for literature by Bengalis, 37–38

Fallen Feathers (*jhara palak*), 48; critical opinion of, 276; influenced by Satyendranath Datta, 116; JD's opinion of, 48; Middle Eastern imagery in, 123; reviewed in *Kallol*, 50; Sajani Kanta Das suppresses review of, 50–51
Four Arts Club: forerunner of Kallol, 45

Gandhi, Mohandas Karamchand, 41; and national education, 26; and Quit India, 179, 187
Ganguly, Amiya Kumar: editor of *Nirnay*, 256
Ganguly, Narayan: contributes novel to *Swaraj*, at JD's request, 202; JD approaches for teaching position, 258
Ganguly, Narendralal: critical of JD, 151; JD approaches for teaching position, 259; and JD's autobiography, 259
Ganguly, Sunil: on JD's "Dance of Twilight," 153–54; on JD's diction, 69–70; and Poets' Conference, 269
Ganguly, Taraknath: author of *Swarnalata*, 120
Ghai harini: confusion over meaning of, 101. *See also* Doe in heat
Ghosh, Bimal Chandra: and Poets' Conference, 268, 269
Ghosh, Prabhash Chandra: colleague of JD's at Ramjas College, 78, 90
Ghosh, Sagarmoy: editor of *Desh*, 207
Ghosh, Santosh Kumar: general secretary of Contemporary Writers' Association, 252
Ginsberg, Allen, 283; adaptation of JD's "Lighter Moments," 166; on JD, 272, 283
Gitanjali, 161: and Nobel Prize, 39; and prose poetry, 126
Gray Manuscripts (*dhusar pandulipi*), 81; announcement of, 113; Asokananda Das's introduction to the second edition of, 115; and *Bengal the Beautiful*, 89; contrasted with *Banalata Sen*, 132; critical opinion of, 277; JD's introduction to, 113–14; sonnets published in, 89–90, 265
Guha, Bhumendra: ministers to JD in hospital, 271
Guha, Naresh: JD approaches for teaching position, 259; on JD's "Dance of Twilight," 154; and memorial for JD, 273
Gupta, Amritalal: guardian uncle of Labanya Das, 79
Gupta, Atul: and Anti-Fascist Writers' and Artists' Association, 171
Gupta, Dilip Kumar: and Poets' Conference, 268
Gupta, Rohini Kumar: father of Labanya Das, 79
Guru-*candali* error, 54
Gurudeb: epithet for Rabindranath, 39, 62

Haimantika, 237
Haldar, Gopal: joint editor of *Paricay*, 249
Hindu-Muslim relations, 43–44, 72, 73, 196–97, 250; as depicted in JD's novels, 219, 220, 223–25
Hosen, Abul: review of JD's *Banalata Sen*, 181, 186
Howrah Girls' College: JD on the faculty of, 261
Hungry Generation: and respect for JD, 278–80

Imagery: historical-geographic, 49, 121–24; Middle Eastern, 48–49, 123, 127, 130; oxymoronic, 239–42; shift from sensuous to cerebral, 193
Imagists' Manifesto, 126
"In Camp" (*kyampe*): brief history of publication of, 101; compared with

later poetry, 185, 192; JD's defense of, 107–8, 155; and poem by Krishna Dhar, 278; Sajani Kanta Das's criticism of, 106–7

Introduction to Bengali Verse, An (*bamla kabya paricay*): criticized by Buddhadeva Bose, 126; edited by Rabindranath, 126; excluded prose poetry, 126

Islam, Kazi Nazrul, 42; attacked in *Sanibarer Cithi*, 48; influence on JD, 50; in *Modern Bengali Poetry*, 269, 270; and "Kemal Pasha," 44; Rabindranath's telegram to, 42; and "The Rebel," 42. Work: "The Rebel" (*bidrohi*) (excerpt), 42

Jhara palak. See *Fallen Feathers*
Jibanananda daser srestha kabita. See *Jibanananda Das's Best Poems*
Jibanananda Das's Best Poems (*jibanananda daser srestha kabita*), 48, 122, 270; receives Sahitya Akademi prize, 275

Kabir, Humayun, 263: and *Caturanga*, 251; *Darkness of Seven Stars* dedicated to, 235; JD approaches for teaching position, 262
Kali-Kalam: avant-garde journal of the 1920s, 47, 72
Kallol: brief history of, 45, 72; JD's "Blue Skies" published in, 45–48
Kankabati: book of poetry by Buddhadeva Bose, reviewed by JD, 109; folk-tale character and JD's muse, 110, 112
Kathya: and poetic diction, 283. See also Bengali: *sadhu* and *calit* forms of; Poetic diction
Kavita, 72; Buddhadeva Bose's description of, 108–9; editorial on prose poetry, 126; JD's reaction to, 118–19 and *Nirukta*, 173; special JD issue of, 102
Kavita Bhavan: Buddhadeva Bose's publishing concern, 190
Keats: influence on JD, 117
Kharagpur, 258
Kharagpur College: JD on the faculty of, 258

King Lear, 107

Mahabharata, 41, 94, 180
Mahakala: magazine in opposition to *Sanibarer Cithi*, 71–72
Mahaprithibi. See *World at Large, The*
Mailer, Norman: and profanity, 223
Maitra, Heramba Chandra: and Brahmo morality, 76–78; and City College, 40, 72–78; and loss of JD's position at City College, 76–78
Maitra, Jyotirindra, 161
Majumdar, Dipak: and Poets' Conference, 269
Majumdar, H. K.: sublets from JD in Calcutta, 205
Majumdar, Mohitlal: influence on JD, 50; and Rabindranath, 118; theoretician for *Sanibarer Cithi*, 51, 61
Majumdar, Satyendranath: and Anti-Fascists Writers' and Artists' Association, 171
Mamud, Hayat: on JD's lack of acceptance by aristocratic literary circles, 101
Manasa Mangal: and *Bengal the Beautiful*, 34–35, 93–94
Mannan, Qazi Abdul: and JD's "New Entrance," 241
Marksbadi: brief history of, 247–50; critical of Manik Banerjee and Tarasankar Banerjee, 247–48; critical of Ram Mohan Ray through Rabindranath, 253; praises Michael Madhusudan Dutt, Kaliprasanna Simha, and Dinabandhu Mitra, 250
Marxism: and Bengali literature, 146
Marxist: critical opinion of JD softens, 277
Matrabritta. See Meter
Meter, 116; blank verse, 250; *matrabritta*, 166; *payar*, 89, 121, 122, 154; prose meter, 126, 160, 255. See also Datta, Satyendranath
Mitra, Asok: on JD's lack of acceptance by aristocratic literary circles, 101; review of JD's *Darkness of Seven Stars*, 242–43

Mitra, Dinabandhu: called "progressive" by *Marksbadi*, 250
Mitra, Haraprasad: JD writes to, for teaching position, 258
Mitra, Narendranath: joint editor of *Dwandwa*, 251
Mitra, Premendra: and Best Poems series, 270; compared with JD, 63; and JD's "Blue Skies," 47; and *Kavita*, 72, 108, 169; and *Nirukta*, 148, 149, 169; and Poets' Conference, 268; *The World at Large* dedicated to, 191
Modern Bengali Poetry (*adhunik bamla kabita*): published in response to Tagore's *An Introduction to Bengali Verse*, 126, 269–70
Montessori, Maria, 28
Mukherjee, Dhurjati Prasad: on JD's poetry, 155–56
Mukherjee, Hirendranath: coeditor of *Modern Bengali Poetry*, 269
Mukherjee, Jagadish: headmaster, B.M. Institution, 28; influence on JD, 29
Mukherjee, Sarat Kumar: on JD's influence, 277–78; and JD's poetic diction, 283
Mukherjee, Subhas: and Anti-Fascist Writers' and Artists' Association, 171; compared to JD, 181; and Poets' Conference, 268; and *Pratirodh*, 172; protests killing of Somen Chanda, 171; review of *Banalata Sen* (Signet Press edition), 267; solicits essay from JD for the Anti-Fascist Writers' and Artists' Association, 187
Mukul: JD's mother publishes in, 22–23
Muniruddin: Barisal hunter, 105
"My Golden Bengal" (*amar sonar bamla*): Bangladesh national anthem, 15, 50

Nag, Gokul Chandra: coeditor of *Kallol*, 45
National education, 26–28; and B.M. Institution, 27–28
Nirukta, 148, 186–87; JD featured in, 149; and *Kavita*, 173

Obscenity, 75, 76; and JD's "In Camp," 107–8; and Sajani Kanta Das, 55, 70
One for a Pice (*ek payasay ekati*): poetry series, 169, 181, 190. See also *Banalata Sen*
Oxford Mission: JD resides at, in Calcutta, 29

Paricay, 77, 90, 100–101, 146, 194; and JD, 100–102; mouthpiece for Leftist writers, 100, 247; review of *Gray Manuscripts*, 117–18
Payar. See Meter
Pearls, The: feature in *Sanibarer Cithi*, 54
Petrarchan sonnet. See Sonnet
Poetic diction: and JD, 67, 282–84; and Sudhindranath Datta, 101; T. S. Eliot on, 282
Poetic inspiration, 66–67, 110–12, 194–95
Poetry (Chicago): published *Gitanjali* poems, 39
Poets' Conference, 268–69
Pound, Ezra: and Imagists' Manifesto, 126; on Rabindranath, 39
Prabasi: founded by Ramananda Chatterjee, 24
Prafulla Chandra College: JD on the faculty of, 78
Pragati: avant-garde journal of the 1920s, 47, 55, 72
Pratirodh: and Dacca District Progressive Writers' Association, 172; and Somen Chanda's death, 171
Prem Chand: president of All-India Progressive Writers' Association, 147
Pre-Raphaelites: influence on JD, 117
Presidency Boarding: JD resides at, in Calcutta, 47
Presidency College: JD attends, 29; JD seeks position at, 262
Prose literature: emergence of, in Bengali literature, 35–36
Prose meter. See Meter
Prose poetry, 125–26, 244, 273; Sajani Kanta Das ridicules, 52

Purvasa: brief history of, 147–48; resumes publication, 187

Rabibarer Lathi: magazine in opposition to *Sanibarer Cithi*, 72
Sanibarer Cithi, 72
Rabindranath. *See* Tagore, Rabindranath
Raha, Ashokebijay: and Poets' Conference, 268
Rahman, Ataur, 262; and publication of *Darkness of Seven Stars*, 235
Ramdas, 43
Ramjas College: JD on the faculty of, 78–79, 122
Ram Mohan Ray hostel: and City College, 72–74
Ramprasad, 95, 96. Work: "I'm not calling you Mother anymore," 33–34
Ranadive Doctrine: and the Communist Party of India, 247
Rasa, 62, 63, 219
Ray, Annadashankar: and Poets' Conference, 268
Ray, Bani: and appointment of JD at Barisha College, 260; on JD's influence, 277; and memorial for JD, 273
Ray, Bidhan Chandra: ministers to JD in hospital, 271
Ray, Brajasundar: City College professor with Barisal connections, 73, 74
Ray, Gopal Chandra: and appointment of JD at Howrah Girls' College, 260–61
Ray, Manindra: on JD's poetry, 275–77
Ray, Nirendranath: joint editor of *Paricay*, 249
Ray, Parimal: and teaching position for JD, 262
Ray, Ram Mohan: disparaged by Marxists, 253; founder of Brahmo Samaj, 36; mother asks JD to write about, 43
Ray, Sarojendranath: his review of *Fallen Feathers* suppressed, 50; on loss of JD's City College position, 76, 78

Ray, Satyajit: designed cover for *Banalata Sen*, 263
Ray, Subodh, 259
Raychaudhuri, Kusum Kumari: possibly first woman novelist in Bengali, 120
Raychaudhuri, Upendrakishor: contributor to *Mukul*, 23
Reincarnation: in JD's poetry, 59–60, 132, 137, 138
Reminiscences (*jiban-smriti*): JD's unpublished (maybe unwritten) autobiography, 206, 234, 257, 259
Romanticism: and Sanjay Bhattacharya, 147–48, 190
Roy, Jamini: and Anti-Fascist Writers' and Artists' Association, 171
Roy, Nihar Ranjan: and Poets' Conference, 268
Roy Choudhury, Malay. Work: "Against Freedom of Art," 278–79
Rudra, Suhrid: cofounder of *Dwandwa*, 251
Rupasi bamla. *See Bengal the Beautiful*
"Rustlings of the Mind" (*mana-marmar*): JD's feature column in the *Swaraj*, 202

Sabuj Patra: introduces *calit* forms of Bengali to literature, 53; alluded to by Sajani Kanta Das, 55
Sadhu. *See* Bengali: *sadhu* and *calit* forms of
Sahitya Akademi: brief history of, 275; first Bengali prize awarded to *Jibanananda Das's Best Poems*, 275
Sahitya Patra: criticized by *Marksbadi* and critical of Buddhadeva Bose, 248
Samanta, Rabindranath: on JD's "A Day Eight Years Ago," 141–42
Sanibarer Cithi, 48, 51–55; called "literary goon squad," 51; JD curious about, 151
Sankhamala, 91, 96, 99, 132, 133
Sanskrit: and Bengali, 67–68; JD's avoidance of, in prose poetry, 126
Sanyal, Hiran Kumar: and Anti-Fascist Writers' and Artists'

Association, 171; coeditor of *Paricay*, 100
Saraswati puja: and City College, 73–78; and Hindu-Muslim conflict, 73
Sarkar, Alok: critical of *Bengal the Beautiful*, 98
Sarkar, Arun Kumar: and All-Bengal Rabindra Literary Conference prize for JD, 266; on JD's "Dance of Twilight," 154
Sarkar, Jadunath: and City College's Saraswati puja, 73
Sarkar, Susobhan: and *Paricay*, 100
Sastri, Sivanath: Brahmo friend of JD's family, 22; editor of *Mukul*, 22
Satati tarar timir. See *Darkness of Seven Stars*
Sen, Bhowani: and speech to the All-India Party Congress (1948), 247
Sen, Dinesh Chandra: attacked in *Sanibarer Cithi*, 71
Sen, Ramesh Chandra: of assistance to JD in Calcutta, 205; parodied JD's poetry, 151–52. Work: "Is This Alone Solace(?)" (*ei sudhu santwana[?]*), 151–52
Sen, Samar: JD on, 118; and *Kavita*, 108, 109; in *Modern Bengali Poetry*, 269; and Poets' Conference, 268, 269; protests killing of Somen Chanda, 171
Sengupta, Acintya Kumar, 47: and Bicitra Bhavan conference, 61; compared with JD, 62; JD on, 47; JD's letter to, 257; on JD's personality, 196; on loss of JD's City College position, 75–76; and *Mahakala*, 71; and *Nirukta*, 148; and Poets' Conference, 269
Sengupta, Anandagopal: and *Dwandwa*, 251; JD's letter to, 252–53; organizing secretary of Contemporary Writers' Association, 252
Sengupta, Kiran Sankar: and JD's housing problems in Calcutta, 259; JD writes introduction to his *Dream-Desire*, 111, 171; and *Pratirodh*, 171

Sengupta, Naresh Chandra: and Anti-Fascist Writers' and Artists' Association, 171; attacked in *Sanibarer Cithi*, 71; threatens Sajani Kanta Das with legal action, 71
Sengupta, Yatindranath, 274; and Poets' Conference, 268
"Sensation" (*bodh*), 64–67, 277; compared with "A Day Eight Years Ago," 141–42; compared with "Glory" (*garima*), 164
Shelley, Percy Bysshe: and terza rima, 114; "soul's sister" borrowed by JD, 108;
Simha, Kaliprasanna: called "progressive" by *Marksbadi*, 250
Simon Commission, 73
Socialist Party of India: and Contemporary Writers' Association, 251
Sonnet, 89–91; Petrarchan structure, 90, 99–100; terza rima, 114, 115, 265
Soviet Revolution, 168, 180
Spenserian stanzas, 116
Stalin, Josef, 277
Stalinism: and Sanjay Bhattacharya, 187
Sundarban jungle, 108, 130
Sunderland, Jabez T.: author of *India in Bondage*, 70–71
Sutirtha, 205–6, 210–18; and JD's short stories, 87
Swadeshi movement, 26
Swaraj (newspaper) 196, 226, 235; brief history of, 201
Syed, Abdul Mannan. Work: "Jibanananda" (*jibananda*), 280–81

Tagore, Debendranath: mother asks JD to write about, 43
Tagore, Rabindranath: and All-Bengal Rabindra Literary Conference, 266; angered by Sajani Kanta Das, 52–53; on artistic creation, 162; attacked in *Marksbadi*, 247, 249, 250, 253; attends Provincial Conference in Barisal (1906), 26; and Bicitra Bhavan Conference, 61–62; death of, 160; defends City

College, 74; guru of Bengali letters, 112–13; and Indian and Bangladesh national anthems, 38; influence on younger poets, 60, 62, 277; and *Introduction to Bengali Verse, An* (*bamla kabyer paricay*), 269; and JD, 30, 51, 113, 118, 160, 235–36, 273, 276, 283; JD on, 160, 235–36; on JD's "Before Death," 113; and JD's *Fallen Feathers*, 51; and *Kavita*, 109; and Kazi Nazrul Islam, 42; and *matrabritta* meter, 166; in *Modern Bengali Poetry*, 269, 270; and *Mukul*, 23; and *Nirukta*, 148; and Nobel Prize, 39; and *Paricay*, 100, 107; on plight of modern poetry, 149; presides over second All-India Progressive Writers' Association (1938), 147; and prose poetry, 126; resigns knighthood, 25; and *Sanibarer Cithi*, 61, 71; as standard against which poets were judged, 118, 146; and Sudhindranath Datta, 102; warns against Western influence, 52–53. Works (excerpted or referred to): *Balaka*, 155; "Broken Nest, The" (*nasta nir*), 120–21; "Essence of Literature, The" (*sahitya dharma*), 60–61; *Gitanjali*, 38–39, 161; *Last Poem, The* (*seser kabita*), 62, 160; "Literary Innovation" (*sahitye nabatwa*), 60–61; "My Golden Bengal" (*amar sonar bamla*), 15, 38, 80; *Postscripts* (*punasca*), 126

Terza rima. *See* Sonnet

Thomas, Dylan, 283

Tripathi, Dipti: on JD's poetry, 121, 141, 264

Twenty-fifth of Baisakh, The (*pancise baisakh*): commemorative volume on Rabindranath, 161

Vaidya: and Brahmos, 79; and Dasgupta surname, 20, 50; protagonists in JD's novels, 219, 233; and village of Gaila, 22

Vivekananda, 43; referred to in *Marksbadi*, 249, 250

Western influence: criterion of criticism, 52–53; Rabindranath opposes, 52–53, 61; and Sajani Kanta Das, 55

Why I Write (*kena likhi*): publication of the Anti-Fascist Writers' and Artists' Association, 188, 190

World at Large, The (*mahaprithibi*), 122, 132, 190–93, 263; compared with JD's *Darkness of Seven Stars*, 236; critical opinion of, 276; and romanticism, 147, 190

Yeats, William Butler, 39, 248; influence on JD, 117